דוד וסרשטיין

ירושלים חנוכה תשמ"ה

(מהו')

David Wasserstein

Jerusalem 1984

JOSEPH NAVEH   SHAUL SHAKED

AMULETS AND MAGIC BOWLS

AMULETS AND MAGIC BOWLS

Aramaic Incantations of Late Antiquity

by

JOSEPH NAVEH SHAUL SHAKED

THE MAGNES PRESS, THE HEBREW UNIVERSITY, JERUSALEM
E. J. BRILL, LEIDEN

Distributed by E.J. Brill
Leiden, Holland

ISBN 965-223-531-8

Printed in Israel
Typesetting: Yael Kaplan, Jerusalem

CONTENTS

II. Incantation Bowls from Mesopotamia

III. Amulets and Fragments of Magic Books from the Cairo Geniza

LIST OF ILLUSTRATIONS

Figures

(All drawings by Ada Yardeni, unless otherwise noted)

Plates

(Photos on Pls. 1, 12, 14–20, 25, 30–31 by Z. Radovan)

*

Signs used in the transliteration of texts

( ) Uncertain readings
[ ] Restoration of lost writing
< > Omitted by the scribe by mistake
⌜ ⌝ Written above (or outside) the line
{ } Superfluous writing in the text (e.g. in case of dittography)

PREFACE

It was a widespread practice in the area of Palestine, Syria and Asia Minor during the fourth to the seventh centuries of the current era to use talismans written on metal sheets in order to ward off the powers of evil, to heal people, or to gain the love of a person. The common Babylonian practice of the same period was to write incantation texts on earthenware bowls. The number of Mesopotamian texts written in Jewish Aramaic, Syriac and Mandaic on clay bowls published to date reaches about one hundred and fifty, whereas less than ten Aramaic amulets from Palestine and its vicinity have been published so far.

This book developed from the desire of the two authors to do a modest work on a number of Aramaic magic bowls which at that time (almost ten years ago) were in Jerusalem in the hands of dealers and in the collection of the Institute of Archaeology of the Hebrew University. It has developed to its present dimensions as more texts have turned up. Work on some newly found metal amulets has made it necessary to study and revise the readings of the whole corpus of Aramaic amulets from the area of the Holy Land. Thus fifteen amulets have been edited in this volume — all those which can be deciphered with some confidence — and twelve new bowl texts written in Babylonian Jewish Aramaic and Syriac.

In order to understand the terminology and praxis of the texts discussed in this volume, it is essential to refer to contemporary and later texts from other sources: the Greek magic papyri, the early magic literature in Hebrew, and the magic fragments in the Cairo Geniza. Of the last group, so far almost completely neglected, a few selected texts are included in this work: five amulets, and three fragments from books of magic recipes.

The texts are provided with translations and commentaries, and a detailed glossary of all words is given. All newly published texts are accompanied by photographs. It has been our wish to make available to scholars material for the study of popular religious life of Jews and pagans in the crucial period which corresponds to that of the Talmud. Our primary aim has been to provide philologically reliable material, and not to offer a detailed study of the religious implications of these texts.

It is out pleasant task to acknowledge the help received from various institutions and persons in the course of preparing the present study.

The following institutions provided us with photographs and allowed us to publish these texts and we should like to extend our thanks to their directors and staff: the Institute of Archaeology and the National University Library of the Hebrew University; the Israel Department of Antiquities; the Israel Museum; Museum of the Flagellation Convent, Jerusalem; the Jewish Historical Museum of Belgrade; the Metropolitan Museum; the New York Public Library; the Geniza Research Unit, Cambridge University Library.

The persons who made it possible for us to publish texts from their collections are Mr. Victor Barakat, Dr. Reuven Hecht, Mr. Victor Klagsbald, Dr. Wladimir Rosenbaum and Mr. Joseph Sammel.

Dr. Amos Kloner and Mr. Zvi Maoz of the Israel Department of Antiquities, the excavators of Ḥorvat Rimmon and Ḥorvat Kanaf, placed at our disposal their finds and their notes.

Mme. Hélène Lozachmeur has found and put at our disposal the original photos of Amulets 7a and 7b which were used by the late Professor A. Dupont-Sommer. We are very grateful for this help, which came when the book was nearly ready in the press.

Several friends and colleagues have given valuable advice. We should like to mention in particular the late Professor G.G. Scholem, as well as J.C. Greenfield, M. Sokoloff, G. Stroumsa and Y. Sussman.

Mrs. Ada Yardeni has contributed to this volume much more than drawings and layout; in several places she has improved the readings of the text. Mrs. Tamar Naveh has typed the manuscript and has rendered great assistance in the preparation of the book. Mrs. Miriam Shaked has done the editing of the typescript and prepared it for the press.

The staff of the Magnes Press, and in particular its director, Mr. B. Yehoshua, who has taken personal interest in this book, have done their utmost to produce an attractive-looking volume.

Jerusalem, February 1984 *J.N., S.S.*

INTRODUCTION

1. Aramaic Magic Texts: General Description

The Aramaic texts published and discussed in this book are part of a long-standing tradition of magic in the Near East. Aramaic magic literature continues Assyrian, Babylonian and Egytian magic, and is closely related to the rich literature of magic and incantations in Greek, known to us chiefly from Egytian papyri. These texts, taken together, supplement our knowledge of society, religion and culture during the early centuries of the Christian era. The Aramaic magic texts, of which a a group of hitherto unpublished specimens is given here, form a distinct body of material within the corpus of magic in late antiquity, and we shall try to elucidate them mostly within their own terms.

The inscribed magic artifacts in Aramaic, which are usually supposed to date from the fourth to the sixth or seventh centuries C.E., are known to exist in two basic material forms: (a) earthenware bowls, inscribed with ink, usually on the concave side in spiral concentric circles,[1] all of them found, as far as it is possible to tell from controlled excavations,[2] in the area of Mesopotamia and Iran; and (b) metal sheets, of gold,

[1] Exceptions to this method are not rare. Some other techniques of writing are: The inscription, or part of it, is written on the outside surface of the bowl; the inside area is divided into sections, in which the writing is done in columns (e.g. our Bowl 8); some bowls have their writing arranged in circular lines without a spiral connection between the lines. The usual spiral arrangement can begin either in the centre or on the rim.

[2] In some cases (e.g. our Bowl 9) the provenance as given by the dealer is Palestine, but this statement, which cannot be verified, lacks credibility. For a similar claim made with regard to a Mandaic amulet cf. Naveh 1975, p. 47, note 1.

silver, copper or lead,[3] with the inscription incised into the surface of the metal with the aid of a sharp instrument. These latter amulets were designed to be folded, rolled into a narrow strip, and inserted into a container (reminiscent of a *mezuza* in shape), also made of metal, which could be worn as a phylactery on the body of the owner, or placed in a private house or a synagogue, possibly by suspension (see Commentary to Amulet 11). Amulet 10, which was written on a potsherd, and which served not for protection but for arousing love, was presumably designed to achieve its effect by being placed in fire (see Commentary *ad loc.*). Amulets written on a metal sheet are mostly typical of the area of Syria, Palestine and Asia Minor, although they are not entirely absent from the eastern regions, i.e. Mesopotamia and Iran.[4] It may be taken for granted that besides such solid materials as earthenware and metal, soft materials, such as parchment, papyrus or cloth, were also often used for writing amulets, but have not survived. Amulets on papyrus are in fact known from Egypt, written in Greek and Coptic,[5] and incantations on paper, parchment and cloth have been found in the Cairo Geniza (dating to the 10th century and later); some specimens of these latter texts are given in this book. Metal bowls were used for incantations in the Muslim world (Spoer 1935; Reich 1937-38), but this practice is unknown from the earlier period. We come across medallions and gems inscribed as amulets in the Hellenistic and Iranian cultures,[6] but no such objects inscribed in Aramaic have yet come to light.[7]

[3] At least one Nabataean incantation (Naveh 1979a) is written on a large pebble. One Aramaic amulet is done on a potsherd (our Amulet 10).

[4] Metal amulets written in Syriac have been found in the area of Luristan (a photograph, without decipherment or identification, published in Vanden Berghe 1970). Several Mandaic amulets on sheets of lead have been found; cf. Lidzbarski 1909; Macuch 1967, 1968; Caquot 1972; Naveh 1975.

[5] The most comprehensive collection of the Greek material is in Preisendanz 1928, 1931, 1941.

[6] For the Hellenistic material, cf. chiefly Mouterde 1930; Bonner 1950 and 1951. The rare Pahlavi amulets are discussed in Pope 1938, among the Sasanian seals. Bivar 1967 discusses a Parthian amulet while adducing other Iranian material.

[7] There are some Samaritan amulets written on metal pendants and rings, cf. Ben-Zvi 1976; Kaplan 1967.

Among Semitic amulets from Palestine and its environs we have texts written in three languages, Jewish Aramaic (Amulet 1–3, 5, 7–15), Hebrew (Amulet 4), and Syriac (Amulet 6). The first two varieties, Jewish Aramaic and Hebrew, were presumably written by Jews; they use the regular Hebrew script of the period, whereas the Syriac amulet, which seems to have been composed by a Christian, is written in Estrangelo.

As to the magic practice which accompanied the use of the bowls, different opinions have been expressed. Many bowls were found placed in their original position upside down, a fact which has led scholars to assume that they may have served as traps for demons, being meant to keep the evil spirits imprisoned inside them. This view may gain some support from the fact that in some cases two bowls were found placed facing each other forming between them a closed sphere.[8] Such an enclosed ball-shaped area might be an ideal prison for evil spirits. This theory was rejected by Gordon,[9] who argued that it would be absurd to assume that any house-owner would want to have demons permanently locked in his house. It seems, according to Gordon, much more likely that they would want to get rid of the maleficent spirits and to have them removed from the house. He therefore suggests that the shape of the bowls resembles that of a skull, which may have been regarded as magically effective. We must confess that this argument fails to convince us. The idea of keeping demon-traps in the house need not strike us as more ridiculous than that of placing mouse-traps. In both cases the hated victim, once caught, is incapacitated and is made powerless to cause harm. A harmless demon caught by the bowl constitutes no menace to the safety of the house. The text of the bowls very often talks of chaining and pressing the evil entities; at the same time it may also bid them go away, leave the house and desist from bothering the house-owner. The bowl thus serves both to entrap the evil powers and to reject them; there is no real contradiction between these two propositions.

It may be noted that many bowls, especially in Mandaic, are designed

[8] Pognon 1898, pp. 3 ff.; Hilprecht 1903, pp. 447 f.; Montgomery 1913, pp. 40 ff.

[9] Gordon 1957, pp. 161 f.; Isbell 1975, pp. 13 ff., represents the same view.

as "of the cemetery".[10] This may possibly indicate that some bowls were placed in a cemetery, and this association with the Other World added to their mysterious power. This was by no means the only location which was used in order to increase the efficacy of amulets. The amulets from Nirim (Amulets 11–13) were found in the apse of the synagogue, where the ark of the holy scrolls was presumably placed. It may be assumed that the amulet was put there in order for it to be as close as possible to the spot which served as a gate for communication (through prayer) with heaven. In this connection one may recall that a favourite modern spot for placing appeals to divine help is in the Wailing Wall.

Another theory for the use of the bowls is based on the current modern practice of bowl magic in the Middle East, according to which the bowl is often filled with some liquid and the person who seeks protection or healing is made to drink the water which has absorbed the contents of the formula and has thus been made potent.[11] There is, however, no evidence for such a practice with our Mesopotamian bowls, and it seems rather unlikely that they were used in such a way, which might have effaced the letters or left some other mark on the bowl.

Apart from bowls designed to protect the house and the person of the inhabitants of the house from harm or disease — the most common type — or to arouse love,[12] there are bowls which aim at inflicting evil on an enemy specifically named (e.g. Bowl 9). We have no information as to how these latter bowls were used. One can only try to speculate that they were buried or hidden in the vicinity of the enemy's house, or attached to some personal effect of the victim to be, probably obtained furtively.[13]

[10] Pognon 1898, p. 3, and our Bowl 4:2, which carries the phrase "the spell of the tomb". Some metal amulets were found in tombs; see our Amulet 4 (from Aleppo) and Montgomery 1911, p. 272 (Irbid). See also Montgomery 1913, pp. 40, 43 f.

[11] Canaan 1914, p. 102; similar injunctions in Winkler 1930, pp. 75, 76. Montgomery 1913, p. 45 gives the text of an Arabic brass bowl which also contains a reference to drinking. An early reference to this practice is in the Geniza text T.–S. K1.132: .פתיחת לב
קח קערה חדשה ותכתוב ג̇ ימים בכל יום אלו השימות ותרחוץ אותו במים ותשתה...

[12] Montgomery 1913, Nos. 13, 28. Our Amulet 10 and Geniza 1 and 3 constitute further examples.

[13] We have a recipe for hatred in a late Judaeo-Persian manuscript of magic (JTS 1714,

Three basic Semitic modes of writing are presented by the Babylonian incantation bowls. These are Judaeo-Aramaic, Syriac and Mandaic. A fourth type of writing found on some bowls is Pahlavi, but its interpretation is, unfortunately, extremely difficult. A single bowl which has been seen (at the Yale Babylonian Collection) contains a script looking like Parthian, but its authenticity is questionable and it is likely to be a modern forgery. The different scripts correspond not so much to linguistic or ethnic differences (although such differences also existed), but rather more to distinctions among religious communities; it is therefore interesting to raise the question whether the religious differences are also reflected in the magic texts, or whether one can establish a correspondence between each community's magic and its religious perceptions.

On the plane of language and phraseology we have significant and obvious differences between the various groups. The bowls in Judaeo-Aramaic contain a high degree of material which is derived from the Hebrew scriptures (see the index of scriptural quotations of this volume and Isbell 1975, p. 195). They also contain a small number of peculiarly Jewish concepts of the post-biblical period. The most noteworthy among these is the figure of Yehoshuaᶜ bar (or ben) Peraḥya and the idea, associated often with his name, of giving a *geṭ*, a letter of divorce, to the female demons. This is further elaborated on in some of the texts by the idea of a *geṭ* which is sent across the sea (see below, p. 27). It is remarkable that the figure of Yehoshuaᶜ bar Peraḥya occurs also in two Syriac bowls (Montgomery 1913, Nos. 32–33), where the Jewish term *geṭ* is rendered by the Persian word *dastabīra.*[14] A similar concept which may be of Jewish origin (although it may equally well be a pagan magical concept introduced into the Talmud) occurs in our Bowl 6 (see Commentary to Bowl 6:7–8 **wbyr**...). Several Talmudic associations seem to be present in Bowl 13.

Such elements are specifically Jewish; it is hard to imagine that they could have been composed by non-Jews. One must come to the conclu-

ENA 2326, fol. 1b): ... לשנאה יכתוב על חרס חדש לפּבּפּ עם פּבּפּ בשם... בשם אלו שמות תתנו
The practice accompanying the writing of an incantation for hatred is to bury the inscribed new potsherd in a new tomb. The same instruction with regard to a "new egg" is given in Geniza 6, p. 4:9–11.

[14] On this term cf. Shaked (forthcoming).

sion that the writers of these Jewish-Aramaic bowls were in all probability practitioners of magic who belonged to the Jewish community. This conclusion does not necessarily apply to the clients, who ordered the bowls written for healing, protection or other purposes. There is, in fact, a combination of two factors which makes it likely that not a few of these customers were indeed non-Jews: First, there is the fact that Jewish bowls constitute the great majority of inscribed earthenware bowls from Mesopotamia and Iran, while Jews certainly did not form more than a minority of the population; and secondly, there is the fact that the names of most of the clients were not Jewish, and some of them are theophoric names of Zoroastrian significance. The second fact would not be particulatly significant on its own, since there can be no doubt that many Jews carried Persian and other non-Jewish names. However, when it is combined with the first consideration, it adds some weight to the supposition that magic may have been considered to some extent a Jewish specialization and that pagans and Zoroastrians often turned to Jewish practitioners when they sought an effective remedy, protection or curse.[15]

It may be noted that the amount of Zoroastrian religious influence which may be detected in the Babylonian bowls is very limited; it concerns mostly some names of demons (see Shaked, forthcoming). This observation stands in contrast to the strong presence of Iranian linguistic elements in Babylonian Jewish Aramaic, and to the Iranian influence which may be detected in other spheres of Jewish life.[16] The same may be said of the Syriac bowls, which seem to have been written by pagans (or even by Zoroastrians). Mandaic bowls tend to have some specifically Mandaic terminology (e.g. the divine names **abatur, iurba**), but the same divine and demonic names and concepts are sometimes found also in Jewish bowls.[17] In general, the Mandaic texts follow the same magical conventions as found in Jewish Aramaic and Syriac bowls. In one or two cases Syriac and Mandaic bowls seem to reflect

[15] See further on this in Greenfield 1973a, p.150, and Shaked 1983, pp. 16 f.

[16] This field of study has not yet been treated in a comprehensive study. Sketchy references may be found in Neusner 1968 and 1975.

[17] See Pognon 1898, pp. 93 ff.; Montgomery 1913, p. 96; Yamauchi 1967, pp. 40 ff.

specific Jewish texts.[18] At least one Jewish Aramaic text seems to show clear dependence on a Mandaic *Vorlage* (cf. Greenfield and Naveh's forthcoming article on a Mandaic lead amulet containing four incantations).

2. History of Research : Bowls

The study of the Aramaic magic texts was first begun in the middle of the nineteenth century, when Thomas Ellis translated for Layard six incantation texts in Jewish Aramaic and one in Syriac, inscribed on earthenware bowls which were brought from Mesopotamia to England and deposited in the British Museum (Layard 1853; Levy 1855). Several other texts on bowls, inscribed in Jewish Aramaic and in Syriac, were published afterwards by Rodwell 1873 (for which cf. Halévy 1877); Chwolson 1882; Hyvernat 1885 (with Nöldeke 1885 and Grünbaum 1885); Schwab 1886 and Schwab's later publications; Harkavy 1889; Wohlstein 1893, 1894; Stübe 1895; Lacau 1896. These early attempts at interpretation are often quite faulty, though they paved the way to subsequent research. Towards the end of the century Pognon (1894, 1898) published more than thirty Mandaic incantation bowls found at Khuabir on the Euphrates, west of Baghdad.

The most important single scholarly contribution to the study of the bowls was done by Montgomery 1913, a monumental book containing an edition and translation, with notes and indices, of forty bowls (thirty of them in Jewish Aramaic, seven in Syriac, and three in Mandaic). All of these bowls were found *in situ* in the archaeological excavations conducted by the University of Pennsylvania at Nippur. This fact

[18] See the observations in Greenfield 1973a, as well as the comments above on Yehoshuaʿ bar Peraḥya in Syriac bowls.

enables us to have a unified corpus of inscriptions written (or at least used) in a single town, presumably within a relatively short period of time, often by or for members of the same family. We thus gain an insight into the range of languages and scripts used in Nippur, as well as into the variety and limitations of the magic formulae which were current among the various communities in that town.

Montgomery's work (1913, pp. 16 ff.) has the added benefit of presenting the most comprehensive and solid introduction to the study of the bowls. It gives a detailed survey of earlier publications, thus rendering further discussion of the early studies of the magic bowls unnecessary, and analyzes the most important aspects of the texts and their contents. No attempt will be made in the following to duplicate or supersede Montgomery's treatment of the subject. Only certain points on which new material is available, or on which new suggestions may be offered, will be touched upon in the following pages.

Although Montgomery's readings are on the whole solid and reliable, the book contains a number of textual errors, both with regard to the reading of the bowls and with regard to points of interpretation. Many of these were corrected and clarified in an important review article by J.N. Epstein (1921-1922), which, unfortunately, was not taken into account by many of the scholars who have worked in this field since, with the result that several of Montgomery's patent errors have been perpetuated in the literature.[19]

The next most important name in this field of study is C.H. Gordon, who has in a series of articles,[20] published a great many new bowls from various collections in the U.S.A., Europe and the Middle East. The study of the magic bowls further benefited from the fact that a number of students of Professor Gordon felt inspired to work on this material; as a result there were published several dissertations containing corpora of bowls in Mandaic (Yamauchi 1967), Syriac (Hamilton 1971) and Jewish Aramaic (Isbell 1975), as well as a Handbook of the latter

[19] This observation applies to the work of C.H. Gordon, whose readings are generally reliable, as well as to that of his students Rossell 1953; Yamauchi 1967; and Isbell 1975. In Hamilton 1971 the Syriac texts of Montgomery are corrected in the light of Epstein's comments.

[20] See Bibliography under Gordon. The only work done on the subject in the intervening period between Montgomery's and Gordon's is by Fuÿe 1925.

language, in which a grammatical sketch is included (Rossell 1953). The texts collected in these corpora make up the following total numbers: 72 in Jewish Aramaic, 33 in Mandaic and 21 in Syriac. It may be remarked that not all the published bowls were incorporated into these collections.[21]

The more recent publications of texts in this field include Oberman 1940; Teixidor 1962; Jeruzalmi 1963; Yamauchi 1965; McCullough 1967; [22] Borisov 1969; Kaufman 1973, 1975; Geller 1976, 1980; Harviainen 1981.

3. Amulets Published So Far

The state of study of the Palestinian incantation texts is much less satisfactory than that of the Mesopotamian bowls. One part of the problem is that the small number of Palestinian texts makes their comparative study difficult. Another problem is that these texts were inscribed on small metal plaques (mainly silver, copper and lead), which were rolled up. The unrolling of the generally corroded fragile material and then the reading of the preserved tiny letters, which often consist of shallow scratches on the surface of the material, is by no means an easy task. Among the few generally fragmentary Palestinian amulets five were published at the beginning of this century: one, Amulet 4, is from Aleppo (Schwab 1906); one, Amulet 5, from Emmaus (Vincent 1908) and three from Irbid (Montgomery 1911). Two other amulets, Amulets 7a–b, were found at Ağabeyli in Turkey, near the Syrian border (Dupont-Sommer 1950/51). Still another, of unknown provenance,

[21] Missing from Isbell 1975 are, for example, the texts published in Hyvernat 1885; Harkavy 1889; Wohlstein 1893 and 1894; Stübe 1895; Fuÿe 1925; Borisov 1969. Not all of these were published without facsimiles.

[22] Cf. the reviews by Segal 1970; Yamauchi 1970.

Amulet 8, was published in Testa 1967. The latest publication of an amulet, Amulet 9, is by Klein-Franke 1971. The amulet is in Cologne, Germany, and may have come from Oxyrrhynchus in Egypt.

The amulets preserved in the New York Public Library, of which three were published by Montgomery in 1911, are part of a group of six metal amulets which were donated by Mrs. Henry Draper. Their state of preservation is such that it is very difficult to improve much on Montgomery's readings (which in some cases are evidently wrong).[23] We have therefore decided to leave them out of the present publication, which otherwise aims at giving a complete corpus of the known Aramaic amulets. Apart from Aramaic amulets we have included here one amulet in Syriac, published by Dupont-Sommer 1946, where we believe we can offer an improved reading and interpretation. Otherwise, because of the geographical definition which we have found useful to adopt with regard to amulets, namely those coming from the region of Palestine and adjoining countries, we have excluded from this corpus metal amulets from Iran and Mesopotamia in Mandaic and Syriac (see above, note 4).

The first amulet of this kind to be published, found near Aleppo (Schwab 1906; our Amulet 4), is one of the longest Palestinian amulets known. It contains some manifestly Jewish elements (e.g. the figure of 248 limbs, some biblical allusions, and many Hebrew phrases), together with the usual magic terminology (e.g. Ablanathanalba, Marmaraot, **ʾwgryt**). A prominent symbol which occurs in the text is strongly reminiscent of the Christian monogram XP. It has led scholars to believe that we are faced here with a Judaeo-Christian monument, though this does not seem proven, as the symbol may have been widely used outside Christian circles and may have preceded Christianity.

Vincent published in 1908 a fragmentary amulet of some five lines

[23] As an example for lines where the readings of Montgomery 1911 may be improved upon with some confidence, cf. the beginning of New York Public Library, Hebrew amulet No. 3 (Montgomery's amulet A) where one may read:

1. ובחטרה דמשה ובציצה דאהר[ן]
2. כהנה רבה ובעזקתה דשלמה ו(ב)[מג]
3. נה דדויד ובקרנתה דמדבחא ובשמ(ה)
4. [ד]אלהא חיה וקימה ד(תי)גע[רון]

The combination **bḥwṭrʾ dmšh nbyyʾ... wbʿzqtyh dšlmh br dwd mlkʾ dyś** [**rʾl**] occurs in the Geniza fragment ENA 3513.11a.

found in Emmaus (our Amulet 5). Vincent's readings, which have been followed by subsequent scholars, have proved upon inspection to be in need of emendations, which are included in the edition presented here. We encounter in this amulet some divine names (Masagiel, Shamriel) and the magic term **krqṭyry**ʾ "magic characters, magic signs".

It has been the bad luck of this material, perhaps because of its rarity and the difficulties inherent in its decipherment, that it suffered in some cases from fanciful interpretations and unreasonable speculations. Thus, one amulet (our Amulet 6) was heralded upon its first publication as containing a gnostic doctrine relating to the letter *waw* (Dupont-Sommer 1946); subsequently it has been shown (by Gordon 1949, 1953) that not even once does the name of this letter occur in the text. Another text (our Amulet 7) was understood to allude to the Great God, who would be different from the God of Israel (Dupont-Sommer 1950/51, p. 208 on lines 15–16), but this was shown to be inexact (Scholem 1965, pp. 84 ff.). In both these cases the new reading offered here tends to confirm the revised interpretations, and in some measure it adds new details which improve our understanding of the amulets. Thus, the Syriac amulet (our Amulet 6) is now shown to contain an allusion to three deities, who are named Bar-Theon, Rabbā Ḥasīnā and Qaddiš Īlā "who stand in the great ford of the sea". It talks of a demon, called apparently Tarpas-dukh. In the Aramaic amulet (our Amulet 7) we may eliminate the speculation as to the "womb to be blessed" as well as to Metatron, as we can recognize the name of the client Shalluna bar Demetrion in lines 7–8. On the other hand there is a possibility of reading (in lines 14–15) a reference to words which rise "beside (or behind?) the throne", an allusion which brings to mind the notion of the angel whose name, Metatron, indicates that he is "beside or behind the throne".

A similar scholarly controversy has arisen with regard to an amulet which was apparently found near Jerusalem (our Amulet 8). The scholar who first published it regarded it as a blessing of the "oil of faith" (Testa 1967), but this interpretation was rightly rejected by Milik 1967 in favour of the more likely reading of the plaque as an incantation. We can see from the new reading that a demon by the name of Marten daughter of Qoriel is adjured in the name of the angel Agirat.

Finally, an amulet here reprinted with some corrections (our Amulet 9) adjures a spirit called "Fever and Shivering", evidently with the aim of healing the client, a certain Marian daughter of Esther.

4. The Newly Found Amulets

The corpus of amulets presented here is enriched by nine newly discovered texts, all, except three (Amulets 1,14,15) coming from controlled excavations in Israel, two from Ḥorvat Kanaf, near the Sea of Galilee (Amulets 2–3), one from Ḥorvat Rimmon, north of Beer-Sheba (Amulet 10) and three from Nirim in South Western Israel (Amulets 11–13). The last six amulets (Amulets 10–15) reached us at a stage when the corpus was ready for the press, and the numbers assigned had to follow at the end of the group.

As to the dating of the amulets, the archaeological data converge around the fifth-sixth centuries C.E. This dating is provided very clearly in the case of Nirim (Amulets 11–13), where the late Roman and Byzantine coins help in defining the period from which the amulets stem. The conclusion reached by L.Y. Rahmani as to the period of the small finds places them in the sixth century C.E. A similar conclusion was reached by the excavators of Ḥorvat Rimmon (fifth-sixth century C.E.) and Ḥorvat Kanaf (same period).

Amulet 1 is designated for healing the client. It contains several Jewish formulae, such as are encountered in the prayer before sleep *(Qeri'at shemaʿ ʿal ham-miṭṭa),* as well as biblical quotations. It also has a series of magic names, and an interesting sequence of nouns, each one preceded by the word **mʿyn,** which may mean either "from the eye of..." or "in the form of...".

Amulet 2, more specifically formulated for healing, commands "the fever and the shiver, the female demon and the spirits" to be driven out from the body of its owner.

Amulet 3 is for the protection of "Rabbi Eleazar..., the servant of the God of Heaven". This title is quite unusual in our amulets. Some of the text seems to suggest that the amulet is designed for protecting the owner on the road: "In every place where this amulet will be seen, you (the evil spirit) should not detain Eleazar, son of Esther. And if you detain him , you will be cast immediately into a burning furnace". Other parts seem to beg for the healing of the owner: "Send healing and cure to Eleazar". This amulet also contains verbal allusions to the Bible.

Amulet 10 is a love charm. It is written on an unbaked potsherd, which must have been meant to be thrown into the fire after the writing of the amulet, and was probably used in this way, as far as we can tell from the black areas caused by fire on the surface of the sherd. The evidence for writing amulets on unbaked clay comes from the Judaeo-Arabic texts of the Geniza, where the term *nayy* "uncooked" occurs. The subsequent burning in fire was alluded to in the text of this amulet (and in Geniza amulets of similar nature) by the words: "Just as this sherd burns, so shall burn the heart of..."

Amulet 11 is for curing its owner from headache, which is called here by the Greek term κεφαλαργία, written **qplrgy**ʾ. The pain is considered to go into the bones (?) of the chest.

Amulet 12 is designated for the protection of a woman and her child. Here too Jewish formulae are quite conspicuous. The female customer is called Shlamṣu, a hypocoristic form of Shlomṣiyyon.

Amulet 13 is for a woman called Esther daughter of Tatis. Esther is the most widely attested feminine name in these amulets. The amulet is designated to save her from evil spirits, and much of the text is taken by a quotation from Exodus 15:26.

Amulet 14, which is very fragmentary, is remarkable for its combination of Hebrew-Aramaic with Greek.

Amulet 15 is based on an interesting *historiola,* or magic story, which is also available to us in a Babylonian version in Bowls 12a and 12b. This story enjoyed widespread popularity in Christian magic literature of the East, where the name of the helper was identified with Saint Sisinnius. The names of the helpers in this amulet were perpetuated in late Jewish magic under the form Sanoy, Sansanoy and Samangalof, in amulets which are used for the protection of a new-born baby and its mother. The names of the main actors in our amulet are partly metaphorical: The woman is called Smamit (= spider or lizard), the attacking fiend Sideros (=iron), while the names of the helpers, **swny, swswny** and **snygly,** have not yet received satisfactory explanation. It may be significant that all names begin with the letter *s.*

5. Magic Bowls in the Present Volume

The present volume contains most of the legible bowls available in Jerusalem. These are bowls which form part of the collection of the Institute of Archaeology of the Hebrew Universty (Nos. 2–4), as well as those of the Israel Museum (Nos. 5–8). In addition we have included a bowl recently presented to the Jewish National and University Library in Jerusalem (No. 12a), together with a parallel text which occurs in a bowl at the New York Metropolitan Museum (12b). We are also publishing two bowls seen in the hands of an antique dealer in Jerusalem, Mr. Victor Barakat (Nos. 1 and 9), although the present whereabouts of these latter bowls is unknown. The texts of two unpublished bowls at the Jewish Historical Museum in Belgrade, Yugoslavia, photographs of which have been sent to Jerusalem for study and publication, have also been included (Bowls 10, 11). A last addition to this group of bowls comes from the Klagsbald Collection, Jerusalem (Bowl 13).

Several points of interest are brought out by the new bowl texts which are published in this volume. Two bowls contained in this collection are in Syriac, 1 and 10. Bowl 1 contains basically a well-known text, occurring on three Syriac bowls so far published (see Commentary to Bowl 1). The parallel text presented in this new bowl allows us to complement and improve certain readings in the previously published texts, and it confirms some of J.N. Epstein's conjectural readings (cf. Commentary to lines 3–4). A point which can be made on the basis of this text and which clarifies a formula in Aramaic bowls is the possibility of eliminating the figure of Hermes where it does not belong. It is clear that in Montgomery Nos. 2 and 27 what was regarded as an allusion to the Greek god is actually a reference to steel (cf. Commentary to line 12). It is a recurrent phrase in the bowls that the sorcerer is surrounded by a wall of pure steel, or clothed with a garment of pure steel.

Bowl 10 uses some interesting metaphors for the demons who are to be abjured. They are to be like birds who fly and change places (which is why they should leave the body and person of the client), and they should be like wax which melts in fire. It is not unlikely that such formulae were accompanied by suitable magic practices of the sympathetic kind.

Our Bowl 2 (in Jewish Aramaic) has five parallel texts already published. The new text again helps establish the correct readings of the formulae. From the study of Bowls 1 and 2 we may learn something of the mechanism of the transmission of magic formulae, which is not entirely that of a scribal tradition, but is akin in some respects to oral transmission. The combination of the two modes of transmission is clearly visible in the list of eleven names of angels (see Commentary to lines 6–7), where we can see certain modifications which may be attributed to copying, while others are only comprehensible in terms of free oral tradition.

Bowl 2 also affords a possibility of establishing the original form of the divine (or angel) name which occurs in Mandaic as **iurba,** identified with Adonai. The element **yw** in **ywrbʾ** is certainly a development of the divine name Yah, Yahu etc. (which occurs here as **yyy**), with the epithet *rabbā*. Although this figure is apparently defined here as an angel, there are eleven names of other angels who assist him against the demons, a fact which establishes his lofty position as a deity.

The international character of this magic is apparent in the expression **byt ʾylhy wbyt knyštʾ** (line 5), which seems to refer to pagan temple(s) and to Jewish synagogue(s).

Bowl 3 has a glaring example of Hebrew spelled from hearing, without acquaintance with the traditional spelling, when Num. 10:35 is given as ...וחיחי בין נסוע הארון וימר מושה קומה יהוה ויפוצו איבאך וינסו מ מיפנך

Bowl 4 has a curious illustration of an undefinable human figure. The ribbons waving to the left of the figure may be associated with the ribbons which constitute a symbol of royalty in Sasanian iconography; cf. Göbl 1971, pp. 11f. If this was intended in the picture, it may be possible to regard **mlknʾ** (in line 4) as signifying "I am king" or "I rule", rather than "I advise", as preferred in our translation.

Yehoshuaʿ bar Peraḥya is a well-known figure in the Aramaic incantation bowls. He occurs in Bowl 5, where he is associated, as is usual, with the practice of giving a deed of divorce (*geṭ*) to a female demon, named Lilit; the legal complication which arises in this situation is similar to that of a *geṭ* sent across the sea, which is valid. However, the *geṭ* lacks force because the man who writes it does not know the name of the woman. This is rectified by the divine powers, who add the name in the blank space. The situation is used to make the exorcism valid in all cases, "both when I know the name, and when I do not know the name" (line 4). The point about the name of the demoness being unknown is so far only attested in this text, but it may explain the particular difficulty of the *geṭ* which comes from across the sea, with an incomplete name.

Bowl 6 presents a curious introductory text which seems to be moulded partly on the Book of Jonah, but also uses other biblical allusions (e.g. Ps. 115:4–6), as well as what looks like an association with a phrase in the Babylonian Talmud (Taʿanit 8a; see Commentary to 6:7–8). A sequence of chronological designations, which has parallels in other magic texts, is included, and also a reference to groups of people "who sit in market places and streets, and who go out on the roads". This kind of enumeration is reminiscent of the various lists of nationalities which occur on some bowls; see e.g. Kaufman 1975, where the spirits of different nationalities are mentioned.

Bowl 7 is so unusually formulated that it partly defies translation. The translation provided is to a large extent conjectural. It provides us, nevertheless, with some interesting parallels to late Jewish magical literature. The phrase **kmypl ḥysyʾ mn ṭwrʾ** etc. can be understood in the light of *The Sword of Moses* (Gaster 1898), which in its turn also gains in clarity by this comparison.

Bowl 8 has an unusual arrangement in columns radiating from the centre cross-like. This is the only text in our collection which has already been published (it was first printed in a Hebrew article by Narqis 1935), and it is re-edited in order to complete the collection of the Jerusalem bowls, as well as for rectifying some minor points in the reading.

Bowl 9 is particularly interesting in that it provides a rare example of a text devoted to imprecations addressed by name against an enemy, Judah bar Nanai. The language of the curses is based on biblical verses, and in some cases it invents non-existent biblical phrases; **wlʾ thʾ ʾswth lmḥtm** betrays the intention of the writer, since he fell into the trap of using Aramaic words where he obviously thought he was writing in good Biblical Hebrew. A list of diseases, not all of them understood by us, is an interesting feature of this bowl.

Bowl 11 provides us with some new features. A seemingly Iranian term for a magic formula, **mhryn**, occurs here for the first time, as well as such unusual forms as **pydgmy** and **ʾryswtʾ** (the latter denoting a magic bane). Two biblical verses are intertwined for magical purposes in lines 6–7 by giving a word of each successively.

Under number 12 two bowls which have a similar text are given in parallel columns, together with the text of Amulet 15, which contains the same story. For some comments on the story of Smamit and her helpers see above in the description of Amulet 15 (p. 25).

The main interest of Bowl 13 is in its large size and very long text as well as in some features of its contents. It contains a unique description of the physical appearance of the demon addressed in the incantation, apparently the demon Bagdana, "head of sixty kingdoms, whose power is the power of a blast, whose heat is the heat of fire" and so on. Besides these attributes of power and of the terror which he arouses, we have such concrete details as "his head is that of a lion, his molar teeth are those of a she-wolf, his teeth are those of a tiger, the draughts of his mouth are furnaces of fire" and so on. The text of this bowl is also remarkable by the fact that it has a well defined structure of parallel passages, which begin with similar formulae, although the precise significance of the dialogue formed by these passages is not entirely clear. All in all, the text of this bowl presents a unique incantation formula, which has no parallel in other magic texts as far as we know.

6. **Other Texts of Magic and the Geniza Material**

The objective of this study was to publish the texts of our amulets and bowls with readings and intepretations which would be as exact and thorough as possible. While doing this work we checked previously published incantation texts (as far as possible from photographs or facsimile drawings) without relying too much on previous editions. Thus we could suggest revised readings not only for the amulets which we have re-edited (Amulets 4–9), but also for several phrases in the previously published Mesopotamian bowl texts.

In order to get acquainted with the whole magical literature in antiquity, major publications of Greek magic papyri and various magic books which have survived, such as the Christian Syriac *Book of Protection* (Gollancz 1912) or the Jewish *Sword of Moses* (Gaster 1898) and *Sefer ha-razim*, which was found among the Geniza materials, were checked. However, among the fragments which survived in the Cairo

Geniza there are many amulets and pages of magic books which have not yet been treated by scholars. We have found it necessary to go through some of this material and compare it with other Jewish magical texts, although we have not aimed at completeness in this field.

The Geniza amulets and magic books were written in the Middle Ages, generally in Egypt itself, but some presumably in the neighbouring countries, as e.g. Palestine. The writers of these texts spoke Arabic (in certain cases Persian, and in one case a Persian dialect), but their magic texts were written in an interesting mixture of Hebrew, Aramaic and Arabic (including some Greek terms and words). As for the contents, it is obvious that the magic of the Geniza follows in general the Palestinian tradition. Thus it is possible in some cases to understand phrases in the Palestinian amulets and restore the fragmentary love charm from Ḥorvat Rimmon only by comparing them with the formulae used in the Geniza magic texts. A selection of five Geniza amulets (Geniza 1, 3–4, 7–8) and three fragments of magic books (Geniza 2, 5–6) is given here. Apart from these texts, some occasional phrases from further unpublished Geniza fragments are quoted in the Commentary. The use of the Geniza texts is designed to help in elucidating certain obscurities and to add paralled material to the formulae discussed in the main parts of the book (mainly in connection with the amulets).

7. Notes on the Language of the Texts

Short sketches of the three main dialects of the bowls are provided in the following publications: Rossell 1953 (Jewish Aramaic); Yamauchi 1967 (Mandaic); and Hamilton 1971 (Syriac). Useful remarks on some expressions will be found in Epstein 1960, p. 14; Levine 1970; Greenfield 1973a and 1973b. On some formulae there are also remarks in Niggemeyer 1975 (which is mainly concerned with those in *Sefer harazim*); Gruenwald 1980; and Niditch 1979. Mention should also be made of the observations by F. Rosenthal 1939, pp. 218 ff., 233 ff. Some points of detail have been dealt with by Schiffman 1973 and Sperber 1966.

In discussing the language of the bowls and the amulets published in this volume, we have to distinguish three groups of texts: Syriac (Bowls 1 and 10 and Amulet 6); Babylonian Jewish Aramaic (Bowls 2–9, 11–13); Palestinian Jewish Aramaic (Amulets 1–3, 5, 7–15). In Amulet 4 the Hebrew element is predominant.

a. The Syriac Bowls

The three Syriac texts are not written in the same script: the script of Bowl 1 is Proto-Manichaean, more akin to Palmyrene cursive (cf. Montgomery 1913, Nos. 31–37), while Bowl 10 and Amulet 6 are in Estrangelo. All three Syriac texts share some common features: the determined state is always written with a final *alef* and the masculine plural det. st., -*ē*, is expressed by *alef* (generally marked by a *seyāme*). *Alef* as a medial *mater lectionis* occurs in Bowl 1, cf. **y'tẅh** (in line 6), **ym'm'** (line 13). *ʿAyin* and *ḥet* are weak , cf. **šm'** (for **šmʿ** in 1:8); **mbʿd'** (for **mʿbd'** in Bowls 1:11; 10:8); **bwtk** (for **bʿwtk** in Amulet 6:10); **ḥdyn** and **ḥd'** (for **hdyn** and **hd'** in Bowl 10:7, 11, 13); *he* is sometimes omitted, cf. **nywn** (10:10). Moreover, in Bowl 10 *ʿayin* is used as an initial *mater lectionis* for the designation of the vowel *e/i,* cf. **ʿmm'** (line 4) **br-ʿm'** (line 6), **ʿtqṭlw** (line 12), etc. This trait is characteristic also of Mandaic (cf. Yamauchi 1967, pp. 75f.).

Further features of the orthography of the Syriac in Bowl 1 are: a line over the final part of words usually marks the participle (e.g. **mḥw'** line 6, **mtqr'** line 9). The *seyāme* is sometimes used for marking forms which are only reminiscent of the plural (e.g. **y'tẅh,** Bowl 1:6). The third person singular in both bowls has the typical Syriac **n-** prefix, e.g. **nhw'** (1:8), **nḥdrh** (1:11); **nytnṭr** (10:6) etc. If the reading **lkbyšwh** (10:13) is correct, *lamed* occurs for the *nun* prefix in this case.

b. The Bowls in Babylonian Jewish Aramaic

The language of the bowls written in the Jewish script has the clear features of Babylonian Jewish Aramaic. The plural masculine, for example, has quite often the -*ē* ending, as in Syriac, but here it is expressed by a final *yod*: cf. **kwkby wmzly** (Bowl 2:3); **byšy wtqypy** (Bowl 6:2), etc. The final -*ā* designating the determined state (in singular masculine and in singular and plural feminine) is generally marked by an *alef,* but there are quite a number of words ending with a final *he* (as in Palestinian Jewish Aramaic), cf. mainly the word **ʾrʿh** in Bowls 2:8; 3:4; 5:2; 7:8; but also **bny ʾynšh** (6:2,5); **ywblh** (6:7); **byryʾth** (6:9); **ʾswth** (11:7); **ršyʿh** (12a:3); **nḥšh** (12b:3); **rbh** (12a:6); **mqdšh** (12b:6). For this phenomenon, cf. Rossell 1953, p. 36.

Bowl 6 has the characteristic Babylonian Jewish Aramaic *paʿʿel* infinitive **lštwqy wlskwry** (line 1), but in line 5 there occurs **lštqʾ**. Rossell 1953, p. 53 has already remarked on this: "the infinitive may be *qaṭṭālā,* or more commonly, *qaṭṭōlē*".

It has been pointed out that in Babylonian Jewish Aramaic the *qamaṣ* was quite often pronounced *o.* In the bowl-texts there is sometimes a *waw,* where an *ā* is expected (cf. Rossell 1953, p. 20). This trait is quite prominent in Bowl 12a, cf. **smwmyt** (line 1), **wʿwl** (line 5), **ywtyh** (lines 5, 6, 7), **qwmw** (line 6), and in Bowl 13, cf. **qwmk** (line 2), **qwmh** (line 8) and perhaps **ywyty** (line 1). Since this phenomenon occurs in a limited number of bowls only, it may justify the assumption of Sharvit 1974, p. 555, according to which Babylonian Jewish Aramaic possessed two contemporary pronunciations of the *qamaṣ*, probably distributed by areas, one where we may observe the development *ā* > *ō*, while in another area the *qamaṣ* was pronounced *ā*. A similar division had been suggested for Palestine. On this problem cf. also the study by Boyarin 1978b.

The *shwa* was sometimes written with a *yod.* This is attested not only with regard to the conjunction **wy-**, the prepositions **by-**, **ly-**, and the relative pronoun **dy-** (cf. Rossell 1953, p. 21 and our Commentary to Bowl 2), but also within the words themselves as **pyryšw** (Bowl 5:4–5); **tyštqwn** (*paʿʿel* imperfect, Bowl 6:9). This trait occurs also in Amulet 3:4, **tyḥšyn** (*paʿʿel* imp.).

Alef is often elided in the bowls; examples are **dyttʾ** (2:9), **ytyttʾ** (2:9), **dymʾ** (2:4).

Besides the older form of the possessive suffix of the third person singular masculine attached to a plural noun, **-why**, which is attested in forms like **ḥzwhy** (Bowl 9:13), we have the younger form with **-yh,** e.g. **šqyh** (Bowl 9:3) and **kkyh, šynyh** (Bowl 13:4), **ʿynyh** (Bowl 13:5) and similar forms in Bowl 13. In Syriac we have such a form in **bnyh** "his sons" (Bowl 10:6). For this phenomenon cf. Epstein 1960, p. 123; Rossell 1953, p. 38. In addition we have the interesting hybrid form **(h)dmyhwʾ** (Bowl 9:13). With regard to the preposition **ʿl**, again, both suffixes for the third person singular masculine are used, sometimes in one and the same bowl; cf. **ʿlyh** (Bowl 9:7), **ʿlwhy** (Bowl 9:14). In contrast, the Palestinian forms attested in the amulets tend to show this ending as **-wy** (Amulet 3:15, 16; 5:5,7; 15:16). Amulet 1:22 has the full form **bgydwhy wbgrmwhy.**

c. The Amulets

Since Amulets 2, 3 and 10–13 were found in excavations carried out in Palestinian sites, they may be considered — together with the synagogue inscriptions (Naveh 1978) — as a reliable witnesses for the description of Palestinian Jewish Aramaic. Similar traits can be found in Amulets 7 and 9, although they stem from Ağabeyli (in southern Turkey) and Oxyrrhynchus (in Egypt). The other amulets (with the obvious exception of 6, which is in Syriac), may be presumed to derive from Palestine or its immediate vicinity.

In most Palestinian texts the determined state is generally marked by *he,* but the Nirim amulets display a preponderance of *alef.*

The negative *lā* is spelled **lh** in two amulets: Amulet 3:4 and 9:6.

A typical Galilean Aramaic trait is the absence of initial *lamed* in the infinitives, cf. **mʾsyh** and **mgʿwr** in Amulet 2:1,11. This can be compared to **dʿtyd mʿbd mṣwth** in the inscription of the synagogue at Tiberias (Naveh 1978, No. 26). The above-mentioned form **mʾsyh,** i.e. the *paʿʿel* infinitive with an initial *mem,* is also characteristic of Galilean Aramaic. For **plṭʾ**, where the existence of a prefix is uncertain, see Commentary to Amulet 13:4.

The form **šwmyh** in Amulets 3:6 and 9:5 is well-known in Palestinian Christian Aramaic (Schulthess 1903, p. 209), and it occurs in two synagogue inscriptions (Naveh 1978, Nos. 20, 70).

As in the synagogue inscriptions, there are here signs for the weakening of the gutturals, cf. **ʾwryth** in Amulet 9:1 (for **ʿryth,** occurring in Amulet 2:2,12 and **hʿryh** in the Hebrew text of Amulet 4:29; but see Commentary to Amulet 9:1. A case of *ʿayin* for *alef* occurs in **mrʿšy** (Amulet 14:8), as part of the same phenomenon. The *alef* was left out by the writer of Amulet 9: cf. **mryn brth dstr** (9:2), as against **rby ʾlʿzr brh dʾstr** (Amulet 3:5).

Incidentally, the Palestinian form **rby** (cf. Naveh 1978, p. 58) occurs in Amulet 3, whereas the Babylonian form **rb** occurs in a bowl text (cf. Harviainen 1981, p. 5:8,9). For the title of the well-known authority on magic , R. Joshua bar Peraḥya, the form attested on Babylonian bowls seems to be invariably *rabbi,* as in the Palestinian tradition, presumably because this is a name borrowed into Babylonia from Palestine. This is also the case in our Bowl 5. (Montgomery 1913, Nos. 32, 33, reads in the Syriac text **rb yyšwʿ**, but an examination of the facsimiles suggests that the correct reading should be **rby,** followed by **yšwʿ**; in Montgomery No. 17 Yehoshuaʿ ben Peraḥya is not given a title). Cohen 1981, p. 78, collected forms of the title **rby.** In about five cases the "Babylonian" form occurs in Palestine.

The expression **ytḥzh yt** in Amulet 3:14, i.e. the accusative particle **yt** after a passive verb, has some parallels in the Targum.

A typical Palestinian form is the plural imperative **ʾswn** (Amulet 3:22), whereas the third person plural feminine perfect **slqh** (Amulet 7:14) occurs in *qeri* Biblical Aramaic and the language of Onqelos.

d. Contacts Between Palestine and Babylonia

There were, no doubt, strong connections between the magical tradition of Jewish Palestine and that current among the Jews of Babylonia. This is demonstrated by various phrases and expressions which are common to both the amulets and the bowls. The opening formula of Amulet 3 occurs in three of the magic bowls (Isbell 1975, Nos. 67 and 69; Isbell 1976, p. 23). The use of the phrase from Zach. 3:2, which is quite common in the bowls (cf. our Bowl 11:5–6), occurs in Amulet 1:5–6. The story told in Amulet 7:16–22 has close parallels in two bowls dealt with by Gordon 1971, pp. 233 f. and 236 f.

This connection between the two traditions is also visible in the orthography. It has already been noted that in the bowls there are some *he* endings for marking the determined state. On the other hand, in the amulets there are several *alef* endings.

The overlapping between the Babylonian and the Palestinian traditions may occasionally be noticed in some points of vocabulary. Thus the verb **ḤMʾ** occurs in the Babylonian Bowl 6:4, although it is generally considered to belong to western Aramaic (cf. Kutscher 1971, cols. 270, 274). This is, however, a verb which is known to occur outside the area of western Aramaic (cf. Tal 1975, p. 199 and note 24).

Amulet 15, with Bowls 12a and 12b, present a concrete case of a Palestinian-Babylonian contact. The formula contained in these magic texts certainly travelled from west to east. Along with the formula and the names of the heroes of the story some typical Palestinian expressions were adopted by the writers of the Babylonian bowls: cf. **ʾrtq** (for which see Kutscher 1971, col. 274). In other cases, the writers of the bowls made the necessary linguistic adjustments to translate the language of the formula into Babylonian Aramaic: e.g. Palestinian **kl hn d-** "everywhere" (Amulet 15:19) corresponds to **kl ʾtr d-** in Bowl 12:VIIIb.

8. Magic in the Palestinian Amulets and their Religious World

While this book aims to give, for the first time, a full and accurate reading and interpretation of all the legible amulets from Palestine and the neighbouring areas, it seems proper to try and attempt an interpretation of the world of religion and of the occult as it emerges from these texts. Of the period in which these amulets were written we do not have too many direct epigraphical traces in Palestine, especially not in Aramaic.[24] And yet this is a period of great importance in Jewish history: it is the period in which post-exilic Judaism crystallized, the Jerusalem Talmud emerged, and to a very large extent the final shape of late Judaism was determined. The study of these texts, however short they are, and however fragmentary, should therefore prove to be of considerable interest.

The Jewish influence in the magic of the period is conspicuous. This can be seen both in the Greek and Coptic papyri from Egypt and in the Mesopotamian bowls which use non-Jewish scripts (see above, p. 18). For its own part, however, "Jewish" magic, i.e. magic written by Jews and using the Hebrew script, is also cosmopolitan, containing as it does religious elements borrowed from other cults and cultures, as do other types of magic written in other scripts. It partakes with other forms of neighbouring contemporary magic the use and address of such prominent magical figures as Abrasax, Marmaraot, Ablanatanalba, Sesengen

24 The most important epigraphical material is the collection of synagogue inscriptions, some of them extremely short; see Naveh 1978. Apart from these, there are a number of funerary inscriptions; See Frey 1952, though the latest finds have not yet been collected.

Bar Ferenges. It contains allusions to such concepts and *topoi* of magic as the great importance of iron and copper, the careful inclusion in the incantation of a reference to all possible directions: right, left, front, behind, and above (with the deliberate omission of the world underneath; see Amulet 1). It makes use of magic letters and magic figures, of a comprehensive number for the limbs of the body (usually 248, but there are other figures), and sometimes of a list of specific limbs, of careful references to divisions of time (day, week, month, year), and of other themes of a similar nature.

Within this general web of magical elements, there are elements which may strike us as Jewish. Some of these have become part of the general non-Jewish magic tradition, e.g. names such as Yah, Yahu, Sabaoth, El, I-am-who-I-am, as well as formulae such as Amen, Selah, etc. More to the point are the direct biblical quotations and the biblical allusions, and sometimes the made-up biblical verses, which underline the fact that the amulets were composed in a *milieu* where the Bible was the sacred scripture, and quoting it, or at least pretending to quote it, was deemed to be of special magic power. It is of course important to bear in mind that we have to do here in most cases with a popular type of practice, and with a level of learning that does not go very deep.

Can any doubt be raised as to the orthodoxy, in terms of Jewish religion, of the people who wrote and used these amulets? Contemporary Jewish sources, notably the Talmudic and Midrashic literatures, are notoriously ambiguous about magic.[25] It must be recalled that we should not take the utterances of the sages in the matter of magic at face value. Magic is officially condemned, but many people who practised what we call "magic" would deny that they indulged in a practice which was against Jewish law. They would say that they practised healing, protection, etc., and that they relied not on magical powers, but on the power of God and His angels. The argument about the legitimacy of magic, among Jews just as in other cultures, sometimes revolves around the definition of terms.

Of more fundamental importance is the question as to what powers are invoked in the Jewish amulets, and what position they are deemed to occupy. In the Jewish bowl texts from Mesopotamia, the divine names

[25] See L. Blau 1898, pp. 19 ff.; Urbach 1975, pp. 97 ff.

appealed to include, besides Yahweh and his epithets, and the Jewish angels Gabriel, Yehoel, Yequtiel, Michael, Nuriel, etc., also names of pagan gods such as the Greek Hermes (see Montgomery 1913, p. 99); the Mesopotamian and Syrian Belti, Nereg, Nanai, Shamish, Dlibat and Mot (see Index here and in Montgomery 1913); the Iranian Anahid, Danahish, Bagdana, and others.

The Palestinian amulets in Jewish script do not contain references to such pagan deities. In the amulets, as far as we can make out, the various powers invoked are apparently conceived as being magic agents dependent on or subordinate to Yah the God of Israel. This seems to be the case in most amulets, though in some of them (Nos. 5, 8 and 10) the God of Israel is not mentioned at all. Amulet 3:11 speaks of "Yahu **krmsys,** the great God"; whatever the actual identity of this **krmsys,** it seems to figure here as an epithet of Yahu, and not as an independent power.

Abrasax is very frequently invoked in the Palestinian charms (see Amulets 1:9; 2:3; 12:2). According to *Sefer ha-razim* IV:3 Abrasax is the first among some thirty angels directing the sun during the day. In the same chapter of *Sefer ha-razim,* a Greek prayer addressed to Helios, the sun god, is given in Hebrew transcription. The text says: "Holy, eastern Helios, good sailor, highest governor, most exalted, who of old regulate the heavenly wheel, holy umpire, controller of the poles, Lord, glorious guide, master, soldier".[26] It may be mentioned in this connection that in the mosaic pavement of three synagogues of the fourth to the sixth centuries, those of Bet Alpha, Hamat-Tiberias and Naʿaran, Helios is shown in the centre of the mosaic, riding his chariot in the middle of the zodiac. The reason for this prominent display of Helios in Palestinian synagogues has been the subject of extensive scholarly discussion.[27] The basic question is whether it may be assumed that Helios was worshipped alongside, or independently, of God in these synagogues. The evidence of our amulets, while not decisive in itself, tends to strengthen the position that Helios, like so many other supernatural powers who were treated with great respect, did not seriously encroach upon the supreme position of God. Amulets 11–13 were found in

[26] *Sefer ha-razim* IV:61–63; translation by M. Smith 1982, p. 210*.

[27] See some references in Smith 1982.

another synagogue of the same period, in Nirim, and they were placed in or close to the holy ark. The syncretistic mixture which they display, while perhaps not universally approved of in rabbinic circles, was nevertheless part of the everyday piety of the age, and the angels mentioned in them are all subservient to God.

We know from the Talmudic sources that the use of this magic was not confined exclusively to the ignorant classes of society, but may have been shared partly by people who belonged to the circles of the learned. It is interesting, nevertheless, to have this confirmed by one of the amulets of Ḥorvat Kanaf, which was made for the benefit of a certain "Rabbi Eleazar son of Esther, the servant of the God of Heaven" (Amulet 3:6–7). Specialists in Talmudic literature may try to identify the person in question, but it is sufficient to note that this title, which is not too common in magic texts, occurs here for the client of an amulet. S. Cohen 1981 discussed all the evidence for people called Rabbi in epigraphical sources. Cohen makes a distinction between two senses of the title "Rabbi": It may be used either as a general honorific title, or for a tradent of Talmudic tradition. It is obviously impossible to decide here which usage is relevant, but the pious formula "the servant of the God of Heaven" no doubt indicates that "Rabbi" is here used in a religious sense.

The one amulet in our collection which is clearly not Jewish, the Syriac amulet No. 6, displays a spirit which stands in sharp contrast to that of the Jewish amulets from Palestine. It talks of three deities, and these are given high epithets. If this contrast is anything to go by, the distinction between Jewish and non-Jewish magic in Palestine and its environs is strongly pronounced. However, since we possess no more than a few specimens of what must have been a very extensive literature of magic in that area, it would be rash to base far-reaching conclusions on so little material.

TEXTS AND COMMENTARY

I. Amulets from Palestine, Syria, Asia Minor and Egypt

Amulet 1

Provenance unknown
Collection of Dr. R. Hecht, Haifa
Plate 1; Figure 1

1 [מ]ימינך הרבה מאד משמאולך עוזי(א)[ל]
2 [מ]לפניך סוסיאל ומאחריך מנוחה
3 [ו]מלמעלה מאלה שכינת אל הצילה (א)[ת]
4 [קוזמ]ה בן סלמינו מפגע מרגע מנגע
5 [ויאמ]ר ייי אל השטן יגער ייי בך ה[שטן]
6 ויגער ייי בך הבוחר בירושלים (אמ)[ן]
7 [מ]לך יונון נימוס וכל מסוסין ברא[...]
8 ישמעאל רבא גיברא (ודחילא) מאמ...
9 ולידפת ולוזפת ומרהפתיס אברסקוס
10 [ר]וחא רובא רביא יה יה אתאסנ[י]
11 [ב]ר סלמינו מכל מכאובא מן יומא [דן]
12 [וע]ד לעלם אמן אמן סלה אנה כתבת יי[יי]
13 [י]אסי בשם סתריאל עזריאל גרגו (...)
14 [...](ר)ע רקיעה דהוא מ(...)ל (ת)מידה בכלין (ה)[וא]
15 ישלח באסיותיה דקוזמה בר סלמינו [...]
16 vacat (זמורה) ומעין ברוקה מעין לוחשה [ומעין]
17 שיחה מעין ביתה ומעין ברא ומעין ה[...]
18 באסיותיה מן קדם מרי שמיה אמן אמן (ס)[לה]
19 [...]ת אחד (ו)עלוה אחד הרי שנים אמן אמן (ס)[לה]
20 [ברוך] המכה והמרפא לרוח גרמיה קמיע [טב]
21 משבענה עליך רוח גרמיה דהיא מהלכ[ה]
22 בגידוהי ובגרמוהי דקוזמה בר סלמינ[ו]
23 עליך בחי | האל || אלהי | ישראל למן קדמין (...)
24 [צב](אות) מלך מל[כי ה]מלכי[ם]

Amulet 1

Translation

1 On your right are very many, on your left is Uzziel,
2 in front of you is Susiel, behind you is Repose.
3 Above these is God's Divine Presence. Save
4 [Quzm]a son of Salminu from affliction, from (bad) fate (?), from plague.
5 "And God said unto Satan: May God rebuke you Satan
6 and may God who has chosen Jerusalem rebuke you" (Zach. 3:2). Amen.
7 King **ywnwn nymws** and all **mswsyn** ...
8 Ishmael the great, mighty and terrifying. ...
9 **wlydpt wlwzpt wmrhptys ʾbrsqws**
10 Ruḥa, Ruba, Rabia, Yah, Yah. Be healed,
11 Bar Salminu, from all pain from this day
12 to eternity. Amen, Amen, Selah. I have written, God
13 will heal. In the name of Satriel, Azriel, ...
14 ... heaven, who ... wine in vessels (?), h[e]
15 will send forth the healing of Quzma son of Salminu ...
16 ... from the eye of cataract (?), from the eye of a spell, [and from the eye of]
17 a talk, from the eye of the house, and from the eye of the open space (?), and from the eye of ...
18 in his cure on behalf of the Lord of heaven. Amen, Amen, Selah.
19 ... one and on top of that one, then there are two. Amen, Amen, Selah.
20 [Blessed be] He who afflicts and heals the spirit of the bones. A [good] amulet.
21 I adjure you, the spirit of the bones, that walks
22 within the tendons and the bones of Quzma son of Salminu.
23 (I adjure) you by the God who lives, God of Israel, from the beginning ...
24 ... [of Hos]ts, king of the kings of kings ...

This amulet was incised with a sharp instrument on a narrow silver sheet, rolled from the upper part to the bottom; it was placed in a container, which has been preserved with the amulet. Nothing is known of its provenance. Its surviving height is 4.5 cm., width 3.3 cm.

1–3 The first phrase is reminiscent of Geniza 5, p. 2, lines 9–10 and that of the prayer "*Qeri*ʾ*at shema*ʿ on the bed": מימיני מיכאל ומשמאלי גבריאל ומלפני אוריאל ומאחורי רפאל ועל ראשי שכינת אל "On my right Michael, on my left Gabriel, in front of me Uriel, behind me Raphael and above my head the Shekina of El". See also Amulet 14:8. This formula found its way into Christian Syriac (Gollancz 1912, p. 5, § 7; p. 6, § 8) and Muslim Arabic (Goldziher 1894, pp. 359 f.) sources. See also Winkler 1930, pp. 20ff.

4 The name of the client Quzma — Cosmas is well known among the Syriac Christians (Payne-Smith, col. 3515). The name of the client's mother **slmynw** is unknown; can it be a variant of Σαλώμη? Cf. also Frey 1952, Nos. 1236–1237, 1459.

mpgʿ mrgʿ mngʿ is a pun. Only **pgʿ** and **ngʿ** have the sense of "affliction" and "plague". **rgʿ** means generally "moment"; it may mean here "a sudden calamity".

5–6 This verse from Zach. 3:2–3 is common in magic bowls and occurs in "*Qeri*ʾ*at shema*ʿ on the bed"

7–10 The names in the frames are of angels: **nymws** is Greek νόμος "law"; **mswsyn** means perhaps "healers", a *saf*ʿ*el* form of the root **ʾSY.** Cf. Brockelmann 1928, p. 464b.

lwzpt: See Isbell 1975, 69:7 and Isbell 1976, p. 23 **llyzpt.**

mrhptys: This may be an inversion of a Greek compound word such as ἑπτῆμαρ or ἑπτημέρος.

ʾbrsqws is generally written **ʾbrsks**; see Amulet 2:3 as well as the Geniza amulet 7:29 and a fragment from the magic book, Geniza 6, p. 1:11–12: **ʿbrsks mlʾkh rbh** "Abrasax the great angel". This angel is well known in the Greek magic papyri from Egypt, where it is listed with Yau the God Sabaoth, Adonai, Michael, Suriel, Gabriel and Raphael (Preisendanz 1928, I, p. 36; pp. 10, 158). See also in the bowls Isbell 1975, Nos. 3:8–9; 4:3–4 and in the Syriac bowl Montgomery 1913, 34:9 as well as *Sefer ha-razim,* pp. 8 and 96 (IV, 13).

8 **rbʾ gybrʾ wdḥylʾ**: The reading of the last word is dubious. One seems

Fig. 1. Amulet 1

to see **drwqyl**ʾ, but this may be considered to be a corruption of **wdḥyl**ʾ. The whole formula brings to mind the expression in the ʿAmida prayer: **האל הגדול הגבור והנורא**. For the phrase **rb**ʾ **gybr**ʾ **wdḥyl**ʾ, which seemingly uses *rabbā* as the substantive epithet for the deity, followed by two attributes, cf. Amulet 6:1–2 **rb**ʾ **ḥsyn**ʾ (one of a trinity of deities); Bowl 6:9 **mšbʿn**ʾ **ytkwn byšmyh ⌜d⌝rb**ʾ **wdḥyl**ʾ; and Amulet 7:15 **bsṭr krsyh d**ʾ**lh rbh ḥsynh wdḥylh,** where the sequence **rbh ḥsynh wdḥylh** may possibly be taken as an apposition to ʾ**lh**.

12–13 **ʾnh ktbt yyyy yʾsy**: See Isbell 1975, 1:14–15 **ʾnḥnʾ ktbnʾ wšmyh ysyk** "we have written, and his name will heal you", or Isbell 69:8 **ʾnʾ ktbyt wʾlhʾ mʾry kwlʾ ysy yt**[...] "I have written, and God the Lord of All, will heal [...].

14 If one may reconstruct **[t]rʿ rqyʿh** we may compare it with **trʿy šmyʾ** in 4QLevi, I:18 (Fitzmyer and Harrington 1978, p. 90) and Hebrew **šʿry šmym**.

14, 16–17 The readings and the interpretations in these lines are uncertain. **brwqh** may mean "lightning", but it may also mean "cataract" as **brwqtʾ** in Gaster 1896, p. XIII:3; *Sefer ha-razim* II:182 (p. 91) **rwḥ hbrqt**; see **brqyt** in Jastrow, p. 197a and **bruqta** in Drower and Macuch, p. 70a: **aina bruqtia** "eye with cataract". In Syriac there occurs the phrase **wbrq brwqʾ bḥṣh wpqʿt mtnh** (Gollancz 1912, p. 8,§10), which the editor translated "he hurt (?) his back, his loin ruptured" (p. XXXI). **mʿyn** could conceivably also be translated "in the form of", but the formula in the printed amulet (Warsaw 1867), where

Amulet 2

Provenance: Ḥorvat Kanaf
Golan Archaeological Museum, Qaṣrin, No. 3164
Plate 2; Figure 2

1 קמיע טב מאסיה יאיתה בר[תה]
2 דמרין מן אשתה ועריתה ועינה
3 בישתה אברסכס יה יה יהו
4 אל אל אל קקקקקקקקקק צצצצ
5 צצצצ ץץץץץץץץץץ ה/א ה/ח ה/א
6 אות או אוא יה יה יה יה
7 יהו יהו יהו יהו (*4 magic signs*)
8 געורו אשתה ועריתה שידתה
9 רוחתה מן פגרה דיאיתה ברתה
10 דמרין בשם אהיה אשר אהיה

we have a series of **ʿynʾ** indicating various forms of evil eyes (Fig. 21 on p. 133), suggests that here too a similar concept is probably present.

20 For [**brwk**] **hmkh whmrpʾ** see Gordon 1941, p. 352 **brwk mkh wrwpʾ** "blessed is he who smites and heals"; Bowl 12b:13 **brwk ... mk(h) wrwph**; as well as Isaiah 30:26; Jer. 14:19. See also Geniza 7:2–3 **ʾl mwḥṣ wrwpʾ** "smiting and healing God", and Geniza 8:21.

20–22 **rwḥ grmyh** "the spirit of the bones" is the actual sickness, that "walks within the tendons and the bones of Quzma". For **gydwhy wgrmwhy** see the Geniza fragment at the Jewish Theological Seminary in New York ENA 3381 fol. 7b: אנה משבע יתכון שמהתה דאסרין לי פֿל וגידוי וגרמוי ; see also Amulet 5 below.

23 See Geniza 5, p. 1:2–3 **mšbʿnʾ bšm ḥy hʾl** and I Sam. 25:34 and I Kings 17:1 חי יהוה אלהי ישראל and Dan. 12:7 וישבע בחי העולם.

24 **mlk mlky hmlkym**: This is a frequent expression; see Jastrow, p. 791a.

Amulet 2

Translation

An amulet proper to heal Yaʾitha the daughter
of Marian from the fever and the shiver and the evil
eye. Abrasax Ya Ya Yahu
El El El **qqqqqqqqq**, **ṣṣṣṣṣ**
ṣṣṣṣṣ, (final) **ṣṣṣṣṣṣṣṣṣ** **hhh** **ʾḥʾ**
ʾwt (letter) **ʾw ʾwʾ** Ya Ya Ya Ya Ya
Yahu Yahu Yahu Yahu Yahu *(4 magic signs)*
exorcise the fever and the shiver, the female demons
(and) the spirits from the body of Yaʾitha the daughter
of Marian. In the name of I-am-who-I-am

11 אמן אמן סלה קמיע טב מגעור
12 אשתה ועריתה ודקיקתה מן
13 יאיתה ברתה דמרין בשם כריאל
14 כסיאל זריאל צצצצצצ בשם
15 קקקקקקק בשם מיכאל]
16 עזריאל]

Amulets 2 and 3 were found in the excavations at Ḥorvat Kanaf by Mr. Zvi Maoz of the Israel Department of Antiquities, who kindly entrusted us with the publication of these texts. The essential details about the archaeological context of these amulets, as communicated by Z. Maoz, can be summed up as follows:

> Ḥorvat Kanaf is situated on a lofty spur, descending from the basalt plateau of the Golan, 3.5 km. off the north-eastern shore of the Sea of Galilee. In 1885 Lawrence Oliphant found here a fragmentary Aramaic inscription with Hebrew characters, which was part of an inscribed lintel of the ancient synagogue (Naveh 1978, No. 19). Systematic excavations began at the site in 1977 by Zvi Maoz. During four seasons two areas were unearthed: (A) The synagogue and the adjacent area on the top of the hill; (B) Building 300 on the lowest terrace of the southern slope below the synagogue.
>
> The two amulets were found in two rooms in Building 300. Amulet 2, that of Yaitha, was unearthed in a shallow pit in the north-western corner of Locus 301, together with an iron ring and a bronze ring that lost its inlay. Amulet 3, that of Eleazar, was found in the earth fill in the centre of Locus 308, 1.35 m. above the floor level. It probably had fallen from somewhere above.

According to the stratigraphy provided by Z. Maoz, Building 300 was erected in the early Byzantine period (350–500 C.E.), while the synagogue was erected in the middle Byzantine period (c. 500–551 C.E.). In the late Byzantine period (c. 551–630 C.E.) there took place the restoration of the synagogue and the division of Building 300. It seems likely to us that the two amulets belong to the later part of the occupation of Building 300, i.e. late 6th or early 7th century C.E.

11 Amen Amen Selah. An amulet proper to exorcise
12 the fever and the shiver and the hectic (fever) from
13 Yaʾitha the daughter of Marian. In the name of Kariel,
14 Kasiel, Zariel **ṣṣṣṣṣṣṣ**; in the name of
15 **qqqqqqq**; in the name of Michael [ ]
16 ʿEzriel [ ]

Amulet 2 is written on a copper sheet, incised with a pointed instrument. Only the first 18 lines are preserved. The surviving portion measures *c.* 6x6 cm. Fuller commentary on Amulet 2 will be found in Naveh 1983.

1 **qmyʿ ṭb** "a proper amulet". These two words, which are repeated here in line 11, appear also at the beginning of the Aleppo amulet (No. 4), and they occur in the Geniza fragment of a magic book, Geniza 5, p. 1:7 as **qmyʿ ṭwb**.

mʾsyh "to heal", infinitive of the root **ʾSY** (*paʿʿel*). The lack of the *lamed* (see also **mgʿwr**, line 11) and the initial *mem* in the *paʿʿel* infinitive are characteristic of Galilean Aramaic (Dalman 1905, p. 281).

yʾyth is a feminine personal name meaning "the nice/beautiful (girl)"; cf. **špyrh**, a well known name in the first two centuries C.E., in Amulet 14:1.

2 **mryn** is a quite common Palestinian feminine personal name; see Amulet 9 and Montgomery 1911, p. 273f. lines 15, 22. **mryn** is a by-form of **mrym**. See Kutscher 1976, pp. 61–62.

ʾšth wʿryth: These nouns seem to be synonymous. Whereas **ʾšth** is well known in all Aramaic dialects as "the fire" or "the fever", **ʿryth** is rare. In Syriac, however, the root **ʿRY** means *inter alia* "to be seized with illness, to swoon"; in *paʿʿel* "to become numb with cold"; **ʿryʾ** "cold, frost, chill'; and **ʿrwytʾ** "the shivering fit of an ague". The latter meaning fits **ʿryth** in our text. **ʾyšth wʿryth** occur in the British Museum incantation bowl No. 91745 (cf. Gordon 1941, p. 341). Cf. also **hʾš whʿryh** in Amulet 4:28–29. In Amulet 9:1 the word **ʾwryth** seems to be a misspelling of **ʿryth** (but see also Commentary *ad loc.*). The sequence **ʾ(y)š(ʾ)tʾ** and **ʿrwytʾ** occurs also in the Geniza fragment T-S K 1.95 as

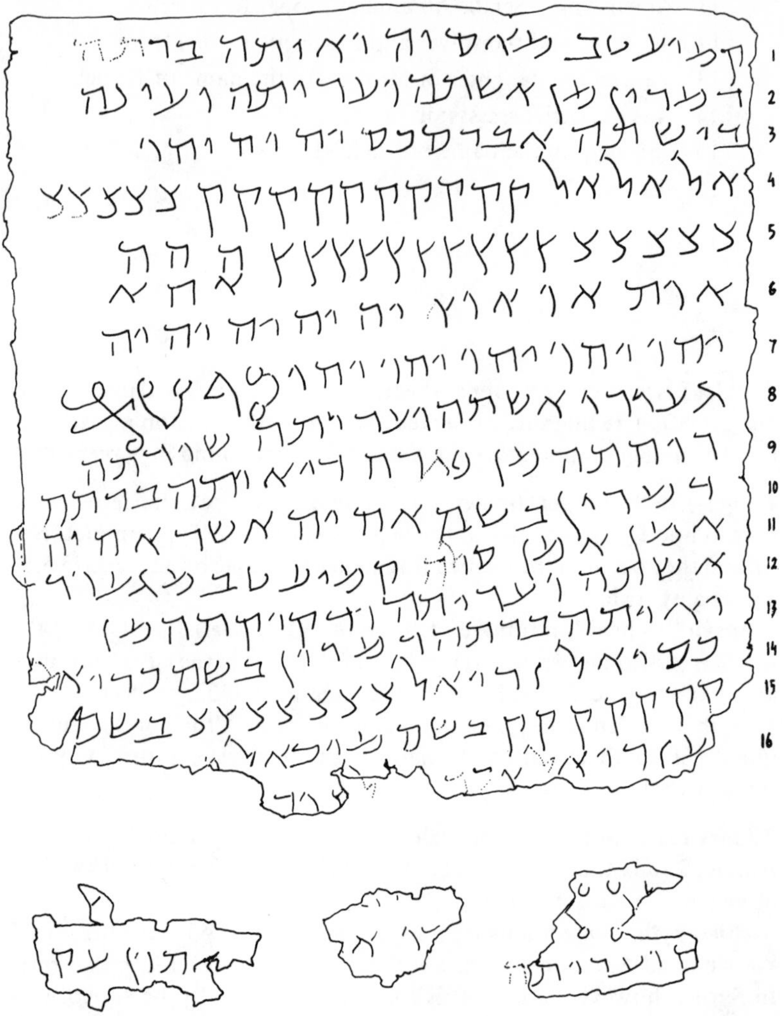

Fig. 2. Amulet 2

well as in Geniza 7:16. The combination **ʾštʾ ʿrwytʾ** together with other diseases occurs in a late Syriac magic book, Gollancz 1912, p. 8 f., § 11. The Samaritan Targum of Lev. 26:16 and Deut. 28:22 renders **qdḥt** by **ʿrbyth** (Tal 1980–81).

3 Abrasax is followed by a series of divine names and letters. It seems likely that in a prototype of this incantation these names were followed by a phrase like אתון אתייה קדישייה "You holy letters"; אתון שמהתה קדישייה "You holy names", which appear quite frequently, as in Geniza 6; or אתון כלקטירייה קדישיא "You holy characters", as in Geniza 1. For a similar phrase see Amulets 7:4 and 10:3. The plural imperative verb **gʿwrw** (line 8) implies such an address. For Abrasax see Commentary to Amulet 12:2.

4–5 The letters *qof* and *ṣade* may represent Is. 6:3. On the other hand, *qof*, medial *ṣade* and final *ṣade*, each repeated ten times in succession, may represent the root **QṢṢ** "to cut, break, fell, scrape, mutilate" (possibly addressed against the evil spirits of disease?).

8 For the verb **GʿR** in the sense of "to drive away, to exorcise" cf. Greenfield 1980, pp. XXXVIII f., as well as Geniza 4:3. Further discussion in Naveh 1983.

10 For the phrase אהיה אשר אהיה cf. e.g. Amulets 3:2–3; 11:1; 12:6, 40; Isbell 1975, Nos. 67:2, 69:3–4 and Geniza 4:5–6; 7:7.

11 **mgʿwr** instead of **lmgʿwr;** see above, Commentary to line 1, **mʾsyh**.

12 **dqyqth** is the rendering of the Samaritan Targum to Deut. 28:22 **ḥrḥr**; the Arabic equivalent given in *Ha-Meliṣ* is **ʾldq** (see Ben-Ḥayyim 1957, p. 473b). Bar-Hebraeus, pp. 13, 28, translates the phrase **ʾštʾ dqyqtʾ** in the Peshiṭta version of Ben Sira 26:26 as Greek ἑκτικός. In the Geniza fragments we have various corruptions of this word: **rqyqtʾ** (Geniza 5, p. 1:1), **zʿqh** (Geniza 6, p. 3:12) and **dnwqh** (Geniza 6, p. 4:2).

Amulet 3

Provenance: Ḥorvat Kanaf

Golan Archaeological Museum, Qasrin, No. 3163

Plate 3; Figure 3

1 שיר תשבחות למלך עלמ[יה]
2 [י]ה יה יה יחיש עולמים אהיה
3 אשר אהיה מלך ממל<ל> ברוז פרוש
4 אל כל רוח בישה ומבאשה דלה
5 תיחשין לרבי אלעזר ברה דאסתיר
6 עבדה דאלה שומיה חזק וגער
7 שרד ופרת טרגין אסתד ובקתה
8 סלסלירה קללקם יקיפס צוריאל
9 רפאל אביאל אנאל נהריאל
10 נגדיאל אפפאל ואננאל מס
11 פס יקרנדריס יהו כרמסיס
12 אלהא רבה תחתה גחגה טחטה
13 מרמר פספס יהוה קדש בכל
14 אתר דיתחזה ית קמיעה דן
15 לא תעכבין עלוי על אלעזר
16 ברה דאסתיר ואן תעכבין עלוי
17 בה בשעתה תתרמין לאתון
18 נורא יקדתה ברוך אתה אדוננו
19 הרופא כל הא־רץ שלח רפוי
20 אסו לאלעזר בוברית תבריט
21 [ו]בשתארות מלאכיה דמ[מנין]
22 [ע]ל אשתה ועריתה אסון אל[עזר]
23 [ב]מאמר קדיש

This amulet is written on a copper sheet, incised with a pointed instrument. The sheet measures *c.* 7.5×5 cm. The writing seems to have been preserved almost intact. It was found by Mr. Zvi Maoz in the excavation of Ḥorvat Kanaf. For a description of the Ḥ. Kanaf amulets see Commentary to Amulet 2.

Amulet 3

Translation

1 A song of praise to the King of the Worlds
2 Yah, Yah, Yah, Yaḥish of the Worlds, I-am-
3 who-I-am, the King who speaks with distinct mystery
4 to every bad and evil-doing spirit, that you should not
5 cause pain to Rabbi Eleazar the son of Esther,
6 the servant of the God of Heaven. **ḥzq** and **gʿr**,
7 **šrd** and **prt**, **ṭrgyn**, **ʾstd** and **bqth**,
8 **slslyrhʾ**, **qllqm**, **yqyps**, Suriel,
9 Raphael, Abiel, Anael, Nahariel
10 Nagdiel, Aphaphel and Ananel **ms**
11 **ps yqrndrys** Yahu **krmsys**
12 the great god **tḥth ghgh ṭḥṭh**
13 **mrmr psps** Yahweh, sanctity. In every
14 place where this amulet will be seen,
15 you (the evil spirit) should not detain Eleazar
16 the son of Esther. And if you detain him,
17 you will be cast immediately into a burning
18 fiery furnace (Dan. 3:6). Blessed are you our Lord,
19 the Healer of all (people on) earth, send healing
20 (and) cure to Eleazar. **bwbryt, tbryṭ**,
21 **bštʾrwt**, the angels that are [appointed]
22 over fever and shivering, cure Ele[azar]
23 by a holy command!

1–3 The opening phrase, which consists of a mixture of Hebrew and Aramaic words, is very similar to that which occurs in the magic bowls published by Jeruzalmi 1963 (see Isbell 1975, Nos. 67 and 69) and by Isbell 1976, p. 23, where the correct reading is שיר תשבחות למלך עלמיה יהוה צבאות צור עולמים אהיה אשר אהיה מלך ממליל ברזי (בראזי) פרישתא. This similarity constitutes a further indication to the existence of contacts between Babylonian and Palestinian Jewish magic formulae.

2 **yḥyš** (or **yḥwš**): Probably connected to the "name" **yḥwš**, which developed from an appeal to speed, so common in magical invocations; cf. Scholem 1980/81, p. 266, notes 84–85. Our Geniza material illustrates the transition from the verb **ʾḥyšh** in Ps. 55:9 to the divine name. The verse is prominently used in Geniza 5, p. 2:6–7; 7:23–25 (where the verse occurs twice, straight and backwards). The divine name occurs in Geniza 8 in the formula **yh ʾhh ḥsyn yh yḥyšh**, repeated several times with slight variations (lines 6f.; 8f.; 10f.; 13f.).

4 **ʾl** is Hebrew, for Aramaic **ʿl**; **dlh** is sometimes written for **dlʾ**, cf. Amulet 9:6.

5 **tyḥšyn** is probably a causative form of ḤWŠ/ḤŠŠ "to feel (pain), to suffer"; the *yod* after the *taw* shows that it cannot be an *afʿel*, but rather a *paʿʿel*, the *yod* standing for a *shwa mobile*. At any rate it is a second person feminine imperfect meaning "you will cause pain".

5–6 The client is called Rabbi Eleazar son of Esther (note the *plene* spelling **ʾstyr**), the servant of the God of Heaven. This is one of the rare examples in which the client of a magic text bears the title Rabbi. Cf. also Harviainen 1981, p. 5:8,9 **rb ywsp br ʾymʾ dʾymh**.

6–10 **ḥzq wgʿr šrd** ... can be a series of verbs: "strengthen and drive out, cause to remain...", but this sequence does not make much sense. Therefore, it may perhaps be assumed that **ḥzq wgʿr šrd** is a sequence of corrupt words based on a formula such as we have in Isbell 1975, 67:3 **byʾl ḥzq wgybwr šlḥ byd** "By God, strong and mighty, send by the hand...", where it is followed by a series of angels: Shlomiel, Michael, Raphael etc. Here we may reconstruct something like **ʾlh šwmyh ḥzq *wgbwr *šdr** "...God of Heaven, strong and mighty, send..." The words **prt ṭrgyn ʾstd**...until **yqyps** may be names of angels (or *nomina barbara*); they are followed by Suriel, Raphael etc.

10–13 **msps** is an Atbash reversal of **yḥwḥ** and **psps** for **wḥwḥ** i.e. Yahweh; Cf. Montgomery 1913, p. 60.

krmsys has been explained by Jeruzalmi 1963, pp. 25,40 as Hermes. The text there says: **[bšmyh] dkrmsys yh šmh rbh mpršh.**

mrmr is reminiscent of Marmaraoth.

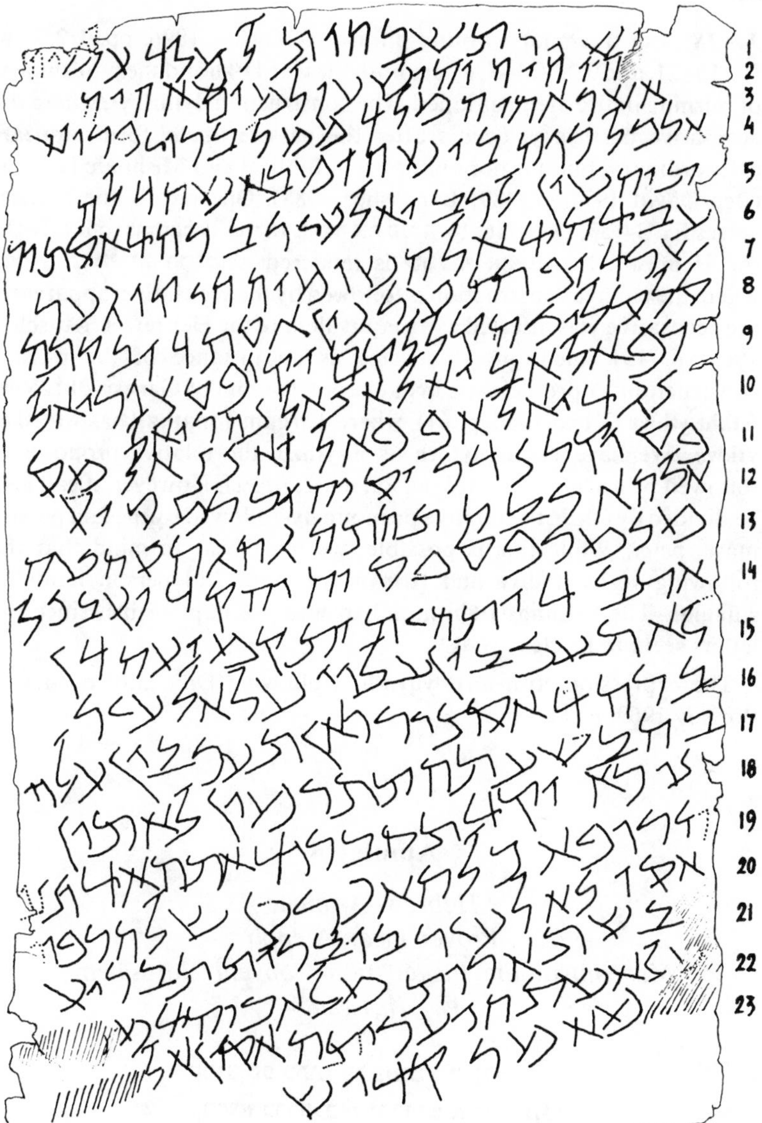

Fig. 3. Amulet 3

14–18 For a similar warning phrase see Gaster 1896, pp. I:25–28; III:13–21, and XXV:4–7, where both the word **tʿkb** and the punishment of burning in fire are mentioned. The construction **dytḥzh yt**, where the accusative particle **yt** occurs after the passive *itpeʿel* form, appears extraordinary, but it is not unknown in Biblical and Mishnaic Hebrew (Ben-David 1971, p. 489; Bar-Asher 1983). One recalls the biblical verses Ex. 34:23; Deut. 16:16 **יֵרָאֶה את פני ה'**. In the Targums to Ex. 16:12 the Hebrew...**שמעתי את תלונות** is rendered...**שמיע קדמי ית תרעמת**, where the passive construction is followed by the accusative; apparently the accusative **yt** is inserted as an equivalent of the Hebrew **ʾt**. Kutscher 1969, p. 151, mentions this verse as an instance of the passive construction. A problematic instance is a Targum of Genesis 38:25 **wlʾ ʾštkḥt ythwn** (Klein 1980, p. 61), where Targum Jonathan has **wlʾ ʾškḥt ythwn**. We have taken **dytḥzh** as **d+ytḥzh**, the relative pronoun **d-** followed by an imperfect 3rd person masc. *itpeʿel*. However, it can also be divided **dy+tḥzh**, the relative pronoun **dy-** followed by the 2nd person masc. *peʿal*. While this is possible, we must bear in mind that the following verbs, **tʿkbyn** and **ttrmyn**, are both 2nd person feminine singular. The readings **tʿkbwn** and **ttṛmwn** are implausible, since the letters seem to be clear *yod*s.

The expression **ʾtwn nwrʾ yqydth** (following Dan. 3:6) occurs in Borisov 1969, p. 11.

Amulet 4

Hebrew–Aramaic
Provenance: Aleppo
Museum of the Flagellation Convent, Jerusalem
Plate 4; Figure 4

1 קמיע טב כתום פי פתגמא הד[ן]
2 קדישא ברבר<ב>ן ובקדישיא שמו (נכ)[בד]
3 רמיאל מפאר יה עזרי אהיה א
4 אחמה אהיה אחמה יה שדי ח
5 אל (ח)י הוא אתו מאשו (מ)כרעי
6 טלמי ו(כ)מא במנא (כ)ל נדרך ה

19 **hrwpʾ kl hʾrṣ**: This blessing formula is unknown; but it can be compared with רפא חולי כל בשר (in Isbell 1975, 42:12) and רופא חולי עמו ישראל (in the ʿAmida prayer). In Gen. 18:25 we have, somewhat differently, השפט כל הארץ. There is a curved line (possibly the beginning of a *ṣade*) between the *alef* and *resh* in the word הא־רץ.

20 The first word in this line can be read either **ʾsy**, *paʿʿel* imperative, or **ʾsw**, the absolute state of the noun meaning health, healing, cure. The latter may serve as a gloss on the Hebrew word **rpwy**.

21–22 The reconstruction **dmmnyn ʿl** is based on the phrase which occurs in several magic texts; cf. Amulet 12:2; the Geniza fragment T-S K 1.160 ואלן מלאכיה דממנין על לילותא; *Sefer ha-razim* V:13–14 ואלה הם הממונים על שנים עשר חודשי השנה; Gaster 1896, Sword of Moses XX:4 שם סרא דממנא על מלאכי רוגזא.

22 **ʾšth wʿryth**: See above, Amulet 2.

ʾswn = pl. imperative; the final *nun* is typical of Galilean Aramaic, see Dalman 1905, the paradigms on pp. 402 ff. This word seems to be followed by a *lamed* somewhat ligatured with the following *alef*, but it is perhaps only a highly drawn right bar of the *alef*; whether we read with or without *lamed* the meaning is the same.

23 **bmʾmr qdyš**: In Isbell 1975, No. 42:6 we read **bdbr ʾylwh wbmʾmr qwdwš** "by the Word of God and by the holy commandment".

Amulet 4

Translation

1 A proper amulet. Write (?) this phrase,
2 the holy one. His name is venerated through great ones and through the holy ones.
3 Ramiel adorns Yah. My help is I-am,
4 I-see, I-am, I-see. Yah, Shaddai,
5-6 living God. (*An incomprehensible sequence of words; in the following such words are indicated by dots*)

7 דן יהוה אהיה יהוה אל שדי אשר
8 אל × יש (ח)י × חי  אהיה ומלך
9 מכר × מנצח × ים אש(ר) מקצפו ה
10 ארץ רעשה | הר | סר | הר הבמה
11 והר יהו יה × ה זמרו לדו(י)ד ודר
12 הי × שם לעולם ועד (ד)רום ופנים
13 ושמאול ומערב לאחוז בכנפות
14 הארץ וינערו רשעים ממנה כן
15 תנער הטלנית ורוח זכר ונקבה
16 מן אקמו ברתה דאמרבן ממאתים
17 וארבעים ושמונה אבריה ומארבע
18 מאות עם קרבין ובל תשית לב נכל
19 עליה בפיה תיחל מן זולתו כצל
20 חמה כמועט לבנה וכמזלותיה ×
21 ×××××××××× יהפש יה
22 פש ×× יה ××××××××××××
23 אמן אמן סלה ×× הללויה
24 אלהי מערכות ובשם אוגרית מר
25 מרמאות יפא ובמלכות אבלנה
26 אלבלה נאתה לבאת קטב נרקי
27 (מ)ראות הדר

(three suns and seven stars
are given here as magic figures)

28 משביע אני עליכם הפג<ע> והק[
29 והאש והעריה בין מיום לי[ום]
30 בין משבת לשבת בין משנה
31 לשנה בין מחדש לחדש משבי[ע]
32 אני עליכם בשם ימינו וכח [קדשו]
33 תוקפו ביה יה ביה יה בין[ ]
34 צבאות אלהי ישראל [ ]
35 ....

7 ... **yhwh**, I-am, **yhwh**, God, Shaddai, who (is)
8 God. ... Living, ... I-am and king
9 ... "At his wrath the
10 earth shall tremble" (Jer. 10:10) ...
11 ... Sing for David ...
12 <May the> name of God be for eternity. South, east,
13 north and west. "That it seizes the corners
14 of the earth, and shakes the wicked out of it" (Job 38:13), so
15 will be shaken the shadow-spirit and the male and female spirit
16 from Aqemu daughter of Em-rabban, from her
17 248 limbs, and from (her)
18 400 ... (?) entrails. Do not place an evil man's heart
19 over her. With her mouth she shall expect (?) from someone else. Like the shadow
20 of the sun, like the diminution of the moon, and like her zodiacal signs.
21-22 (*magic characters and combinations of letters*)
23 Amen, Amen, Selah, Hallelujah.
24 God of battles. And by the name of Ugrit, Mar-
25 marma'ot **yp'** and by the kingdom of *Ablanatanalba
26 ... **qṭb nrqy.**
27 Visions of splendour.
(*three suns and seven stars*)
28 I adjure you, affliction and ...
29 and fever and shiver, whether it is from day to day,
30 or from week to week, or from year
31 to year, or from month to month, — I adjure
32 you, by His right hand and the might of [His holiness].
33 His vigour, **byh yh byh yh by[h** Lord of]
34 Hosts, the God of Israel ...
35 ...

Amulet 4

This text was incised on a silver sheet, folded and placed in a bronze tube. It was found in a tomb near Aleppo.

The text was first published by Schwab 1906, and again 1916/17, p. 624. It was reproduced by Frey 1952, No. 819, and discussed in Testa 1962, pp. 52 ff.

The translation is given here with great reservation, as the text is largely obscure. We have examined the original at the Museum, and have had the benefit of a fresh photograph, kindly supplied to us by Father Michele Piccirillo O.F.

1 **ktwm py** seems a better reading than Schwab's **ktwm (ḥtwm) bw. py** may be a dittography on the following **ptgmʾ. ktwm** may be a corruption of **ktwb**.

2 **brbr<b>n**: Schwab read **brbwn**.

6 **bmnʾ kl**: Cf. Schwab **kmw ʾpl.**

8 This line contains the so-called "monogram of Christ". Deissmann 1927, p. 255 n. 4, remarks that it was in use long before the time of Christ. Testa 1962, p.55, regards it as an evident Christian symbol, following Avi-Yonah 1940, p. 112. See also Budge 1930, p. 347 f.

10 Schwab reads *waws* where the amulet seems to have vertical strokes.

11 **zmrw ldwyd** seems to be written. One might expect **l<y>hwh** as occurs frequently in the Psalms.

12 **pnym** signifies "east", cf. Kimron 1980, p. 41 f.

13 **śmʾwl** is written with a *waw* following the *alef*, as in Amulet 1. For **śmʾwl** in the sense of "north"cf.Kutscher 1957, p.32, and Kimron 1980.

15 **ṭlnyt**: This species of demons is quite widely attested. In our texts they occur in Amulets 7:6; 11:8; 13:8. For other occurrences in bowl texts see Gordon 1941, p. 279; Borisov 1969, p. 7:4, and the discussion in Scholem 1965, pp. 85, 88. The Targum of Cant. 4:6 has **ṭlny** as a species of demons (reference kindly supplied by Dr. E. Kimron). The same sense occurs in Mandaic **ṭulaniata** (pl.), cf. Drower 1946, p. 332, line 2. The transition from the sense of "shadows" to that of "demons" is illustrated by a passage in the *Schatzhöhle*, where a number of natural

Fig. 4. Amulet 4.
After Testa 1962

elements worshipped are listed: **wmnhwn byd ṭʿywthwn lšmšʾ sgdyn hww wmnhwn lshrʾ wlkẅkbʾ wmnhwn lʾrʿʾ wlḥyẅtʾ wlpr̈ḥtʾ wl̈rḥšʾ wlʾÿlnʾ wlk̈ʾpʾ wlṭln̈ytʾ wlmÿʾ wl̈rwḥʾ** (Bezold 1888, II, p. 130).

16 **ʾmrbn** is probably to be read Em-Rabban.

17–18 While 248 is רמ״ח, the traditional Jewish figure for the number of limbs, 400 followed by **ʿm** is incomprehensible.

20 **mwʿṭ lbnh** may be connected with Heb. **mʿwṭ** "diminution, waning". The juxtaposition *ḥammā-levānā* occurs in Is. 24:23; 30:26; Cant. 6:10. The whole expression is reminiscent of the phrases in the Qiddush Levana prayer.

wkmzlwtyh was not read correctly by Schwab.

24 **ʾlwhy mʿrkwt**: Cf. Geniza 4:2–3.

ʾwgryt, which occurs in Bavli Pesaḥim 111a (see Margaliot 1945, p. 204), is also attested in Amulet 8:6.

Amulet 5

Provenance: Emmaus
Present location unknown
Figure 5

1–2 *(magic characters)*
3 [ ](מ)שג־אל שמראל אלהא [... אתון]
4 [כרק](ט)יריא קדישיה בטלון כל (ח)[ ]
5 [מן ע]ינוי מן נו(חר)ה מן רישה מן גידו[י]
6 [מן ר]יסיא בשם *(magic figures)*
7 [ ] ומן ...נוי ומן בניה ... [ ]

This amulet was found in 1896 in a tomb in Emmaus and was acquired by Herbert Clark for his collection. It is written on a thin silver sheet. It was first published (with a facsimile drawing only) by Vincent 1908; and then again in Frey 1952, No. 1185; cf. also Testa 1962, pp. 64–66. Our

25 We have here the familiar Marmaraot, and afterwards the formula Ablanatanalba (lines 25–26), Scholem 1965, p. 94. Cf. also *Sefer ha-razim*, p. 8.

26 For **qṭb nrqy** cf. **qṭb mryry** in Deut. 32:24. For the use of the biblical formula in magic, cf. *Midrash Tehillim* (*Shoḥer Ṭov*), ed. S. Buber, Vilna 1891, p. 397 (on Ps. 91:3); *Midrash Rabba, Bammidbar*, Jerusalem 1965, fol. 87b (Parasha 12:3).

28 Cf. **mpgʿ mrgʿ mngʿ** in Amulet 1:4.

29 **hʾš whʿryh**: Cf. **ʾštʾ wʿrytʾ** in Amulet 2.

29–31 On the time divisions in this magic usage cf. Commentary to Bowl 6:7–8.

32 Cf. הושיעה לו ימינו וזרוע קדשו (Ps. 98:1).

33 For **yh byh** cf. Commentary to Bowl 6:2.

Amulet 5

Translation

1–2 *(magic characters)*
3 ...Masagiel, Samriel, the God [... You]
4 holy [charac]ters, annul all [the...]
5 [from] his eyes, from his nostril, from his head, from his tendon[s,]
6 [from the eye-]lids. In the name of (*magic figures*)
7 ... and from ... and from her sons...

reading is based on the drawing in Vincent; we have no information about the present whereabouts of the object, and have seen no photograph of it. It does not appear to be in the Clark collection, which is kept at the Y.M.C.A. in Jerusalem.

3 **mšg'l**: See *Sefer ha-razim*, VI: 14 **msgy'l**. In Greek amulets we have Μυσαγαω[ϑ], Preisendanz 1928, p. 34 (III:56); Μυσαγωϑ, Preisendanz 1930, p. 51 (IX:2). For **šmr'l** see the late Jewish amulet in Shachar 1971, No. 2.

3–4 The reading is based on Geniza 1:2 and similar texts.

4 **bṭlwn**: A *he* is written above the line; hardly to be read **bṭlhwn**.

5 Vincent followed by Frey read **nwhrh** "son intelligence".

7 Vincent read unconvincingly, **wmn 'wznwy bṣyh** "et de ses oreilles et de ses testicules".

Amulet 6

Syriac

Provenance and present location unknown

Plate 5; Figure 6

1 + ואו • בר תאון • רבא
2 • חסינא • קדיש אילא •
3 הלין • תלתא • קימין • ב(מ)
4 עברתא • רבתא • דאוקינ
5 וס • ומדברין • מיא • וע
6 למא • במעברתא • דע
7 למא • ○ מוממנא ○ בך
8 ○ רבו ○ אקים זבאות ○
9 פרקי ○ טרפסדך ○
10 דיוא ○ אנהר ○ בותך
11 ○ או ○ בר ○ תאון ○ אילא ○
12 ארזם ○ בך ○ רבון ○ אק
13 ים זבאות ○ פרק ○ טרפס
14 דך ○ דיוא מן תלטא ומן
15 * דמוללך ○ בנק(ו)תא
16 ...

Fig. 5. Amulet 5. After Vincent 1908

Amulet 6

Translation

1 O Bar-Theon, mighty
2 Lord, the holy one of God!
3 These three are standing in the
4 great ford of the ocean
5 and directing the water and the
6 world in the ford of the
7 world. I adjure you,
8 Greatness, Aqem Zabaoth.
9 Loosen Ṭarpas-dukh
10 the demon. Illuminate your desire,
11 O Bar Theon the God!
12 I invoke (?) you, the Lord
13 Aqem Zabaoth. Loosen Ṭarpas-
14 dukh the demon from the sea (?) and from
15–19 (undecipherable)

This amulet is inscribed on a silver sheet in Syriac in Estrangelo characters. It was acquired in 1925 in Beirut by Charles Virolleaud. The object was lost in 1926 when it was sent to A. Cowley in Oxford for examination, and the first editor, A. Dupont-Sommer, and all subsequent scholars who have worked on it, have had to rely on photographs only.

The inscription was first published with an extensive commentary by Dupont-Sommer 1946, who sought to understand it as an expression of a gnostic adoration of the letter *waw*. This theory was contested by Gordon 1949, who suggested a new reading of the inscription. Dupont-Sommer 1951 defended his original interpretation, and a further article by Gordon 1953 concludes this debate. See further Del Medico 1949; Testa 1962, pp. 59–64.

One problem in the interpretation of the text is the use of word-dividers. There are two devices used for this purpose in this amulet: a dot and a circle. It should be noted that in the first part of the inscription, viz. lines 1–7, only a dot is regularly used, while the circle is consistently used from line 7 on. After the first word in line 7 the transition from the one system to the other is marked by the fact that a dot followed by a circle are both used to divide **bʿlmʾ** from **mwmmnʾ**. It may be remarked that at this point the introductory invocation is concluded, and the main text of the adjuration begins. It follows from these remarks that the first word in the inscription, after the cross, is probably to be read **wʾw** (as read by Dupont-Sommer), though this does not imply that Dupont-Sommer's interpretation of the word as meaning the letter *waw*, personified or otherwise, is acceptable. **wʾw br tʾwn** corresponds to **ʾw br tʾwn** in line 11 (where **ʾw** follows a clear word-divider in the shape of a circle) and both must be forms of interjection (as seen by Gordon 1953, p. 116). It may be possible to interpret the **wʾw** in line 1 as either a variant form of the vocative particle, otherwise unattested, or, more likely, as the conjunction **w-** followed by the vocative **ʾw**. In the latter case, the initial **w-** begins the text in the same way as does **twb**, e.g. in Bowl 4, and may be translated "again" or similarly.

Resh has a dot over the letter (cf. Dupont-Sommer 1946, pp. 83f.). In **dywʾ** (lines 10,14) the *dalet* has a dot to its right.

1 The cross at the beginning of the inscription may indicate that this is a Christian amulet.

br tʾwn is here written without an internal divider, while in line 11 **br** is

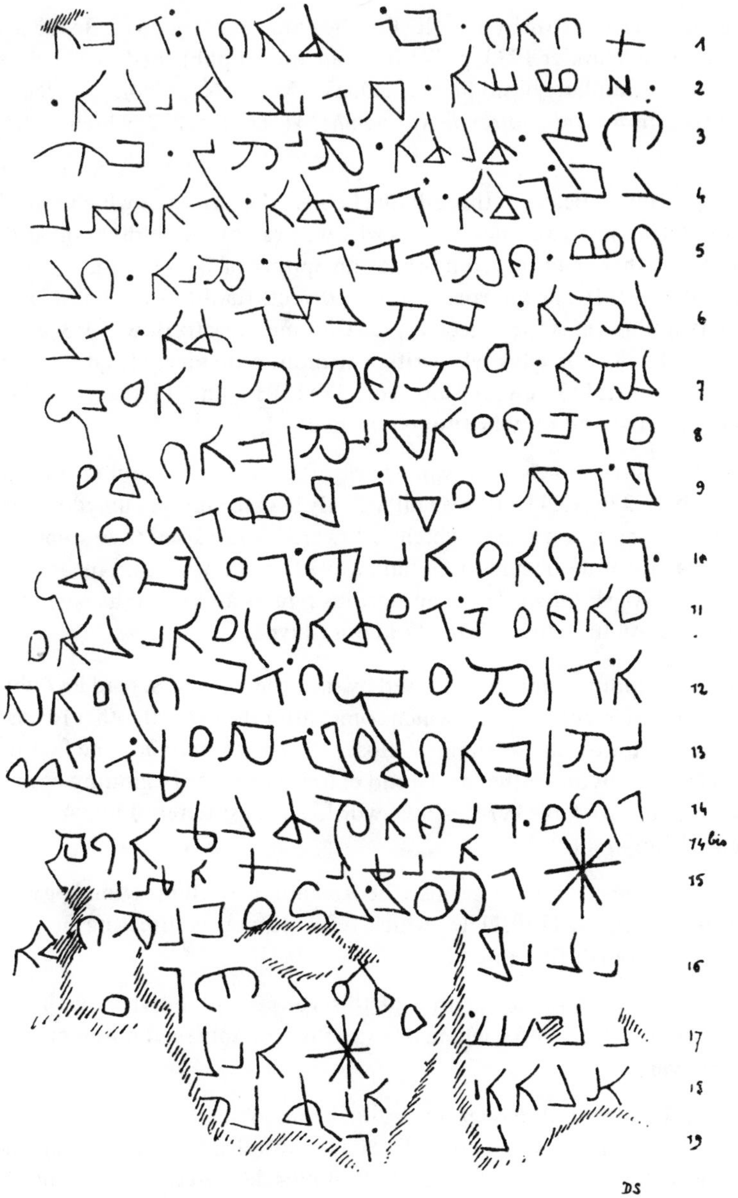

Fig. 6. Amulet 6. From Dupont-Sommer 1946

separated from **t'wn** by a circle. For the name Bar-Theon cf. **Βεραδωνάι** quoted in Winkler 1930, p. 141 from an amulet published by Froehner, "Sur une amulette basilidienne inédite du Musée Napoléon III", *Bull. de la Société des Antiquaires de Normandie*, 4 (1866), p. 272 (which we have not seen).

1–2 Line 3 speaks of three divine beings, the names of which must be sought in these two lines. That is why we prefer to take **rb' ḥsyn'** as one name, rather than regarding **rb'** as an epithet of Bar-Theon.

rb' ḥsyn': If our interpretation is correct, Rabbā is the name of the deity and **ḥsyn'** is the adjective; see Commentary to Bowl 13:3. and to Amulet 1:8. For **qdyš 'yl'** (written without a divider) cf. **qdšy'l**, *Sefer ha-razim*, II:119; **qwdšy'l** op. cit., IV:15. In line 11 the formula is abbreviated and only **br t'wn 'yl'** is invoked.

3 For three angels in a framework of a magic situation cf. Gordon 1934b, p. 326 (C:4 f.) **tlt'hwn ml'k'... tly bsykth dmyšply dmydly** "three angels... hung on a peg which is lowered and raised". A somewhat similar formula occurs in Gollancz 1912, p. 96, where an incantation begins **hlyn šb‘' 'ḥÿn**. Three mysterious figures also occur as part of the incantation in Amulet 7:16–17 **hmwn tlthyn**...

3–4 Dupont-Sommer, followed by the other scholars, read **bh / gbrt'**. A comparison of the letter which comes after the *bet* with other forms in this inscription shows that it is closer to *mem* than to *he*. The fact that there is no divider either at the end of line 3 or at the beginning of line 4 shows that we have here a single word. The first letter of line 4 is quite clearly an *‘ayin*.

5 **mdbryn**: This verb seems to correspond to Hebrew **mnhygym** in *Sefer ha-razim*, IV:9,11,18, which refers to angels directing or ruling over the fourth firmament.

7 **mwmmn'**: Cf. the spelling of this verb in the bowl published by Kaufman 1975, p. 151, where one should probably read **mwmymny** (for **mwmymn'**).

8 **rbw** lacks a dot over the *resh*, hence a reading **dkw** should be considered. However, in line 12 we have **rbwn** clearly written in the same combination. **rbw** and **rbwn** are both nouns derived from the same root as **rb'** in line 1, a fact which may strengthen our interpretation of **rb'** as an independent divine appellation. For **rbw** cf. Gollancz 1898, p. 95:

bʿynn mnk wmtkšpynn lrbwtk "we beg you and implore your greatness".

ʾqym zbʾwt: The first word may be a form of the verb **QWM** in *afʿel*, which recalls the frequent personal names mainly in Palmyrene: **ʾqmt** (Stark 1971, p. 72), **mqym, mqymw, mqymy, mqymt, mqmw** (Stark 1971, p. 96). What appears to be the same name occurs in Amulet 4:16, **ʾqmw brth dʾmrbn**.

The reading **zbʾwt** (see already Gordon 1949, pp. 340f.) is based on the assumption that this form can be a reflection of Hebrew **ṣbʾwt**, as Syriac **zdyq** corresponds to Hebrew **ṣdyq**. This goes against the fact that **ṣbʾwt** is the usual Syriac spelling of this word; cf. e.g. Macler 1908, p. 20. In Bowl 10:5 **bšwm ṣbʾwty ṣbʾwty ḥyʾ wqymʾ**, we have in the same phrase both **ṣbʾwty** and **qymʾ**, which are reminiscent of **ʾqym zbʾwt**. Arabic magic texts also have **ṣbʾwt**; cf. Goldziher 1894, p. 358.

The presumed spelling of a *ṣade* with a *zayin* may gain some force from the Greek form Ζεβυϑ which occurs in the formula Ιαβεζεβυϑ (the Paris magical papyrus, lines 1798 and 2000, quoted by Blau 1898, p. 134 and footnote 4), if indeed this compound name means **yhwh ṣbʾwt**. The phenomenon of Greek *zeta* corresponding to *sigma* in such names may similarly be attested in the two names Σουτιήλ and Ζωτιήλ as suggested by Peterson 1926b, p. 419, No. 114; cf. also there p. 402. J.C. Greenfield would regard the expression **ʾqym zbʾwt** as equivalent to **ʾlhym ṣbʾwt** (Ps. 59:6; 80:5 etc.), but this seems problematic.

However, a different reading of our word is possible: **zkʾwt**. This word would be the equivalent of classical Syriac **zkywtʾ**, which renders Hebrew **ṣdqh**; see Brockelmann 1928, p. 196. This reading may be supported by the divine name ʾΙαω Ζούχα which occurs in the Paris magic papyrus, line 1983, cf. Peterson 1926b, p. 402, No. 41. The whole epithet **ʾqym zkʾwt** may then mean "establish justice", or with an initial vocative *alef*, "he who stands (in) justice".

9 **prqy** is a feminine singular imperative, perhaps addressed at **rbw** which is a feminine noun; its emphatic state would be **rbwtʾ**.

ṭrpsdk: The first element of this word was explained by Dupont-Sommer 1946, p. 21 as Greek τρόπος "façon, manière". Gordon connects it with **ṭrps lybʾ** "pericardium" and adduces the meaning "(metal) sheet". It seems to us that **ṭrpsdk** is a Persian form, Tarpas-dukh, with the typical Persian suffix for "daughter". A similar formation is e.g. **zrdwk dywʾ** (Gollancz 1912, p. 89, §25). The first part of the compound may be interpreted as **ṭrps** in Judaeo-Persian, which means "backwards". For a different interpretation of **ṭrps** one may try to connect it with the Greek form ϑραφιαρι (Preisendanz 1928, p. 94, VI:652; cf. variants in Preisendanz 1941, Register XII, p. 257). A demon **ṭarpis** is attested in Mandaic, see Drower 1943, pp. 2 f.; **dwrps** occurs on a bowl: Jeruzalmi 1963, p. 128: 4 (Isbell 1976, No. 69).

10 **ʾnhr**: The same verb occurs in Myhrman 1909, p. 146 (=Montgomery 1913, p. 151) **wmnṭrnʾ lkwn wmnhrnʾ lkwn wmḥtymnʾ lkwn**.
bwtk seems to be a defective writing of **bʿwtk**.

11 There seems to us no reason to assume an omission of **rbʾ ḥsynʾ qdyš**, as does Gordon 1949.

12 **ʾrzm bk** corresponds to **mwmmnʾ bk** in line 7 (cf. Gordon 1949, p. 341), thus establishing the meaning of the verb **RZM** (a variant of **RMZ**, cf. Job 15:12 and for Targumic Aramaic cf. Jastrow, p. 1482, s.v. **RMZ**). The verb **RMZ/RZM** has a magic connotation, e.g. in Mandaic **kup raza urimza uraza** "bow thyself, mystery and winking and mystery!" (Drower 1937, p. 596; translation on p. 610). A discussion of words derived from **RMZ** in a magic connotation is in Pognon 1898, pp. 91 f. In Montgomery 1913, No. 19:8 we have the phrase **wbšm srpyʾl mry dynʾ**

Amulet 7

Provenance: Ağabeyli, Turkey
Present location unknown
Plate 6; Figures 7–8

7a

vacat שויו רחמין מן שמיה
לשלונה בשם מיכאל רפאל
עזאל עזריאל אריאל ס(רר)ו
רבה אתון מלאכיה קדשיה דקימי[ן]
קדם כרסיה דאלה רבה דיתכלון
רוחה בישתה וטלניתה ושידה
אן דכר ואן נקבה מן שלונה
בר דמיטרין בשם ...

(emended by Epstein 1921, pp. 49 f. to **rwzʾ**, though doubtful) **wrymzʾ**, where the last word is obviously a magical technical term.

rbwn: This is evidently a variant of the form **rbw** in line 8, although **rbw** seems to be the absolute form of the feminine abstract "greatness", while **rbwn** appears to be an absolute form of a word meaning "master". On this latter word see Kutscher 1963, pp. 268–271; Ben-Ḥayyim 1967, pp. 37 ff.; Kutscher 1968, pp. 403 f. This may be the reason why the imperative following **rbwn** (in line 13) is in the masculine singular form **prq**, as opposed to **prqy** in line 9 following **rbw**.

14 **tlṭʾ**: Del Medico 1949, p. 182, recognized here the Greek word for sea ϑάλαττα, which makes sense as it corresponds to "ocean" and "water" in lines 4–5.

15 The reading is difficult. It is possible that the star at the beginning of the line is a pictogram representing the noun which should follow **wmn** in line 14. Del Medico 1949, p. 180, in fact translated it as "le Soleil".

dmwllk may be a defective writing for **dnmwllk** "may he crush you". The following word might possibly also be **bnqmtʾ** "with vengeance".

Amulet 7

Translation

7a

1 Put mercy from heaven
2 on **šlwnh**. In the name of Michael, Raphael,
3 Azzael, Azriel, Ariel, the great
4 dominion (?), you, the holy angels who stand
5 in front of the throne of the Great God. May there be extinguished
6 the evil spirit and the shadow-spirit, and the demon,
7 whether male or female, from **šlwnh**
8 son of Demetrion. In the name of...

9 ששקופות וסמרוטוש עקרמכמרי
10 סוסגון ברפרונגס אסטר ושב[ן]
11 תחת יהוה בשמך אלה מקדשה
12 דיתכלון רוח<ה> בישתה ושידה
13 וטלניתה ומזקה ומחבלה בשמ[ך]
14 אלה דישראל לרקיעה מליה סלקה
15 בסטר כרסיה דאלה רבה חסינה ודחילה
16 מקדשה ומגדלה מ<פ>ארה ומרומה המון
17 תלתהין חדה כפנה ולא אכלה חדה
18 צחיה ולא שתיה וחדה נימה
19 ולא דמכה אמרת לכפנתה למת
20 כפנה ולא אכלה לצחיתה למת צחיה
21 ולא שתיה לנאמת<ה> למת נימה ולא
22 דמכה גיזו תלתיהן ואמרן דאן

7b
1 vacat לרחמין מן קדם כרסיה [דאלה רבה]
2 [ד]יתכל מזקה ומחבלה וד(ש)[ ]
3 [ו]שידה טלניתה אן דכר ואן נק[בה]
4 [מ]ן (ש)[ל]ונה בר [ד]מיטרין (ב)[שם]
5 ...

Amulets 7a and 7b are two silver sheets inscribed in Jewish Aramaic. They were found by peasants in the market village Ağabeyli in the valley of Bertiz not far from Maraş, placed in a cylindrical bronze container. The circumstances of the discovery are described by Anstock-Darga 1950/51. The larger sheet (our Amulet 7a) measures approximately 50×58 mm. Amulet 7b, of which only a fragment is preserved, measures about 43×12 mm. The *editio princeps* was by Dupont-Sommer 1950/51. A new interpretation was offered by Scholem in 1960 (see Scholem 1965, pp. 85 ff.) Further elucidation was given by Levine 1970, pp. 360 f. A comment on a part of the text is in Sperber 1966. We have tried to present in the following a better text, but in view of the fact that the

9 **ššqwpwt wsmrwṭwš ʿqrmkmry**
10 **swsgwn brprwngs ʾsṭr** and...
11 under **yhwh**. In your name, sacred God,
12 may there be extinguished the evil spirit and the demon
13 and the shadow-spirit and the tormentor and the destroyer. In your name
14 God of Israel, may the words rise up to heaven
15 at the side of the throne of the great, powerful, aweful,
16 sacred, magnified, praised and exalted God. Those
17 three: one who is hungry, but does not eat, one who
18 is thirsty, but does not drink, and one who is drowsy,
19 but does not sleep. I said to the hungry one: Why are you
20 hungry, but you do not eat? (I said) to the thirsty one: Why are you thirsty,
21 but you do not drink? (I said) to the drowsy one: Why are you drowsy, but you do not
22 sleep? The three vanished and said: **dʾn**.

7b
1 For mercy in front of the throne [of the great God.]
2 [May] there be extinguished the tormentor, the destroyer and ...
3 [and] the demon and the shadow-spirit, whether male or female,
4 from **šlwnh** son of Demetrion. In [the name of]
5 ...

photographs reproduced in Dupont-Sommer 1950/51 are not sufficiently legible, we have had to rely largely on Dupont-Sommer's drawings (Fig. 7), which seem to be accurate. [But see *Addendum* at the end of this Commentary, on p. 76.]

1 It is noteworthy that in both amulets there is a space left on the right hand side of the first line. It seems therefore unjustified to assume that something is missing at the beginning of Amulet 7b.

Dupont-Sommer read **šwy wrḥmyn**, which he translated "prix (?) et amour". Scholem suggested an emended reading **šyyl rḥmyn** "begging mercy", which is unlikely as an Aramaic phrase and is contradicted by

Amulet 7b which starts with **lrḥmyn**. Levine suggests that **šwy wrḥmyn** be interpreted "accord and mercy", the first word connected with **šwyt'**, which occurs in Montgomery 1913, No. 16:6. While Levine's interpretation may be correct, it seems at least equally possible and perhaps better to read the first two words **šwyw rḥmyn** from the verb **ŠWY** "to place, put", which was recently discussed in connection with Samaritan Aramaic by Margain 1979. The usage "put mercy" would be analogous to the Hebrew **śym šlwm** in the ʿAmida prayer, rendered into Aramaic **šwy lyšlm'** (Gaster 1928, III, p. 56), with its counterpart in Bowl 1:10 **dmšw' šlm' zk' bdyn'**. A similar expression is in Mandaic **šauia asuta** "one who makes a remedy" (Drower 1946, p. 326). For the form **šwyw** see Gen. Apocryphon 21:26. In 7b the shorter formula, **lrḥmyn**, is used. It is easier to explain **lrḥmyn** as an abbreviation from **šwyw rḥmyn** than from a formula such as **šwy wrḥmyn**. For the whole expression compare **wlrḥmn yśmnk qdm drywhwš mlk'** "and may He give you favour before Darius the king" (Cowley 1923, No. 30:2).

šwy, which corresponds to Hebrew **šwh**, could also mean "at once" (cf. Ben-Ḥayyim 1943, p. 119; Lieberman 1962, p. 135; Kutscher 1961, pp. 124 ff.; Ben-Ḥayyim 1967, p. 69, n. 23), though such an interpretation seems unlikely in the present context. Similarly, it is possible to interpret **šwyw** in the sense of "make haste", cf. Ben-Ḥayyim 1967, p. 69, n. 23, where we have in a Samaritan liturgical poem **nšwy khln wnptḥ pwmynn** "let us hasten all of us and open our mouths"; **'šww... mʿbd** "they did at once". This construction hardly fits in here, as it seems normally to require another verb or infinitive which is qualified by the verb **šwy**.

2 **lšlwnh**: Dupont-Sommer, followed by Scholem, read **lšlw zh**, which is impossible because: (1) the text is purely Aramaic, (2) the Hebrew phrase suggested is nowhere attested and is quite unlikely in the sense of "he who possesses this (amulet)". The letter *nun* is not sharply distinguished from *zayin* and in this case it merges with the preceding *waw*. The name **šlwnh** may be compared to **šlwn**, Greek Σαλων, a feminine proper name (cf. Sukenik 1930). A name **slwn'**, in Syriac, is rendered by Chabot 1898, p. 303, line 183, "Sylvain"; see also Payne-Smith 1890, p. 2641, s.v. **slw'n'**. A name CHΛONO(C) appears in a tomb-stone inscription from Italy (Frey 1936, p. 433, No. 596). For the correspondence of Aramaic *shin* to Greek *sigma* cf. Krauss 1898, pp. 7 ff. The masculine name **šlwnh** may be a variant of the masculine Jewish name Shallum. On the variation of **m›n** in word-final position cf. Kutscher 1976, pp. 58 ff.

7a

7b

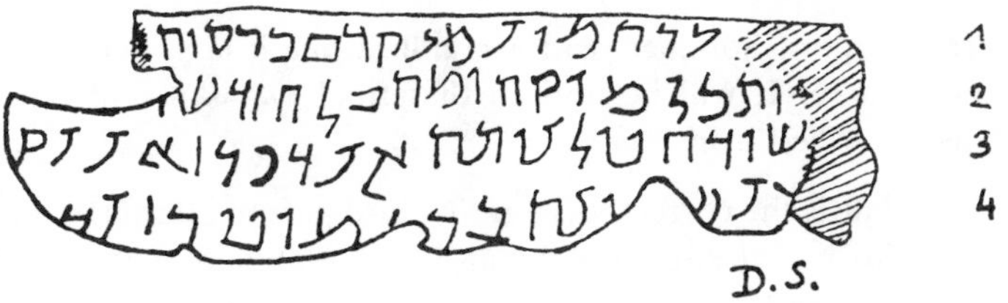

Fig. 7. Amulets 7a and 7b. From Dupont-Sommer 1950/51

Sokoloff 1982, p. 114 quotes an oral remark by Kutscher according to which the name in our amulet should be read as **šlw** (Shallu, an abbreviated form of Shallum). Kutscher accepted the reading **zh**, which follows the name as a demonstrative pronoun. It seems to us unlikely that the Hebrew demonstrative would be used in this Aramaic text.

4 **ʾtwn mlʾkyh qdšyh**: Here again the combination of *waw* and *nun* misled previous scholars. Dupont-Sommer read **ʾtt mlʾky hqdš wḥd**, which mixes Aramaic with Hebrew and makes an impossible sentence. For the phrase **ʾtwn mlʾkyh qdšyh** cf. Amulet 10:3 and the Commentary to Amulet 2:3.

dqymyn: Cf. Amulet 6:3, where the same word is used for angels.

5 **qdm krsyh dʾlh rbh**: We assume that **qdm krsyh** stands in contrast to **bsṭr krsyh** in line 15. A similar contrast is found in Stübe 1895, p. 26, lines 56 ff.; Lacau 1896, p. 50: ובשום גבריאל ומיכאל ורפאל ובשמיה דעניאל דקאים אחורי גלגלי שמשא ובשום דוקיאל ופרקיאל ודרקיאל וערכיאל דימשמשין קדם כורסיה דיקרא דאלהא

6 For **ṭlnyth** see Amulet 4:15.

7–8 **mn šlwnh br dmyṭryn:** Dupont-Sommer read in line 8 **brk myṭryn** "bénis une matrice". Scholem translated this "blessed be Meta[t?]ron". See also Niggemeyer 1975, p. 146, n. 28. The reading given here, which presents the full name of the owner of this amulet, is quite well established. The Greek name Δημήτριος, which seems to underlie here the parent's name, is generally attested for men, although we normally would expect the mother's name to be mentioned in an amulet. As a Jewish name, Demetrius is found in inscriptions; see Frey 1936, No. 682 and Lifshitz in Frey 1975, Prolegomenon, p. 85, No. 715 i.

9–10 For these magical names see Scholem 1965, pp. 89, 94 ff.

11 Dupont-Sommer read **bšm dʾlh**, while it is preferable to read as given here. It will be noticed that final *kaf* is not always carefully distinguished from *dalet*.

14 **slqh** is the correct form of the third person plural feminine perfect in Jewish Palestinian Aramaic. See Dalman 1905, paradigm on p. 402 (**slyqʾ**).

15 **bsṭr** has been explained as "at the side of". However, it is possible to take it as an equivalent of Syriac **bstr** "backwards, behind" (which may be of Persian origin). "Behind the throne" would then be the perfect counterpart of μετὰ ϑρόνον. **bsṭr** stands in contrast to **qdm** in line 5.

A recent discussion of the etymology of Metatron by S. Lieberman is contained in Gruenwald 1980, pp. 235 ff. Lieberman argues that μετάϑρονος, though unattested in Greek sources, is the equivalent of σύνϑρονος and was preferred by Jews for the name of the angel. An earlier detailed discussion of the term is in Odeberg 1928, pp. 137 ff.

rbh ḥsynh wdḥylh: We have here the same sequence as in Amulet 1:8 (see Commentary there). A similar sequence **rbʾ ḥsynʾ qdyš ʾylʾ** occurs in Amulet 6:1–2.

16 This sequence of adjectives is reminiscent of the series of verbs in the Qaddish prayer, as noted by Scholem 1965, p. 90. See also T–S AS 143.143 מלך מפואר מרומם מלא כל הארץ כבודו נורא תהלות נשגב נפלא ...

hmwn: The form is not mentioned in the grammars of Palestinian Aramaic and Syriac (e.g. Dalman 1905, Kutscher 1976, Schulthess 1924), but it is attested in Biblical Aramaic for the masculine and once (Dan. 2:34) for the feminine.

16–22 For the theme of three mysterious figures we have numerous analogies in magic texts. We may refer, e.g. to Gollancz 1898, pp. 92 f., where three evil forms, a man, a wolf and lion, meet Moses when he tends his sheep.

A very close analogy to our story is found in the Iraq Museum bowl, No. 9731 (published in Gordon 1941, p. 349, and Gordon 1978, pp. 236 f.) and in a bowl in the Zion Research Library in Boston, No. 48 (published in Gordon 1978, pp. 233 f.). A recently published parallel version is in Scholem 1980/81, pp. 263 f. In these Jewish texts we have the story of the sorcerer (who speaks in the first person) going up to the roof at night and talking to some mysterious figures addressed as **ḥršyn byšyn wrʾzyn ʾpwkyn** "evil magicians and overturned mysteries". He says to them "If you are hungry, come eat! If you are thirsty, come drink! If you are dried up, come be oiled! But if you are not hungry, or thirsty, or dried up, go back the way you came, enter the house from which you went out, and the mouth from which you went out". The first to notice this parallel was Levine 1970, pp. 360 f., who suggested as an interpretation the observation "that providing hospitality for demons was a duty that could not be overlooked. Like many hosts the exorcist is saying, in fact, that unless there is more coming to the demons by the way of official hospitality, they had better be on their way". Gordon 1957, pp. 171 f. (followed by Niggemeyer 1975, pp. 70 f.) also speaks of hospitality offered to demons. Our context, however, brings to mind that we have to do with a somewhat different situation. The demons come to the house probably masked as human beings, but they do not partake of food and drink as human guests normally do. They can be unmasked by putting to them the embarrassing question: why do you not eat, drink or sleep; when they are found out they must depart. There are Jewish discussions of the problem whether demons can eat and drink; according to Bavli Ḥagiga 16a they can. On this question see Shaked (forthcoming).

22 **gyzw**: Dupont-Sommer read **ḥzy** which does not conform to the signs visible. The form **gyzw** is difficult. We might have expected **gyzn**, the feminine plural of the active participle "they vanish", or **gzn**, the third person fem. plural perfect.

tltyhn is an error for **tlthyn**; see line 17.

ʾmrn: Active participle (or perfect?) plural feminine.

dʾn may be connected to the magic word mentioned in Tosefta Shabbat 7:3 and Bavli Shabbat 67b: **dny dny**, which is explained by Lieberman 1957/58, p. 188 as Greek δέννω, δέννω or δένο, δένο "I bind, I bind". **dʾn** could also be interpreted as **d-+ʾn** "(they say): yes!".

[*Addendum*: When the book was already set in the press we received from Mme. Hélène Lozachmeur the original photographs of the two amulets (7a and 7b) which the late Prof. Dupont-Sommer had used. On the basis of enlargements made from these photographs (Pl. 6), Mrs. A. Yardeni has made a fresh drawing (Fig. 8). A study of both the enlargements and the drawing brings out the following new readings:
Line 1 of 7b. Read at the beginning בעון רחמין "ask mercy".
Line 15. Read בסטר כרסיה דאלה רבה תקיפה ודחילה.
Line 22. For גיזו read ענו, which makes better sense and removes most of the difficulties. The translation is: "The three answered and said: **dʾn**".]

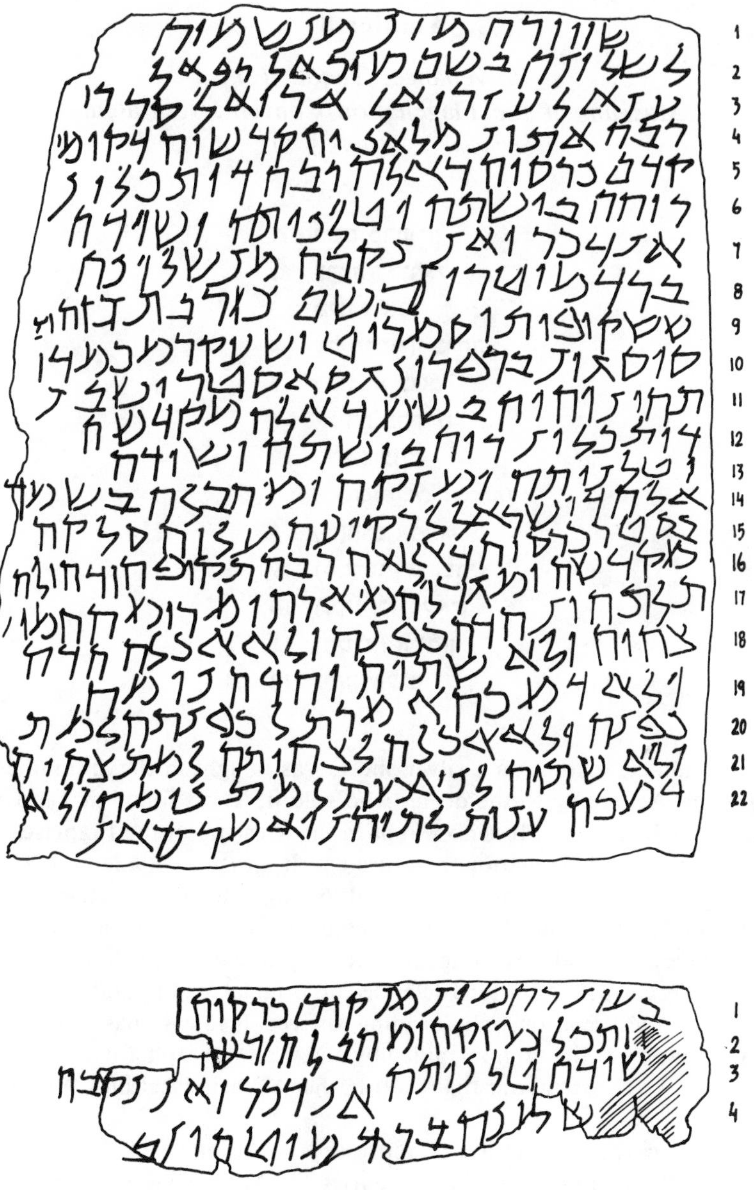

Fig. 8. Amulets 7a and 7b.

Amulet 8

Provenance: Teqoaᶜ (?)
Museum of the Flagellation Convent, Jerusalem
Plate 7; Figures 9–10

1 לשם מרת(י)ן
2 ברתה דקוראל
3 משבע אנה
4 על מרת(י)ן ברתה
5 דקורלא בשם
6 אגירת מרתי פ
7 ללא ויב(ך)

(magic characters)

8 (מ)חרב אנ<ה>
9 (סטרסוק שאפתי)
10 (נקימנס וסקאי)
11 (חטרב) אי(ת)ה
12 ניחה שלום

This amulet, written on a silver sheet, was bought in the antiquities market. According to the dealer who sold it, it was found at Teqoaᶜ south of Bethlehem. It is now kept in the Museum of the Franciscan Convent of the Flagellation in Jerusalem. It measures 60×24 mm. The first publication of the text by Testa 1967 suggested that it refers to an unction of sick people. Milik 1967 recognized that the text is an amulet, and gave an emended reading and interpretation of it, which we regard as largely correct. Testa 1968 defended his original reading and attacked Milik's interpretation. The reading offered below is based on an examination of the original, aided by a new photograph, for which we should like to extend our thanks to Father Michele Piccirillo, O.P.M.

1 **lšm mrtyn**. The amulet is addressed at the name of the demon Marten ("our lady"?) daughter of Qoriel. For Marten one may compare Μαρθήνη Αστερία in Mouterde 1930, p. 124, line 15, where it occurs as a feminine proper name. The title Marten occurs also in Montgomery

Amulet 8

Translation

1 To the name of Marten
2 daughter of Qoriel
3 I adjure
4 against Marten daughter of
5 Qoriel. In the name of
6 Agirat, my lady,
7 **pllʾ**...
(*magic characters*)
8 I destroy
9 ...
10 ...
11 ...bring (?)
12 rest. Peace.

1913, No. 19:5–6 **wbšmyk mrtyn ʾybwlyt mlktʾ rbtʾ dʾystrʾtʾ**. The name is known from the triad of deities in Hatra (Marēn, Martēn and Bar-Marēn), for which cf. Drijvers 1980, pp. 176–179. Palaeographically Milik's reading, **mrtwn=mrt(h)wn** "their lady", is also possible. It seems, however, preferable to connect this word with a well-established divine name.

2 Qoriel is well-known as a name of an angel. It occurs in the Geniza fragment JTS ENA 1177, fol. 16:13 **qryʾl**. In the unpublished Aramaic bowl Metropolitan Museum, New York, L. 66.6, line 8, we have **bšwm qwryʾl glglyʾ**. In Greek there occur the forms Κουριήλ in Preisendanz 1928, IV:86; Καρα(α)ήλ, Καριήλ, cf. Peterson 1926b, p. 405, No. 59.

6–7 For **ʾgyrt** see above Amulet 4:24. Each of the names **ʾgyrt, mrty, pllʾ** and **ybk** seems to have a counterpart in the list of angels in *Sefer ha-razim* 4:13–16...**mʾryt**...**yʾbwk**...**ʾgrytʾl**...**plʾwʾl**. If this correspondence is correct, **pllʾ** (for ***plʾl**) displays the same transposition of

Amulet 8

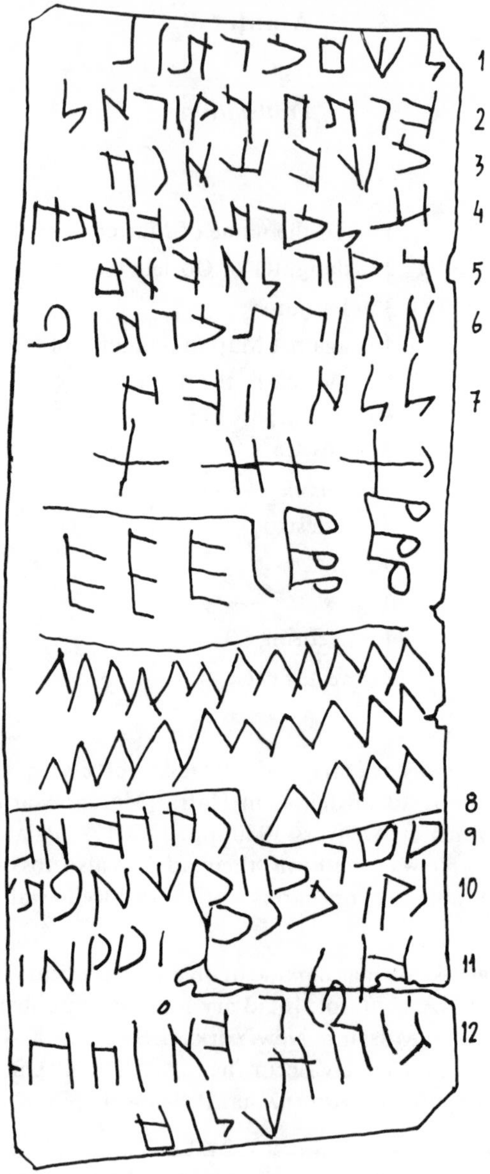

Fig. 9. Amulet 8

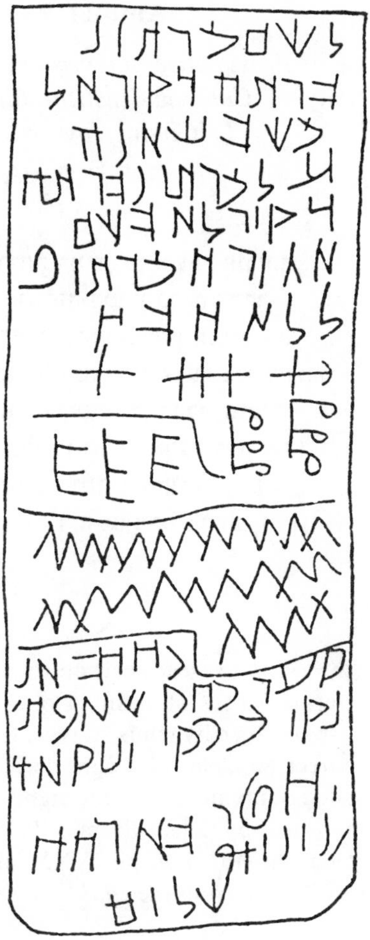

Fig. 10. Amulet 8. From Milik 1967

letters as we have in **qwrlʾ** for **qwrʾl**. For **mrty=mʾryt** cf. Peterson 1926, pp. 40 f., No. 75 **Μοριάϑ**, etc. **mrty** may be at the base of the name **mrtyn**.

8 Our transcription follows that of Milik, though the traces do not give an unequivocal reading.

11–12 **ʾyth** is doubtful, whereas **nyḥh** is quite safely established.

12 **šlwm** as a concluding formula, although it is frequent in epitaphs and dedicatory inscriptions, is quite unknown in amulets.

Amulet 9

Provenance: Oxyrrhynchus (?)
University of Cologne, Institut für Altertumskunde,
T. Colon, Inv. No. 6
Plate 8; Figure 11

1 עליך רוחה דמתקריה אשתה אוריתה
2 אגער מן גופה דמרין ברתה דסתר
3 מן מתין ותמניה וארבעין אברין
4 דבה משבע אנה עליך אגער מנה בשמה
5 דמן דחיה וקימה דמן דתלה שומיה
6 דלה בשלשלן ואקים ארעה דלה [על]
7 עמודין וימה ומדברה ת(מהי)ן מן
8 ק[ד]מוי וטוריה וגלמתה מזד(ע)[זעין]

This amulet, inscribed on a lead sheet and measuring 93×46 mm., is now in Cologne, Germany (T. Colon, Inv. No. 6). It was presumably found in the cemetery of Oxyrrhynchus, Egypt, from which the rest of the collection of Greek amulets in Cologne derives. The original text seems to have consisted of no more than the eight lines that are preserved. It was first published by Klein-Franke 1971 and was subsequently discussed by Greenfield 1979, pp. XXXVIII f. Our readings are in several points different from the *editio princeps.*

1–2 **ʿlyk**: This word was read **lyk** by Greenfield 1979, but Klein-Franke is certainly right in seeing an *ʿayin* at the beginning of the line. Although an invocation beginning with **ʿlyk** is not elsewhere attested, it seems clear that this is the actual beginning of the text. For a similar beginning compare Amulet 8:1 **lšm mrtyn**...The construction is elliptical, and one has to assume an implied **mšbʿ ʾnh**, as in line 4. According to Greenfield **lyk** is the direct object of **ʾgʿr**, which he understood as the first person singular imperfect of *peʿal.* However, it seems preferable to explain **ʾgʿr** as imperative singular masculine *itpeʿel* from **GʿR**, to be read as *iggĕʿar* (<**itgĕʿar*). The root **GʿR** occurs very

Amulet 9

Translation

1 Against you, the spirit which is called fever (and) shivering:
2 Be exorcised from the body of Marian the daughter of Esther,
3 from the two hundred and forty eight limbs
4 which are in her. I adjure you, be exorcised from her, in the name
5 of He who lives and exists, of He who suspended the sky
6 without chains, and set up the earth without
7 pillars, and the sea and the wilderness are terrified (?) from
8 His presence, and the mountains and the hills tre[mble].

often in the *itpeʿel* form; see the examples adduced in Greenfield 1979. For the assimilation of the *taw* to the *gimmel* cf. Dalman 1905, pp. 103 and 252 f. It is noteworthy that the form of the verb **ʾgʿr** is masculine, although **rwḥh** is described by the feminine participle **dmtqryh**. **rwḥʾ** of course can be either masc. or fem., cf. Geniza 4:3, **rwḥyn byšyn**, as against **rwḥʾ bʾyštʾ** in the Gen. Apocryphon (see Greenfield *loc. cit.*). For **GʿR** cf. Amulet 2:8.

ʾšth ʾwryth: The meaning of these two words is established by Amulet 2:2 (see Commentary there). Geniza 6, p. 4:2 displays another corruption of the formula. The spelling with *alef* for *ʿayin* is caused by the loss of the gutturals; cf. Kutscher 1976, pp. 67 ff. The peculiar spelling **ʾwrytʾ** occurs possibly also in Hyvernat 1885, p. 116: **ובעיזקתיה דמיכאיל גברא מלכא עיסרא דאוריתא ... ובעיזקתיה דגבריאיל גברא מלכא** ... **עיסרא דנורא** .... The parallel **ʾwrytʾ//nwrʾ** recalls our **ʾšth ʾwryth**. It has been noted (Grünbaum 1885, p. 223; cf. also Margaliot 1945, p. 118) that Michael represents water and hail, while Gabriel is fire. Montgomery 1913, 24:2 should be read **dtytsy brḥmy šmyʾ mn ʾšytʾ wmn ʾrytʾ**, which gives us a third instance of the spelling with *alef*. Since Biblical Hebrew has **ʾwr** in the sense of "flame", one wonders whether the spellings

ʾwryth, ʾwrytʾ, ʾrytʾ do not represent a contamination of two words of different origin, the root **ʿRY** and the word *ʾūr* (?).

mryn: See above, Commentary to Amulet 2:2.

dstr: The reading seems certain. The initial *alef* of **ʾstr** was elided. The same name, spelled *plene* (**ʾstyr**), occurs in Amulet 3:5, 16.

3 **mtyn**: Here too the *alef* was omitted.

5 **dḥyh wqymh**: Cf. Bowl 10:5.

5–6 דתלה שומיה דלה בשלשלן ואקים ארעה דלה [על] עמודין: References to the earth and the firmament, which are said to be either supported or unsupported by pillars and chains, are frequent in magical and early mystical Jewish literature. Lieberman 1962, pp. 80 f. quotes from *Shir ha-shirim Rabba* 7:8 דברייתא משתבעין ואמרין במאן דאקים ארעא על תלתא עמודים. Niggemeyer 1975, p. 153, n. 32 quotes various sources, where the world is said to rely on the arm of the Lord. Wertheimer 1980, I, p. 28 וכל העולם כולו עומד על עמוד אחד; p. 41 ירושלים ובית המקדש עומדים ותלויים בשלשלאות של אש בין שחקים לזבול (in *Seder Rabba di-Breshit*).

Arabic invocations have references to the same theme; cf. e.g. "und bei 'Allah, der die Himmel erhöht hat ohne Säulen' (Sura 13:2) und ohne ein Band" (Winkler 1930, p. 60, translation on p. 64; and a similar phrase in Winkler 1931, p. 9).

The idea is attested also in Zoroastrian Pahlavi: "I am thankful to the good, bounteous, beneficent and merciful Creator, who, when he created Asmān (the sky), which is well-formed, bright, of wondrous substance, wondrously adorned, fully ornamented, fashioned by the spirits, which stands in *mēnōg* without pillars (*a-stun*) and without being held from above (*an-abar-dāštār*)..." (*Zand-i khūrtak avistāk*, p. 256:5–10).

Amulet 10

Provenance: Ḥorvat Rimmon
Israel Department of Antiquities, No. 80.880
Plate 9; Figure 12

1 |הראות| |אתבאות| |קולהון|
2 |ספתון| |סוסגר| [ ]

For the spelling **šwmyh** cf. the inscription in the Engedi synagogue (Naveh 1978, No. 70:15) and cf. **šwmy**ʾ (op. cit., No. 20:5).

7 **wymh wmdbrh t(mhy)n**: The reading of the verb is uncertain. The root **TMH** is used in Biblical Hebrew, *inter alia*, for the terror and trembling of the earth or the pillars of heaven in the presence of God. In Job 26:11 עמודי שמים ירופפו ויתמהו מגערתו is rendered in the Jewish Targum עמודין דשמיא מזדעזעין ורתתין מן מזופיתיה. The Peshitta has עמודי שמיא רעלין ונתמהון מן כאתה. Syriac **TMH** is used to render Hebrew **ḤRD** "fear, tremble" in Gen. 42:28, where the Jewish Targums have **TWH** instead.

8 **glmt**ʾ: The word seems to be typically Palestinian. It is attested in the Palestinian Targum, where it renders **gbʿh** and **ʿmq**. It also occurs in Palestinian Syriac.

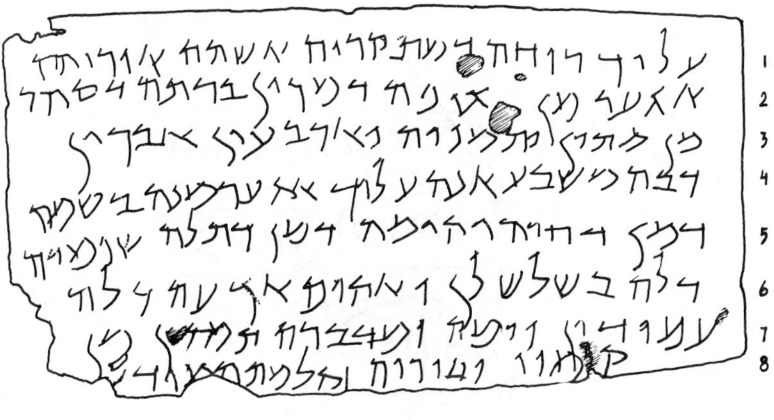

Fig. 11. Amulet 9

Amulet 10

Translation

1 **hrʾwt ʾtbʾwt qwlhwn**
2 **sptwn swsgr** [ ]

Amulet 10

3 אתון מלאכיה קד[ישיה (ותקיפיה)]
4 [משבע אנה] יתכון כמ[ה דיקד חספה]
5 [הדין כן] יקוד לבה דר[... ברה/ברתה]
6 [דמר](ין) בתר(י) אנה (יו)[... ותהפכו]
7 [לבה והו](נה ו)כוליתה ו[י/תעבד]
8 ציביוני בהד[ ]מוד [ ]
9 *(magic characters)* [ ]

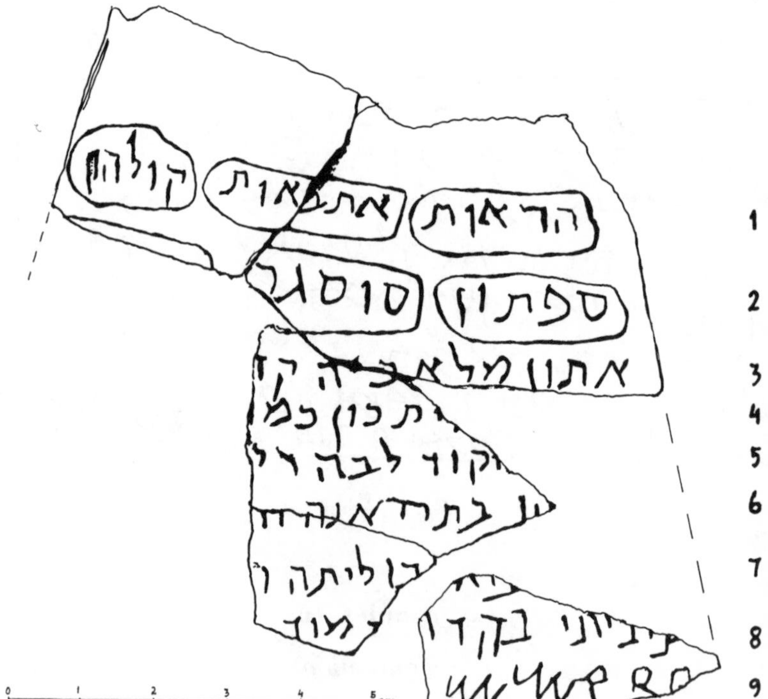

Fig. 12. Amulet 10

3 You ho[ly (and mighty)] angels
4 [I adjure] you, just as [this sherd]
5 [burns, so shall] burn the heart of R[... son/daughter of]
6 [Mar]ian after me, I ..[...and you should turn]
7 [his/her heart and mi]nd and kidney, so [that he/she will do]
8 my desire in this [ ]
9 (*magic characters*)

This amulet is inscribed on a potsherd. It was found in the excavations at Ḥorvat Rimmon (Kh. Umm er-Ramamin, Map Ref. 13721/08677), *c.* 1/2 km. south of Kibbutz Lahav and *c.* 13 km. north of Beer-Sheba, by Dr. Amos Kloner of the Israel Department of Antiquities, who kindly entrusted us with its publication. Dr. Kloner also communicated the following details about the archaeological context of the amulet:

> The potsherds under discussion were found in Locus 148, in the Ḥorvat Rimmon excavations in 1980 (cf. Kloner 1980, 1981). Locus 148 is in the north-eastern corner of the enclosure, which contains the synagogue and its adjoining area; this enclosure was created in the fifth century C.E. by the erection of a surrounding wall. The area of Locus 148 was excavated through a filling of debris down to the bed rock. Two different strata were distinguished within the debris: the upper stratum, 80 cm. in thickness, contained numerous fragments of jars, cooking pots and lids, oil-lamps, roof-tiles, glass objects, iron nails and animal bones, as well as an axe-like iron instrument and fragments of a chancel screen and a chancel post. All of these finds date back to the Byzantine period. The lower stratum (20 cm. in thickness) contained potsherds from the Second Temple period and later (1st century B.C.E. — 2nd century C.E.). The five fragments of the amulet (registered as 858/572; 858/559/1–2) were found scattered in different places in the upper stratum of the fill. It seems that the upper stratum of the debris accumulated at the end of the Byzantine period. The amulet under consideration is thus to be dated to the fifth-sixth centuries C.E.

The amulet consists of five broken pieces, four of which can be attached to each other, forming line 1 and parts of lines 2–8. The fifth piece contains parts of the last two lines (lines 8–9), but it cannot be properly joined to the other fragments, as there seems to be a tiny piece missing. As a result we do not have a consecutive text of line 8. Mrs. Ada Yardeni, who suggested how the fifth fragment should be joined to the amulet, based her idea on an observation of the pattern of the thickness and of the wheelmarks.

In contrast to other potsherds, this is not an accidental fragment of a broken pot. It seems that the potter deliberately cut deep incisions on the surface of the jar before firing it, and that he broke the jar along the same incisions. Marks of the incisions are visible along the edges of the fragments, where about half the thickness of the clay is smooth and the rest is rough. The writing must have been executed when the clay was still soft, before it was baked.

This observation brings to mind the injunction which occurs in several magic recipe books, especially in connection with love charms, to use "a new sherd". Cf. e.g. the *Sword of Moses*, Gaster 1896, p. XV:17–18, where we read **לגברא דייתי בתרך סב חספא חדתא וצבע במורא אוכם ואמר על שמיה מין אתוֹמי עד פנכיר ואיזיל ולא תצפי לאחורך** "If a man is to follow thee, take a new potsherd and dip it in black myrrh and pronounce over his name the words from **ᵓtwmy** until **pnkyr** and walk without looking backwards" (Gaster 1896, p. 184; "black myrrh" is Greek *zmurnomelan*, cf. Margaliot in *Sefer ha-razim*, p. 2). The idea of a new piece of clay on which the charm is written occurs as a fixed formula in Mandaic incantation bowls, e.g. **ᶜl glala dlbzᶜia ᶜtib wᶜktubinin ᶜl kasa hdta d̲phara uᶜšadrinin lluṭata d̲laṭu**... "on the rock that is not split I will sit and I will write them on a new bowl of clay and I will send the curses (back) to those who cursed..." (Yamauchi 1967, No. 18c:5–8; see also Nos. 7:24–26; 12:34–39; 19:16–18; 26:20–22). In the Mandaic instances the texts are not love charms. Similar injunctions occur with regard to using "a new piece of cloth" **kyrqh gdydh** (in Geniza 6, p. 1:15). An example for such an amulet on a piece of cloth exists in Geniza 1, another love charm.

In some Geniza fragments of magic books we have a more specific instruction, which relates to love or hate charms. The expression used is not "a new sherd", but **šqph nyh** (Geniza 5, p. 3:12), **pkr ny** (Geniza 6, p. 1:3, 4:4), or **kzph nyh** (Geniza 2, p. 2:). These expressions signify "an unbaked piece of pottery"; the Arabic *nayy* (like Hebrew *nāᵓ*) means "uncooked". For a charm against an enemy we have in Gaster 1896, p. XXII:29:30 the following instruction: "to break an enemy write the Sword (=amulet) upon a potsherd that has not yet been burned (**šlʾ nkns lʾwr**)..." (op. cit., p. 193). In a Geniza fragment, T–S K 1.153, p.1:11, we have: לאהבה סב חסף לא צלי וכתוב עלוי ... וכד את מטלק חספה בנורה אמור היך דאלין כתביה מתיקדין כן יתיקד לביה דפלנית ברת פלנית בתר פ̇ב̇פ̇. Our amulet was apparently prepared according to such an instruction.

The amulet bears marks of black areas which were perhaps caused by exposure to fire. It was perhaps thrown into the fire as part of the sympathetic magic rite alluded to in the text: "Just as this sherd burns, so shall burn the heart of...". This is a frequent formula which occurs in love charms, such as our own amulet. On this point see further below, Commentary to lines 4–5.

1–2 These lines contain the names of six angels surrounded by a frame. **qwlhwn** and **sptwn** remind one of **qlhwn** and **swptyn** in T-S K 1.160, whereas for **swsgr** see **ssgn**, **ssngnys** in *Sword of Moses*, Gaster 1896, IX:21, **swsgwn** in Amulet 7:10. See further Scholem 1965, pp.94 ff.

3 **ʾtwn mlʾkyh qdyšyh**: See Amulet 7:4 and Commentary to Amulet 2:3.

4–5 The reconstruction is based on the Geniza fragments Nos. 2, 5–6, which are pages from magic books, as well as on the Geniza amulets Nos. 1 and 3, which are love charms. In all these texts the angels are invoked and asked to cause the heart of a certain person to burn in love for the client just as this potsherd burns in the fire. The words **yqwd lbh dr[** "the heart of R... should burn" are sufficient for the suggested reconstruction. Moreover, the word **kwlyth** "his/her kidney" (line 7) has also been preserved, and this word occurs in Geniza 6, p. 1:13–14 **lbh whwnh wkwlyth dp** "the heart, the mind (?) and the kidney of X".

6 It is possible to read **btr dʾnh** "after that I", but in this case the reconstruction suggested here is difficult. **btr dʾnh** would hardly be "after Dana", as we would expect a name to be followed by **br** or **brt** and the name of the parent (usually mother).

8 For the phrase **yʿbd/tʿbd ṣbywny** cf. Geniza 6, p. 1:2; Gaster 1896, p. VIII:5. If this reading is correct, **bhd[h]** might mean "in this matter". Alternatively, it is possible to supplement **[ytʿbd] ṣbywny bhd[yn]/bhd[h]** [personal name] "May my desire be accomplished with regard to this [person]".

Amulet 11

Provenance: Nirim
Israel Department of Antiquities, No. 57.733
Plate 10; Figure 13

1 [אהיה [א]שר אהיה בשם ק[   ]ה ש(נ)רון ארסכיאל (נ)]
2 [אל מש(נ)ידה שמגרון סכסך דוקון דוקון ואן]
3 [אל [ב](ר)קיאל אוריאל מלחמיאל אה אה אה [א]ה אה א]ה
4 [א דתתעקרון מן רישה דנתרון ברתה דשאר[ה] אמן א]מן
5 ד]מתקרייא קפלרגיא ועלא בכורכוריא ד(נ)יא ולא]
6 בש]מה ד[נ](ג)דיאל מלאכה דכביש בשושלן דלא ד[נ]חש וב(ש)]
7 ד]לא דפורזיל ובשמה דנחשור ובשמה דסור(י)א[ל] מלא]כה
8 [זיקין ומזקין וטלנין יערקון מנה יואל יואל]
9 נ](ת)רון ברתה דשארה בשם אוה (ה)לוסא אל באל רב]
10 [תעקרו מן כורכוריא דניה ומן רישה]
11 ...]

Amulets 11–13 were discovered among the "small finds" in the apse of the ancient synagogue excavated in 1957–58 near kibbutz Nirim in the North Western Negev (see S. Levy and others 1960). This site has been identified as that of ancient Maʿon (Menois; cf. S. Levy 1960, p. 6). The group of 19 bronze amulets were deposited in the store-rooms of the Israel Department of Antiquities, where for many years they lay unopened. The three amulets given here have now been unrolled with relatively little damage in the chemical laboratories of the Israel Museum, thanks to the efforts and expertise of Dodo Shenhav and David Bigelajzen.

The synagogue is remarkable for its beautiful mosaic, covering the whole width of its nave (on which cf. Avi-Yonah in S. Levy and others 1960, pp. 25 ff.), in which an Aramaic inscription is inlaid, probably executed by a craftsman ignorant of the Hebrew alphabet (cf. S. Yeivin in S. Levy and others 1960, pp. 36 ff., and Naveh 1978, No. 57).

As for the dating of the amulets, since they were found in the apse of the synagogue, they are likely to belong to a late period in its use.

Amulet 11

Translation

1 ...I-am-who-I-am. In the name of... **š(n)rwn, ʾrskyʾl...**
2 ...] el, **mš(n)ydh, šmgrwn, sksk, dwqwn, dwqwn** and ...
3 ...]el, Barqiel, Uriel, Milḥamiel, **ʾh, ʾh, ʾh, ʾh, ʾh, ʾh...**
4 ...that you should depart from the head of Natrun, the daughter of Sarah, Amen, Amen...
5 ...called *kephalargia* and goes into the bones (?) of the chest and does not (?) ...
6 ...In the name of Nagdiel the angel who is bound by chains, which are not of bronze, and...
7 ...not of iron, and in the name of Naḥšur and in the name of Suriel the angel...
8 ...blast-demons, tormentors and shadow-spirits should flee away from her. Joel, Joel...
9 ...Na]trun, daughter of Sarah. In the name of **ʾwh, hlwsʾ**, El, Bael...
10 ...remove from the bones (?) of her chest and from her head...
11 ...

Rahmani 1960, p. 18, summarizes his discussion in the following words:

> These finds show that the synagogue was built in an area settled in the fourth century; also that the floor, and probably the whole building as well, were not later than 538. This suggests an early date of construction in the reign of Justin I, or Justinian I, at any rate before A.D. 538. It is probable that the synagogue was still in use about A.D. 582.

S. Levy (in S. Levy and others 1960, p. 11) concludes from the ceramic finds that the synagogue was used in "the sixth century A.D. with a possible continuation into the early seventh century A.D."

As mentioned by Rahmani 1960, p. 15, the amulets were "rolled tightly into a little scroll", and "on some of the amulets fragments of an outer wrapping of some woven material can still be seen; one still has the remains of the thread by which it was suspended, tied round one end. This shows that it was worn on the body, most probably around the neck". Alternatively it may be supposed that some of the amulets were suspended from the wall near or behind the Ark of the Law, or even from the Ark itself (see the description of the place of the find in S. Levy 1960, p. 7). See above, p. 16.

The maximum dimensions of Amulet 11 are 130×45 mm. It is clear that one or more lines are missing before the first preserved line.

3 Barqiel and Uriel occur in *Sefer ha-razim* (see index there).

4 **šʾrh** seems to be a curious spelling of Sarah.

5 **qplrgyʾ**: This is obviously Greek κεφαλαργία "headache". The same word may be present in a quotation from the lost *Midrash Yelamdenu* to Ex. 4:10 (Kohut 1955, VII, p. 165a): אינו עשוי לקופלארגיא הזו הוי לא איש דברים אנכי. Kohut explains **qwplʾrgyʾ** from Greek κουφολογία "light, empty talk". Jacobson 1980, p. 59, has suggested that the Greek derivation should be from καλοπραγία "noble, heroic acts". The word in ther *Arukh* is spelled practically in the same manner as the word in our amulet, and the sense obtained may be acceptable: "He is not made for this 'headache'", although such a usage is apparently otherwise unknown in Greek.

kwrkwryʾ: There seem to be two possible ways to explain this word: (1) A word of Greek origin in Aramaic (κερκίς, κερκίδος = staff, rod, weaver's comb, shuttle") gives in Jewish Aramaic a variety of forms **krkr, krkd, kyrkwr** etc.; see Jastrow, p. 670b. This word acquired in Syriac the additional meaning of "the bone of the upper arm, or of the upper leg". (2) A word of Semitic origin attested in the Hebrew and Aramaic root **KRKR** "to go around in circles", from which one might hypothetically derive a word meaning "a circle, a disc". None of these explanations seems entirely satisfactory.

(n)yʾ: The reading here gains from the comparison with the same expression in line 10. In contrast to Syriac **nʿʾ**, Jewish Aramaic has **nyʿʾ**, our form **nyʾ** may have developed from the latter.

6 **ngdyʾl**: The reading of this word is based on Amulet 3:10.

dkbyš: This verb often comes in association with **KPT** and **ʾSR** (e.g. Bowl 5:3); hence its use here in a context which implies tying or binding.

6–7 **šwšln dlʾ d[n]ḥš... dlʾ dpwrzyl**: The designation of the suppressing object as being "of iron" is fairly frequent (e.g. Bowl 13:13–14), but the negation of metals is much rarer. Compare, however, the phrase in Mandaic **zariz napšaikun bzaina dla hwa mn parzla** (*Ginza Y.*, p. 25:20), "arm yourselves with a weapon which is not of iron". For the

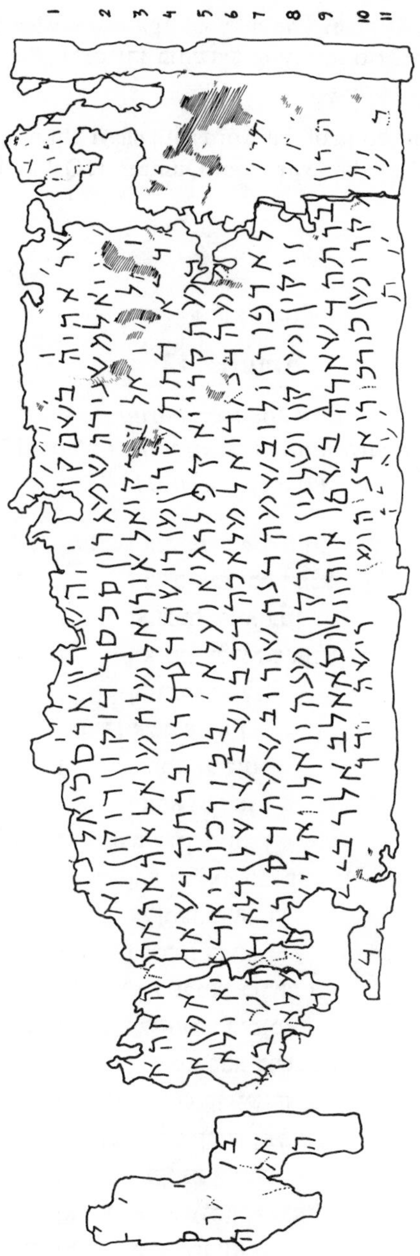

Fig. 13. Amulet 11

expression **bšwšln dl' dnhš** one may compare **w'srwhw bšlšln dnḥš** in Targum Judges 16:21 translating **ויאסרוהו בנחשתים** , "and they bound him with (fetters of) brass".

7 **nḥšwr**: The connection of this word with **nḥšyr** "hunt, eschatological war" in the Scroll of the War from Qumran (1QWar I:9, 10, 13) is unlikely.

Amulet 12

Provenance: Nirim

Israel Department of Antiquities, No. 57.739

Plate 11; Figure 14

1 [משבע] אנה על כול רוח ועל כול [ ] [
2 [ ] בשם אברסכס דממני ע[ל]
3 [ ]א ונטר טליא במ[ן]
4 [ ]יא טור ולד[ה דש]למ[צו]
5 [ ]ה דברכתא לנ[ ]
6 [אהיה] אשר אהיה [ ]
7 [ ]דאמה ובש[ם]
8 [ ] ארא וכף א[ ]
9 [אשב]עת עליך רוחא [ ]
10 [ ]תא דל<א> תכ<פ>ין ו[לא]
11 [ ]של[מצו ברתה ד[ ]
12 [ ] ולרוח באתא [ ] דלא]
13 [תתח]מין לשלמצו ב[רתה ד]
14 [לא ב]ליליא ולא בימ[מא]
15 [ ] בשמא רבא ב(ש)[ם]
16 [צבאו]ת קדוש קד[וש קדוש קדוש]
17 [קדו]ש קדוש קדוש [אל נקמות]
18 [ייי] אל נקמות [הופיע]
19 [אדו]ני אל אל(וה)[י ישראל]
20 [מלך] מלכי מלכי[א]

8 **ṭlnyn**, though masculine in form, seems to be the plural of **ṭlny** (see below Amulet 13:8). See further Commentary to Amulet 4:15.
ywʾl is a variant of **yhwʾl**; see Bowl 5:8 and the discussion there.

9 **ʾl bʾl** could be compared with **yh byh** (cf. Amulet 4:33) and the personal proper name **bryk yhbyh**. See the detailed discussion in the Commentary to Bowl 6:2.

Amulet 12

Translation

1 I [adjure] against every spirit and against every...
2 ... In the name of Abrasax who is appointed over ...
3 ... and the guardian of the boys ...
4 ... guard the child [of Sh]lam[ṣu]
5 ... of the blessing ...
6 [I-am]-who-I-am ...
7 ... of his/her mother; and in the name...
8 ...
9 [I ad]jure you, spirit, ...
10 ... that you should not force (?) and [not]...
11 ...[Shla]mṣu daughter of ...
12 ... and to the spirit that is lodging... [you should not]
13 [be] seen to Shlamṣu dau[ghter of]...
14 [neither at] night nor at day[time]...
15 ... In the great name ...
16 [of Host]s Holy, Holy, Ho[ly, Holy,]
17 [Hol]y, Holy, Holy ["God of vengeance]
18 [Lord] God of vengeance [appeared"] (Ps. 94:1) ...
19 [the Lord] God, God of Israel (Gen. 33:20?) ...
20 [King of] the Kings of King[s]...

...	23-21	...
[ ]אל צבאות ש[ ]	24	... God of Hosts ...
[ ] יחיש יחי[ש]	25	... **yḥyš yḥyš**...
...	26	...
[ ] שדי ש[ ]	27	... Shaddai...
[א]לוהים אל [ ]	28	... The God, God of ...
[ ]יה יה יה [ ]	29	**yh yh yh**
...	30	...
[ ] (ג)יבור [ ]	31	... hero ...
[אשבע]ת עליך רוח [ ]	32	I [adjure] against you, spirit ...
[דלא ת]תחמין ולא [ ]	33	[that you should not] be seen and not ...
[ ]ולדה ד(ש)[למצו]	34	... the child of [Shlamṣu]...
...	39-35	...
[אהיה א]שר אהיה[ ]	40	[I-am-]who-I-am ...
[ ] אדוני א[ל]	41	... the Lord God ...
...	42	...
[ ] ל ל ל ל [ ]	43	**llll**...
[ ] קדוש [ ]	44	... Holy ...
...	45	...

For a general description of the Nirim amulets see Commentary to Amulet 11. The maximum dimensions of the extant fragment of Amulet 12 are 115×38 mm.

2 **ʾbrsks**: See Amulet 2:3, as well as Montgomery 1913, No. 7:9 (with parallel) **wʾbrks rbʾ mnṭrnʾ drwḥy ṭbʾtʾ wmḥblnʾ drwḥy byšʾtʾ**. A discussion of Abrasax is in Dieterich 1891, p. 46; *Sefer ha-razim*, p. 8.

11 **šlmṣw** is attested as a hypocoristicon of Shlamṣiyyon, cf. Jastrow, p. 1587a; Frey 1952, No. 1253.

12 **bʾtʾ** seems to be the feminine singular active participle of **BYT/BWT**.

18 The reading **yyyy** for God's name is according to Amulet 1:5 etc., but another spelling is also possible.

Fig. 14. Amulet 12

Amulet 13

Provenance: Nirim
Israel Department of Antiquities, No. 57.744
Plate 11; Figure 15

[...   ]
[ק](מ)יע טב לאסתר
[ב](ר)תה דטאטיס
[ל](פ)לטא יתה מן
[מ]זקין [בי](ש)ין
[מן] עין בישה
[מן] רוח מן שיד
[מ]ן טלני מן
[כל] מזקין ביש[ין]
[מן] עין רעה מן
[   ] מן רוח טמ[אה]
[   ]אם שמו[ע]
[ת]שמע בקול י[ייי]
[א]להיך והישר
[ב]ע[יני]ו תעשה
[והאזנת]ה
[למ]צוותיו
[ו]שמרתה כל ח[וקיו]
[כל] (ה)מחלה א(ש)[ר]
[שמתי במ]צרים
[לא אשים עליך]
[כי אני ייי רפאך]
[...

For the Nirim amulets see Commentary on Amulet 11.

The maximum dimensions of the extant fragment are 88×35 mm.

1 Only faint traces are visible.

Amulet 13

Translation

1 ...
2 An amulet proper for Esther,
3 daughter of **ṭʾṭys**,
4 to save her from
5 evil tormentors,
6 from evil eye,
7 from spirit, from demon,
8 from shadow-spirit, from
9 [all] evil tormentors,
10 from evil eye, from
11 ... from imp[ure] spirit,
12 ..."If thou wilt diligently
13 hearken to the voice of the Lord
14 thy God, and wilt do that
15 which is right in his sight,
16 and wilt give ear
17 to his commandments,
18 and keep all his statutes,
19 I will put none of these
20 diseases upon thee, which
21 I have brought upon the Egyptians.
22 For I am the Lord that healeth thee" (Ex. 15:26).
23 ...

2 **qmyʿ ṭb**: See Amulet 2:1 and the Commentary there.

3 **ṭʾṭys**: For this name cf. the feminine pr. n. Tation in a synagogue inscription from Ionia; Frey 1952, No. 738. A masculine proper name

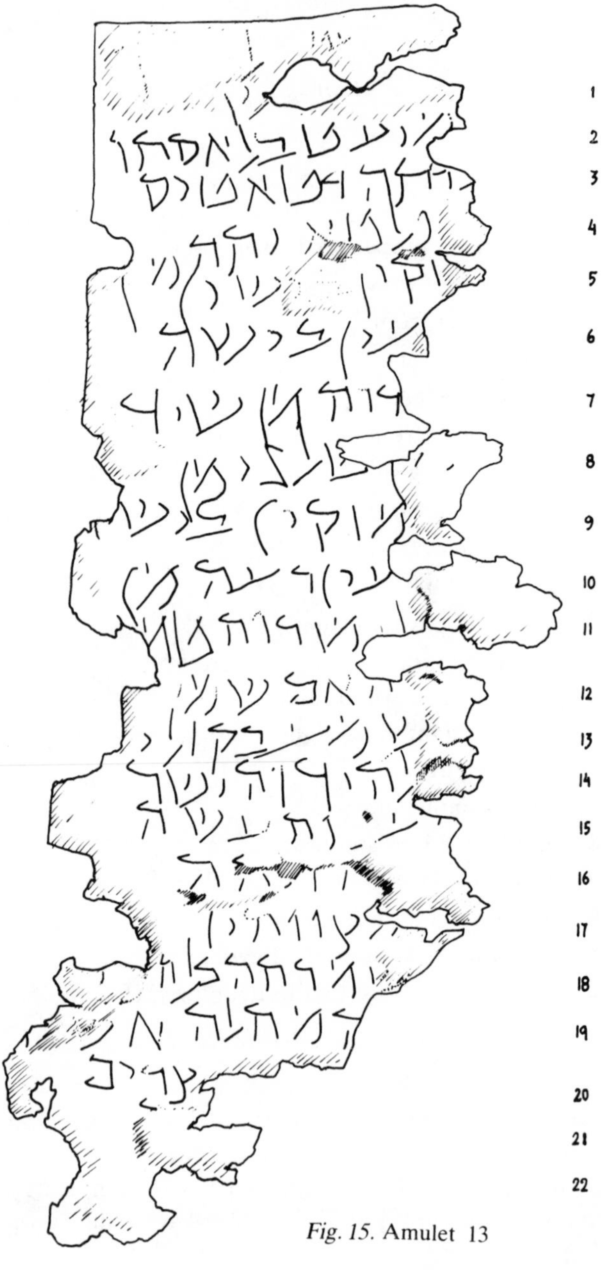

Fig. 15. Amulet 13

Tettius is attested on a Jewish tombstone in Rome (Frey 1936, No. 480).

4 **[l]plṭʾ**: Infinitive of *paʿʿel*. The reconstructed letter could also be *mem*; **mplṭʾ** would then follow the pattern of Galilean Aramaic (see Commentary to Amulet 2:1). The root **PLṬ** corresponds to **hṣylh** in Amulet 1:3 and **ṭwlw wšyzbw** in Geniza 8:11.

5–11 The evil entities here have all indefinite forms, as in Amulet 14 and Geniza 8. The sequence **rwḥ wšyd wṭlny** occurs also in Scholem 1980/81, pp. 252 f. The same sequence occurs in Amulet 7 with the definite forms. For **ṭlny** see also above, Amulet 4:15.

The list of evil entities is partly repeated, given first in Aramaic and then in Hebrew (**mzqyn byšyn** serves both in Aramaic and in Hebrew). Geniza 7 displays a somewhat parallel phenomenon, giving a full incantation in Hebrew, which is then partly repeated in a similar text formulated in Aramaic.

12–22 The same biblical verse concludes also Geniza 8, which has other parallels with our amulet.

For the reconstruction **yyyy** see the Commentary to Amulet 12:18.

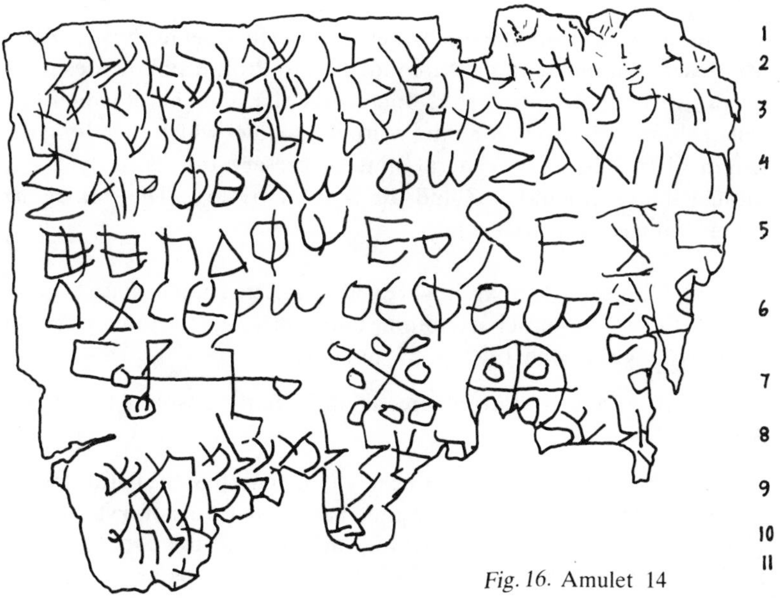

Fig. 16. Amulet 14

Amulet 14

Provenance unknown
Collection of J. Sammel, Munich
Plate 12; Figure 16

1]](ש)[מ]עון בן שפירא על כל
2]](דל)לא וסטן ועיין בישא ואשא
3]]רו(ח) דמרתתא בשם אל(וה)ה דישראל
4] ZAIP ΦΘΑΩ ΦΩΖΑΧ(ΩΤ)[
7-5 *(magic characters)*
8]]אל שכ[ינ]ת אל למעל מרעשי
9]](ג)עו[ר] סטן מן
10]]צב[אות] אלהי
11 [ישראל...]

This amulet was brought to the Israel Museum for opening by its owner, Mr. Joseph Sammel, and we are indebted to Prof. Yaʿakov Meshorer for drawing our attention to it. It consists of a silver sheet which was rolled along its narrow side. The writing is in lines which run along the length of the sheet. Its general state of preservation is fairly good, though the right-hand side and the bottom are lost. The size of the extant fragment is *c*. 4×3 cm.

1 Both Shimʿon and Shappira are widely attested names since Second Temple times. Shappira is a feminine name, meaning the same as Yaʾita (Amulet 2). Cf. Naveh 1980, p. 57, note 12.

2 The list of nouns is given here, as often, in the absolute forms; see Amulet 13.

3 At the beginning of this line one might imagine that the natural word to follow **ʾšʾ** is **ʿryʾ**, **ʿrwy**, the presumed absolute forms of **ʿrytʾ**, **ʿrwytʾ**; see Amulet 2:2 and the commentary *ad loc.,* and the corresponding Hebrew form **ʿryh** in Amulet 4:29.

Amulet 14

Translation

1 [This amulet is for Shim]ʿon son of Shappira against every
2 ...and Satan and evil eye and fever
3 [and shiver...and every] spirit that shakes. In the name of the God of Israel
4 Zair phthaò phozakh(ot).
5–7 (*magic characters*)
8 [...]el, God's Divine Presence above my head.
9 ...exorcise Satan from
10 [...God of] Hos[ts...] God
11 [of Israel...]

ʾl(wh)h dyśrʾl: The reading of the first word is not entirely clear. An alternative reading may be **ʾl(ʾ)h**.

4 We owe the reading of this Greek line to Professor Morton Smith, as well as most of the following comments on this line.

The first word may be read ΖΑΙΡ or ΣΑΙΡ (if we assume that the upper stroke of the *sigma* merged with the leg of the *lamed* in the preceding line). Prof. Smith suggests that the word may be a reflection of the biblical toponym Śeʿir (Septuaginta Σηειρ) in Jud. 5:4. We wonder whether an association with biblical *śaʿir* "satyr, demon" (cf. e.g. Is. 34:14) is to be excluded.

ΦΘΑΩ is explained by Prof. Smith as the name Ptah with an ending.

For ΦΩΖΑΧ(ΩΤ), Prof. Smith comments: "ΦΩΖΑ is a word found in two spells: Preisendanz 1931, p. 164 (XXXVI:44) and p. 170 (XXXVI:228). In both it follows πεφϑα/πεφνα and πεφρα is followed in Preisendaz 1931, p. 14 (VII:312) by ζαωϑ. Both spells in XXXVI are for personal favour, that in VII:312 is for protection from dreams and demons".

8 We have here a sequence which is reminiscent of the text of *Qeriʾat šemaʿ ʿal ham-miṭṭa*, as in Amulet 1:1–3, although what is left of the formula here conforms more closely to the traditional text. We should therefore expect the words which survive in our amulet to be preceded by an enumeration of four angels on each side of the person to be

Amulet 15

Provenance unknown
Israel Museum, No. 69.3.146
Plate 13; Figure 17

1 [ ] סממית יל⌈י⌉דת בנין [... קטלהון]
2 [סד]רוס ערקת מן ק[דומוי]
3 [ ] קמת (ל)ה ברא(ש)[ ]
4 [ ]בנת לה בית ברא[ ]
5 [ל]ה תרעין דפרז(ל)[ה]
6 [ ]ה וטרדת בא[ ]
7 [י]ת תרעה לידא סוני [וסו]
8 [וס]וני וסניגלי ארתקו על [ ]
9 [ ]בין נעבר וניעל לע(ל)[ ]
10 [קמ]ת ופתחת להון על עמ(ה)[ון]
11 [סד]רוס וקטל לברה וצו(ח)[ת]
12 [ע](ל)יהון סוני וסוסוני
13 [וס]ניגלי מה עבד (הכין ש)[מע]
14 [סד]רוס ופתח וער(ק) מ(נ)[הון]
15 [מן] חזין רדפו בתרה וא[ש]
16 [כ]חוי בפלגוס דימה (והנ)[ ]
17 [ל]מקטול יתה אמר להון [אנה]
18 (מ)שתבע לכון במן דאכ[יל]
19 (מ)יה בשעולה דכל הן דן[ ]
20 [ ]ן מדכרין {ש} שמה דס[וני]
21 וסוסוני וסניגלי לא א[קטול]

protected; either as in the traditional formula (Michael, Gabriel, Uriel and Raphael), or as in Amulet 1.

mrʿšy: The interchange of *alef* by ʿ*ayin* is noted by Kutscher 1976, p. 80.

9 **(g)ʿw[r]**: See Amulets 2:8,11; 9:2,4.

Amulet 15

Translation

1 Smamit gave birth to sons. [They were killed by]
2 [Side]ros. She fled from h[im.]
3 ...Ṣhe stood in...
4 ...She built a house for herself in...
5 [She provided it with] gates of iron...
6 ...and she locked...
7 ...the gate...**swny** and
8 **swswny** and **snygly** knocked on...
9 ...We shall pass and get in...
10 [She stood] up and opened (the door) for them. There came in with [them.]
11 [Side]ros and killed her son. She cried
12 [at] **swny** and **swswny**
13 and **snygly**: Why did (he) do (so)? [Side]ros
14 [heard], opened (the door) and fled from [them.]
15 [Having] seen (him), they chased him and found
16 him in *pelagos* of the sea ...
17 to kill him. He said to them: [I]
18 swear to you in (the name) of He "who has measured
19 the water in the hollow of his hand" (Is. 40:12), that wherever
20 [people] mention the name of **swny**
21 and **swswny** and **snygly**, I shall not [kill]

22 לאנטונינה ברתה ד(נ)[ ]
23 [ ] (וב)רה ברוך אתה י[ייי]
24 (אל) קים מלך העולם [יגער]
25 הרוחות מלפניך

This is an amulet on a thin silver sheet, measuring 35×82 mm. It was purchased by the Israel Museum in 1969 from an antique dealer in Jerusalem, but the provenance of the object was not transmitted. By its language, orthography, the material on which it is written and its place of purchase there can be little doubt that this is a Palestinian amulet.

The amulet, which forms a parallel to Bowls 12a and 12b, came to our attention at a late stage in the preparation of the book when it was going to press. The commentary to Bowls 12a and 12b has had to be somewhat modified in view of our better understanding of the text and of the history of the formulae which occur here. However, it was impossible to rewrite the whole commentary, and some inconsistency in the treatment of these texts may have remained.

At the same time, since the amulet is fragmentary and its decipherment has been very difficult, due to the fact that the letters are crowded together and the text is often elliptical, it might have been impossible to reach a clear understanding of the text of Amulet 15 without the benefit of previous acquaintance with the story from Bowls 12a and 12b (and the other parallels).

The text of Amulet 15, like that of Bowls 12a and 12b, is based on a story of Smamit (lizard or spider; see below, Commentary to line 1), whose sons were killed by an evil agent; the name of that demon may be reconstructed from Bowl 12a: Sideros. She flees to a place, which, if it conforms to the detail in Bowl 12, would be a mountain, and there three helpers, **swny**, **swswny** and **snygly**, enter her house, unwittingly admitting with them the fiend, who kills her (new-born) son. She cries at her helpers, but the fiend flees. They chase him and find him in the midst of the sea. When they wish to kill him he swears that wherever the names of **swny**, **swswny** and **snygly** are mentioned, he will not kill the client of this amulet and her new-born son. This story obviously serves for the protection of a woman giving birth and of her child. The details of the story and the comparison to other versions of the same story in

22 Antonina, daughter of...
23 ... and her son. Blessed art Thou y[yyy]
24 the living God, King of the world. [May He exorcise]
25 the spirits from your presence.

medieval and later times will be discussed in the Appendix to this amulet.

In order to facilitate the textual comparison, we have set the three Aramaic texts — Bowls 12a and 12b with Amulet 15 — in parallel columns, in the section which deals with Bowl 12 (p.188–193).

1 A word was probably lost before **smmyt**. Two possible reconstructions of the lost word have been considered: **ḥdh** ("one") and **hdh** ("this"). The first alternative would have required an indefinite form **smmy**; the second alternative seems to go along better with the form **smmyt**, although it lacks the determined ending, on the assumption that **smmyt** is already used as a proper name. For **hdh** before a proper name cf. e.g. **hdh rḥl**, *Berešit Rabba*, 70; ed. Theodor-Albeck, p. 817.

smmyt (Bowl 12a **smwmyt**, 12b **smmyt**ʾ) is related to Biblical Hebrew *śmāmīt* (Prov. 30:28), which is variously interpreted as a lizard or a spider; the Targum and the traditional Jewish commentaries favour the latter rendering, while the Septuagint has *kalabōtēs* "spotted lizard". In Lev. 11:30 *lĕṭāʾā* is rendered by the Jonathan version *śmāmītā*, which the medieval commentary on Jonathan says is a spider. In Talmudic Hebrew and Aramaic, **smmyt/śmmy** seem to mean uniformly "spider" (cf. Kohut 1955, VI, pp. 72b f.; Jastrow s. vv.). Our context could bear either interpretation, but the preponderance of the sense "spider" in Hebrew and Aramaic in the period corresponding to the writing of our texts seems to weigh in favour of this interpretation (see also Löw 1912, pp. 140 ff.). A late Jewish amulet from Tunis (cf. Casanowicz 1917, p. 50) mentions a negative figure called **zmzwmyt**, probably unrelated to our **smmyt**. One may also recall the grasshopper figure in Islamic wonder stories (cf. Goldziher 1872, p. 767).

bnyn [...]: It is possible that the number of sons followed, although it is not certain that there is room for a number. The number should have normally preceded the designation **bnyn**. In the bowls the number of sons killed is twelve, while in the late Greek version given in the Appendix the number is six.

2 **[sd]rws**: The name is reconstructed on the basis of Bowl 12a. That the name Sideros ("iron") is original is demonstrated by the Ethiopian Werzelya (see Appendix).

3 **br'(š)** [ ]: One may be tempted to reconstruct here and at the end of line 4 **br'(š) [ṭwr']** "at the top of a mountain", following the indication in Bowls 12a and 12b, section III.

4–6 The details about the construction of a house with gates and the shutting of the gate are not mentioned in Bowls 12a and 12b, though they are implied in the story given there. All of this is explicitly found in the late Greek version (see Appendix).

7 **lyd'**: This is a puzzling expression in this context. **yd'** might signify "handle", but would not make a meaningful translation. **lyd** normally means "at, near"; **mn yd** or **myd** means "immediately". One wonders whether **lyd'** could not mean "near there" or "at that time"?

swny etc.: The three names are clearly divided in lines 12–13 and 20–21. The same division seems to occur in Bowls 12a and 12b, and it is continued in the later tradition of this story; e.g. in the late Hebrew amulets **snwy, snsnwy wsmnglp**, and in the Greek stories (Perdrizet 1922, p. 16: Sisinios, Sinēs and Sēnodōros). For further discussion of these names see Appendix.

8 **'rtqw**: This verb has been identified as typical of Galilean Aramaic (Kutscher 1971, col. 274). In Bowls 12a and 12b this verb lost its meaning, and it seems to be used as part of the name of the helpers.

9 A portion of the story seems to have been contracted here. The parallel stories tell of the request of the helpers to enter, the initial refusal of Smamit, their insistence, and her final acquiescence. Here we only have the helpers' insistence.

13 The reading of the final part of the line is uncertain.

14 The verbs "[heard]...opened (the door), fled" are not found in Bowls 12a and 12b.

15 For the reconstruction **[mn] ḥzyn** (the verb is in the active participle pl. m.) see Kutscher 1976, pp. 51 ff.; the alternative construction, with

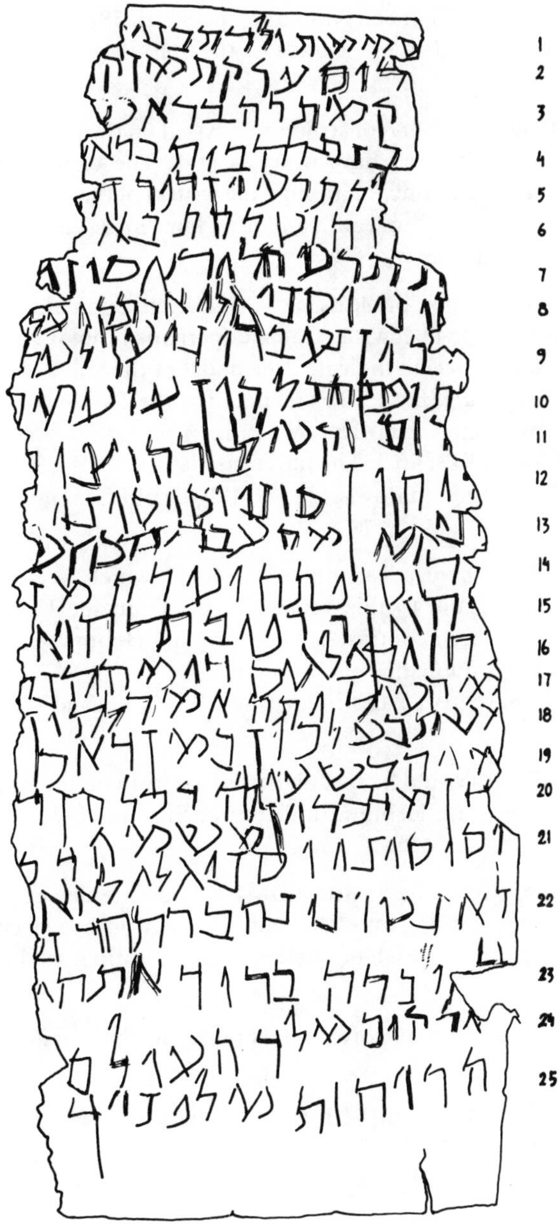

Fig. 17. Amulet 15

kd, is not attested in Galilean Aramaic (op. cit., p. 58). However, as we should have expected to see a trace of the *nun*, the reconstruction is doubtful.

15–16 **w'[šk]ḥwy**: The reconstruction is based on the parallel versions of 12a and 12b, where we have **w'drykw ytyh**. The verb **DRK** in *af'el* should mean there "to find", although the writers of the bowls probably understood it to mean "to lead", and used **lgw** "into (the Great Sea)", instead of **bgw** "in".

16 **bplgws dymh**: This double usage — Greek and Aramaic — seems to be a constant phrase in Jewish Aramaic (perhaps more particularly in the Palestinian dialect) to indicate "the midst of the sea". The Hebrew expression *bĕ-lev yām* (Ex. 15:8) is rendered by the Targum of Jonathan b. Uzziel **bgw pylgws dym' rb'**. A similar translation occurs in the Aramaic version of Ps. 46:3. The phrase is also attested in *Lev. Rabba*, section 12, beginning. In Bowls 12a and 12b the phrase is **lgw plgws ym' rb'**.

18–19 We have here a version of Is. 40:12 which is close to the Peshitta. The Targum to this verse diverges from the Hebrew text. Bowls 12a and 12b, in contrast, use the original Hebrew; in Bowl 12b the whole verse is quoted.

kl hn d- is apparently a Palestinian usage. Bowls 12a and 12b use **kl 'tr d-** instead.

20 The first word could be reconstructed as **['tw]n** on the basis of the phrase in parallel late Hebrew amulets; see Shachar 1971, p. 19, No. 4: כשמזכירים אתם את שמותינו

22 **l'nṭwnynh**: Antonina is attested as a feminine Jewish name in Rome; see Frey 1936, Nos. 236 and 416. Antoninos occurs as a masculine name on a Jewish tombstone from Palestine; see Frey 1952, No. 970.

23–24 The blessing here corresponds partly to the blessing in Bowl 12b, section X.

24–25 The reconstruction **[yg'r]** is based on the Qumran Scroll of the War X:31 ורוחי [גו]רלו גערתה מפנינו

In **mlpnyk** the suffixed pronoun refers probably to the client.

Appendix to Amulet 15

The story on which the texts in Amulet 15 and Bowls 12a and 12b are based is interesting because of its wide-ranging connections. It tells of a *smamit*, i.e. a lizard or a spider (see Commentary to Amulet 15:1), which gave birth to (twelve) children, who were killed by Sideros (the wicked).[1] Bowl 12b has the name **srgys** (Sergius?) instead. There is no clear explanation to the name Sergius in this connection, except by assuming that it is a corruption of Sideros. The latter name is clearly the Greek *sideros* "iron", a sense which gets a gratifying confirmation in the Ethiopian versions (see below).

The bereaved mother flees to a mountain "the name of which is unique in the world", to quote the phrasing of Bowl 12a. According to the two bowls she performs magic rites of copper and iron,[2] but this detail is absent from the amulet. Three new persons, **swny**, **swswny** and **snygly**, appear on the scene as friendly helpers; in the Christian version they are usually described as the woman's brothers. The meaning of these names is obscure. One might think of some Greek connection, e.g. σαύνιον "javelin"; σείσις "shaking, concussion", but such explanations lack proof.

swny, **swswny** and **snygly** knock on the door and ask the woman to open the door for them, but she refuses. At their insistence,[3] she opens, and then the wicked Sideros enters with them and kills the child which has evidently been born in the meantime. When she raises a cry, the helpers chase Sideros and reach him in the midst of the sea. They seek to kill him, but refrain when they are told by Sideros that if they spare him, he will undertake by oath to desist from killing the client and her son wherever the name of the helpers is mentioned.

The story told here has many parallels in medieval Christian literature, in Greek, Coptic, Ethiopian, Armenian, Rumanian, Slavonic

[1] The name Sideros is attested once as an angel name in the Geniza fragment T-S N.S. 329.972: אסידרוס רוחה רבה. It seems also to occur once in Mandaic, cf. Macuch 1967, p. 118:37 f., 43, but the context there is not entirely clear.

[2] The magic combination "iron and copper" occurs in Amulet 11:6–7 and in Montgomery 1913, No. 19:10.

[3] The argument which they use and which ultimately convinces her to open the door is not made explicit.

and late Syriac, as well as in Arabic and Hebrew. The various versions are discussed in detail by Peterson 1926a, pp. 109ff. and by Winkler 1931. A Greek version of it exists in a number of late medieval manuscripts. We are reproducing the Greek text given by Perdrizet 1922, pp. 16 ff.:[4]

Ἐπὶ τῆς βασιλείας Τραϊανοῦ τοῦ βασιλέως ἦν τις γυνὴ ὀνόματι Μελετινή, ἥτις ἐγέννησεν παιδία ἕξ, καὶ συνέλαβεν αὐτὰ ἡ μιαρὰ καὶ ἀκάθαρτος Γυλλοῦ · καὶ πάλιν ἐν γαστρὶ συνέλαβεν ἡ Μελετινή, καὶ εἰσῆλθεν εἰς τὰ λεγόμενα Χαλκοπράτια, καὶ κτήσας πύργον ὑψηλόν, καὶ καθηλώσας αὐτὸν καὶ μολυβδώσας, καὶ λαβὼν ιβ´ θεραπαίνιδας διῆγεν μετ' αὐτῶν καὶ ἐμβὰς ἐν αὐτῷ, ἔτεκεν ἐκεῖ τὸ παιδίον.

Ἐν μιᾷ οὖν τῶν ἡμερῶν ὁ ἅγιος Σισίνιος, Σίνης καὶ Σηνόδωρος κατῆλθον τοῦ ἐπισκέψασθαι τὴν ἀδελφὴν αὐτῶν, καὶ γινόμενοι πλησίον τοῦ πύργου ἔκραξαν αὐτὴν λέγοντες · ἄνοιξον ἡμῖν, ἀδελφὴ Μελετινή. Ἡ δὲ εἶπεν · παιδίον ἐγέννησα καὶ φοβοῦμαι ἀνοῖξαι.

Ἐπὶ πολὺ δὲ αὐτῶν ἱσταμένων καὶ τῶν ἵππων χαλινοκτυπούντων, κατῆλθε τοῦ ἀνοῖξαι αὐτῶν . Ἡ δὲ μιαρὰ Γυλλοῦ συνεισῆλθε σὺν τοῖς ἵπποις ὥσπερ μυῖα · καὶ περὶ μέσης τῆς νυκτὸς ἀπέκτεινε τὸ παιδίον. Ἡ δὲ Μελετινὴ ὠλόλυζεν πικρῶς, λέγουσα · ὦ Σισίνιε, Σίνη, καὶ συνοδία, οὐκ εἶπον ὑμῖν ὅτι παιδίον ἐγέννησα καὶ φοβοῦμαι ἀνοῖξαι; ἦλθεν ἡ μιαρὰ καὶ ἀπέκτεινεν αὐτό. Τότε οἱ ἅγιοι προσευχὴν ποιήσαντες πρὸς Θεόν, κατῆλθεν ἄγγελος ἐξ οὐρανοῦ καὶ εἶπεν αὐτοῖς · εἰσηκούσθη ἡ δέησις ὑμῶν πρὸς Θεόν · καταδιώξατε αὐτὴν εἰς τὰ μέρη τοῦ Λιβάνου.

Τότε λέγουσιν πρὸς τὴν ἀδελφὴν αὐτῶν · μὴ λυποῦ, ἀδελφὴ Μελετινή, ἡμεῖς γὰρ ἐν ὀνόματι τοῦ Θεοῦ γενόμεθα ὡς κυνηγοί, καὶ κρατήσωμεν αὐτήν. Τότε καθίσαντες ἐπὶ τοῖς ἵπποις αὐτῶν, ἔτρεχον αὐτήν. Ἡ δὲ μιαρά, ἰδοῦσα τοὺς ἁγίους ὄπισθεν αὐτῆς, ἔδραμεν πρὸς τὴν θάλασσαν, καὶ ἔλασαν οἱ ἅγιοι

[4] Another closely related Greek story was published in an English translation by M. Gaster 1900, pp. 142 ff., from the text in Leo Allatius, *De templis graecorum*, 1645 (not available to us). Perdrizet seems to have been unaware of this earlier publication. These Greek stories are probably the origin from which are derived the Slavonic and Rumanian versions discussed in M. Gaster 1900. Perdrizet 1922, p. 19, note 1, mentions a related Arabic text which occurs in a Vatican Ms. Arab. 118. Winkler 1931, pp. 97 ff., gives the text of Cod. Arab. 117 in the Vatican, which is a prayer by St. Sūsniyūs for the protection of small children. Some further bibliography is provided by T. Gaster 1971, pp. XXXIV f., and in his articles of 1942 and 1955.

τοὺς ἵππους αὐτῶν, καὶ ἔφθασαν αὐτήν. Καὶ ἀπέλαβεν αὐτὴν ὁ ἅγιος Σισίνιος ἐκ τοῦ πλευροῦ αὐτῆς, καὶ ἤρξατο βασανίζειν αὐτήν· ἐὰν μὴ μοῦ ὁμολογήσῃς ποῖον θεὸν σέβεις καὶ ποῦ τὴν δύναμιν ἔχεις, ἐκ τῶν χειρῶν ἡμῶν οὐκ ἀπόλυσαι, ἕως οὗ ἀποδώσεις ἡμῖν καὶ τὰ ζ' τέκνα Μελετινῆς ζῶντα, ὥσπερ ἔλαβες. Τότε ἡ μιαρὰ λέγει τοῦς ἁγίους· Ἅγιοι τοῦ Θεοῦ, ἀδύνατόν ἐστιν δοῦναι τὰ παιδία, ἐὰν μὴ πίω γάλα ἐκ τῶν μασθῶν Μελετινῆς. Καὶ στραφεὶς ὁ ἅγιος Σηνόδωρος πρὸς τὴν ἀδελφὴν αὐτῶν, ἀνήγγειλεν αὐτῇ τὸ γεγονός, καὶ ἔδωκεν γάλα τὸν ἅγιον. Καὶ ἐλθὼν αὐτὸς εἰς τὸν τόπον ὅπου ἐκράτησαν τὴν μιαράν, καὶ ποτίσαντες αὐτὴν τὸ γάλα, καὶ κατ' οἰκονομίᾳ Θεοῦ ἐξέρασεν τὰ παιδία ζῶντα. Τότε ἤρξαντο μαστίζειν αὐτήν· ἡ δὲ μιαρὰ λέγει τοὺς ἁγίους· Ἅγιοι τοῦ Θεοῦ, μὴ μὲ πολυβασανίσετε, καὶ ὀμνύω σας εἰς τὸν κύκλον τοῦ ἡλίου καὶ εἰς τὸ κέρας τῆς σελήνης, ὅτι ὅπου γράφεται τὸ ὄνομά σας καὶ ἀναγινώσκεται ἡ πολιτεία σας, καὶ τὰ ιβ' ἥμισυ ὀνόματά μου, οὐ μὴ τολμήσω προσεγγίσω ἐν τῷ οἴκῳ ἐκείνῳ, ἀλλὰ ἀπὸ τριῶν μιλίων φεύξομαι ἐκ τοῦ οἴκου ἐκείνου. Τότε λέγουσιν αὐτήν· Ἀνάγγειλον ἡμῖν τὰ δώδεκα ἥμισύ σου ὀνόματα. Τότε ἡ μιαρὰ πυρὶ φλεγομένη ἔλεγεν· Τὸ μὲν πρῶτόν μου ὄνομα καὶ ἐξαίρετον καλεῖται Γυλλου, τὸ δεύτερον Αμορφους, τὸ τρίτον Αβυζου, τὸ τέταρτον Καρχους, τὸ πέμπτον Βριανη, τὸ ἕκτον Βαρδελλους, τὸ ἕβδομον Αἰγυπτιανή, τὸ ὄγδοον Βαρνα, τὸ ἔνατον Χαρχανιστρέα, τὸ ι' Ἀδικία, [τὸ ια'...], τὸ ιβ' Μυΐα, τὸ ἥμισον Πετομένη (1). Καὶ ἀκούσαντες ταῦτα τὰ ὀνόματα, οἱ ἅγιοι ἐθαύμασαν, καὶ ἀνέσπασαν τὸν δεξιὸν πλόκαμον τῆς κεφαλῆς αὐτῆς ποιήσαντες σχοινία τοῖς ἵπποις αὐτῶν, καὶ λαβόντες τὰ ἰδιόχερα αὐτῆς ὀνόματα, καὶ τὰ παιδία ζῶντα ὥσπερ ἔλαβεν, καὶ ἀπόλυσαν αὐτήν. Καὶ εἰσελθόντες εἰς τὴν Πόλιν, πᾶσα ἡ πόλις ἐδόξαζεν τὸν Θεὸν τὸν ποιοῦντα θαυμάσια διὰ τῶν ἁγίων αὐτοῦ.

Ὁ ἔχων τὴν ἀποστροφὴν αὐτῆς οὐ μὴ ἀδικηθῇ.

In the reign of Trajan the King there was a woman by the name of Meletinē. She gave birth to six children, and the abominable and impure Gyllou carried them off. Meletinē became once again pregnant, and went to those (places) called Khalkopratia, where she acquired a lofty tower; she bolted it (with nails) and sealed it with lead. Having taken twelve maids, she lived amongst them and entered into it, and she gave birth there to the child.

One day Saint Sisinios, Sinēs and Sēnodōros came down to visit their sister. Having drawn close to the tower, they called her saying,

"Open the door for us, our sister Meletinē". But she said, "I have given birth to a child and I am afraid to open the door".

But as they stood there for a long time, and as their horses stamped upon the wood, she descended to open the door for them. The abominable Gyllou came in together with the horses in the form of a fly, and toward midnight he killed the child. Meletinē cried bitterly, saying: "O Sisinios, Sinēs and company! Did I not tell you that I had given birth to a child and that I was afraid to open the door? The abominable one has come and killed him". The saints then addressed themselves to God in prayer, and an angel came down from heaven and said to them: "Your petition has been heard by God. Pursue her as far as the Lebanon".

They then told their sister: "Do not be distressed, Sister Meletinē, for we are going to be pursuers in the name of God and we shall seize her". Then, seated on their horses, they ran after her. The abominable one, however, seeing the saints behind her, ran into the sea. The saints drove their horses and overtook her. Saint Sisinios took her from her side and started to torture her: "If you do not promise to tell me which god you worship and where you derive your power, you will not escape from our hands until you give back to us the seven children of Meletinē, as much alive as they were when you snatched them". The abominable one then says to the saints: "Saints of God, it is impossible for me to give the children as long as I do not drink milk from the breasts of Meletinē". Saint Sēnodōros returned to their sister and recounted to her that which had happened, and she gave milk to the saint.

Having come to the place where they were holding the abominable one, they gave her the milk to drink, and, by God's disposition, she vomited the children alive. Then they started flogging her. The abominable one said to the saints: "Saints of God, do not torture me too much, and I swear to you by the disc of the sun and the horn of the moon that wherever your name is written and your association is known, and my twelve and a half names, I shall not dare approach that house, but shall keep away from that house to a distance of three miles". Then they said to her, "Disclose to us your twelve and a half names". The abominable one, burning in fire, said: "My first and special name is called Gyllou; the second Amorphous; the third Abyzou; the fourth Karkhous; the fifth Brianē; the sixth Bardellous; the seventh Aigyptianē; the eighth

> Barna; the ninth Kharkhanistrea; the tenth Adikia; (...) the twelfth Myia; the half Petomene". Hearing these names, the saints were surprised. They tore off the right-hand braid of her head, making cords for their horses. Taking the names revealed by herself, and the children, alive just as they had been when she had snatched them, they let her go. Having entered the City, the whole city praised God who made wonders by the hand of His saints.
>
> This device against her will not cause any harm to him who uses it.

Here we have nearly all the essential elements of our Aramaic story: Several children killed by the fiend; the flight of the mother to a fortified and lofty place;[5] the three helpers[6] coming and not being admitted; they insist; the tricky fiend sneaks in with them; the new-born baby is killed; the appeal to the helpers; the chase into the sea; and the promise of the fiend not to harm anyone who uses the helpers' names and those of the fiend. The differences are mostly of secondary character: the name (and proper identity) of the attacked mother;[7] the name[8] and gender of the

[5] The Greek text has εἰς τὰ λεγόμενα Χαλκοπράτια, which Perdrizet explains as follows (p. 17): "Quartier de Constantinople, avec une église fameuse, où était conservée, entre autres reliques, la ceinture de la Vierge". While this identification of the place name seems valid, one wonders whether Khalkopratia does not contain a reminiscence of something like Χαλκοπράγματα=חרשין דינחשה, as in Bowl 12a.

[6] The number is not uniform in the different versions. Three is still the number used in the Greek story just quoted, although it is sometimes blurred, as in the case when Meletine addresses the helpers by the words "Sisinios, Sines and their party" (ὦ Σισίνιε, Σίνη καὶ συνοδία). Other Greek versions (e.g. those given by Leo Allatius, cf. Gaster 1900 and Winkler 1931, pp. 109 f.) speak of only two helpers: Sisinios and Sisynodoros. In some versions there is talk only of a single helper, who is the woman's husband or brother (e.g. the Arabic version given below). In a similar way there is a single helper in the late Jewish and Christian sources, where the function is relegated to Elijah, Michael, or Gabriel.

[7] A certain zoological association may nevertheless exist: Meletine may be connected with the Greek word for a bee (μέλιττα). The fiend has a strong association with a fly (Greek μυῖα), which is both the form it assumed when it entered with the brothers' horses and one of its names. *Smamit*, as noted above, is a spider or a lizard.

[8] Gyllou (or Gellō, Gelō) is considered by some to be the origin for Arabic Ghūl. Cf. Sophocles, *Greek Lexicon*, s.v. γελλώ etc.; Perdrizet 1922, p. 25; M. Gaster 1900, p. 148. On the Babylonian origin of this demon cf. Frank 1910, pp. 161 ff.

fiend, as well as its identity ("iron");[9] the number of offspring killed by the fiend (12+1 in the bowls, 6+1 in Greek);[10] the helpers are designated in Greek as the mother's brothers,[11] while in the Aramaic there is no relationship mentioned. Other points of divergence may seem to be mere enlargements or embellishments of an original version.

Apart from the great similarity of structure and plot, the Greek versions present a striking similarity to the Aramaic text in the names of the helpers. Sisinios, Sinēs and Sēnodōros bear great resemblance to **swny**, **swswny** and **snygly** in their sound pattern. All three names, in the Greek as well as in the Aramaic, play about with the phonemes *s* and *n*.

The identity of the fiend, Sideros=Iron, was lost in the Greek version. It survives, however, in a group of stories which are current in Ethiopic amulets and which probably derived from Coptic. They were summarized in Worrell 1909, pp. 165 f.; the interesting feature of that story for our purpose is that the attacking fiend is called *Werzelya*, while the helper, who is the woman's husband, is called in the Ethiopic stories *Susneyos*, a form resembling the Aramaic and Greek versions. Werzelya is not an Ethiopic word, and several suggestions have been put forward by scholars to explain it; it was compared to Ursula, Epilepsia, Basileia, as well as the Hebrew *Barzel*.[12] In light of the Aramaic text we are now discussing, there can be no doubt that Werzelya is actually a reflection of Aramaic Parzĕlā or Hebrew Barzel "iron". It is curious to note that the Aramaic name is preserved in Ethiopic, while the Aramaic texts present a Greek form. The surviving Greek versions, on the other hand, have lost all memory of Sideros.

[9] The name Sideros may well lie behind the sixth name of Gyllou, Bardellous, which is reminiscent of Ethiopic Werzelya, cf. below. See also Perdrizet 1922, p. 21.

[10] The theory that interprets the Sisinnius story as an astrological allegory can of course make better use of the number 12 than 6. Cf. Peterson 1926a, pp. 125 f. and the discussion by Winkler 1931, esp. pp. 126 f. The mother indeed has 12 servants and 12½ names (the additional half-name is perhaps analogous to the thirteenth baby just born).

[11] Some versions make the helper the brother of the fiend and the husband of the bereaved mother. Cf. Fries 1893, pp. 62 ff., quoted in Winkler 1931, p. 96, and see also pp. 127 ff. See also note 6 above.

[12] For a summary of views and references cf. Worrell 1914/15, p. 137. See further Aešcoly 1932, pp. 39 ff., 126; Winkler 1931, pp. 175, 186. The latter connects it with the Babylonian Labartu.

A much contracted version of this story occurs in an Arabic synaxary, based on the Coptic rite, which gives under the date Barmūda 26 the martyrdom of St. Sūsniyūs, who is said to have been the son of Sūspatros, of the retinue of King Diocletian. The relevant portion says:

> He returned to Antioch where he found a sister of his who had given birth to a hideous-looking son. Before him she had given birth to a daughter whom she had killed and whose blood she had sucked. Satan dwelled in her, and she assumed by witchcraft the shapes of birds and snakes. Whenever a child was born to the inhabitants of the town she would descend on it, kill it and suck its blood. When the holy man saw this, he took a lance in his hand and killed his sister and her son, for he was Satan's son, as well as her husband and his father, for they were sorcerers.[13]

Fig. 18. ʿAbd–Išoʿ and "the accursed Satan", who wears the "likeness of a hateful woman of dark appearance". From a Syriac book of magic (Gollancz 1912)

[13] Cf. Basset 1922, pp. 336 ff., particularly p. 337. Quoted in Winkler 1931, pp. 129 f., where further references are given for the Ethiopian version based on the Coptic.

It is clear that a modified version of our story is given as part of the biography of this martyr; it has indeed become a standard element in the hagiography connected with St. Sisinnius.[14] Other reflections of the same motif are found in the various Arabic Islamic charms connected with the figure of Qarīna al-Tābiʿa, Umm al-Ṣibyān,[15] and discussed at length by Winkler 1931; as well as in the late Syriac figure of *emmā ḥanoqṭā d-ṭalyē* "the mother who is a strangler of children" (Gollancz 1912, pp. 60–65), represented in the manuscripts as being killed by ʿAbd-Išōʿ: she is "the evil spirit in the likeness of a hateful woman of dark appearance" (see Fig. 18).

It may be remarked that we seem to have a late Jewish echo of this motif in the trio of magical names which are used to protect a woman at childbirth and a new-born baby: instead of סוני וסוסוני וסניגלי we have in late Jewish magic סנוי וסנסנוי וסמנגלף. The suggestion that these names are connected with Sisinnius has already been made by Moses Gaster;[16] the story in which these names occur in *Alphabetum Siracidis*,[17] is close enough to our own so as to suggest literary dependence. A typical late Jewish amulet in which the same story is used may be given in its outline as an indication for the survival of this motif in Jewish magic (see Shachar 1971, No. 3;[18] reproduced here in Fig. 19): Elijah,

[14] Cf. e.g. *Bibliotheca sanctorum*, XI, col. 1246 f.

[15] The corresponding Hebrew term אם התינוקות occurs in the Geniza fragment ENA 3381, f. 8.

[16] Gaster 1900, pp. 155 ff. (=1928, pp. 1031 ff.). Cf. also Trachtenberg 1961, pp. 101 f., where an amulet for the protection of mother and child during childbirth using these names is given in the frontispiece; also in Schrire 1966, p. 118.

[17] Fol. 23a, quoted in English by Gaster, ibid. Lilith in this story is depicted as a witch whose task is to destroy little babies; she is chased into the sea, and promises to desist from harming children if the names of the three angels are used on an amulet. Other elements in *Alphabetum Siriacidis* diverge from our base story.

[18] See also Shachar 1971, Nos. 2 and 4. The same story occurs also in Montgomery 1913, pp. 258 ff., from notes made earlier by Richard Gottheil. The provenance of that amulet is uncertain, but there can be no doubt that it is not part of the Nippur excavation material, despite Montgomery's wavering on this point. The language and style are clearly late medieval or modern (Scholem 1948, p. 166, n. 25). Montgomery's text seems to come from an area where Spanish was used. The name of the young mother to whose house Lilith goes may be read as Mercada who is known as (ד״מ is probably for דמתקריא) Vida (?), daughter of Donna. The first line should be read סנוי סנסנוי סמנגלף אדם וחוה קדמונה חוץ לילית as in other amulets of this kind. A very similar text is in M. Gaster 1900, p. 149 (=1928, p. 1025).

walking on the road, met Lilith and her companions and said to her: "You and your companions are impure, where are you going?" She said: "I am going to the house of X daughter of Y, the woman in childbirth, to kill her and take away her son, to drink his blood, to suck the marrow of his bones and to eat his flesh". Elijah put a ban on Lilith, but she asked him to release her and in exchange she promised not to harm that woman and her son wherever the names of Lilith which are enumerated[19] are mentioned. This amulet as usual carries the names of the three angels סינוי וסנסנוי וסנמנגלוף, after the regular heading אדם וחוה חוץ לילית חוה ראשונה.[20]

Fig. 19. A Jewish amulet printed in Germany in the 18th century. From Shachar 1971, No. 3

[19] Some of the names of Lilith in this text and in Montgomery 1913, pp. 285 ff. can be identified with the names in the Greek and other versions: אמורפו is evidently Morphous, שטריחה may be Striga. It may be noted that among the names of the demoness in the Greek text of Allatius (see Winkler 1931, p. 109) we have Pelagia, reminiscent of our "Pelagos, the great sea".

[20] For a psychoanalytical discussion of these stories see Hurwitz 1980.

The general outline of the probable development of the versions we have discussed may be set forth as follows. An early Palestinian Aramaic version of the story of Smamit, Sideros (=iron) and the three helpers of the childbearing woman survives in Amulet 15. This version of the story is marked by the presence of the Greek term *sideros*. This may suggest the existence of a Greek story on which the Aramaic formulation was based, but such a conclusion is not strictly obligatory. A similar Palestinian Aramaic text found its way to Mesopotamia and was copied in Bowls 12a and 12b (possibly also in Gordon 1941, p. 346), where a number of corruptions and perhaps some Babylonian linguistic features were introduced into the text. The Palestinian Aramaic story gave rise to several Christian Oriental versions, the common feature of which is the fact that the helpers assume the shape of Christian saints. The bereaved mother in these versions is a woman related to the helpers. At least one of the Christian versions (the Ethiopian one) used an

Fig. 20. A fresco at Bawit, Egypt. From Perdrizet 1922

Aramaic or Hebrew text, where the Greek name Sideros was replaced by its Semitic equivalent. A parallel Jewish and Christian legend existed, in which the role of the helper is essentially fulfilled by the Prophet Elijah or by the Archangel Michael,[21] who are secondarily identified with the phonetic equivalents of **swny**: Sanoy (etc.) on the Jewish side, Sisinios (etc.) in the Greek tradition. There seems to be a tendency in the Christian tradition to conflate this helper figure with St. George.[22] The evil agent is Iron in the early Greek-Aramaic form of the story, but this was largely forgotten in the later versions, where the evil power is a female figure, Gyllou in Greek and the dependent versions, Lilith in the Jewish tradition. Iron only stays on as a reminiscence, in the name *Barzelya/Werzelya, and in the various practices using iron in connection with child birth.[23] Many versions retain the sea as the place where the demon is vanquished. A constant feature of most forms of the story is the promise made by the evil power that wherever the name of the helpers (later coupled with those of the evil figure) should be invoked, no harm would befall the woman in child-birth and her new-born baby, on whose behalf the amulet is being prepared.

Perdrizet 1922, pp. 13 ff. tried to develop the thesis that the origin of the Coptic and Greek legend is Parthian, adducing the name Sisinnius, which was also the name of Mani's famous disciple, and the Parthian costume of this figure in the Fresco at Bawit in Egypt (Fig. 20). The

[21] See Reitzenstein 1904, pp. 298 f. (Winkler 1931, p. 112), where the Archangel Michael, who is the helper, is also identified with Sisinios and Sinodoros. In Winkler 1931, p. 111, the helper is Gabriel.

[22] Cf. Viaud 1928, p. 112, who uses Perdrizet 1922.

[23] The use of iron for the protection of a woman at child-birth is very widespread. The earliest attestation in Jewish literature seems to be in Tosefta Shabbat 7:4 והקושר ברזל בכרעי המיטה של חיה ... הרי זה מדרכי האמרי; see Lieberman 1961/2, p. 84. See further Blau 1898, pp. 159 f. For ethnological data on the Jews of Afghanistan Brauer 1944, p. 337; on Jewish practice in Karlsruhe, Scheftelowitz 1920, p. 77. In nineteenth-century Poland iron was used for the protection of women at child-birth with the explanation that Heb. *barzel* represented the initial letters of Bilha, Rachel, Zilpa and Lea (*Jahrbuch für jüd. Volkskunde*, I, 1923, p. 217; Trachtenberg 1939, p. 313, n. 14). We have information about the magic use of iron in child-birth, e.g. among Armenians (Hambroer 1962, pp. 32 ff., 105 ff.) and among Arabs in Morocco (Westermarck 1926, index s.v. iron, steel). On the efficacy of iron against demons in general see Abt 1908, pp. 159 f., where further literature is given; Doutté 1908, pp. 41 ff.; Goldziher 1907; and Trachtenberg 1939, p. 160.

name Sisinnius, as can be seen from our Aramaic material, is not original, and the Parthian costume in a pictorial representation may indicate nothing more than that an Oriental figure is intended. The theory of the Manichaean affiliation of the story (see M. Gaster 1928, pp. 1252 ff.; Winkler 1931, p. 123) can also be safely disposed of. Even without the evidence of the Aramaic text the Manichaean connection might have seemed too tenuous, but it is now clear that Sisinnius has nothing to do with the original form of the story, and that this name is merely a transformation of the mysterious names **swny**, **swswny** and **snygly**.

II. Incantation Bowls from Mesopotamia

Bowl 1

Syriac

Formerly in the possession of V. Barakat, Jerusalem

Plates 14-15

(1–2) [מזמן הנא כאסא לחתמתא ונטרתא] ד(בי)תה ודד(ו)רה [ודפגרה דחונא בר כופיתי דתיזה מנה מ]בכלתא וחילמ̈א ו[לוטתא] ונידרא וחרשא (3) [ומעבדא] (ושידא) ודיוא ולליתא וקרוביא וסרודתא רז שמיא בשמיא קביר ורז א[רעא] (4) בא[רעא קבי]ר ורזה דביתא הדין אנא אאמר על כל דאית בה על שיד̈א ועל ד̈יוא ועל חרשא̈ (5) ועל מעבד̈א ועל כל אזגנד̈א דפתכרותא ועל כל גנד̈א ועל חומר̈א ועל איס̈תרתא ועל כל שיד̈א תקיפ̈א (6) ועל כל סטנא̈ תקיפ̈א ועל כל ללית̈א תקיפתא̈ פתגמא הדין לכון מחוא̄ דמקביל יאתו̈ה טבתא משכח ודביש לא מקביל (7) מל̈א רז̈א ומלאכ̈א רוגזא אתין עלוה וסיפא̈ וחרבא̈ וקדמוהי קימין וקטלין לה נורא חדרה לה ושלהביתא אתיה עלוה (8) דפתגמא שמא ויתיב בביתא אכיל ומוכיל שתא̄ ומשקא̄ חדא̄ ומחדא̄ אחא לאחא̈ נהוא̄ ורחמא לדירא̈ ביתא חברא לדרדקא̈ הוא̄ (9) ומרוביא מתקרא̄ צותא לבירא הוא̄ וגדא טבא מתקרא̈ שלמא קבילו מן אבוכון דבשמיא ושבא [ש]למא̈ מן אלהא̈ דיכ̈רא ומן איסתרת̈א (10) נקבתא דמשוא̄ שלמא זכא בדינא ודמשוא̄ חבילא מתקלא בנורא

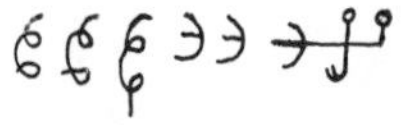

ניתחת[ים וניתנ]טר ביתה ודורה ופגרה דחונא בר כופיתי (11) ותיזה מנה מבכלתא וחילמא̈ בישא̈ ולוטתא ונידרא וחרשא̈ ומבעדא̈ (!) ושידא ודיוא̈ וללי̈תא קרוביא (וסרו)דתא וניתכביש כורחנה ונחדרה שורא (12) דאדמסא דכיא לחונא בר כופיתי {וניתכביש} (ונ)תכביש כורחנה ושידה ודיוה דחונא בר כופיתי (13) ונתנטר בלליא ובימאמא אמין

Bowl 1

Translation

(1–2) [Appointed is this bowl for the sealing and guarding] of the house, dwelling [and body of Ḥuna son of Kupitay, that there should go out from him the tormentors, evil dreams, [curses,] vows, spells, (3) [magic practices, devils,] demons, liliths, encroachments and terrors. The secret of heaven is buried in heaven, and the secret of the e[arth] is (4) b[uried in the ear]th. I say the secret of this house against all that there is in it: against devils, demons, spells, (5) magic practices, all the messengers of idolatry, all troops, charms, goddesses, all the mighty devils, (6) all the mighty Satans, all the mighty liliths. I tell you this word. He who accepts it, finds goodness, and he who is bad (and) does not accept (7) the mystery words, angels of wrath come against him, and sabres and swords stand before him and kill him. Fire surrounds him, and flame comes against him. (8) Whoever listens to the word sits in the house, eats and feeds, drinks and pours drink, rejoices and causes joy, he is a brother to brethren and a friend to the dwellers of the house, he is a companion of children (9) and is called educator, he is an associate of cattle and is called good fortune. Accept peace from your Father who is in heaven and sevenfold peace from male gods and from female (10) goddesses. He who makes peace wins the suit. He who causes destruction is burnt in fire *(magic characters).*

Seal[ed and guar]ded shall be the house, dwelling, and body of Ḥuna son of Kupitay, (11) and there shall go out from him the tormentors, evil dreams, curses, vows, spells, magic practices, devils, demons, liliths, encroachments and terrors. His sickness shall be pressed down, and a wall (12) of pure steel shall surround Ḥuna son of Kupitay. The sickness, devil and demon of Ḥuna son of Kupitay shall be pressed down (13) and he will be guarded by night and by day. Amen.

The interest of this new find is in the fact that it constitutes a welcome addition to a small group of bowls in Syriac which carry basically the same text. Since none of the bowls gives an unequivocally clear reading of the whole incantation, and since the text contains several problems, a new version helps to elucidate and sometimes to confirm earlier hypotheses. The texts parallel to our new bowl are the following:

1 A text read by T. Ellis in Layard 1853, pp. 443 f., No. 6. The bowl is now in the British Museum, B.M. 91712 (cf. Hamilton 1971, No. 10).

2 A bowl from Nippur at the University Museum of the University of Pennsylvania, published by Montgomery 1913, pp. 242 ff., No. 37 (cf. Hamilton 1971, No. 9).
These two texts benefited from the insights and comments of Epstein 1922, pp. 56 ff., who discovered their similarity, and managed, by comparing them to each other, to restore much of the mutilated text and to elucidate the meaning of the fragmentary formulae.

3 A bowl at the Iraq Museum (No. 44107), first published by Teixidor 1962. Teixidor did not notice the connection between this text and the previously published ones, and his reading was therefore somewhat fragmentary. The identification of the similarity is due to Hamilton 1971, No. 14, who offered some improvements to Teixidor's readings.

We have re-checked the British Museum bowl by the aid of a photograph, and having at our disposal our new text, we believe it is possible in some points to complete and correct Epstein's readings and reconstructions, which are on the whole confirmed by this text. The state of preservation of our bowl is good enough to make an almost continuous reading possible, apart from the opening words, which are illegible. Whereas our new text and Montgomery No. 37 are written in proto-Manichean characters,[1] Ellis 6 and Teixidor's bowl (as well as our Bowl 10) are written in Estrangelo.

The text begins in the centre and goes, by spirals, towards the circumference. This is, with some exceptions, the normal practice in the

[1] See Lidzbarski 1916; Teixidor 1962, pp. 61f.

magic bowls. On our bowl the two opening lines are so faint as to be largely illegible. They can, however, be reconstructed by comparing the similar formula in lines 10–11, and the opening phrases of such other Syriac texts as Montgomery 1913, Nos. 31, 32 and 35. The three parallel texts, Ellis 6, Montgomery 37, and Iraq Museum 44107, are all too defective at the beginning to be of any help.

3 The two words, **qrwby' wsrwdt'**, obviously denoting evil spirits, are also attested in line 11. The Syriac word *qrūḇyā* means "approach, attack, accusation", a cognate of *qrāḇā* "war", and could possibly serve as the proper name of a demon. No form corresponding to **srwdt'** is attested in Syriac, but Jewish Aramaic provides it in Gaster 1896, p. XII:35. The verb **SRD** "to fear" and the noun *sūrādā* "terror" are, however, familiar in Syriac, and occur in a magic text published by Hamilton 1971 (20:8): **nytsrwd bswrd' dl'lm** "may he be struck by eternal terror". **swrd'** occurs more than once in the charms published from Syriac manuscripts by Gollancz 1898. Thus we have, for example, the sequence ...**wdḥlt' wzw't' wrtyt' wtwht' wswrd' wrny'**...(p. 79) "...fear and trembling, terror and surprise, dread and anxiety..." (a similar sequence on p. 86). Derivatives of the same verb occur also in Mandaic, although the verb "to fear" in Mandaic, affected by both a metathesis and an enlargement by **-n-**, is **SNDR** (Drower and Macuch, p. 334a, where however the etymological references to Jewish Aramaic and Modern Syriac words meaning "sieve" seem out of place). The causative verb in Mandaic has the form **SRWD** (like the reflexive verb in the Syriac text of Hamilton 1971, quoted above; cf. Drower and Macuch, p. 337a, where the reference to **SRD** as an "inversion of **SDR** II" is not clear, since **SRD** is the basic form of the verb, as it is indeed presented on p. 334a). A Mandaic noun which is very close to our own is **saruadta**, translated by Drower and Macuch as "(a) fright, alarm (esp. nightmare), terror, (b) loneliness" (p. 315). The examples given there support a somewhat different translation. The phrase **saruadta ḏ-'umama** indicates "terror of the day time", perhaps personified, as opposed to **sahria ḏ-lilia** "night-demons", and the phrase **bsibutḫ usaruadtḫ timut** need not compel us to introduce a new meaning "loneliness" for the word. It can perfectly well be rendered "she will die in her old age and in her fright". The plural feminine form **saruata** indicates a class of demons associated with ruins and destruction (cf. Drower and Macuch, p. 315b). Cf. also Bowl 13:13.

3–4 The phrase רז שמיא בשמיא קביר ורז ארעא בארעא קביר was reconstructed by Epstein 1922 for Montgomery No. 37, and it is gratifying to have it fully confirmed by our bowl.

4 From this point Epstein managed, by comparing the two bowls with each other, to make an almost complete reconstruction of their text. Our bowl is very close to Montgomery's text, offering only minor variations, which will be noted below. For **ʾʾmr** Montgomery has **ʾymr**.

5 On the basis of our text it is possible to suggest in Montgomery, line 5, to complete **[wʿl kl ʾzgndʾ]** (6) **dptkrwtʾ**.

6 **ptgmʾ hdyn**: Epstein conjectured in Montgomery 37:7 **pytgʾmʾ syt[rʾ]**, which Hamilton read **pytgʾmʾ hnʾ**. The correct reading of Montgomery 37:7 seems to be, like here (though in *plene* spelling), **pytgʾmʾ hydy[n]**, with the demonstrative written exactly as in Montgomery 37:5 **[r]ʾzh dbytʾ hydyn**.[2] It may be noted that the demonstrative **hdyn** is not usually recorded in Syriac texts; it is a form which is normal in Jewish-Aramaic (cf. Epstein 1960, p. 23; Rossell 1953, p. 27).[3] This may suggest that our present text is based on a Jewish-Aramaic version; see also **ytwh**.

mḥwʾ has a mark above the word to indicate the participle. In Montgomery 37:7 and in Iraq Mus. 44107:2 the form is **mḥwynʾ**.

dmqbyl yʾtwḧ: For the first word Montgomery has **dmqbl**. For **yʾtwh** both Ellis 6 and Montgomery 37 have **yʾth**. The accusative particle is quite unusual in Syriac, and is characteristic rather of the Jewish Aramaic texts. For the particle with pronominal suffixes, one can note a wavering in Jewish Aramaic between a singular-type declension and a plural one. For the singular cf. e.g. **yʾtky** (Gordon 1934a, p. 141, line 6); **ytyh** (Montgomery 3:7, 9); **ytkwn** (Montgomery 15:7); for the plural-type declension cf. **ytyky** (Gordon 1934c, p. 469, G:5; Montgomery 17:3). The variation **yʾth** as against **yʾtwh** demonstrates the two forms of treatment of the particle. It seems strange, though, to see a plural mark (*seyāmē*) over **yʾtwh**.

[2] There is an error in Hamilton's edition and translation of this line. **ḥdyn** occurs in Bowl 10:13, cf. Commentary to Bowl 10:7.

[3] In Babylonian Jewish Aramaic **hydyn** is used only for the interrogative "which one"; see Epstein 1960, pp. 29 f.

dmqbyl y'twh ṭbt' mškḥ wdbyš l' mqbyl: The B.M. text, Ellis 6, provides the clue to the puzzling sentence. Ellis 6:5 should read: **[d]mqbyl y'th ṭbt' mškḥ wdbyš wl' m(q)[byl]**. The phrase **l' mqbyl** is thus an apposition to **wdbyš**.

7 **mï' rż'**: This is also the obvious reconstruction of the text in Montgomery 37: **[m]l' r'z'** (or **r'zy**), rather than **'r'zy**. *Mellē rāzē* is used here in the sense of incantations.

wsyṗ' wḥrḃ': The correct reading in Montgomery 37 seems to be the same as here. Montgomery read the first word **wdsyp'**; Epstein preferred to read **[b]syp'**. The two nouns are best taken as standing in juxtaposition to **wml'k̈' rwgz'**.

wqdmwhy: See Epstein 1922, p. 56, where it may be seen that Montgomery's text has **qdmwh**, while Ellis has **wqd[m]why**.

nwr' ḥdrh lh "fire surrounds him": **ḤDR** is used with other prepositions, **ḥdr b-** "to retract" and **ḥdr ʿl** "to return" (cf. Levine 1970, p. 350). In our text, line 11, the same verb occurs with a direct object in the sense of "to encircle".

8 **šm'** is written here, corresponding to Montgomery **šmʿ'**, which is equally wrong. The Iraq Museum text has the correct form, **šmʿ**. The correspondence between our new text and Montgomery No. 37, here and elsewhere, shows that they both were copied from the same source.

wytyb bbyt': The initial *waw*, which does not exist in Montgomery and Ellis, is our scribe's mistake.

'ḥ' l'ḥ̈' nhw': Ellis 6 and the Iraq Museum text have here **'ḥ' l'nš' hw'**. One other case in which Ellis and the Iraq Museum text join together against the reading of Montgomery and of our new text is in the preceding line, where they have **wšlhbyt' npl' ʿlwhy** (according to Iraq Mus.; Ellis has minor variations and a dittography), against **wšlhbyt' 'tyh ʿlwh** (according to our text; Montgomery has minor variations). **nhw'** has a diacritic sign which marks it as a participle, perhaps to indicate that it is used for the present tense.

9 **wmrwby'**: This seems to be a copyist's error for **wmrwbyn'** attested in Montgomery 37. Ellis and Iraq Mus. spell the word **wmrbyn'** (cf. Hamilton 1971, p. 55). The correct identification of this word was made by Epstein.

ṣwt' lbyr' hw': This phrase is still puzzling. It is written in this manner in Montgomery 37 and in Iraq Mus. 44107, where it would have the sense of "he is an associate of cattle" (**byr'** for *bʿīrā*), which seems curious. In Ellis the text shows in effect **lgld'** (or **lglr'**), which Epstein, followed by Hamilton, read **lgʿr'**, assuming a corruption **bʿr'** > **gʿr'**. It is possible to consider a variant form of *būrā* "uncultivated, simple, stupid", which might correspond to *gʿīrā* "hateful, hideous", although one can hardly account for the sense obtained "he is an associate of the hateful, ignorant". An argument in favour of this interpretation, however, is the fact that it comes parallel to the preceding phrase, which states that he is "a friend of children and is called an educator". Here he may be termed "a companion of the simple-minded (or of those excluded), and is called good luck", possibly some kind of auspicious magical situation.

wgd' ṭb' mtqr': The scribe of Montgomery 37 omitted the word **ṭb'**.

šlm' qbylw mn 'bwkwn dbšmy': Epstein's reconstruction of Montgomery's text is unacceptable. He read it **šlm[' mn] bl 'bwkwn**. It would seem more plausible to reconstruct there too **šlm[' q]b[y]l[w]**, and to assume that **mn** was omitted by a scribal error. The same text may underlie the letters preserved in the Iraq Museum bowl. Ellis 6 has a completely different version at this point.

wšb' [š]lm̈': Epstein followed the word **dbšmy'** by a reconstructed **[w'r](ʿ)'**. However, it seems more reasonable to reconstruct for Montgomery 37 the same phrase which occurs in our text. Indeed, the traces visible allow very well to reconstruct **[wš](b)'**. The same applies to the text of the Iraq Museum. It reads **wšbʿ' w[...]šlm'**.

dmšw' šlm' zk' bdyn': Epstein's correct reading is re-confirmed by our text, in addition to the support brought by the Iraq Museum bowl. The initial letter is undoubtedly **d-**, as in Teixidor 1962.

wdmšw' ḥbyl' mtql' bnwr': As the verb was not visible in Montgomery's text, Epstein had to invent one, and he chose **mtyqyd**. The Iraq Museum bowl and the new Jerusalem text concur in using the verb **QLY**, which should of course also be reconstructed in Montgomery 37. Teixidor's reading (followed by Hamilton) of the Iraq Museum text should be corrected as follows: **wdmšw' ḥbl' mytql' bnwr'**.

10–12 The closing formula does not occur in the parallel texts, just as the Iraq Museum bowl closes with a formula which does not occur elsewhere. The formula of our text has corresponding texts in other magical bowls, such as Montgomery Nos. 31–35.

The client of this bowl is Ḥuna bar Kupitay. The name Kupitay occurs also in some other texts, cf. Montgomery Nos. 2, 4, 12, 16.

11 The spelling **mbʿdʾ** for **mʿbdʾ** is another instance for the weakening of the *ʿayin*; cf. above **šmʾ** in line 8 and **šbʾ** in line 9.

kwrḥnʾ: This word is written here twice with a *ḥet*, though it occurs with a *he* in Montgomery 7:11 (in Jewish Aramaic). Syriac has normally only the spelling with a *he*.

11–12 **wnḥdrh šwrʾ dʾdmsʾ dkyʾ**: The reading is quite clear and unequivocal. **ʾdmsʾ** is a loanword from the Greek **ἀδάμας** which consists of a privative **α-** with a derivative of the verb **δαμάω** "to conquer". The Greek word thus means "unconquerable" and designates the hardest substances: steel or diamond.[4] The word occurs also in Syriac (cf. Brockelmann, *Lex. Syr.*, s.v. **ʾdʾmws**), and in Mandaic, where the phrase **šura d̲-dmasa** is attested several times (Drower and Macuch, p. 111b). The word is also found in Persian and Arabic *almās* in the sense of "diamond", and in Manichean Middle Persian under the form **ʾrmʾs** for "steel" (cf. Nöldeke 1892, p. 44; Bailey 1943, p. 134).[5] It can be shown that **ʾdmsʾ**, **ʾrmsʾ** does indeed refer to some metal by comparing the parallel phrase in Montgomery No. 4:6 (in Jewish Aramaic): **wšwrʾ rbʾ dnḥšʾ ʾḥdryt lh** "and I have surrounded it with a great wall of bronze".

The same word, **ʾdmsʾ**, occurs, we believe, in three other Jewish incantations, where it has not been recognized. The texts in question are Montgomery 2 and 27, and Gordon 1941, p. 273 (11:3). Montgomery 2 and 27 were re-studied by Epstein 1921, pp. 30 f.; his reading and translation are quoted and amplified by Levine 1971, pp. 361 f. as follows:

> תוב אזלנא אנא פ׳ בר פ׳ בחילי דנפשי בקומתי גציצא דפרזלא קרקפתי דפרזלא קומת דנורא דכיא ולבישנא לבושא דארמסא דכיא וממללא
>
> "Again I come, I, X. son of Y., with my own might. On my body are arms (or hands) of iron, a head of iron, a body of pure fire. I don the pure-white and simmering robe of Hermes".[6]

[4] For the occurrence of *Adama* and its derivative in Greek magic cf. Peterson 1926b, p. 393.

[5] A striking parallel is found in a Manichean magic text in Middle Persian, where we have: **ʾwm šfšyr ʾwd [cy]lʾn ʿy hswd ʿy ʾrmʾs [ʿ]y pʾk pyrʾmwn ʾwbʾyyd** (Henning 1947, p. 40, lines 32–34) "I am girt with a whetted sword and a dagger of pure adamant".

[6] Epstein did not commit himself on the word which was read by Montgomery as **ʾrmsʾ**. The warlike character of such magical operations recalls the similar motif in the Chaldaean Oracles; cf. Lewy 1978, pp. 194 f.

The text of Gordon 1941, p. 273 (No. 11) is basically the same, though somewhat shorter.[7] However, although the name Hermes does occur on incantation bowls,[8] it is most unlikely that it occurs here. **ʾdmsʾ** "steel" is clearly the preferable reading, giving the translation "a robe of pure steel", which goes along with other indications of iron and fire. In Gordon 1941, p. 273, we might read not **lbwšʾ dʾrmys wddbyh**, but rather **lbwšʾ dʾdmwsʾ dkyh.**[9]

Another point worth examining is the adjective **mmllʾ**. Levine suggested the translation "simmering", as of coals, but this seems doubtful. One might rather seek the explanation in the Mandaic phrase **parzla nimalil ʿlẖ**, probably to be translated "iron will crush him" (cf. Drower and Macuch p. 273b, s.v. **MLL** III). Hebrew **MLL** also has the sense "to crush, squeeze" (cf. Jastrow s.v.). **ʾdmsʾ dkyʾ wmmllʾ** could therefore very well mean "pure, crushed (=forged) steel".[10]

Montgomery 19:7 was corrected by Epstein 1921, p. 49, to read **wbšwm mryʾ mlylʾ wmʾmlʾ dʾrmsʾ**. However, an examination of two unpublished parallel texts (University Museum of the University of Pennsylvania, both bearing the number 18059), shows that the correct reading is **mryʾ klylʾ wmgdlʾ dʾrmsʾ**.

[*Addendum*: When the book was in the press we noticed the article by Harviainen 1978, which had escaped our attention before. It contains in Estrangelo script another parallel text to our Bowl 1. The parallel to our text goes as far as our line 10, with no significant deviations, and it confirms the restorations proposed above.]

7 We must recall that Gordon was probably unaware of Epstein's insights on this text.

8 The one safe example is Montgomery 7:8, which is the equivalent of Myhrman 1909, p. 346, line 4. The correspondence established by Montgomery is: **ʾyrmys=hrmys**. On Hermes in Jewish writings cf. also Lieberman 1947, pp. 53 f.; Milik 1976, p. 336, follows Montgomery's wrong interpretation.

9 In Montgomery 25:4 **[ʾr]msh myṭṭrwn** is not entirely certain.

10 It seems possible that **mmllnʾ** occurs also in the sense of "pure", at least in the phrase **pwrdysʾ mmllnʾ**, Black 1954, fol. 72b (cf. p. 61: "Paradise of the Word", which seems inadequate). The interpretation of **mmllʾ** as meaning "crushed, forged" does not exclude the much more common usage of the word in the sense of "speaking, talking", as in Jeruzalmi 1963, p. 115; Isbell 1976, p. 23, where we have **mlkh mmll brʾzy pryštʾ**; **mlk mmlyl brzy pryštʾ**; cf. our Amulet 3:3.

Fig. 21. A Jewish amulet printed in Warsaw in 1867

Bowl 2

The Hebrew University of Jerusalem, Institute of Archaeology, No. 1401

Plates 16–17

Inside the bowl:

(1) (ליט ....) הפיכי (הפיכא הפיכא) (2) הפיכא הפיכא הפיכא ארעא (3)
וי(שמ)יא הפיכי כוכבי ומזלי הפיכא שעתא דכול בני אינשא (4) הפיכא לוטתא דימא
ויברתה דכלתא ויחמתה הפיכא לוטתא דגברי וינשי (5) דקימין בדברא ויבמתא
ויבטורא ובית אילהי ובית כנישתא אסירא ויחתימא לוט(6)תא דלטת בישום ביתיאל
ויקותיאל ובישמיה דייי רבא מלאכה דיתליה חדעסר שמין ססכבא (7) כבבא כנברא[1]
סדיא סודאריא מריריא אנקפא אנס[2] פספס כביבי בנורא כול מן דעבר על הלין
שמהתא (8) מלאכי אילין אסירין ויחתימין כול שידין ושופטין וכול דלרעא קריא וכול
דלישמיא מציתא שמעית קל ארעה שמיה (9) דימקבלא כול נישמתא מין הדין עלמא
שמעית קלה דיתתא דלטת ושדרית עלה מלאכין נכיר נכיר יי נקום ניקמת יי נגיל ונגיל
יי כיסס צצצ טימא יתיתתא דלטת ושדרו וחבילו יתה מין ענין דבר(ת)א[3] דלא תיקום
ולא תילוט

Outside:

(10) דכיא בר קיימתא וימחלפא בר (דויד) ושרכה (בר) אלי(ש)תא[4]
(10a) (א) דכיא בק[5]
(11) מרים בת חורן

[1] An alternative reading could be **kkbrʾ**. [2] An alternative reading could be **ʾks.**

[3] This word is seemingly written **dbrdʾ.** [4] Another possible reading is **ḥlyptʾ**.

[5] This looks like being the first attempt to write the name, abandoned because of a mistake, and re-done subsequently above.

Bowl 2

Translation

Inside:
(1) (Cursed [?] . . .) Overturned, (overturned, overturned,) (2) overturned, overturned, overturned, overturned is the earth (3) and heaven, overturned are the stars and the planets, overturned is the talk of all the people, (4) overturned is the curse of the mother and of the daughter, of the daughter-in-law and of the mother-in-law, overturned is the curse of men and women (5) who stand in the open field and in the village, and on the mountain and the temple(s) and the synagogue(s). Bound and sealed is the cur(6)se which she made. In the name of Betiel and Yequtiel, and in the name of **yyy** the Great, the angel,[6] who has eleven names: **sskbʾ**, (7) **kbbʾ**, **knbrʾ**, **sdyʾ**, **swdʾryʾ**, **mryryʾ**, **ʾnqpʾ**, **ʾns**, **psps**, **kbyby**, **bnwrʾ**. Whoever transgresses against those names, (8) these angels, bound and sealed are all demons and evil spirits. All that is of the earth calls, and all that is of the heaven obeys.

I heard the voice of the earth, [and of] the heaven (9) which receives all soul(s) from this world. I heard the voice of the woman who cursed, and sent against her the angels **nkyr nkyr**, **yy** take vengeance, **yy** let us rejoice and rejoice, **yy kyss ṣṣṣ ṭymʾ** the woman who cursed. And they sent and injured her (away) from the eyes of the daughter, that she may not avenge nor curse.

Outside:
(10) Dakyā son of Qayyamtā and Maḥlepā son of (David?) and Šarkā daughter of Alištā (?)
(11) Miriam, daughter of Ḥoran

[6] Or possibly "his angel".

Bowl 2

The text starts at the centre, where a circle is drawn, and runs in spirals towards the circumference. Near the rim of the bowl a large circle surrounds the text. No client's name is contained in the text of the incantation, but such names occur, quite unusually, on the outer surface of the bowl.

The text has a number of parallels, both complete and partial. These are as follows:

1 B.M. 91720 = Layard 1853, pp. 438-440 (Ellis 2). Layard does not contain a drawing, but we have been able to use a photograph kindly provided by the British Museum authorities to check the readings. The portion of this text which provides a parallel to the Jerusalem bowl begins at the fifth line.

2 B.M. 91727 = Layard 1853, pp. 440-441 (Ellis 3). This text has been re-edited by Schwab 1890, pp. 306-310 (Text B), and by Jeruzalmi 1963, pp. 52–63, and it has been incorporated into Isbell 1975, pp. 131-133 (Text 58). Again we have been able to consult a photograph of this bowl. The text which corresponds to the Jerusalem bowl begins at line 5.

3 B.M. 91745. Portions of this text were published by Gordon 1941, pp. 339-341, without photograph or drawing. The same text had been published without indication of its present location by Schwab 1892, pp. 139-142 (Bowl G), but Gordon did not notice that Schwab's text was the same as B.M. 91745, which he re-edited. A reader would not notice this identity by comparing the two editions, which are quite divergent, unless he had the benefit of a photograph, as we did. Only by collating the two editions with the photograph of B.M. 91745 can one conclude, with a high degree of certainty, that both scholars worked on the same original. Yamauchi 1965, when he studied parallels to his text (cf. No. 5 below), treated the versions provided by Schwab and Gordon as if they constituted two different texts. It may be noted that in several cases Schwab's readings are better than Gordon's, a tribute to that pioneer in the research of magic bowls.

4 Iraq Museum 9726, studied by Gordon 1941, pp. 348-349. Only a partial reading and translation is given, and no photograph or hand-copy.

5 A private bowl in the possession of Mr. E. Safani, published by Yamauchi 1965. From line 3 we have parallels to our Jerusalem bowl, but the second half of Yamauchi's text is again divergent.

The bowls enumerated 3 and 4 begin, like the Jerusalem text, with the word *hafīḵā* repeated several times, while the other parallels have a longer introductory text.

The text contains a number of formulaic elements which recur in other bowls. It may be convenient to list them:
(a) The formula: **hpykʾ hpykʾ ...** with a list of (negative) objects to be reversed, especially the curses of relatives and other men and women.
(b) An invocation of angels, in particular a group of eleven names which constitute the person of **yyy** the Great.
(c) The formula which asserts the efficacy of the invocation: "All that is of the earth calls, and all that is of the heaven obeys".

All three elements recur in the parallel texts (=PT) 2, 3 and possibly also 5, where element (c) is not visible. The same may be true of PT 1, where the third element is missing, and of PT 4, of which only a portion is given by Gordon.

Some particular features of our bowl may be indicated. The spelling **wy-** for the conjunction, **by-** and **ly-** for the prepositions, and **dy-** for the relative particle are frequent in this text. Rossell 1953, p. 21, refers to the spelling **wy-** indicating that it occurs before a vowelless consonant. This is not true either of the Jerusalem bowl (cf. **wybrth, wyḥmth, wynšy,** etc.), or of Montgomery No. 1 (see Epstein 1921, p. 29). The same is to be said of **by-** for the preposition **b-**, cf. **byšwm.** Similarly in Montgomery 2:7 we have **byptkry** (assuming that the first syllable is *pat-*).

The elision of an initial *alef* following a prefixed element also characterizes this text: cf. **dymʾ** (*=d-ʾimmā*), **dytlyh** *(=d-ʾīṯ lēh),* etc.

There is a seemingly careless alternation of *alef* and *he* in final position for the *status emphaticus,* but it may be, at least in some of the cases, a conscious use of the possessive suffix of the third person singular feminine: **lwṭtʾ dymʾ wbrth dkltʾ wyḥmth** (line 4) "the curse of the mother and her daughter, of the daughter-in-law and her mother-in-law", although in the parallel versions all these nouns end with *alef.* At the same time we also have the interchange of **dlrʿʾ, dlyšmyʾ**, as against **ʾrʿh, šmyh,** with no apparent difference in function.

The spelling of the plural **gbry, nšy** seems an East Aramaic feature, while the use of the preposition **yt** for the accusative is more typical of West Aramaic; cf. Rossell 1953, pp. 11, 37; Tal 1975, pp. 28–30 (see also above, Commentary to Bowl 1:6).

2–3 In PT 4 the formula, as read by Gordon, is: **ʾwpykh {ʾrʿ} ʾrʿh**

hwpyk' šyd', where in view of all the parallel versions, the last word is likely to be a wrong reading for **šmy'**.

3 The word **š‘t'** in our text corresponds to **š‘wt'** in PT 3 (B.M. 91745, correctly read by Schwab, but wrongly read by Gordon as **bw‘wt'**),[7] and to **š‘whwn** (for **š‘w<t>hwn**) in PT 2 (B.M. 91727). The translation as given by Schwab "que la [mauvaise] heure soit renversée" was followed by subsequent scholars, but it seems wrong. This is most probably a form of the noun derived from the verb **Š‘Y**, cf. Bab. Aramaic and Syriac **'št‘y** "to tell, talk". We thus have Syriac *taš‘ītā* "story", as well as *še‘yā, šu‘āyā* "play, joke", *šū‘ītā* "story", etc., Mandaic **šuta** (from **š‘wt'**) "talk, speech, conversation".[8] In all the parallel versions of this text we have the sequence **hpyk' š‘(w)t'/š‘w(t)hwn dkl bny 'ynš'** "that the discourse of all the pepole be overturned". This corresponds in PT 4, according to Gordon's copy, to **hwpykh lwṭt' dkl bny 'ynšh.** Nothing like this occurs in PT 5 (Yamauchi's bowl), though the phrase **hpyk' kl myly** can be regarded as conveying the same idea (if it is not to be read **mzly**).[9]

4 **lwṭt' dym' wybrth:** PT 2 has here **lwṭt' d'b' wdym' wdbrt'**, while PT 1, 4 and 5 have a version similar to the one on our bowl, without the father being mentioned.[10] Our version is unique in the distinction it makes between the suffix of *immā* and of *bartāh,* if it is intentional (see above). A similar formula with the possessive suffixes is found in the printed amulet (Warsaw 1867), where we have **משביע אני עליכם כל מין עינא בישא ... עינא דאיש ואשתו עינא דאשה ובתה עינא דאשה ואחותה עינא דאשה וקרובתה ...**; for the same incantation with minor variants see Hanauer 1907, pp. 318 ff. (see Fig. 21 on p. 133).

5 **dqymyn bdbr' wybmt' wybṭwr':** A similar sequence occurs in each one of parallel versions, but none is identical. **ṭwr'** and the two following

[7] The correct reading was already suggested by Jeruzalmi 1963, p. 59.

[8] Cf. Drower and Macuch, p. 458. For the Mandaic verb cf. Yamauchi 1967, p. 360 s.v. **Š‘'**.

[9] In a note on the word *millā* as a magic term in Hebrew, Sperber 1966 commented on PT 3 as published by Gordon 1941. The word does not exist there; Schwab read it correctly as **mzly,** the same word that we have in the Jerusalem bowl.

[10] PT 3 reads according to Schwab **hpyk' lyṭt' d'b' wdym'**, and according to Gordon **hpykh lwṭt' d('b)' wdymh,** while the bowl clearly has **hpykh lwṭt' hd' d'ymh.**

terms are unique to our bowl. On the other hand, we lack here a reference to "near" and "far", which occurs in other versions.

wbyt ʾylhy wbyt knyštʾ: These terms are also unique to our bowl in this formula. Both terms seem to present plural nouns, although the main part of the genitive construction is in the singular. For a similar phenomenon in Syriac one may quote from the Julian Romance: **wpqd dntpthwn byt ptkr̈ʾ wntbnyn ʿlwthwn...wnttqnn byt knwštʾ dyẅlpnʾ ṭ̈ʿyʾ dʿqyr̈n ḧwy wsḥypn** "He ordered that the idol temples be opened and that their altars be constructed ... and that the schools for erroneous doctrines, which had been overthrown and destroyed, be repaired" (Gottheil 1969, pp. 1 f.). The Syriac phenomenon is treated in Nöldeke 1898, pp. 83 f., § 141.

6 **lwṭtʾ dlṭt:** The absence of an explicit subject for the verb may suggest a passive form. What goes against such an assumption is the observation that in PT 2 the form which occurs is a masculine active form: **dlṭ** (line 6), and further **wbpwmh lṭʾ** (line 7), apparently in the feminine. Another argument against taking this form as a passive participle is the phrase further down in our bowl: **ṭymʾ ytyttʾ dlṭt** (line 9), where *ītta* seems to be the subject of the verb. The subject, when it is not specified in the texts, could well be a demon, which can of course be either masculine or feminine.

bytyʾl wyqwtyʾl: PT 3 has here **byʾytyʾl wyqwtyʾl** though the two names were quite erroneously read by both Schwab (who read **byʾwhyʾl mmnḥyl**) and Gordon (who read **ʿzʾ wḥyʾl ḥqytyʾl**). Yamauchi's text PT 5 seems to have **šdyhyʾl wyqtyʾl** (the first word was read by Yamauchi as **ṭšhyʾl**). PT 1 has (as correctly read by Ellis) **btyʾyl wyqtwʾyl.** There is nothing corresponding to it in PT 2, and Gordon does not quote a similar formula from PT 4 (Iraq Museum).

wbyšmyh dyyy rbʾ mlʾkh dytlyh ḥdʿsr šmyn: The corresponding expression in the other bowls has caused considerable trouble to previous editors, and the contribution of our bowl may be said to be chiefly in clarifying this phrase. In PT 2 Ellis read **bšmrwt kʾ mlʾkh,** while Schwab, in a completely different conception of the letters, read here (beginning from the preceeding word) **mn kwl mdyntʾ mlʾkh.** Jeruzalmi greatly improved on his predecessors, but this particular expression was read by him **bšmrytkʾ mlʾkh.** He cannot be blamed for his reading, because the error is obviously the magician's own, who miscopied from his original, where the formula must have been correctly written. The ancient scribe wrote **bšmk ytbʾ mlʾkh,** for the obviously correct **bšmk yy**

rb' ml'kh. Paleographically the mistake is easy to understand. The same mistake was done by the scribe of PT 3: **wbšwm ytb' ml'k' d'yt lyh ḥd 'šr šmht'.**[11] Both scribes may have used a similar original, although PT 2 has the indefinite plural form **šmhn** for PT 3 **šmht'** (our **šmyn,** which has the indefinite masculine plural ending).

One may remark in passing that the process of transmission of the magical formulae was not apparently one of careful copying from a bowl or a notebook, but something like a free adaptation from existing written (or oral) formulae. Hence the great variations even when we deal with a text which is basically the same. In a sense the process of transmission is more like one of oral tradition than in almost any other form of written tradition. At the same time, **ytb'** from **yy rb'** could only come about by erroneous interpretation of written signs.

Once the correct formula is established, it is easy to see that in Yamauchi's bowl (PT 5) we should read **byšmk yy rb' ml'kh,**[12] where Yamauchi read, with hesitation, **ywrb'**. Similarly one recognizes without undue difficulty in PT 1 (Ellis 2) the phrase **wbšmk yrb' rb' ml'k(y)h d'yt lyh ḥd ʿšr šmhn,** where the original formula **yyy rb'** "the Great **yyy**", having given way to a pseudo-word **yrb',** is reinforced with the epithet **rb'.**[13] Not having the benefit that we possess by our comparison, Ellis read here **wbšmry dk' dk' ml'kh.**

The partial transcriptions which Gordon gives of the Iraq Museum bowl (PT 4) do not contain any correspondence to the phrase under discussion.

6–7 The eleven names of **yyy** *rabbā* have been compared by Yamauchi in the different versions which he possessed. As stated above, he was not aware of the fact that Schwab G is the same text as Gordon's rendering of B.M. 91745, and so the two lines C and D in Yamauchi's table constitute but two transcriptions from the same bowl. On the other

[11] This is the correct reading of the word (with Gordon), against Schwab's **šmwt'.**

[12] Yamauchi transcribes by mistake **ml'k'.**

[13] The recurring Mandaic form of the name is **adunai iurba,** where the first element is sometimes omitted. Cf. Pognon 1898, p. 17 = Yamauchi 1967, p. 154; Pognon, p. 22 = Yamauchi, p. 156 (where the text is **aduna rba**); Pognon, p. 23 = Yamauchi p. 158; Pognon, p. 25; Pognon, p. 73 **(bit iurba),** etc. The name is also quite familiar from literary texts in Mandaic. Cf. Lidzbarski, *Ginza,* p. 258 note 1; Drower and Macuch, p. 191. In Gordon 1934a, p. 141, we have **ywdg' ywdb'**, and the second word may well be identical with **ywrb'.**

hand, there is room to add PT 2 (Ellis 3), which also has a similar list, competently edited by Jeruzalmi, as well as our own new text. The Iraq Museum bowl (PT 4) obviously has also a list of eleven names, but this was not copied by Gordon.

If we take the Jerusalem text as basis for comparison, we may make the following table:

1 **sskbʾ**=PT 2: **ssbbʾ,** PT 5: **ssbʾ,** PT 1: **ssbbh,** PT 3: **qsrbʾ.**

2 **kbbʾ**=PT 2: **kkbʾ** (the third in that list), PT 5: **krbʾ,** PT 1: **kkkʾ** (third in that list), PT 3: **kbkʾ** (third in that list).

3 **knbrʾ**=PT 5: **kbkʾ,** while the other corresponding forms are quoted above, under number 2. In PT 2 No. 4, **bpbbʾ** may be compared here.

4 **sdyʾ**=PT 2: **sryh** (second in that list), PT 5: **mrwh,** PT 1: **sryh** (second in that list), PT 3: **srtyh** (second in that list).

5 **swdʾryʾ**=PT 2: **sydryh,** PT 5: **sw** (?), PT 1: **sydryh,** PT 3: **ʿnyny** (?).

6 **mryryʾ** = PT 2: **hydryʾ,** PT 5: **hʿpnyʾ,** PT 1: **ḥryḥ,** PT 3: **ktyš** (?).[14]

7 **ʾnqpʾ**=PT 2: **ʾnqpʾ** (number 9 in that list, read **ʾrqpʾ** by Jeruzalmi), PT 5: **ktypʾ,** PT 1: **ʾnqpʾ** (number 9 in that list).

8 and 9 **ʾns psps** = PT 2: **ʾlsps** (number 10 in that list), PT5: **hls sš pb,** PT1: **ʾnsps** (number 10 in that list?), PT 3: **nttnt pkrps** (?).[15]

10 and 11 **kbyby bnwrʾ** = PT 2: **bmmr nwryʾ** (read differently by Jeruzalmi), PT 5: **kbybn blwrʾ,** PT 1: **kbyby...,** PT 3: **kbybn bnwr.**

We are left with PT 2 **ʿzryh**[16] (No. 7 in the list) and **btwqpʾ** (No. 8) in PT 3.

Even though this is a somewhat cursory comparison, without a proper textual edition of the different texts involved, one sees that with a fairly small movement of items one comes to a grasp of a list which is more or less identical, though it contains the fluidity of an orally transmitted tradition, as noted above.

7 kwl mn dʿbr ʿl hlyn šmhtʾ: The expression occurs in PT 1, and was correctly transliterated and translated by Ellis. The same is true of PT 2, where Ellis read and translated correctly, though Schwab made a wrong

14 Thus read by Jeruzalmi 1963, p. 62.

15 These names recall the very frequent **ʾnqtm pstm pspsym** in late Jewish amulets; cf. Shachar 1971, p. 227, and above, Fig. 21 (p. 133).

16 Jeruzalmi reads this name as **ʿzzyh.**

translation and Jeruzalmi made a mistake both in copying the text, which should read **wlkl dʿbr ʿl hlyn šmhtʾ**, and in its translation, and was followed in this by Isbell. PT 3 has the same phrase, again translated wrongly by Schwab ("à tous ceux qui passent près ces noms") and Gordon ("and each that works **[dʿbd]** by these names"). PT 5 no doubt contains the same phrase, though this was not legible to the editor. PT 4 is not quoted at this point.

As for the expression **ʿbr ʿl** "to transgress", the usage is quite well attested in Mishnaic Hebrew. Cf. B. B. Meṣiʿa 111a: כל הכובש שכר שכיר עובר בה׳ שמות הללו. Tosefta Bava Meṣiʿa 10:8: ועובר על כל שם ושם שיש בו. These contexts demonstrate the meaning of the phrase: "to transgress, to hurt, to injure sacred names", which is somewhat transformed in the rabbinical usage to "to transgress against commandments".

8 **kwl šydyn wšwpṭyn:** Of the other versions, PT 3 has a more extensive list of demons. It contains the following elements, some of which were not quite accurately read by Schwab, but which Gordon rendered very well: **kl šydyn wšwbṭyn wdywyn wlyṭyn wlylyn wsṭnyn wšqwpyn.** The first two elements are identical in the two versions, despite the variation in the spelling of the second. The spelling with a *pe* occurs in Hyvernat's text.[17] A discussion of the term occurs in Montgomery 1913, p. 92. The parallel versions have different sets of names, or no names at all.

wkwl dlrʿʾ qryʾ wkwl dlyšmyʾ mṣytʾ: An analogous phrase is found in the various parallel versions. PT 2: **wkl dlʾrʿʾ qryʾ wkl dlšmyh mṣytʾ** (lines 11 f.); PT 3: **wkl dylʾy dylʾrʿh qry wlyšmyh myṣyt;**[18] PT 1 is too effaced at this point, at least in the photograph, but Ellis managed to read it very nicely (without being able to give an accurate translation): **wkl dlʾrʿʾ [qry] kl dlšmyh mʿyt,** where only the final word should obviously be read **mṣyt.** PT 5 can easily be restituted at this point. The editor read **kl dlʾw**..., which is apparently the beginning of our formula: **kl dlʾrʿh qry (wk)l [dlšmyh] (mṣy)[t]**. The passages copied by Gordon from the Iraq Museum bowl (PT 4) do not contain our phrase. A similar phrase seems to occur in Geller 1980, p. 54, lines 8–9 **wbtqlʾ dqryh wrwḥ mlʾkh rbty dmytwtʾ**: the last word should probably be emended to **dmṣytʾ**

[17] Some other examples for the alternation of **-b-** and **-p-** are given by Rossell 1953, p. 16.

[18] Schwab: **wkl dwlʾy dwlʾ dmw[t] qry wlšmw ḥmwṣyt.** Gordon: **wkl dylʾy dylʾrʿh qdw wlšmyh,** with the translation: "and all... of the earth's... and heaven's".

As to the sense , we have here clearly a formula which asserts that the incantation is effective: "Everything which is in (or on) the earth calls, everything which is in heaven obeys". Similar formulae occur in other bowls. Cf., e.g., Istanbul 5363 in Jeruzalmi 1963, p. 128: **ʾnʾ ktbyt wʾlhʾ mʾry kwlʾ ysy yt...** "I have written (the incantation), and God, the Lord of all, shall heal...", and our Amulet 1:12–13: **ʾnh ktbt yy[yy y]ʾsy** "I have written, God will heal."

8–9 **šmʿyt ql ʾrʿh šmyh dymqblʾ kwl nyšmtʾ mn hdyn ʿlmʾ:** Here again our bowl can provide us with an aid for clarifying parallel passages, and at the same time also instruct us in the ways of textual transmission of such magical bowls. PT 1, according to Ellis's transliteration (since the photograph is unclear at this point) has the following text: **šmr[h] ql ʾrʿʾ dqdḥʾ wšmyh d[ʾtkl]tny š[mhtʾ] mn hdyn ʿlmʾ.** The first three words can without doubt be reconstructed as identical with our text: **šmʿyt ql ʾrʿʾ**. The fourth word seems to be missing from our text. The rest of the sentence can be imagined to be the same text as ours. The contribution of this text is in the addition of a word **dqdḥ** as the verb for the action of the earth.

PT 3 can be read in the following manner: **šmʿyt kl ʾrʿh dʾwqwḥ** (?) **šmh dym(q)b(y)l**[19] **kl nyšmtʾ mn hdyn ʿlmʾ.** The text is quite definitely corrupt, but, like PT 2, it contains what looks like a verb after **ʾrʿh,** and this is an element which the scribe of our bowl must have omitted by mistake. The interesting point here is the error which the scribe of PT 3 committed when he wrote **kl** for **ql.** The reading itself is clear and unambiguous. The second half of the text in PT 3 is basically the same as the one in our bowl, and it seems to have been badly written because the scribe did not understand the meaning of the words. The verb which should be supplemented in our bowl after **ʾrʿʾ** may be the one which occurs in PT 1 **dqdḥ** : "which flees, which escapes".[20] The form **dʾwqwḥ** in PT 3 is somewhat similar in appearance, and may be assumed to be a corruption of the same verb. The full reconstructed sentence should then read: "I have heard the voice of the earth *fleeing, and that of the sky receiving all the souls from this world". The earth "fleeing" may be an allusion, in this context, to the unwillingness of the souls to die.

19 Gordon reads the last three words: **rḥyqyh šmh dymḥbyl.**

20 For the verb **QDḤ** cf. below Commentary to Bowl 5:11.

PT 2 does not have our sentence, but it has some remnants of it. It reads: **šmʿt mn hdyn ʿlmʾ ql ʿyttʾ dš...** This text can be explained as a haplography: **mn hdyn ʿlmʾ** is the termination of the phrase just quoted, while **šmʿyt ql ʾyttʾ...** would be the beginning of the next sentence. In PT 2 the two sentences were conflated.

9 **šmʿyt qlh dytth dlṭt wšdryt ʿlh mlʾkyn:** This phrase too has close parallels. PT 1, according to Ellis's transcription, reads: **ql ʾytʾ [šm]ʿyt dlw[ṭtʾ] wšdrʾ**[21] **ʿlh mlkyn.** PT 2: **šmʿt ...**[22] **ql ʾyttʾ (ks...**[23] **wlṭyʾ wšdrt) ʿlh mlkn (wtqypyn).** PT 3: **qlh šmʿyt šmʿyt ql gbrʾ mšršyʾ br pwrtw dlyṭ wšdryt ʿlhw mlʾky.** No comparable phrase is quoted by Gordon from PT 4, and the final part of PT 5 is not well preserved, but seems not to contain such a phrase. The only significant difference here is that PT 3 refers to a man, while the other texts where the formula appears deal with women.

nkyr nkyr: This name does not occur in Aramaic, as far as we know, outside our text, where it occurs in some of the parallel versions. PT 1 has **nkyr** (once only). PT 3 has **nkr nkr.** The other versions do not have this name, as far as can now be verified. The context suggests that this is the name of an angel sent against the man or woman who curses. The Islamic figure of *nakīr* (usually associated with *munkar*) comes to mind: this pair of Islamic angels are the ones in charge of the *post mortem* trial of people, and their punishment. The origin of the Islamic name has been unknown. We may have here an antecedent to it.[24]

yy nqwm yy ngyl wngyl yy kyss: PT 1 has **wnqwm**[25] **nqmʾ wngl**[26] **nglʾ ww**[27] **ss.** PT 3: **ynqm nyqmt nglh nglh ss ṭwy ss.**[28] The other versions do not contribute parallels, though Ellis reads in PT 2: **ydrk wtqym nqmʾ wngyl nyglʾn wssw mʾ,** which does not seem visible in the photograph.

[21] The passage is not visible in the photograph, but we may conjecture ***wšdryt.**

[22] As explained above, the group of words **mn hdyn ʿlmʾ** probably belongs to the preceding sentence, which was omitted by haplography.

[23] Our reading here differs from Jeruzalmi's.

[24] Cf. *Shorter Encyclopaedia of Islam,* pp. 411 f., s.v. *Munkar.*

[25] Possibly to be emended to **ynqwm.**

[26] Possibly to be emended to **yngl.**

[27] Possibly **yy.**

[28] Schwab's transcription is here wide of the mark.

ṣṣṣ ṭym' ytytt' dlṭt wšdrw wḥbylw yth myn ʿnyn dbr(t)': PT 1: **wss ṭy mn wssṭ mn wd'ytt' dlyṭ' wš[r]y'**[29]... **ksy 'ytt'... mn [ʿ]nn dbryk.** PT 2 (Ellis's reading): **wssym yd'ytt' dlwṭ' wšry' lwṭt' '''.** PT 3: **ṭymw yt mšršy' br pwrtw dlṭ wšdr lwṭtyh lḥwpy dy(?) my' wlyṭwr mdnḥ'...** The word **ytytt'** is clearly a combination of the accusative participle **yt** with **'ytt'.** It seems that this was corrupted in PT 1 and 2 into **yd'ytt'.** All versions apart from our own become muddled and incomprehensible here. **ṣṣṣ** has a parallel sequence of letters in Isbell 1975, No. 65:4 and in Amulet 2:4–5,14.

dl' tyqwm wl' tylwṭ: PT 1: **dl' tyqwm wl' tylṭ.** PT 3: **dl' mwlyṭ.**

10–11 The names, written on the outside, are an unusual feature of incantation texts, where they are usually incorporated into the text. Here the text is entirely impersonal. The mother's name may well be read Qayyamtā. The masculine name **qywm'** occurs in a Nabataean inscription published by Milik and Starcky 1975, pp. 121 f.

From Bowl 9

[29] Perhaps one should read here ***yd'ytt'...*wšdrw.**

Bowl 3

The Hebrew University of Jerusalem, Institute of Archaeology, No. 1399

Plate 20

(1) אסותא מן שמיא למאאדאראפרי בת (2) אנושאי ידמכון בעפרא חבילי נידרא
דכוליה דוכא (3) וכל טלא וכל מידיעם דביש ומעיק לה למאדאראפרי בת מאנושי (4)
חרשות ועבדין דמיתעבדין יתכבשון ויטמרון בארעה מן קדומיה (5) בעוז גדודהו
וחיחי בין נסוע הארון וימר מושה קומא יהוה ויפוצו איבאך וינסו מ[vacat] מיפנך
אקדד ואברא אמן אמן סלה

This is a plain bowl, with a crude square in the centre, and a fairly short inscription. Much of the inscription is taken up by a quotation from Numbers 10:35, in a peculiar spelling. No parallels are known to us from other magic bowls for any part of this inscription. The reading begins, as in most cases, in the centre.

1 The name of the client is Madar-Afri. The second element of this name seems at first sight to be similar to the name quite frequently attested in Aramaic incantations **ʾprʾ, ʾprh,** and which is likely to be the same as the name of Shapur's mother in the Babylonian Talmud, **ʾyprʾ-hwrmyz.**[1] The several attempts made at explaining this name may

[1] For the name **ʾprʾ, ʾprh** cf. Montgomery 1913, p. 118, where a Jewish or a Persian origin for the name are both mentioned as equally possible. The Jewish derivation would be from Ephraim as a hypocoristic, the Persian being a reduction from a name beginning with *fra-*. Both suggestions seem equally unlikely. Nöldeke 1879, p. 52, footnote, refers to the name of Shapur's mother by saying: "die erste Hälfte dieses Namens ist mir unklar". B. Geiger in Krauss 1955, pp. 58 f. explains **ʾyprʾ hwrmyz** as Farrah-Hormizd. The name suggested by Geiger actually occurs in Sasanian seals as **plxwʾwxrmzd,** Farrox-Ohrmazd, cf. Gignoux 1978, p. 147.

Bowl 3

Translation

(1) Healing from heaven to Mādar-Āfri daughter of (2) Anušay. May there lie in the dust the injuries of vows of every place (3) and every shaded place. And every evil thing, and whatever oppresses Mādar-Āfri daughter of Manušay, (4) the sorcery and the charms which are cast, (all) will be pressed and hidden in the earth before her (5) by the power of his army. "And it came to pass, when the ark set forward, that Moses said, Rise up, Lord, and let thine enemies be scattered, and let them ‹that hate thee› flee before thee" (Num. 10:35). **ʾqdd wʾbrʾ.** Amen Amen Selah.

be summarized as follows: some derivation from *frēh* "more"; some element connected with the preverb *fra-; āfrīn* "blessing"; or *farr(ah)* "fortune".[2] However, it seems likely that the name **ʾprʾ / ʾyprʾ** is connected with the name of the well-known Sasanian jurist and commentator, which is spelt **ʾplg / ʾplk,** and which has been commonly read Aparak.[3] This reading is not convincing, since it suggests a name derived from the noun for "robber" *(appar)*, though Abarag "superior" is also a possible interpretation. One would rather be inclined to think of a name *Āfar(r)ag* "Fortunate", with the preverb *ā* used in an auspicious sense.[4] Another possibility is the word *Āfurāg,* which could conceivably be attested also with a short *a* in the final vowel, for

[2] A summary of most opinions is given by Geiger in Krauss 1955, pp. 58 f. Cf. also the discussion in Goodblatt 1976, where the derivation from *frēh* is accepted.

[3] He is mentioned, for example, in *Mādigān ī hazār dādestān,* in Avesta commentaries, and in *Šāyast ne šāyast.* Cf. Perikhanian 1973, p. 562, s.v. Aparak. West 1892, p. 472, note 1, reads Afarg. Cf. also Tavadia 1930, p. 29, note 8 on 1.3b.

[4] One thinks of words like *āfrīn, āzād(ag), ābādān,* though they are all derivatives of verbal forms, which is not the case here.

"creator". This could of course be a reference to Ohrmazd, and we know that Ohrmazd is also a name of frequent occurrence. The latter explanation, even if it is not accepted as a solution for the name of the jurist, seems the most likely explanation for the name of Shapur's mother: Āf(u)rā-Hormiz, as well as the name on several magical bowls which may be read Āfrā, with an omission of the final consonant *-k/g,* just as we have the alternation Pāpak, Bābak with Pāpā, Bābā, etc.[5]

The name Mādar-**ʾpry** is however unlikely to be connected with any of the above names. The second element seems to represent either *āfriya* "beloved"; or *āfrī* as a variant on the nominal Middle Persian form *āfrīn* (Parthian *āfrīwan*) from the verb *ā-frī-,* the noun meaning "blessing"; or as a form of the present stem of the verb, in which latter case the compound *mādar-āfrī(n)* would mean "blessing (his) mother". The first alternative, reading Mādar-āfriy(a) "beloved to his mother" seems the more plausible one.[6] As a proper name, or as an element in proper names, *mādar* is not known so far either directly in Iranian or in other languages under Iranian influence. The more familiar forms Mama, Mamay etc. are quite widely attested.[7]

2 Anošay alternates, in line 3, with Manošay, an alternation which is not easy to explain, unless we regard the latter spelling as a contracted

[5] Cf. the names in the index to Montgomery 1913, p. 278. Nöldeke 1892, pp. 309 f., hesitated whether Pāpā is Iranian or Semitic. This hesitation is perhaps no longer justified, since we have it attested already in the Persepolis chert bowls in Aramaic and Elamite; cf. Bowman 1970, p. 130. One may also refer to Benveniste 1966, p. 17, who deduced the existence of Pāp as a variant Iranian name besides Pāpāk; cf. the remarks by Gershevitch 1969, p. 218, and the listing in Mayrhofer 1973, p. 133.

[6] For a final element *-friyā-* in Iranian names cf. Mayrhofer 1973, p. 202, No. 8.1116 Mišbapirriya, and Justi 1895, p. 371 Vispān-friyā. Both are feminine names meaning "beloved to all".

[7] Cf. Bowls 4:7 and 6:3 and the references in Montgomery 1913, p. 278 and Justi 1895, p. 189. Naveh, 1979b, pp. 21 f., has discussed the Semitic names denoting "mother", suggesting that they may be taken to be appellatives rather than proper names. One may refer in particular to Hermopolis **mmh** (cf. Naveh, art. cit., note 21). The ambiguity of this usage may be seen in Bowl 6:6. Nöldeke 1892, pp. 309 f. judged such names to be proper names. A seal published by Layard carries the inscription **lmmh**, cf. Lidzbarski 1902, pp. 137 f. and 97, note 3. It may be noted that the Armenian proper name Mam is derived from Persian *mām* "mother", cf. Hübschmann 1897, p. 50.

form of **mhʾnwš(y)**, a name which is also attested without the final *-ay.*[8] We may then take both forms to be basically variants of the same name, freely interchangeable. The name **ʾnwšʾy** and what seems to be its equivalent **mhʾnwš(ʾ)y** is a feminine name of Iranian origin. It is possible to regard the final element, apparently *-ay,* as the very common ending of many Iranian names in the Aramaic tradition, an ending which is attested in both masculine and feminine names, and is thus similar in function to the ending *-oy.*[9]

The base element of Anušay is almost certainly *anōš,*[10] attested in New Persian *nōš, nōšīn* "sweet, pleasant", as well as in loan-words and loan forms of proper-names in Armenian *(anoiš),*[11] in Syriac,[12] and in Arabic.[13] In the Aramaic magic texts we have the proper names **dwktʾnwš, bbnwš** (with variants **bʾbnwš, bbʾnwš), zʾdʾnwš,**[14] **kwʾrʾnwš** and **mhʾnwš.**[15] Most or all of these names can be explained as compounds denoting "beloved by, sweet to —", with the first term referring in most cases to some close family relationship; daughter (perhaps meaning "the other daughter", i.e., the sister), father, son (cf. New Persian *zāda*),

[8] Cf. **ʾnš, ʾnwšy** in Montgomery 1913, p. 274, and **mhnwš, mhʾnwš** op. cit. p. 278. All occurrences are in Mandaic, partly from Pognon 1898, where, on pp. 101 f., Barthélémy's explanations are quoted. Montgomery 1913, p. 254, offers an impossible explanation of **mhʾnwš** as containing the name Mithra. The names are also discussed in Nöldeke 1898b, p. 144. Cf. also Hamilton 1971, text 19, for the name **mʾhʾnw[š]** in Syriac.

[9] For this ending cf. Nöldeke 1888, pp. 413 ff. and 1898b, p. 145. Salemann 1930, p. 49, derives *-ōy, -ōya* from **-avya-ka-.*

[10] For a possible occurrence of this word in Pahlavi cf. Shaked 1979, pp. 254 f.

[11] Cf. Hübschmann 1897, pp. 99 and 18 f. Earlier the word was identified with the term for "immortal", cf. Fr. Müller 1891, pp. 264 f., 356; Horn 1893, p. 30, No. 128.

[12] Cf. Gōšaqanōš, Hoffmann 1880, pp. 25 f.; Rādanōš, Hoffmann 1880, p. 68.

[13] Duxtnōš, cf. Nöldeke 1898b, p. 144. The name Anōšagzād is explained by Nöldeke 1879, p. 467 as "von Unsterblichem geboren"; he was actually the son of Xusrau Anōšag-ruwān.

[14] Cf. **ʾnwšzʾtʾ** in a Sasanian clay sealing, Gignoux 1978, p.114, No. 10.30b. See also the preceding note.

[15] In Montgomery 1913, p. 218 (No. 29:5) we propose to read **mhʾnwš** for Montgomery's **mtʾnyš**. The same applies to Geller 1980, p. 49. In Jeruzalmi 1963, p. 160, there seems to be a name **mhʾnš**.

sister (**kwʾr** may well be a contraction of Middle Persian *xwāhar*),[16] perhaps parents (*meh* "elder"). A similar impression is formed by some of the compound proper names containing *anoiš* in Armenian: Aršanoiš, Sahakanoiš, Smbatanoiš. In all of these cases the first element alludes to the name of the father of the dynasty. For the Mandaic names, Nöldeke 1898b, p. 144, suggests a conflation of the Iranian word with the biblical name Enosh, which became the name of a Mandaean genius. Against this theory one may note that the names containing this element are definitely Iranian, not Semitic, and that they are commonly attested also outside Mandaean texts.

ydmkwn: The verb **DMK** is attested in the Berlin bowl No. 2417; cf. Wohlstein 1894, p. 34, where the meaning is not pejorative as it is here, although the text is not quite clear. In the absence of a photograph or a drawing in Wohlstein, one can only guess what the text might read: **myty dbytʾ d[šky]byn bʾrʿh *wdmkyn bʾprʾ *qdḥw lkwn** "the dead of the house, who lie in the earth and sleep in the dust (or 'in the ashes'). Go away...". The whole of this unusual incantation is addressed at the dead who are asked to abandon the house of *Bābay son of **bydwn** (?) and resort to the house of Asmēn daughter of Iday. In Amulet 7:21–22 there is an opposition **DMK: NWM,** in which the latter means "to doze off", while the former means "to sleep properly".

ḥbyly nydrʾ: This combination could also possibly mean "bundles of oaths", though it has been the custom to translate the first term as "injury, harm" in the magic texts. Cf. also Mandaic **giṭria ḏhbila** (Lidzbarski 1909, p. 354, lines 32 f.; Yamauchi 1967, No. 22) "die Knoten des Verderbens".

3 **ṭlʾ:** The context suggests that we have here a contrast between **dwkh** "(open) place" and **ṭlʾ** "shade, shaded place", although this expression is so far unique in the magic texts. Montgomery 1913, No. 29:9, has the phrse **šydy bny ṭyly,** which he translated: "ghostly shades"; but this may rather mean "ghosts of shaded areas". By a different interpretation one may, however, connect **ṭlʾ** to the well-known term for a species of demons, usually called **ṭlnytʾ, ṭwlnytʾ.** In this case the sentence may be

[16] Nöldeke 1898b, p. 144 denies this explanation and regards the first element as *xwarrah.*

translated: "and every shade-spirit (**ṭlʾ**) and every evil thing which afflicts her..." (J.C. Greenfield's suggestion).

mydyʿm dbyš wmʿyq lh: A fairly close parallel for the usage is found in Gordon 1937, p. 87 (H:13) **wkl zyqyn wmzyqyn byšyn dymʿyqyn lh l...**

4 **ḥršwt wʿbdyn:** Cf. the sequence in Gordon 1941, p. 123 (5:4 f.) **kl ḥršy byšy wkl mʿbd[y] tqypy dʿbydyn bh wdmytʿbdyn bh.** Cf. also our Bowl 12:III **wʿbdt lḥršyn dy nḥšʾ wʿbdyn dprzlʾ.**

wyṭmrwn: The verb has not been attested so far in the magic texts.

5 **bʿwz gdwdhw:** A puzzling phrase, appearing in Hebrew in the midst of the Aramaic text and looking like a quotation from a sacred source, though no source has been identified.

wḥyḥy byn...: A quotation from Num. 10:35, badly written. This verse is yet unattested in the magic bowls, though it is familiar from late Jewish and Samaritan magic.[17]

ʾqdd wʾbrʾ: The second word looks like the name of an angel, cf. *Sefer ha-razim* 1966, p. 88, line 118. The two words could also be taken to be verbal forms in *afʿel* from the roots **QDD** and **BRY,** meaning respectively "to penetrate" and "to soak through" (J.C. Greenfield's suggestion).

From Bowl 12a

[17] T-S AS 142.13; Schrire 1966, p. 131, No. 36. The words **qwmh yhwh**, deriving from the same verse, are quoted in Samaritan bronze amulets and other inscriptions; cf. Ben-Zvi 1970, pp. 179, 187 f., 193, 200; Kaplan 1967, pp. 158 f.

Bowl 4

The Hebrew University of Jerusalem, Institute of Archaeology, No. 1402

Plates 18–19; Figure 22

Inside the circle in the centre:

(1) תוב הדין א(א)א א (2) איסרא דקברא (3) אמן אמן סלא

Around the central design:

(4) פעיח פעזיח מלכנא קלקלא מלכנא קלקלא מלא משמלא קליה די מצמדנא די
סכת פדנא היך מג<ל>א (5) מחת ליה בליביה דפומיה לא יאימר וליביה {לא יאדע} לא
יאידע אמי פת לילי לילי הי לילי יצב יצב בנן בנן (6) אף על פרטדוך ליטא לתהפכי
חרשיא ולוטתא ומשקיפותא מין מחדד בר (7) ממא ומין {בת} ברזוך בת ממא ומין
מחזידוך בר ברזד וך ומין קיימתא בת ק(בנ)י ומין נני (8) בר קימתא ומין ביתא בת
ברזדוך ומין בתי חיא וקינין חיא למעבד חי פו(גריה)

In the centre is a drawing of a human face, perhaps with the body of an insect. Two ribbons are shown on the left side of the face, and what looks like three insect-like legs are at the bottom. Encircling this design are a number of figures, which include a serpent and two reptiles as well as a cross which ends at its four corners with circles.

We should like to acknowledge the intelligent help of Mrs. Ada Yardeni, who drew the script shown in Figure 22 and who made a number of important suggestions for the reading.

The text of the incantation contains a number of obscure expressions, and is not easy to make out. It may have been intended for protecting a tomb, if we take the expressions **ʾysrʾ dqbrʾ** and **lmʿbd ḥy pw(gryh),** which open and close the incantation, in a literal sense. But the expression is

Bowl 4

Translation

(1–3) Again. This is ''''' the spell of the tomb. Amen Amen Selah.

(4) **pʿyḥ pʿzyḥ** I advise (?). A voice I advise (?). A voice fulfils (and) completes. The burnt (thing) which I attach, which (is) the coulter of the plough, like a sickle, (5) shall introduce into his heart, that his mouth shall not speak and his heart shall not know.

Immi the daughter of Lili who is Lili Lili. **yṣb yṣb bnn bnn.**

(6) She also curses Fratadukh, that you may turn away spells and curses and afflictions from Māhdād son of (7) Mama, from Barazdukh daughter of Mama, from Māh-ized-dukh son (!) of Barazdukh, from Qayyȧmta daughter of Kabnay, from Nanay (8) son (!) of Qayyamta, from Bita daughter of Barazdukh, from the houses of life and the livestock of life, to make his body alive.

common in incantations, cf. Commentary to line 2. **pwgrʾ** can of course refer either to a living body or to a corpse.

1 **twb** is a common opening word in Aramaic. It occurs, for example, in the opening of the text in Montgomery 1913, p. 121 (2:1): **twb ʾzlnʾ ʾnh...** Cf. also Rossell 1953, pp. 61 f.

''''': The second *alef* looks like **yt,** but **ʾytʾʾ** would not give any meaningful reading.

2 **ʾysrʾ dqbrʾ:** The idea of an incantation connected with a cemetery or a tomb is quite common; cf. Pognon 1898, p. 3. **ʾysrʾ** is a regular term for a magical spell.

4 The text begins with a series of magical combinations which cannot be precisely translated. It is not clear where this sequence ends, and the translation given of this line is largely hypothetical.

For **pʿzyḥ** one may compare **pʿzyʾl**, one of the names given to Meṭaṭron in the Hebrew Book of Enoch, cf. Odeberg 1973, Hebrew section p. 71 (48D: 1).

mlknʾ: We have translated the word as derived from **MLK** "to advise"; it could equally well be analysed as *malkā anā* "I am king", or *mālek anā* "I rule". See further in the Introduction, p. 27.

qlqlʾ: This formula occurs in Montgomery 1913, p. 178 (13:9), cf. also p. 181, and Epstein 1921, pp. 45f.; Levine 1970, p. 352. In Mandaic, cf. Pognon 1898, p.59 **qal qal...**; Drower 1945, p.173 **qal arqa dbakia uqal šumia.** In Ginza Left, Petermann 1867, I, 2, p. 117:7 f. we have **qal qala qala qala ḏtrin qalia šumit qala ḏtrin qalia ḏiatbia ubanin qal ruha uqal nišimta...** In T–S AS 143.12 we have **wmh qlh bšmyʾ ql ʾrʿʾ dgʿyt wql ʿmwdy šmyʾ ʾtprqw ʾlʾ qlh dkwnnwt kwnnwt kd nḥtyt mn šmy mrwmʾ lqlqlh lstmh wlṭmṭmh lbhy wʿyynyhy..**; Rettig 1934, p. 48 **qlh qlh drbw rbh.** There is a manifest tendency to play on the similarity of the word for "voice" and that for "corruption, spoiling". Cf. on this the note by E.S. Rosenthal in Lieberman 1974, p. 139, addendum to p. 51, where Hebrew **qwl** is shown to be used in the sense of **qlqwl** "disapproval, condemnation, abuse".

mlʾ mšmlʾ: A reading *mellē mašma‹ʿ› lēh* "words he utters" might also be considered. Cf. Levine 1970, pp. 355 f. One wonders whether *ma-li-e mi-il-in-ni,* presumably *mālē millīn,* in the cuneiform Aramaic tablet from Warka, has any relevance. Cf. Dupont-Sommer 1942/44, p. 44, and Epstein's suggestion that the Talmudic idiom **mmly myly** "adversaries" be adduced. Cf. Epstein 1960, p. 11, n. 4; Gordon 1937/39, p. 106, n. 4. In Gordon 1934b, p. 324 (B:9) we have **ql myly myly.** It seems, however, best to read the two verbal forms as derivatives of **MLʾ**, i.e. *mālē mšamlē***,** with the second verb taken as a *šafʿel* participle (cf. Brockelmann 1928, pp. 389 f.).

qlyh, as rendered here, refers to the following **skt pdnʾ** as a burnished iron. Other possibilities of interpretation exist. **qlyh** could be "his voice". The word **qly** (Kali) is attested as the name of an angel. Cf. Montgomery 1913, pp. 258, 262; Gaster 1900, p. 149 (=Gaster 1928, II, p. 1025); Schrire 1966, p. 130; **qlyʾ** in Gordon 1934b, p. 324 (B:1). The formula **ʾpypʾ qly qlylʾ** (T-S K 1.120) may belong here. In Montgomery 1913, p. 141 (6:11 f.) we have a similar word in a somewhat obscure

Fig. 22. The text on Bowl 4

context: **wnyzym bmyzm nḥšh nyzyl qlyh bgygly šmyʾ wnyhwy *dwryh *bsbb** [read so!] **šʾwl *rymh** "and may he be bound by a muzzle of brass; may his **ql(y)** go in the spheres of heaven, and may his habitation be in the vicinity of the grave (and) of worms". Cf. also on this passage Epstein 1921, p. 34. The word **qlyh** is unlikely to be "his voice", as the context requires a pejorative sense. It is possible to think of the word **ql** "voice" in the sense explained by Rosenthal (cf. above, comment on **qlqlʾ**), viz. "abuse, state of abjectness".

It is of course possible to divide the sentence in our bowl differently from the way done here. One other possibility is to read: **mlknʾ qlqlʾ, mlknʾ qlqlʾ, mlʾ mšmlʾ qlyh,** which may be translated: "(His) wisdom (or counsel) is corruption, (his) wisdom is corruption, he fulfils and completes his abuse".

mṣmdnʾ could possibly be a word meaning "yoke" or the like.

skt pdnʾ: For this expression cf. Jastrow 1950, p. 988, s.v. **skʾ**. A similar expression was read by Cross 1973, pp. 126 f. in an ostracon from Heshbon.

hyk mg<l>ʾ: This seems the best solution to a puzzling sequence of letters. An earlier reading which was considered was ***ḥwkmtʾ**, regarding the *gimel* as a badly written *taw* (or as a scribe's error). This earlier reading would give the translation "shall introduce wisdom into his heart". However, the following phrase, "that his heart shall not know", does not go well with such an interpretation.

5 **mḥt:** The active participle of **NḤT** in *afʿel.*

dpwmyh lʾ yʾymr wlybyh lʾ yʾydʾ: The words **lʾ yʾdʿ** were first written and then re-written under the spelling **lʾ yʾydʿ**, presumably because the first spelling might have sugggested a participle form, while the corrected one shows a *ṣere* in the first syllable, and denotes the imperfect. Babylonian Aramaic has numerous expressions in which the pair **lybʾ—pwmʾ** go together, cf. e.g. Jastrow 1950, p. 686.

ʾmy: This is the name of what seems to be a female demon, **ʾymy bt rbqʾ**, associated with **lyly** and **mr**, the sons of **ʾymy**, in the Berlin bowl No. 2416, cf. Wohlstein 1894, p. 11; Stübe 1895, p. 22; cf. Wohlstein 1894, pp. 20 f., who quotes Bavli Pesaḥim 112a, where Immi may well be the name of a female spirit. Here Immi is the daughter of Lili, the latter being perhaps a variant on the name Lilith. Immi is of course also mentioned as a regular human proper name. Cf. Gordon 1941, p. 12 (4:2) reproduced in Isbell 1975, p. 97; Gordon 1937, p. 93 (L:11), reproduced in Isbell 1975, p. 127.

6 **prṭdwk** is an Iranian name which occurs here for the first time. The name may be explained as Frāta-, cf. Old Persian Frāda (cf. lately Mayrhofer 1979, II, 20), though the spelling with **-ṭ-** is problematic. It may alternatively be connected to Av. Parāta-, cf. Bartholomae 1904, p. 856, or to *Frahāta-, cf. Justi 1895, pp. 101 f.

lthpky: The form is unclear. One would have expected a **d-** at the beginning, instead of the **l-**; the latter may be merely a scribal error for **d-**.

mšqypwtʾ: An unusual form for **šyqwptʾ, ʾyštqwptʾ.**

Māhdād occurs also in B.M. 91710, cf. Layard 1853, pp. 437f. (Ellis 1); Schwab 1890, pp. 299 f.; Montgomery 1913, pp. 168 f.; Jeruzalmi 1963, pp. 65 ff., in line 3, where it was wrongly read by previous editors.

For Sasanian seals, cf. Bivar 1969, p. 70, No. DB2; Gignoux 1978, p. 27, No. 3.11; p. 88, No. 4.11b. Other attestations are listed in Justi 1895, pp. 185 f. Cf. also Hinz 1975, p. 156 s.v. *māhīdātā-; Gignoux 1979, p. 69.

7 For Mama, cf. above, note 7 to Bowl 3.

myn bt brzdwk bt mm': The first **bt** is surely a scribal error.

brzdwk: This reading was suggested by Mrs. Yardeni. The name is probably to be vocalized Barāz-dukh, associating it to the common Iranian proper name Warāz/Barāz, for which one may refer to Justi 1895, pp. 348 f.; Mayrhofer 1973, p. 190, Nos. 8.965, 967 ff.; Hinz 1975, p. 255; and to **wl'cdwxty** in ŠKZ, cf. Gignoux 1979, p. 87. The alternative reading **brwdwk** seems less likely both palaeographically and as an Iranian name, though it could be compared to the name **brd'kt** in the Syriac bowl published by Hamilton 1971, pp. 121, 159 ff. and Geller 1976, pp. 422 f. A proper name Bằra seems to be attested at a very early time. Cf. Grantovskij 1970, pp. 216 f.; Hinz 1975, p. 63. It is to be noted that on the Syriac bowl the suffix *-duxt* is spelled **-d'kt,** cf. also **šhd'kt,** and possibly also **mhgwšnyd'(k)t,** though this latter name is read by Geller **mhgwšnwd'yt.** The spelling **-d'kt** betrays an *-o-* pronunciation for long Syriac *-ā-,* as in Western Neo-Syriac, for which one may refer to Nöldeke 1898, p. 5, §4. Hence it may be deduced that the spelling **-d'kt** indicates a pronunciation *-doxt* for the ending of these Persian names, not unlike the usage of Standard New Persian for original short *u* vowels.

mḥzydwk: This name is unattested so far. It might seem possible to explain it by referring to the suffix *-čya-* in Old Iranian, which may give a form *Māhī-čyằ-, perhaps a form of endearment from the word for Moon, which is also the name of a deity. The Elamite proper name Bakizza (etc.), which is reconstructed as Iranian *Bagaiča- (cf. Mayrhofer 1973, p. 138, No. 8.229; Hinz 1975, p. 56) may be compared, as well as the place name Bagiziš from hypothetical *Bagaičya- (Hinz 1975, p. 56), which are assumed to be "Koseformen" derivatives from the divine name Baga. A similar explanation has been proposed for Elamite Takaziya from Iranian **taxmačya-* (Hinz 1975, p. 232); cf. also **tigračya-* in Hinz, p. 236; **kafačya-,* op. cit. p. 144; *maryaičya-,* op. cit. p. 174.

However, a simpler solution offers itself and seems preferable. One could read the name as Māh-ized-dukh, assuming the omission of a *yod* after the second letter, and the quite common haplography of *dalet.* The deity Māh-izad or Māh-yazad is quite well known in the Manichaean texts. Cf., e.g. Andreas and Henning 1932, p. 220, s.v. **mʾhyzd.** The spelling **yzyd** for the second part of this compound name is not surprising. In Mandaean we have both **yʾzyd** and **yzyd** as a name, cf. Pognon 1898, p. 99, taken by this scholar to be the similar-looking Arabic name Yazīd, cf. pp. 14, 103, and claimed by Montgomery 1913, p. 277, to be an unexplained Aramaic name. What proves **yzyd** to be the Iranian name Yazed is the compound form **yzydʾd** "Created by Ized", Montgomery 1913, p. 150; Justi 1895, pp. 147, 149. In Arabic, Ṭabari III, p. 371, we have the spelling **ʾzdʾd;** in Syriac (Assemani III, 226; cf. Justi, p. 149), **yzydʾd,** both for Yazed-dād. The spelling **yzyd** for Ized occurs also in early Judaeo-Persian, cf. in the Dandan-uiliq letter, Utas 1968.

For the haplography of the *dalet* one may refer also to the name **ʾyzdwk**=Izad-dukh in our Bowl 11. It is quite likely that **myrdwk** in Montgomery 1913, p. 152, is not Mithra-dukh, as stated there, but

Bowl 5

Israel Museum, No. 80.1.1

Plate 21

(1) [ב](ש)מך אני עושה הדין קמיעא דיהי לה לאסו להדין לאסקופת (ביתה) [.......]
(2) (וכל קנין דאית) לה כפתינון לכיפי ארעה ואסרתינון לרזי (רקי)עא כבשתינון
[.........] (3) [... כפ]תינון אסרתינון כבשתינון {כל} לכל שידי ומזיקי כולהון דאית בה
בעלמא בן דכר ובן נקבא (מרבר)[בי]הון ועד (4) דערדקיהון מעולימיהון ועד סביהון
בין דידענא שמה בין דלא ידענא שמה כבר פירישו (לי) משבעה יומי
(5) בראשית ודלא פירישו לי משבעת יומי בראשית כבר פרישו לי בגיטא דאתה לכא
*מן[1] עיבר ימא דכתבו ושדרו לה לרבי יהושוע בר (6) פרחיה כד הות ההיא ליליתא
ד(ח)נקא לבני אינשה ושדר עלה יהושוע בר פרחיה שמתא ולא קבילת מחמת דלא הוא

[1] **mn:** written **bn.**

rather Merd-dukh, from the Iranian word *mard/merd* "man".

mḥzydwk br brzdwk, like **nny br qymtʾ**, share the peculiarity that the name of a woman is followed by **br,** and not by **bt.** The same confusion of genders occurs in Geniza 3:6,10.

qbny: The reading is uncertain. The name obtained could be compared to the widely attested name **kpny, kpnʾy.** Both our **qbny** and **kpn(ʾ)y** might be variant forms derived from a noun meaning "small, little", like the Aramaic name Zuṭra and similar names. Kabnay could be derived from Old Iranian *kamna-,* cf. Bartholomae 1904, col. 440. This old Iranian element has been used by Benveniste 1966, pp. 85 f. for explaining the Elamite forms Kamnakka, Kampiya, though the explanation has not been widely accepted (cf. Gershevitch 1969, p. 198, and Mayrhofer 1973, pp. 174 f.). A Middle Persian name which may belong here occurs on the Paris seal 3.31, where the reading is uncertain. Cf. Gignoux 1978, p. 30.

Bowl 5

Translation

(1) [By] your name I make this amulet that it may be a healing to this one, for the threshold (of the house... (2) and any possession which) he has. I bind the rocks of the earth, and tie down the mysteries of heaven, I suppress them... (3) I rope, tie and suppress all demons and harmful spirits, all those which are in the world, whether masculine or feminine, from their big ones to (4) their young ones, from their children to their old ones, whether I know his name or I do not know it. In case I do not know the name, it has already been explained to me at the time of the seven days of (5) creation. What has not been disclosed to me at the time of the seven days of creation was disclosed to me in the deed of divorce that came here from across the sea, which was written and sent to Rabbi Yehoshuaʿ bar (6) Peraḥya. Just as there was a lilith who strangled human beings, and Rabbi Yehoshuaʿ bar Peraḥya sent a ban against her, but she did not accept it because he did not know her name; and her

דידע שמה וכתבו שמה (7) בגיטא וכריזו עלה ברקיעא בגיטא דאתא לכא מן עיבר
ימא אף אתון כיפיתון אסיריתון כבישתון כולכון תחות כיפי רגלה דהדין מרנקא בר
קלא בשום (8) גבריאל גבר תקיף דקטל כל גיברי כולהון (ד)נצחין בקרבא ובשום
יהו(אל) דסתם פום כל גי(ב)[רי כ]להון בשום יה יה יה צבאות אמן אמן סלה

This is one of a group of three bowls donated recently to the Israel Museum by members of the family of the late Mr. Alqanayan, a collector and businessman in Iran, executed by the revolutionary regime of Khomeini on the charge of supporting the State of Israel. Bowls 5–7 in the present publication are from the Alqanayan collection. Bowl No. 5 contains eight lines of inscription written spirally from the centre. The text is quite close to that of Montgomery 1913, Nos. 8 and 17, where the sage Yehoshuaʿ bar Peraḥya is also mentioned as having issued a letter of divorce to the demons.

1 For the reading of the opening formula compare for example Wohlstein 1894, p. 27 (No. 2426, line 1): **mšmk ʾny ʿwšʾ hdyn ʾswtʾ nṭrtʾ *wqywmtʾ,**[2] "By your name I do this healing, protection and preservation". Wohlstein's formula may be compared in its turn to a Syriac incantation first published by Montgomery 1917/18, and again by Hamilton 1971, p. 99a: **mzmn hnʾ qmtyh** (for ***qywmth**?) **kbšʾ wʾswrʾ wḥtmtʾ wnṭrtʾ dbytʾ dyly ...** "Designated is this preservation (or 'oath'), spell and bond and sealing and protection of my house ..."

For our opening formula compare also Wohlstein 1893, p. 328 (No. 2422, line 1): **byšmk ʾny ʿwšh ʾswtʾ mn šmyh l...**, and Gordon 1941, p. 119 (2:1): **lyšmwk ʾny ʿwšh ʾswtʾ mn šmyʾ tyhwy l ...** "By your name I do (this amulet). May there be healing from heaven for ...". In

[2] Wohlstein read this **wḥyy mtʾ**. Our emendation is conjectural without seeing the original. **qywmtʾ**, like **ʾswtʾ** and **nṭrtʾ**, may refer to the amulet or incantation itself. In that case we may translate it by 'oath', cf. Jastrow, p. 1356. For **qaiamta** "Festigung" in Mandaic cf. Lidzbarski 1920, p. XXIV.

name was written (7) in the deed of divorce and an announcement was made against her in heaven by a deed of divorce that came here from across the sea; so you too are roped, tied and suppressed, all of you under the feet of this Marnaqa son of Qala. In the name of (8) Gabriel, the mighty hero, who kills all heroes who are victorious in battle, and in the name of Yeho'el who shuts the mouth of all [heroes]. In the name of Yah, Yah, Yah, Sabaoth. Amen, Amen, Selah.

Montgomery 1913, p. 183 (14:1) we have the enlarged formula: **byšmk ᵓny ᶜwšh yhwh ᵓylhᵓ rbᵓ hdyn ksᵓ nyhwy lḥtmtᵓ l...**"By your name, YHWH the great God, I do this bowl. May it may be for the sealing of..."[3]

The absolute form **ᵓsw** is rare, though not unattested. Cf. Jeruzalmi 1963, p. 128 (5363:1–2): **dyn qmyᶜᵓ dyhwy lᵓsw l...**; and p. 141 (5366:1–3): **lyšmk ᵓny ᶜwšh hdyn ktbh yhwy lᵓsw lbyth dkwrkšyd**[4] **lh wlᵓtth**[5] **wbnh...**"By your name I do this writing . May it be for healing to the house of Xwarxšēd, to him and to his wife and son...".

2 The phrase **kptynwn lkypy ᵓrᶜh** corresponds to an incantation text on a printed amulet (Warsaw 1867; Fig. 21 on p. 133), where we have עינא דכל עיינין בישין אתכפיין ואתטמרין מן קדמוהי גו כיפין. A similar text occurs in Hanauer 1907, pp. 318 ff. Cf. also in a Mandaean magic text **arbikuk uširiuk ᶜl kipia d̲prat udiglat** (Drower 1937, p. 593, after line 190) "They have made you kneel and set you on the banks of the Euphrates and the Tigris". It is doubtful whether the phrase **kypy hqšt** (Odeberg 1928, Hebrew text, p. 36, ch. 22c:4, 6, 7) has anything to do with our text. The most likely interpretation for our **kypy** is that it is connected

[3] Isbell 1975, p. 39, is right in saying that there is no need to supplement **hdyn ksᵓ** before the first word of the formula, as is done by Montgomery.

[4] This proper name should be read thus, viz. Xwarxšēd, meaning in Middle Persian "Sun" (cf. NPers. *xuršīd*), with the preservation of the cluster **-xš-** in the compound. The same name occurs also, unrecognized, in Gordon 1941, p. 342 (British Museum 91776): **ᵓnᵓ hw *kwrkšyd gwšns br dwstᵓy...** The name was transliteated by the editor **kwrbšyd.**

[5] The last two words were not read correctly by Jeruzalmi and Isbell 1975, No. 70:3.

with the Aramaic word for "rock, stone". A play on the similarity of the sounds of the verb **KPT** and the noun **kypy** may have been intended. The difficulty of the translation is caused mainly by the fact that "the stones of the earth" does not give a very good parallel in sense to "the secrets of heaven". In line 7 **kypy rglh** is apparently a different word.

4 **dʿrdqyhwn** has a parasitic *ʿayin,* which is of quite frequent occurrence in Babylonian Aramaic. Cf. e.g. **kʿkʾ** from Persian *kāk,* for which cf. Fraenkel 1886, p. 35. This phenomenon may well be the reverse counterpart of the frequent loss of *ʿayin* in Babylonian Aramaic, for which cf. Rossell 1953, p. 17; Epstein 1960, p. 18. The particular form of **dʿrdq** is however better explained as a contamination of two attested forms of the word, **drdq** and **dʿdq,** both connected with an original form **dqdq,** cf. Syriac *daqdqā.*

For the formula **byn...byn** cf. in Gordon 1941, p. 125: **bn dmyštdryn wbn dlʾ mštdryn.**

5 **mšbʿt ywmy brʾšyt:** A frequent Hebrew idiom, though usually the formula is **mššt ymy brʾšyt** "from the six days of creation", e.g. Bavli Ketubbot 8b, and so it is in Montgomery 1913, p. 170 (11:9): **mn ywmy ʿlmʾ wmyššt** (!) **ymy brʾšyt.** The Mandaean parallel adduced by Montgomery, ibid. from Lidzbarski 1902, p. 104, has: **mršʿšat šit iumia brišit** "vom Uranfange an, seit den sechs Tagen des Uranfanges".

On the *geṭ* formula in incantation texts cf. Montgomery 1913, pp. 159, 179; Gordon 1934, p. 469; Levine 1970, pp. 348 f. The deed of divorce which comes "from across the sea" **(mʿbr ymʾ,** or **mn ʿybr ymʾ)** occurs in Montgomery 1913, Nos. 8 and 17, in both cases associated with Joshua b. Peraḥya.

For Joshua b. Peraḥya cf. Montgomery 1913, pp. 226 ff. Joshua b. Peraḥya occurs in fragments of the Jesus story published by Krauss 1911a (correcting Adler 1911), and further in the fragment recently published by Falk 1978; cf. also Boyarin 1978. A late Kabbala fragment also refers to the role of Joshua b. Peraḥya in the Jesus story; cf. Krauss 1911b.

6 **hhyʾ lylytʾ dḥnqʾ lbny ʾynšh:** Cf. the Mandaean text in Lidzbarski 1902, p. 102: **lilita...diatba bbaiṯ ubʿsqupta dbaiṯ ḏ...uma[hi]a ugaṭla ušaqpa uhanqa dardqia udardqata.** Parallels to this are conveniently given in Gordon 1934, p. 468. Amulet 15 and Bowl 12 provide further examples for the demon who kills children.

The feature which occurs in this incantation for the first time is that the ban imposed by Joshua b. Peraḥya was at first invalid because he did not know the name of that lilith, and only afterwards her name was written in the *geṭ*. In Montgomery 1913, Nos. 8, 11 and 17, the full parentage of the lilith is specified, as is legally appropriate.

mḥmt dlʾ hwʾ dydʿ šmh: In **dydʿ** the first letter seems to be superfluous. The phrase may alternatively be translated "because there was no one (read: **dlʾ hwʾ** <**mn**>) who knew her name".

7 **kypytwn** stands for **kpytytwn**, passive participle plural masculine of *peʿal* + the subject suffix of the second person plural masc: **kpytyn + ʾtwn. kbyštwn** is written for **kbyšytwn.**

8 **bšwm gbryʾl gbr tqyp dqṭl kl gybry kwlhwn:** This phrase is reminiscent of Montgomery 1913, p. 127 (3:2–3) **wytrḥq mynyh dywʾ byšʾ wsṭnʾ byšʾ dmytqry ṣpʿsq ʾbdh gbrʾ dqṭyl gbrʾ mylwt ʾyttyh wʾyttʾ mylwt bʿlh...** "And may there depart from him the evil demon who is called **ṣpʿsq ʾbdh**, the hero who kills a man from the side of his wife and a wife from the side of her husband..." Montgomery reads *abbādā gabbārā* "the Mighty Destroyer", though the first word is nowhere attested in Aramaic. It seems possible that **ṣpʿsq ʾbdh**<**g**> are two names which follow the same principle: in both cases we have a sequence of letters from the alphabet, the first one in a reversed order, and with *qof* coming at the end and out of order. In the second case the *gimel* seems to have been omitted (perhaps by haplography with the following **gbr**). Thus we may reconstruct the two names as badly written for **qṣpʿs ʾbgdh.** Cf. Gaster 1896, p. IX, line 25 **ʾbgdhʾ**.

The play on the element *geber* in the name Gabriel occurs already in Daniel 8:15–16. The epithet *gĕbar taqqīf* (or *gibbār taqqīf*) may well be an etymological *midrash* on Gabriel, the two words rendering its two parts.

yhwʾl: The alternative reading of this name, **yḥyʾl**=Yeḥiʾel, proves upon inspection to give a non-existent name of an angel. Cf. Greenfield 1973, p. 156, n. 40 for a correction to Montgomery 1913, p. 207 (25:4). Cf. also Yo'el in Amulet 11:8 and in Shachar 1971, p. 289, No. 974 (a late amulet).

Bowl 6

Israel Museum, No. 80.1.2

Plate 22

(1) רזא רזא דנן לשתוקי ולסכורי פומה (2) דכל בני אינשה בישי ותקיפי דקימין
לקובליה דבריך יהביה בר (3) ממא שלם ליכי מדינתא דעמיה סגי סגי דלא ברינא לכון
ואנה רחימנא יתכון (4) וקרינא לכון גיבריה דארעה כמה דעינין לכון ולא חמתון
אודנין לכון ולא שמעיתון כן תיתנו לי (5) אבן מנכון {כון} לשתקא מיני אנה בריך
יהביה בר ממא {פ} פומה דכל בני אינשה דקימין לקובלי ופום (6) דדגושנסף בר
אימה והון גברי ואינשי ודרדקי ודרדוקתא דקימן לקובלי אנה בריך יהביה בר ממא
יהוון (7) אילמין בפומיהון סמן בעיניהון חרישין באודניהון אבילין בליביהון מריעין
ומבאשין חמשין שני יובלה שבע שני שמיטתא (8) תלתין יומי ירחא שבעה יומי
שבתא שבתא כסא וריש ירחא בשום חדריאל ושכניאל וביר ואבן ובור משבענא יתכון
משבענא (9) יתכון בישמיה ˹ד˺רבא ודחילא דתישתקון מן בריך יהביה בר ממא פומה
דכל בני אינשה כתבי סיפרי יתבי אקרי יתבי שוקי קרנתא וביריאתה (10) ונפקי
אורחתא ידבוק לישניהון בפומיהון ולא ימללון עלי מלל ביש בישמיה דאמר והוה
אמן אמן סלה

For the provenance of this bowl see Bowl 5.

1 **lštwqy wlskwry** are regular Babylonian Aramaic infinitive *pa‘‘el* forms. In line 5, however, we have **lštq'** in the same function.

2 For the name **bryk yhbyh br mm'** cf. the nearly identical name **bryk yhbyh br m'my** in Montgomery 1913, p. 209 (26:4). We have transcribed the first name as a composite: Bĕrik-Yehabyah. An alternative reading

Bowl 6

Translation

(1) Mystery. This mystery is for silencing and shutting the mouth (2) of all evil and violent people who stand against Bĕrik-Yehabya son of (3) Mama. Peace be on thee, a city whose population is very numerous, whom I have not created, and whom I love, (4) and whom I call the mighty of the earth. In the same way as you have eyes but do not see, as you have ears but do not hear, so shall you give me (5) a stone from you to silence from me, I, Bĕrik-Yehabya son of Mama, the mouth of all people who stand against me, as well as the mouth of (6) Dād-gušnasp son of his mother. And the men and women, boys and girls, who stand against me, I, Bĕrik-Yehabya son of Mama, may they be (7) mute in their mouths, blind in their eyes, deaf in their ears, mournful in their hearts, sick and corrupt, for the fifty years of the jubilee, for the seven years of the *šemiṭa,* for (8) the thirty days of the month, for the seven days of the week, on the Sabbath, the full moon, and the day of the new month.

In the name of Ḥadriel, *Šakniel,* the well, the stone, and the pit, I adjure you, I adjure (9) you, in the name of he who is great and frightful, that you may silence from Bĕrik-Yehabya son of Mama the mouth of all people who write books, who sit in forts(?), who sit in market places and in streets, (10) and who go out on the roads, so that their tongues should cleave to their mouths and that they should not speak evil words against me. In the name of He who commanded and it came into being. Amen, Amen, Selah.

may be to regard this name as analogous to the Syriac name Bĕrik-ṣebyānēh, who is attested as the father of Mar Abbā (cf. Chabot 1898, p. 313, note 1): "His will be blessed". In this case we may read Bĕrik-yĕhabēh and translate "His share/load be blessed".

Montgomery (op. cit.) conjectured that **yhbyh** is a way of writing the divine name **yhwh,** an appealing suggestion which lacks proof. It is true that there is a whole series of divine names such as **yhbyh** (Amulet

4:33; Stübe 1895, p. 22, line 15; Gaster 1896, p. IX line 16), **yhwbyhw** (Montgomery 1913, p. 146, No. 7:8), **yhwh byh** (Montgomery 1913, p. 178, 13:7), **byh byhy** (T–S K 23.3, line 5), **ʾl bʾl** (Amulet 11:9), but Montgomery himself makes the more acceptable suggestion that they reflect a phrase such as Yah-in-Yah. Our name could indeed be rendered "Blessed is Yah-in-Yah". It may be recalled that Psalms 68:5 gives God's name as **byh,** and this verse is quoted e.g. in the Geniza text T–S K 1.68, line 10; Montgomery 1913, p. 154 (8:12), if the reading in Isbell 1975, p. 44, is correct. The divine name **byh** is apparently also attested in Stübe 1895, p. 22 line 6: **mlʾkh dbyh.**

One may incidentally observe that Yah-b-yah is also associated with Bahaot, Abaho. which Scholem 1974, p. 421, has adduced in his attempt at explaining the gnostic name Ialdabaot as composed of Yaled-Abaot "Begetter of [S]abaoth"/"of Abaoth". We thus have **wbyšmyh dyhbyh bʾ(ḥʾwt) yhw yhw ʾlhy** (Stübe 1895, p. 22, lines 15 f.), paralleled by Montgomery 1913, p. 146 (7:8 f.): **bšwm yhw byhw wʾbhw rbh.** It is possible similarly to reconstruct in Gaster 1896, p. IX, line 16 **yh byh *byʾwṭ yh hwh,** by simply dividing the words differently. That this name was indeed the functional equivalent of Sabaot in Aramaic incantations can perhaps be shown by a quotation from a Geniza text: **ʾdwn byh byhy yh yw yhw bh ṣbʾ** ʾwt ... (T–S K 23.3, line 5). The conglomeration of names here also presents a sequence Yah-b-Yah(i)... **bh *ṣbʾwt.** Whatever the explanation which prevails for the first part of the compound Ialdabaot, Abaot or Baot can thus be shown to be attested in Semitic, and more explicitly in Jewish magical practice as well.

3 For the name Mammā "mother" cf. above, Commentary to Bowl 3, note 7.

The formula **šlm lyky mdyntʾ dʿmyh sgy sgy** is interesting and quite unusual. The idea is vaguely reminiscent of Jonah and the story of the gourd, where God says to Jonah (4:9): "Are you so angry over the gourd?" Jonah answers positively and God says: "You are sorry for the gourd, though you did not have the trouble of growing it.... And should not I be sorry for the great city of Nineveh, with its hundred and twenty thousand persons who cannot tell their right hand from their left, and cattle without number?" The statement that this is a city with many inhabitants and the further motif that the speaker did not create them are shared in both sources.

4 The term **gybryh dʾrʿh**, though reminiscent of Nimrod's epithet *gibbor bā-āreṣ* (Gen. 10:8), is quite curious. The epithet *gibbār(ā)* is sometimes used in the magic bowls for negative beings. We thus have **dywʾ byšʾ wsṭnʾ byšʾ dmytqry ... gbrʾ dqṭyl gbrʾ mylwt ʾyttyh ...** (Montgomery 1913, p. 127, No. 3:2 f.), and the rather ambiguous **dtmḥyn bṭwpry lybky wbmrnyth ... dqtrys *gybrʾ** ... (Gordon 1934c, p. 468, G:4), where the parallel texts describe this personage as having power over the demons (cf. the parallels printed by Gordon, loc. cit.). A series of "good" angels are described as **gbrʾ mlʾkh** (Gordon 1934b, p. 331, where Gordon's texts E and F are printed in juxtaposition with the bowl published by Hyvernat).

In our text the status of the beings addressed as *gibbārayyā d-arʿā* or with the pronominal suffix: *gibbārah d-arʿā*, is also quite ambiguous, though their support is sought.

The phrase "you have eyes but do not see, ears but do not hear" is reminiscent of Ps. 115:4–6.

6 **ʾymh** is written with a different stylus, and was probably added later. If our translation "Dād-Gušnasp son of his mother" is correct, it may be surmised that the writer's first intention was to adhere to the formula of quoting the mother's name in an incantation; but since Dād-Gušnasp is an adversary who is being cursed, it was not possible to enquire his mother's name of him, and so the vague formula "his mother" was subsequently added. An alternative reading would be to regard **ʾymh** as a proper name Imma; see above Commentary to Bowl 3:1 and note 7 there.

hwn is act. part. m. pl.; cf. Morag 1973, pp. 68–70.

6–7 **yhwwn ʾylmyn bpwmyhwn smn bʿynyhwn** etc.: Cf. **skyryn pwmhwn ... wʿwryn ʿynyhwn wmṭršn ʾwdnyhwn** (Gordon 1941, p. 124, No. 6:1; also Isbell 1975, p. 102; earlier published in Schwab 1886, and in Schwab 1890, pp. 331 ff.).

7–8 The sequence of time designations has a number of parallels in the magic texts. Cf. Gaster 1896, p. XXVI, lines 15 f.; Montgomery 1913, p. 141 (6:5–6).

ksʾ wryš yrḥʾ: The present context makes it clear, by the contrast of **ksʾ** with **ryš yrḥʾ**, that the first term means "full moon", as it indeed does in the Bible and in Syriac. On the other hand, the Rabbinic explanation of the term, in connection with its use for the New Year, associates it with the new moon; cf. *Encyclopaedia Biblica,* IV, col. 216, s.v. *kese;* III, col. 35–41, s.v. *ḥodeš*. It may be remarked that *šabbĕta* could also be argued to belong to the same category as *kese* and *reš yarḥā* as its original Babylonian meaning was "the full moon" (cf. *Encyclopaedia Biblica,* VII, col. 511, s.v. *šabbāt*). At this historical stage, and in the present context, this explanation would seem to be very far-fetched.

Ḥadriel seems to be attested once in the bowls, in Stübe 1895, p. 22, line 6. The name is also mentioned in *Sefer ha-razim,* p. 81 (2:12). For further references cf. Schwab 1897, p. 109; Margaliot 1945, pp. 50 f.

Šakniel is not hitherto attested in the bowls. His name occurs in *Sefer ha-razim,* p. 75 (1:152), and in Kabbalistic literature (cf. Margaliot 1945, p. 194).

wbyr wʾbn wbwr: This sequence of words, with evident magic meaning, is not clear. The second word could possibly be read **wʾkn,** perhaps for Jewish Aramaic **ʿkn, ḥk(y)nʾ** "snake". If this is correct, the phrase could have something to do with the famous theme of the *ḥuldā*

Bowl 7

Israel Museum, No. 80.1.3

Plate 23

(1) מזמנא הדא מילתא על שמיה <ד>מארוי בר (2) באתאי דמיתקרי אבאבאי בר {ר}
אבדימי וכל שמן (3) דאית ליה קרי קרי בעלמא קריא בישא ואכליא קרי ליה דקירית
(4) אישתא בכיריתא ואישתא מן מרירת קברין ומן אמיתא נפקת (5) שחוטין ושגרין
עימו שיר חצוצר פעל בן לא איתכי אובלתיכי ושלחתיכי ושדרתיכי (6) ושגרתיכי
<על> מארוי בר באתאי על כל בלתי לא שמיה ולא תידחלי מצוח פולי עלוהי (7)
כמיפל חיסיא מן טורא כמיפל חיסיא מן טור טורא ויכמבסק גובתא מן דיחלא

and the *bōr,* the two objects certain people believe in (cf. Bavli Taʿanit 8a). The elaboration on this theme, according to which they are to constitute two mute witnesses to a betrothal, is set forth in commentaries on the text. Cf. *Oṣar ha-Geʾonim,* Taʿanit, Perušim, p. 57 (reference kindly supplied by Prof. M.D. Herr).

9 **rbʾ wdḥylʾ:** Cf. Commentary to Amulet 1:8.

dtyštqwn: The verb, to be vocalized *d-tĕšattĕqūn,* is evidently in the *paʿʿel* form.

ʾqry is taken here to be the plural of **ʾqrʾ** "fortress", with the omission of the preposition **b-.** Otherwise it could be connected to **qrytʾ** "town, village".

ytby šwqy qrntʾ is reminiscent of the expression *yošḇē qrānōt;* in our bowl we may have two separate expressions: **ytby šwqy** and **ytby qrntʾ**, which have merged. Cf also Harviainen 1981, p. 5, line 7: **lyḥš dqrntʾ.**

10 **ydbwq** Cf. Ps. 137:6 תדבק לשוני לחכי

Bowl 7

Translation

(1) Appointed is this incantation against (?) the name [of] Maroy son of (2) Batay, who is called Ababay son of Abdimi and all (other) names (3) that he possesses. There has happened, has happened, in the world an evil accident and a perdition(?). There has happened to him that the fire (4) has happened in the ditch and the fire came out of the bitterness of tombs and from the darkness.

(5) **šḥwṭyn wšgryn ʿymw šyr ḥṣwṣr pʿl bn lʾ**

I have brought you, I have led you and I have sent you and I have dispatched you (6) and I have conveyed you [against] Maroy son of Batay [and] against every unnamed Belti.

Do not be afraid to shout. Fall upon him (7) as rocks fall from the mountain, as rocks fall from a high mountain, and as the hill rises from that which is sand (?), and as the sun shines (down) unto (8) the earth.

ויכמדנח שימשא עד (8) {אר} ארעה פולי עלוהי איכולי מן בישריה ואישתאי מן דמיה
דחלי ומררי בשום דיליד ומידחלא עיש אליון (9) כד עבד אישתא וינרג לא שמיה אמן
אמן עלתר

For the provenance of this bowl see Bowl 5.

1 **ʿl šmyh** has been translated as "against the name of", taking Maroy bar Batay to be the adversary. This assumption entails the hypothesis that **ʿl** was inadvertently omitted by the scribe before the name Maroy in line 6, but this is quite uncertain, as are many other points in this rather obscure text. It must be emphasized that we regard certain portions in the translation of this text as mere guesswork. A case could also be made for taking Maroy bar Batay as the client, for whose protection the bowl was wrtiten.

2 Abdimi is known as the name of several Palestinian Amoraim. The *resh* which is written before the name is pure dittography for the final letter of *bar.* The abbreviation *resh* for *rabbi* is never attested in this period.

šmn is a short form for the regular **šmhn,** the absolute plural form.

3 The translation "perdition" for **ʾklyʾ** assumes that it is related to Hebrew *kělāyā.* The phrase **qry qry** etc. contains several ambiguities, which may have possibly been intended as puns. An alternative translation could be: "There has been called, called, in the world an evil call and cry". **ʾklyʾ** may be associated with **ʾklywtʾ**, which in the Targum of Psalms 104:7 renders *raʿam,* and in the Targum of Job 4:10 stands for *šaʾăgā.* Cf. Tal 1975, p. 91, s.v. **ʾkly.**

qyryt is probably the orthography for *qeryat.* Cf. Epstein 1960, p. 95 and note 254, where the Mandaean form **myṭyʾt** is quoted.

4 **kyrytʾ** could mean, following the meanings of Jewish Babylonian Aramaic **kyrh** or **kryʾ**, either "digging, ditch"; "heap, pile"; or "circle, banquet". The most likely translation may, however, be "a stove", which is only attested in Hebrew.

ʾmytʾ seems to stand for **ʾmyṭtʾ** or **ʿmyṭtʾ** ; cf. Syriac **ʿMṬ**. The image of fire coming out of darkness is quite unusual.

Fall upon him, eat from his flesh, drink from his blood, frighten and afflict.

In the name of he who gives birth and frightens, **ʿyš ʾlywn,** (9) while he makes fire, and the unnamed Nereg. Amen, Amen. Immediately.

5 **šḥwṭyn wšgryn** etc. constitutes a strange sequence of words, which we are unable to translate. The first two could be from the verbs **ŠḤṬ** "to stretch; corrupt (as in Syriac); slay an animal", and **ŠGR** "to flow; run; heat, kindle; send".

ʾytky is evidently for **ʾytytyky.** The accusative in this and the following verbs refers to a feminine object, apparently the fire.

6 "The unnamed Belti" is an unusual appellation, but it corresponds in this text to "the unnamed Nereg" in line 9. In both cases, although the combination **lʾ šmyh** is not usual for this kind of expression, there seems to exist hardly a different alternative for translation. On Belti one may refer to Lidzbarski 1916, p. 1217; Février 1931, pp. 64 f.; Du Mesnil du Buisson 1962, pp. 359 f., where (p. 360) it is stated that Belti is not a genuine name: "Le 'vrai nom' de la *Bēltī* à Palmyre est Atargatıs ou Astarté". Since Belti is not the "real name", it is possible to understand how an "unnamed Belti" could be alluded to. In a Jewish context of magic we have Belti Adonay in Gaster 1896, p. VIII, line 20.

wlʾ tydḥly mṣwḥ: The last word is the absolute infinitive of *peʿal.*

7 **kmypl ḥysyʾ mn ṭwrʾ:** A parallel expression in Gaster 1896, p. XVIII, lines 27 f., clarifies the phrase. It says: **wʾm npl ʿlk ḥysyʾ ʾw mplh wʾt tḥwtyh.** Gaster's translation (op. cit., p. 188), "If any burden or weight falls upon thee", is inaccurate. The term *mappālā* is certainly to be connected with Hebrew *mappolet* "falling in, debris" (cf. Jastrow, p. 820). **ḥysyʾ**, as can be seen from the bowl text published here, must mean stones or rocks. Gaster's text might be translated: "If rocks or debris fall on you and you are buried underneath".

ṭwr ṭwrʾ is an expression which imitates *hor hahār* in Hebrew.

wykmbsq may be an error for **mnsq,** or **mysq,** the infinitive of **SLQ.**

For **gwbtʾ** cf. Jewish Babylonian Aramaic **gwbbtʾ, gwpptʾ** etc. The word **gwbtʾ** could also possibly mean "pit", like **gwbʾ**, but its connection in the sentence would then be obscure.

mn dyḥl': On the face of it, one would be tempted to translate here "out of fear", but this would make little sense in the context. We have read **dyḥl'** as containing the relative **d-+ḥl'** ("sand"). By a slight emendation one may suggest reading **by ḥl(t)'** as in B. Shabbat 110a. The phrase would then mean "as the dunes arise from among the sand(s)".

wykmdnḥ šymš' ʿd 'rʿh: One would have expected **ʿl** instead of **ʿd.**

8 "Eat from his flesh" etc.: The idea is not uncommon in incantation

Bowl 8

Israel Museum, No. 69.20.265

Plate 24

I

1 (אס)[רין]
2 שי[דין]
3 (ו)חתמ[י]ן
4 דיוין אסרין
5 פתכריה חת(מן)
6 לילתה בישתא
7 דכר ונוקבה אסרא

II

1 אסריא
2 עינא
3 בישתא מן
4 ביתה דכודאי
5 בר פאלי מן
6 יומא ד[נן ול]עלם
7 אס[ריא עינ]א

III

1 אסריא
2 עינא
3 בישתא
4 מן ביתה
5 דכודאי {ד}בר
6 פאלי מן [בי]תה
7 ומן ב[..]ה (ו)מן

IV

1 אדור
2 אדורדו
3 ומן אדורדו(ך)
4 ומן בניה מן
5 יומא [ד]נן ועד
6 לעלם אמן אמן
7 סלה

texts, cf. Naveh 1975, pp. 48 (lines 18–22), 51.

ylyd is apparently active participle of *peʿal* and **wmydḥlʾ** is presumably active participle *paʿʿel.*

ʿyš ʾlywn looks like a corrupted spelling of Hebrew *īš ʿelyōn.*

9 **ʿltr** presents a form closer to *ʿal-atar* than the usual Jewish Babylonian Aramaic *l-altar.* Compare Geniza 2, p. 2:13, **bpryʿ**, which also occurs at the end of a magic text, after "Amen, Amen".

Bowl 8

Translation

I

Bound are the demons, sealed are the dēvs, bound are the idol-spirits, sealed are the evil liliths, male and female, bound

II

bound is the evil eye away from the house of Khwadāy son of Pālī from this day to eternity. Bound is the evil eye

III

Bound is the evil eye from the house of Khwadāy son of Pālī, from his house and from his..., (and) from

IV

...and from Ādur-dukh and from her sons from this day to eternity. Amen, Amen, Selah.

This bowl was first published by Narqis 1935, with some notes added by the editor of *Tarbiz* at the time, J.N. Epstein. It is here published again so as to complete the collection of magic bowls in Jerusalem, and because the first publication, done in Hebrew, is not easily available to all interested scholars. The present reading contains a number of improvements on the *editio princeps.* It is noteworthy that this text, together with several others (e.g. those published in Stübe 1895), are not included in Isbell 1975, which purports to be "a collection of all the published Aramaic bowls" (p. ix).

The present bowl is remarkable for its arrangement. Instead of circular lines running spirally from the inside or from the rim, as is the usual practice of the magic bowls , this one is divided into four quarters or sections by two lines which go through the centre and form a cross. The incantation goes from top to bottom in each quarter, and from right to left, quarter by quarter. Each quarter contains seven lines. The bottom of each quarter, except the last one, contains the beginning of the next. This principle was partly recognized by Narqis, but he did not

Bowl 9

Formerly in the possession of V. Barakat, Jerusalem

Plate 25

Within the central circle:

(1) אחיד פכר צמר ואקים ג(ב)יה וסריח וכוכבי ומזלי

Outside the circle:

(2) וכל (קיה) ורריה דיהודה בר נני דנ(י)בש לישנה בפומיה ויתמסי רוקיה (3)
בגרגרתיה ויבשון שקיה וגופריתא ואישתא תידלק ביה וילקו גופיה ב(כו)י(א)
ויסת̣(כר) ויתנכיר (4) ויתעכר לעיני כל חזוהי וישתמת ויתבר וי(בד) וישתצי וימגר
וימות ותיתי עליה שלהוביתא מן שמיא (5) וזיעא יחוד יתיה ותברא ידבקיה ומזופיתא

notice that it applies also to the connection between III and IV. At the beginning of IV two failed attempts were made to write the continuation of the inscription, and only line 3 contains the proper text.

II,1 **ʾsryʾ**: This spelling for **ʾsyrʾ** is repeated in III,1.

II,4 The Persian name Khwadāy "Lord" is quite well attested. Cf. Gignoux 1979, p. 59.

II,5 Pālī is not so far attested to our knowledge in this form, but it could be assumed to belong to the Iranian name Pahray (cf. Gignoux 1979, p. 65); or perhaps to Pālīz "Paradise" (cf. Justi 1895, p. 240, s.v. Pālīzbān).

IV, 3 As noted above, this line continues line III,7, while the lines IV,1–2 may be disregarded as containing unsuccessful attempts. The final letter is almost without doubt *kaf*. The name Ādurdukh, which is quite well attested, is explained by Gignoux 1979, p. 76, as "Daughter of Ādur".

Bowl 9

Translation

(1)...and stars and planets

(2) and all the vomit(?) and spittle of Judah son of Nanay, that his tongue may dry up in his mouth, that his spittle may dissolve (3) in his throat, that his legs may dry, that sulphur and fire may burn in him, that his body may be struck by scalding(?), that he may be choked, become estranged, (4) become disturbed to the eyes of all those who see him, and that he may be banned, broken, lost, finished, vanquished, and that he

תידלוק בי(א) ויתקים עליה קראה דכתיב יפלו ולא י(ק)ומו ו(אל) תהה תקומא (6)
למפלתא ולא תהא אסותה למחתם תיחשכנא עיניהם מיראות ומותניהם תמיד המעט
תה טירתם לשמה ואו(הליה)ם אל יהי יושיב ויתקים (7) עליה קראה דכתיב וחרה אפי
והרגתי איתכם בחרב והיו נשיכם אלמנות ו[בני]כם יתומים ותקים עליה על יהודה בר
נני יככה ייי בשחפת ובקדחת (8) ובדלקת ובחרחור ובחרב ובשידפון וב[ירקון]
ורדפוך [עד אוב]דך יככה ייי [בשחין ר]ע על הברכים ועל השוקים אשר לא {יו} יוכל
להירפי מיכ(ף ר)גלך ועד (9) קודקודך [יכ]כה ייי בשיגעון ובעיורון וב[תמהון לבב
ו]אכלתם ב[שר בני]כם וב[שר בנ]ותיכם תוכילו בלועיה דיהודה בר נני לא יבלע
[וג]רגרתיה [ל]א תכול אסכרא (10) יפול ליה על חינכוהי ואכפיא יפול ליה [על פומיה
ועל לישניה ...] ויתַ[קים על]יה קראה דכתיב ויראו גוים ויבושו מיכל גבו[רתם יש]ימו
י[ד על (11) פ]ה ואוזניהם תחרשנה ילחכו [עפר] כנחש כזוח(לי) ארץ [ירגזו]
מימסגרותיהם (ו)לא י[אבה] ייי (סלוח לו) כי אז יעישן אף ייי *וקנאתו באיש ההוא
ו[רבצה בו כל האלה הכתובה] (12) בסיפר הז[ה ומחה] ייי את שמו מיתחת השמים
כין יתמיח שמיה דיהודה בר נני ויתעק[ר דוכרניה] מן עלמה כמא דאיתמחי שמיה
ד[עמלק (?) ...] (13) יתכבשו (ה)דמאיהוא ועב(י)ד ביה (ויתא) דינא את(ה
ו)פורענותא בעגלה בשיחנה בשיחלה בג(רב)א בקלמתא בשחרתא ובירויתא ובכלמתא
[...] (14) [...]יא ליסטא וסט(נ)ה ובשום שש(ערב) מלאכה ובשום מות וירוד ואנהיד
ואיסטר טורא ושתיוי (ור)וחא דשריא בית קברי (כו)להון יסמכו עלוהי על יהו[דה בר
נני ...]

may die, and that a flame may come upon him from heaven, (5) and shiver seize him, and a fracture catch him, and a rebuke burn in him. May the following verse apply to him: they shall fall and not arise, and there will be no power for them to stand up (6) after their defeat, and there will be no healing to their affliction. "Their eyes will darken, so that they see not, and their loins will be made by you continually to shake" (Ps. 69:24). "Let their habitation be desolate, and let none dwell in their tents" (Ps. 69:26). May the following verse (7) apply to him: "And my wrath shall wax hot, and I will kill you with the sword, and your wives shall be widows and your children fatherless" (Ex. 22:23). And the following may apply to Judah son of Nanay: "The Lord shall smite you with a consumption and with a fever (8) and with an inflammation and with an extreme burning and with the sword and with blasting and with [mildew] and they shall pursue you [until you per]ish" (Deut. 28:22). "The Lord shall smite you in the knees and in the legs with a fes[tering eruption] that cannot be healed from the sole of your foot on to (9) the top of your head" (Deut. 28:35). "The Lord shall smite you with madness and blindness and astonishment of heart" (Deut. 28:28). "And you shall eat the fl[esh of your s]ons and the fl[esh of your d]aughters" (Lev. 26:29). The throat of Judah son of Nanay shall not swallow and his gullet shall not eat, choking (10) shall fall on his palate, and paralysis shall fall on [his mouth and tongue...]. The following verse will apply to him: "The nations shall see and be confounded at all their might. They shall lay their h[and on (11) their mou]th, their ears shall be deaf, they shall lick [the dust] like a serpent, [they shall move] out of their holes like worms of the earth" (Micah 7:16–17). "The Lord will not spare him but then the anger of the Lord and his jealousy shall smoke against that man and [all the curses that are written in this] book [shall lie upon him] (12) and the Lord shall blot out his name from under heaven" (Deut. 29:19). So shall the name of Judah son of Nanay be blotted out and [his memory] shall be uprooted from the world, just as was blotted out the name of [Amalek(?)]...(13) may his members be pressed down and may there be done to him (?), judgement will come, omen and misfortune swiftly, with an inflammation, a purulence, an itch, a vermin, a blackening, a shiver, a vermin...(14)...a pirate and a satan. And in the name of **šš'rb** the angel, and in the name of Mot and Yarod and Anahid and Istar Tura and ... and the spirit which resides in the cemetery, all should lean on Jud[ah son of Nanay...]

This bowl is remarkable for the fact that it contains a text which is totally dedicated to cursing a specifically named individual. In this it would join Bowl 7, if our interpretation of that ambiguous text is correct. It is also unusually rich in biblical allusions and direct quotations, and in various terms for diseases and ailments. In the centre is the drawing of a full human figure, surrounded by a circle within which is a short inscription, which for the most part is unintelligible, though it can be quite easily transcribed.

This bowl, like Bowl 1, was at the time of writing in the possession of Victor Barakat. Mr. Barakat could only say of this bowl that it came from a private collection, and that the unnamed collector had told him that it derived from the Bethany area, in the vicinity of Jerusalem. We regard this attribution with scepticism, as the bowl strikes us as belonging basically with the other Mesopotamian bowls.

1 The first words seem to be a corruption of **ʾsyr pkyr ṣmyd**; cf. e.g. the sequence in Harviainen 1981, p. 5:4 **gzyryn ḥrymyn wmšmtyn ʾsyryn pkyryn wṣmydyn.**

2 **qyh:** If the reading is correct, this would be the first attestation of the noun for "vomit" in any form of Aramaic. It is of course well attested in Hebrew and Arabic.

dnybš is in the third person imperfect masculine *peʿal.* Inconsistency as to gender is very common in these texts.

The series of curses here can be compared to Geniza T–S AS 142.214, lines 18f.: ותהי נא עורון בעיניהם וסתום וחתום פיהם קצץ רגליהם...

3–4 **wystkr wytnkyr wytʿkr:** A rhyming sequence of verbs.

5 **qrʾh dktyb:** The following is an inacccurate reference to Jer. 8:4 and Amos 8:14.

wʾl thh tqwmʾ: A paraphrase of Lev. 26:37.

6 **lmḥtm** (like **ʾswtʾ**) is an Aramaic word used in the Hebrew phrase with a Hebrew suffix. The writer may have identified the Aramaic word **mḥtʾ** with the Hebrew *mákkā*, as in Jer. 30:17 וממכותיך ארפאך. The same connection of **mḥtʾ** with **ʾswtʾ** occurs in Montgomery 1913, No. 16:6, **mḥtʾ tḥwt ʾswtʾ.**

hmʿṭ is an error for *hamʿad.*

9 **blwʿyh,** which parallels **grgrtyh,** evidently means "his throat", though **blwʿʾ** is so far unattested in this sense in Aramaic. It seems hardly likely that we have here **b+lwʿ** "jaw".

ʾskrʾ also occurs as a name for a demon in late Jewish sources; cf. R. Margaliot 1945, p. 208. As a term for a situation of distress, together with **nkph,** the equivalent of our **ʾkpyʾ,** we have it in a late Jewish amulet published by Casanowicz 1917, p. 53: ....ומכל מראים (!) בישין ומנכפה ...ומאסכרה. Similarly Nash 1906: ...ממתה משונה ומחולה הנפל בר מינך ...ומחלה הנכפה. Cf. also Gaster 1896, p. XII, line 35 **lʾskrtʾ** (written **lʾsbrtʾ**); Shachar 1971, p. 286, No. 966.

For **ʾkpyʾ** cf. the Commentary on **ʾskrʾ.**

11 ***wqnʾtw** written in the bowl **zqnʾtw.**

12 **ytmyḥ** error for **ytmḥy.**

13 **hdmʾyhwʾ** is seemingly written in the bowl **qdmʾyhwʾ.**

bʿglh: The sequence would have favoured here a word designating some disease or misfortune.

bšyḥnh: Cf. Gaster 1896, p. XIII, line 16 **lšyḥnh;** Gollancz 1912, p. 3, § 5 **ʾsyryn šḥnʾ wmwtnʾ wqws...**

For **šyḥlh** cf. Gen. Apocryphon **rwḥ šḥlnyʾ** and the commentary by Fitzmyer 1971, p. 136.

qlmtʾ: This is the word used by Onqelos to translate Hebrew *kinnim* in Ex. 8:12.

šḥrtʾ: In the same amulet, quoted above (Casanowicz 1917, p. 53), we also have ... ומחולי שחורה ...

rwytʾ: This may be a syncopated form of **ʿrwytʾ**; cf. Commentary to Amulet 2:2.

klmth: This seems to be a mere orthographic variant of **qlmtʾ.**

14 **wbšwm šš(ʿrb) mlʾkh:** One is reminded of various names made up with **šš...** as the first element. Cf. Montgomery 1913, p. 223 (31:17), where one should correct to read as follows: **mrmrʾwt ššqpwt ʾstr mwth.** Cf. also Amulet 7:9–10 **ššqwpwt...swsgwn brprwngs ʾsṭr...**

wrwḥʾ dšryʾ byt qbry: Cf. *Sefer ha-razim,* p. 76 (I:178): רוח קריפורייא החונה בין הקברות. **byt** could possibly mean "among", as in Syriac.

Bowl 10

Syriac
Jewish Historical Museum, Belgrade, No. 243
Plate 26

(3) [ ] שי̈דא ודיו̈א [(4)] חלמ̈א דליליא וחיזונ̈א דעממא מן
חפ[(5) בעי]ריה וביתיה דברימא ב(ר עזדנדוך) בשום צבאותי צבאותי
חיא וקימא בשו[ם ... ב]שום יה יהו בשום הא היהן הא [ ]ן דתיתון (6) ותיבדון
ל(י)ה אסיותא לפגריה דברע(מ)[א בר עזדנד](וך) {ולבנה} ולבניה ולב[נתיה] דעית ליה
[ודניון ליה] (ו)ניתנטר (7) חדא ברשפתא בר אחתבו וניתנטר חדא נט[רוי ...] בר
רביתא וחדא מטריא בר קימתא לביתיה ול(נשׂא ביתיה) לקיניניה ולבעריה (8) ולפגריה
דיליה דברימא בר (ע)[זדנדוך ...] בשום מריא רבא וק[די]שא פרחו ופוקו אנתון
חרשא דמבעדא דד(ו)א ולוטתא ואשלמ̈תא (9) חדתתא וחתימתא ואזילו וסמו
[ ] משדר חבוקא [ ]תון כד נפקיתון בת דמו כציפר̈א דפרחן ונפקן ומשנין
(10) מן (א)תר ל(א)תר הכנא תישנון ותיפקון מן פגריה ד[ברימא בר עזדנדוך...]בניה
ובנתיה דעית ליה ודניון ליה וניתנטר ברשפתא בר אחתבו (11) וחדא רביתא בת חוא
[ ] וניתנטרון (פ)נהקדוך נטרוי וגוש(נ)[סף]ונימישא ו(א)יך שעיתא
דפשרא בנורא קדחו ערוסו ארוקו (12) ועתבטילו ועתקטלו ועתכלו וא(זי)לו ואזילו
מן פגריה דברע(מ)[א בר עזדנדוך ... על ...] ועל משדרניה מן ממלל פומיה ומן עוב̈דא
עדיה בשמיה דקדחיאיל (13) ומפקיאיל וכבשיא[יל] ופרחיאיל א(סיותא) [ ] לא
ולא לכבישוה וניתנטר חדא ברשב.זא בר (אח)תבו וחדין רביתא [ ]

Bowls 10 and 11 are at the Jewish Historical Museum in Belgrade. Dr. L.Y. Rahmani of the Israel Department of Antiquities received photographs of the two bowls from Dr. Vidosava-Neda Nedomački, curator of the Jewish Historical Museum in Belgrade, and referred them to us for study. The information supplied by Dr. Nedomački was that

Bowl 10

Translation

(3)...demons and dēws...(4)...dreams of night and visions of day from...(5)...the cattle and the house of Bar-Immā son of Izdān-dukh. In the name of **ṣbʾwty ṣbʾwty** the living and the existent, in the name... In the name of **yh yhw,** in the name of **hʾ hyhn hʾ**... that you may come (6) and make healing for the body of Bar-Immā [son of Izdān-dukh] and his sons and d[aughters], which he has and which [he will have]. May (7) this Bar-Shapta son of Aḥat-Abū be protected, may that Naṭ[roy...] be protected; ... son of Rĕbītā, and this Maṭriya son of Qayyamtā, to his house and the members of his house, to his property and to his cattle (8) and to the body of Bar-Immā son of [Izdān-dukh]. In the name of the great and holy Lord, flee away, go out, you sorcerers of witchcraft, (who are) dēws and new and sealed (9) curses and spells. Go and put(?) ... sends ... As you go out in the form of birds who fly and go out and move (10) from one place to another, so will you move and go out of the body of [Bar-Immā son of Izdān-dukh, and of] his sons and daughters, which he has and which he will have. May Bar-Shapta son of Aḥat-Abū be protected; (11) and this Rĕbītā daughter of Ḥawwa... May Panāhakdukh, Naṭroy and Gushn[asp] be protected... and like wax which melts in the fire — run away!... flee away! (12) be annulled! be killed! be terminated! go away! go away from the body of Bar-Immā [son of Izdān-dukh!...against...] and against him who sent him, from that which he speaks by his mouth, and from the works that he does by hand. In the name of Qadḥiel, (13) Mappeqiel, Kabshiel, Parḥiel. [May there be] remedy ...that she may not be pressed down. And may this Bar-Shabta son of Aḥat-Abū be protected, and this Rĕbītā...

the two bowls were found in 1912 by a Jugoslav engineer, Janko Milošević, who was working on the building of a railway at a place specified as being 700 metres north of Kadhimain, which lies 6 km. north of Baghdad. The finder, who supplied this information, took the bowls with him to Belgrade. We should like to thank both the Jewish

Historical Museum in Belgrade and Dr. Rahmani for their cooperation.

Bowl 10 is broken, and what survives of it consists of two large fragments joined together in Belgrade. The writing of the lines in the centre, where the inscription begins, is largely effaced. For the reading we used an enlarged photograph of the joined fragments of the bowl (Plate 26), as well as small photographs of each fragment separately, obviously taken before the joining of the two fragments was made.

The language of Bowl 10 is Syriac written in the Estrangelo script (with some cursive modifications), in contrast to Bowl 1, which is written in the Proto-Manichaean script (cf. Commentary to Bowl 1).

4 **ḥlmʾ dlylyʾ wḥyzwnʾ dʿmmʾ**: The same phrase is found elsewhere, cf. in Mandaic, Montgomery 1913, p. 248 (39:10); Epstein 1922, p. 60.

5 Bar-Immā bar Izdāndukh: The Aramaic name of the client is not yet attested in magic bowls. The mother's name, which is Iranian, occurs on Jewish Aramaic bowls with the spelling **ʾyzdndwk;** cf. Montgomery 1913, pp. 145 (No. 7), 212 (No. 27). The name is attested also in Syriac literature, cf. Justi 1895, p. 146. Justi's explanation "(von den) Ized (geschenktes) Mädchen" should probably be revised. The great number of names with *-dukh* seems to suggest that this is a mere suffix denoting "daughter of". The name Yazdān indeed exists as a masculine proper name; references are given by Justi, ibid.

ṣbʾwty: It is not entirely certain whether the final sign in this word, which is repeated twice, is indeed a *yod,* as read here, or merely a final embellishment belonging to the *taw.* For **ḥyʾ wqymʾ** cf. Amulet 9:5.

6 **wtybdwn:** Quite curiously, the radical *ʿayin* is here spelled by a *yod.* The vacillation between *yod, ʿayin* and *alef* is evident in the forms **brymʾ/brʿmʾ, ʿzdndwk, dʿyt lyh, ʾrwqw, ʿtbṭylw, ʿdyh** etc. (cf. in Mandaic, Yamauchi 1967, pp. 75 f.).

wlbnh wlbnyh: The first word was apparently written by mistake and corrected by writing the word again. In **bnyh** for **bnwhy** our bowl follows the form known from the Jewish Babylonian bowls; cf. Introduction, p. 32.

7 **ḥdʾ**: The text uses the demonstrative pronoun *hādā*, which is properly feminine, indiscriminately, and with the curious spelling with initial *ḥet.* One might think of the numeral *ḥdā* (which is feminine), used irregularly for masculine persons, but the occurrence of **ḥdyn rbytʾ** in line 13 decides the issue. *Hādēn* is certainly the masculine demonstrative pronoun, and it is again remarkable that it is used in line 13 for what is a feminine name; cf. **rbyt' bt ḥw'** in line 11.

bršpt' alternates (line 13) with the spelling **bršbt'**. As a name it belongs to the category of names referring to a day of the week, presumably the infant's birthday.

mṭry' is a name of unclear origin. One thinks of the name of a *dihqān* in Ispahan in the early Islamic period, **mṭy'r,** cf. Ṭabāri, IV, p. 295.

8 **prḥw wpwqw:** Further down, in lines 11–12, a longer list of similar imperatives of verbs signifying going away and being annulled is given. A similar list of imperatives occurs in the Iraq Museum bowl 44107, cf. Teixidor 1962, p. 55; Hamilton 1971, p. 117: **zḥw ʿtrw w'tkrzw prḥw *wpwqw** (read thus!).

mbʿd': The metathesis of **mʿbd'** is attested elsewhere too. Cf. our Syriac Bowl 1:11.

9 It seems that **ḥdtt' wḥtymt'** are attributes of **lwṭt' w'šlmt'.**

smw may perhaps be the imperative *paʿʿel* of **SM'** "to blind".

ḥbwq' is not clear.

bt dmw k- is the expression used for "like", "in the form of", corresponding to the regular Syriac **bdmwt.** Compare the Biblical Hebrew **dmwt k-** in Ez. 1:26 etc. Cf. Geller 1980, p. 51, line 4 **wmydmn lhwn bydmw dmw** (thus to be read!) "and they appeared to them in various forms".

dprḥn wnpqn wmšnyn: Cf. Montgomery 1913, p. 238 (36:2) **pwq pwq wšny mn qdm...** (Montgomery read **qdmy,** but only **qdm** is visible in his drawing).

10 **dʿyt lyh wdnywn lyh:** Compare **[wkl d'y]t lh wdhwyn lh,** Montgomery 1913, p. 242 (37:3). See also Bowl 12:IX

11 **pnhqdwk** is an Iranian name not yet attested. The main part of the name, Panāhak, is obviously derived from *panāh* "protection". Naṭroy seems to be a Semitic proper name (it looks like the Semitic equivalent of Panāhak). The third name could be completed as Gušnay or Gušnasp.

'yk šʿyt' dpšr' bnwr': Cf. Peshitta to Ps. 88:2 **'yk dmtpšr' šʿwt' mn qdm nwr'** and similarly Ps. 97:5.

qdḥw: Montgomery 1913, p. 194 argued in favour of reading this fairly common magic verb as **qrḥ** in order to connect it to the formula in Bavli Pesaḥim 110a **qrḥ qrḥyyky.** Jeruzalmi 1963, p. 74, taking up this idea, translated **wqrḥw wʿyryqw** by "soyez chauves (perdez votre efficacité en tant que magiciens) et éloignez-vous". Isbell 1975, No. 19:7; 20:9; 22:7 read the verb **QDḤ**, though in the glossary, p. 180, Isbell quotes inexplicably **QRḤ** for text 20:9. Our text, which has a clear distinction between *daleth* and *resh,* settles the ambiguity in a decisive manner in favour of the root **QDḤ**. Even without this evidence it would be fairly clear that a verb with the meaning "to flee" and not "be bald" is required. Mandaic has **uqda upuq uʿruq** (Yamauchi 1967, p. 230, line 12) in the same context. See already Epstein 1921, pp. 41 f., who establishes the basic meaning of the word " to pierce, rise". For the other meaning of **QDḤ** "to wail, moan" see Bowl 13:20.

Bowl 11

Jewish Historical Museum, Belgrade, No. 242/1

Plate 27

(1) [ ] ולשלהפתא ולש(ח)מתא ול[ ] לאיסקופתיה דכוסרו
לבר[אידא בר] איזדנדוך [(2)](כ)יר ולבראידא בר איזדנדוך
ולאי[ ]כתבו ש(מן) [(3)] מן צערי ומן מרעי ומן (כורהניא)
ביש(יא ומן) חסמתא ומן מהרין תקיפין ומן ממלא (ב)ישא [ ] ומן כל
פידג(מי) דכסיי סניי (4) (ד)דחילי ומן [ ]א (ח)ברי ותקיפי ומן לוטתא ומן
אשלמתא ומן אריסותא ומן [ ] ומן פ[ ] (ד)ליטי סניי ומן כל (5)
מידיעם דביש אמן אמן סלה ויאמר יהוה אל הסטן יגער יהוה בכא ה[סט]ן יגער
יהוה בכא הבוחיר (6) בירושלי{של}ם (הלו) זה {אוד} אוד מוצל מ(אש) שמע יושב
יישראל בסתר יהוה עליון אלהינו בצל יהוה (7) שדי אחד יתלונן אמן אמן סלה תוב
אסותה מן שמיא לאיסקו(פתיה) דכוס(רו) בר (8) איז(דנדוך) דיתסי ברחמי שמיא
וכל שום דאית ביה [(9)] איסקופתיה דכוסרו בר איז(דנדוך)
[ ] אמן אמן אמן סלה

ʿrwsw is not clear, and seems to be a mistake for **ʿrwqw,** which is indeed written immediately afterwards, but with a new modification, substituting *alef* for *ʿayin.*

12 **mšdrnyh** could mean "they who sent him".

mmll pwmyh: This seems to be a verbal noun, **mmllʾ.**

qdḥyʾyl, mpqyʾyl, kbšyʾyl, prḥyʾyl: A series of names derived from verbs denoting the chasing out or the subordination of the demons.

13 **lkbyšwh:** The first letter looks like a *lamed,* although in Syriac one should have expected a *nun.*

Bowl 11

Translation

(1)...to the threshold of Khusrau, to Bar[-Ida son of] Izdān-dukh ... (2) ... and to Bar-Ida son of Izdān-dukh and to ...wrote names ... (3)...from pains and illnesses and evil sicknesses and from jealousy and from mighty spells and from evil speech (?) ... and from all the words which the frightening enemies (4) are hiding and from...sorcerers and mighty ones and from curses and from spells and from submission (?) and from ...and from...which the enemies curse and from (5) all evil things. Amen, Amen, Selah. "And the Lord said unto Satan, The Lord rebuke thee, O Satan: even the Lord that hath chosen (6) Jerusalem rebuke thee: is not this a brand plucked out of the fire?" (Zach. 3:2). "Hear, O Israel, the Lord our God is one Lord" (Deut. 6:4). "He that dwelleth in the secret place of the most High shall abide under the shadow of the Almighty" (Ps. 91:1). Amen, Amen, Selah.

Again, may there be healing from heaven to the threshold of Khusrau son of (8) Izdān-dukh, so that he may be healed by the mercy of heaven, and any name that is in him [...(9)...should be removed from] the threshold of Khusrau son of Izdān-dukh... Amen, Amen, Amen, Selah.

For the provenance of this bowl cf. Commentary to Bowl 10.

Although the bowl itself is intact, the inscription written on its inner surface is badly effaced. Having only the photographs at our disposal, we avoided readings which seemed speculative, and have concentrated on those which have seemed relatively certain. The writing begins in the outer rim and ends in the centre, going around an illustration which is not clearly discernible. It may be a human figure with two smaller drawings to its left.

1 **šlhpt'** seems to be an unusual spelling for **šlhwbt'** "flame", cf. Montgomery 1913, p. 183: **lgw nwr' yqydt' wylšlhwbt 'yšt'**. In Bowl 1:7 we have **šlhbyt'** and in Bowl 9:4—**šlhwbyt'.**

šḥmt' may mean "blackening" or "heat". It also occurs in Geniza 6, p. 3:6–7, where it seems to indicate the blackness caused by fire. If **šlhpt'** means "fever", it is possible to take **šḥmt'** as indicating some other symptom of disease, perhaps like **šḥrt'** in Bowl 9:13.

Khusrau son of Izdān-dukh and Bar-Ida son of Izdān-dukh may be brothers. It is interesting to note that the client of Bowl 10 is Bar-Imma son of Izdān-dukh. The two bowls, though written in two different scripts, may stem from the same family. If this is so, we have here another indication for the hypothesis that the script (and language) of a bowl does not represent the language used by the client, but only that which was used by the sorcerer. The sorcerer may have belonged to a different religion or nationality. Cf. Introduction, p. 18.

2 **š(mn)** cf. Bowl 7:2.

3 **(kwrhny'):** See above Commentary to Bowl 1:11.

mhryn: This is the first occurrence of this word in Aramaic to our knowledge (the reading might also be **mhdyn**). Our reading is based on the assumption that this is a loan-word from Iranian; cf. Middle Persian *mahr,* Avestan *manthra-* "(sacred) word".

mml' perhaps an error for **mmll'.**

pydg(my): If the reading is correct, this is a form of **ptgm/pytgm** on the way to becoming **pugdama,** as in Mandaic.

dksyy snyy: The first word is active participle *pe'al* plural masculine, while the second is plural of *san'ā/sanyā.*

4 **ʾryswtʾ**: If it is not a graphic variant of **ʾsyr,** would be connected to the notion of the submission of an *aris* "tenant".

lyṭy is the active participle *peʿal* of **LWṬ.**

6–7 The two verses, Deut. 6:4 and Ps. 91:1, are joined together into a single text by taking one word from one verse followed by one word from the other text. The same procedure is also used in Schwab 1891, p. 592 (Bowl O); Gordon 1978, p. 233; and T–S K 1.95.

8 **wkl šwm dʾyt byh:** The usual formula is with the preposition **lyh,** cf. Bowl 7:3. The use of **byh** may be influenced by another formula such as we have in Bowl 5:3 **kl šydy...dʾyt bh bʿlmʾ.**

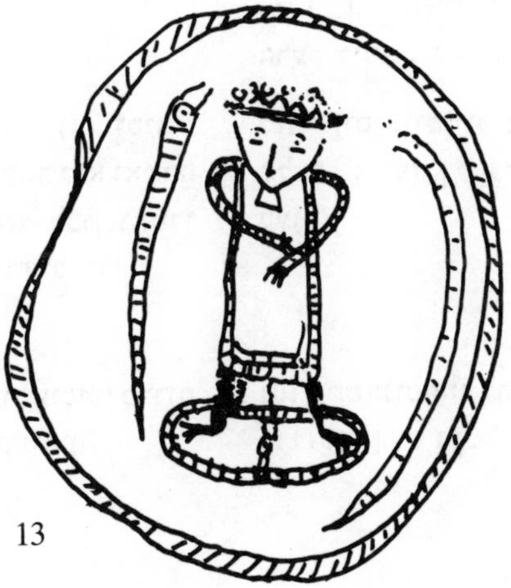

From Bowl 13

Bowl 12

	Amulet 15 *see p.104*	*Bowl 12a* *Jewish National and University Library, Jerusalem, Heb. 4° 6079* *Plate 28*
I		
II	[(1)] סממית יל⌈י⌉דת בנין [... קטלהון] (2) [סד]רוס	(1) סמומית ילידת תרי עשר בנין וכולהון קטל יתהון (2) סדרוס רשיעה
III	ערקת מן ק[דומוי] (3) [...] קמת (ל)ה ברא(ש)[...] (4) [...] בנת לה בית ברא[...] (5) [...ל]ה תרעין דפרז(ל)[ה...] (6) [...]ה וטרדת בא[...] (7) [...י]ת תרעה לידא	וקמת וערקת מן קדומוהי ואזלת לחד טורא (3) דימיחד בעלמא שמיה ועבדת לחרשין דינחשה ועבדין דפרזלא
IV	סוני [וס(8)וס]וני וסניגלי ארתקו על [...] (9) [...]בין נעבר וניעל לע(ל)[...]	ואתא סאוני וססאוני (4) וסנגרו וארתיקו ואמרו לה פתח לנא ואמרת להון לית אנא פתחא לכון ואמרו דוכתא דנעבר (5) וניעול עלה
V	(10) [קמ]ת ופתחת להון על עמ(ה)[ון] (11) [סד]רוס וקטל לברה	וקמת ופתחת להון ועול עימהון סדרוס וקטליה ליברה וחנק יותיה
VI	וצו(ח)[ת] (12) [ע](ל)יהון סוני וסוסוני (13) [וס]ניגלי מה עבד (הכין ש)[מע] (14) [סד]רוס ופתח וער(ק) מ(נ)[הון]	וקמת וצוחת עלוהי אסאוני (6) וססאוני וסנגרו וארתיקו מא עבדו ליה

Bowl 12

Bowl 12b
Metropolitan Museum,
New York, No. 86.11.259
Plate 29

Translation
of the Bowl texts

(1) אסירת וחתימת אנתי מבכלתא בישתא (2) (ד)לוית (?) עים זבינו בר זוני ועים (דותי אינתתיה) (3) בת גוסי וימשצטמת בן דוך (?) ון[ ] ליה (4) לזונא בר דותי

Bound and sealed are you, the evil Mevakkalta, who associates(?) with Zabinu son of Zuni and with Duti his wife, daughter of Gusi, ... to Zuna son of Duti.

סממיתא ילידת תרין עשר בנין כולהון קטל יתהון (5) סרגיס

Smamit gave birth to twelve sons. All of them were killed by Sideros the Wicked [*N. Y.:* Sergi(u)s].

קמת וערקת מן קודמוהי ואזלת לה לטורא חד מאחיד שמיה ועבדת (6) מקדשה דינ(חש) ועבדין דיפרזל·

She got up and fled from him, and she went to a mountain, whose name is unique in the world [*N. Y. var.*]. She performed sorceries of copper and magic acts of iron [*N. Y. var.*].

ואתא סוני וסאסוני וסינגרו וארתיקו ואמרו (7) לה (פתחי לנא) ואמרת לית אנה פתחא ואמרו (ד)רכיה נעבור ונעול עליה

There came **s'wny wss'wny wsngrw w'rtyqw** and said to her: Open (the door) for us. She said to them: I shall not open (it) for you. They said: This is a place (for us) to pass through and enter into.

וקמת ופתחת (8) להון ועל עימהון סרגיס וקטליה ליברה {ונ} וחנק יתיה

She stood up and opened (the door) for them. With them there came in Sideros [*N. Y.:* Sergi(u)s]. He killed her son and strangled him.

וקמת ויצוחת עלי סוני (9) וסאסוני וסינג[רו וא]רתיקו מא עבדו לה

She stood up and cried at him: O **s'wny wss'wny wsngrw w'rtyqw!** What have they done to him?

	Amulet 15	*Bowl 12a*
VII	(15) [מן] חזין רדפו בתרה וא[ש](16)[כ]חוי בפלגוס דימה ו(הנ) [...] (17) [ל]מקטול יתה	**וקומו ורדפו בתריה ואדריכו יותיה לגו פלגוס ימא רבה ובעו (7) מינהון למיקטל יותיה ולמיחנק יותיה**
VIIIa	אמר להון [אנה] (18) (מ)שתבע לכון במן דאכ[יל] (19) (מ)יה בשעולה	**ואמר להון שבוקו מיני ואנא מישתבענא (לכון) במי שמדד בשעולו מים**
VIIIb	דכל הן ד[...] (20) [...]ן מדכרין שמה דס[וני] (21) וסוסוני וסניגלי לא א[קטול]	**דכל אתר דדכרין שמיה (8) דסאוני וססאוני וסנגרו וארתיקו אנא לא איקטול ולא איחנוק ולא איחבול**
IX	(22) לאנטונינה ברתה ד(נ)[...] (23) [...] (וב)רה	**בביתיה דאגבלתא בר קרקוי וכל בנין דאית להון ודהון להון לקאקאי בת (9) (פ)וזיקתוי ולאגבלתא בר קרקוי**

Bowl 12b

Translation

קמו וירדפו בתרוהי {לגו} ואדריכו יתיה לגו פלגוס ימא (10) רבא למיקטל י[תיה ו]למיחנק יתיה

They stood up and chased him and found him *in pelagos, the great sea, [*Jer. adds:* and they sought of them] to kill him and strangle him.

ואמר שבוקו מיני ואנא מיש⸢ת⸣בענא לכון במי שמדד בשועולו מים (11) ושמים בזרת תיכין וכל בשליש עפר הארץ ושקל בפלס {ויגע} ויגבעות במואוזנים

He said to them: Let go of me, and I swear to you in the name of He "who has measured the water in the hollow of his hand [*N. Y. adds:* and meted out heaven with the span, and comprehended the dust of the earth in a measure, and weighed <the mountains> in scales and the hills in a balance]" (Is. 40:12),

דכל אתר דידכר שמיה (12) דסוני וסאסוני וסינגרו וארתיקו איתרח(ם) ולא {אינ} איחנוק ולא א⸢י⸣קטול

that wherever the name of **s'wny wss'wny wsngrw w'rtyqw** is mentioned I shall [*N. Y. adds:* have pity and shall] not kill or strangle [*Jer. adds:* or injure]

the house of Agbalta son of Qarqoy and any children whom they—Qaqay daughter of Poziqtoy and Agbalta son of Qarqoy—have and will have.

ליבנין דזבינו בר זוני (ו)אינתתיה בת (13) גוסי דאית להון וידהון להון מן יומא דנן ולעלם אמן סלה הללויה

the children of Zabinu son of Zuni and his wife daughter of Gusi, those whom they have and those whom they will have from this day to eternity, Amen, Amen, Selah, Hallelujah.

	Bowl 12	Amulet 15	Bowl 12a
X		ברוך אתה י[ייי] (24) (אל) קים מלך העולם [יגער] (25) הרוחות מלפניך	
XI			אסירא ליליתא אסירא מבכלתא אסיר שתא א[ ] אסיר [ ] אסיר (זב)נא אסיר פתכרא אסירין כל מזיקין בישין דאית (10) בביתיה דאגבלתא בר קרקוי [ ] שישים גיבו(רים) [סביב לה מגבורי ישרא]ל כו[לם אחוזי חרב] מלמדי מלחמה [איש] חרבו על יריכו מיפחד בלילות

The Jerusalem bowl (12a) has been recently received by the Jewish National and University Library. It is unusual in that it contains a story which occupies the best part of its text, and in certain other features. The bowl was donated to the Library by the late Professor Gershom Scholem. Professor Scholem had received it as a gift from Dr. Wladimir Rosenbaum, an antique dealer in Ascona (Switzerland).

The most striking feature of this text, as already pointed out, is the fact that it is built around a story with a magic effect, a *historiola,* to use the term applied to it by Heim 1892, p. 495 (cf. also Maas 1942, pp. 37f.). Such stories are practically unknown in other Aramaic magic bowls, although certain bowls contain brief allusions to story situations. Such is the allusion to Yĕhoshuaʿ bar Pĕraḥya and his deed of divorce to the female demons in certain bowls, e.g. in our Bowl 5 and Montgomery

Bowl 12b	*Translation*
ברוך אתה יהוה אלהינו מלך העולם מכ(ה) ורופה (14) את זבינו בר זוני ואת (דותי) בת גוסי ואת זונא בר דותי אמן אמן סלה שריר וקים	Blessed art Thou **yhwh** our God, King of the world, who smites and cures Zabinu son of Zuni and Duti daughter of Gusi and Zuna son of Duti, Amen, Amen, Selah. True and sound.
	Bound is Lilith, bound is Mevakkalta, bound is **šṭ'** ... bound is ... bound is ... bound is the idol, bound are all the evil harmers who are in the house of Agbalta son of Qarqoy ... "Sixty valiant men are around about it, of the mighty men of Israel, all girt with swords, and expert in war, every man has his sword upon his thigh, because of the fear by night"(Cant. 3:7–8).

1913, No. 32 (see also Gordon 1978, pp. 233 f., and our Amulet 7). Incantations with fairly elaborate *historiolae* are, however, quite common in Greek and in Syriac magic literature (cf. Heim 1892, pp. 495 ff.; Gollancz 1912, pp. 14f., 85, 87, 89).

Another interesting feature of this bowl is the fact that it contains a number of Greek words. This is a feature which is totally unknown in other Mesopotamian bowls, and one which has raised initial doubts as to the authenticity and original provenance of the bowl, as most Aramaic incantation bowls whose provenance can be ascertained derive from the area of Mesopotamia and Iran, where the number of Greek elements is rather limited. Although the provenance of our new bowl is unknown, it can be established by parallel material that it is Babylonian. The Metropolitan Museum in New York possesses an unpublished bowl (our Bowl 12b) whose text closely resembles that of our Jerusalem bowl, although the names of the clients are different, and the opening formulae are also cast differently. The Museum records note that the bowl in question, No. 86.11.259, was acquired in 1886 by Mr. Ward, a curator of the Metropolitan , while he was on a journey in Mesopotamia. Another bowl which undoubtedly has the same story was published in Gordon 1941, pp. 346 f., from the Hilprecht Collection, and it "presumably comes from Hilprecht's excavations at Nippur". Gordon could only read a few detached phrases in that bowl, and we have not seen the bowl itself, but the extracts given by Gordon leave no room for doubt that it is in fact the same basic text as in 12a (with the same orthographic peculiarities), although, like the New York bowl, it has a dedication to a different client preceding and following the story.

The *historiola* which forms the basis of the incantations contained in these bowls has numerous parallels in Greek, Ethiopian, Coptic, Hebrew, Rumanian and other texts (see Appendix to Amulet 15). A striking parallel to the texts of these bowls has reached us when the book was ready for publication. Amulet 15, which is in the Israel Museum, turned out to have the same story in a shorter version, but with some details which are certaily more original than their counterparts in the Babylonian bowls. For further details see the commentaries and the Appendix to Amulet 15, as well as the text of Amulet 15 printed above in a parallel column to the texts of Bowls 12a and 12b.

In contrast to the phrasing of Amulet 15, it may be noted that although Bowls 12a and 12b have borrowed certain key expressions from a Palestinian source (the Greek name Sideros, the hybrid Greek Aramaic expression **plgws [d] ymh rbh,** the verb **ʾrtq**), the language of the bowls has nevertheless come under the influence of Babylonian Aramaic (e.g. **ʿly – ʿlwhy; btryh – btrwhy;** the use of *waw* for original *qamaṣ* in Bowl 12a, and other orthographic features). The most important aspect which emerges from the comparison of Bowls 12a and 12b with Amulet 15 is a certain number of textual misunderstandings in the bowls (e.g. **wʾrtyqw** was taken to be a proper name; **wʾdrykw...lgw** for **bgw,** in section VII). For further discussion see the Commentary below.

Some general differences of style and language can be noticed between the Jerusalem bowl and its New York counterpart:

(1) The orthography of the Jerusalem bowl has several peculiarities

which the New York one does not share. The *qamaṣ* vowel is frequently spelled in the Jerusalem (and in the Hilprecht) text with a *waw* indicating presumably that it tended to be pronounced *o*. Thus **smwmyt** (N.Y. **smmytʾ**), **qdwmwhy** (N.Y. **qwdmwhy**), **wʿwl** (N.Y.: **wʿl**), **ywtyh** (N.Y.: **ytyh**), **qwmw** (N.Y.: **qmw**). This way of spelling is not unusual in the Aramaic magic texts, and it has been claimed to be a feature of Babylonian Aramaic in general (cf. Rossell 1953, pp. 20 f., § 3.15 and the literature adduced in Morag 1979, p. 115, n. 21 and p. 116, n. 25). See further Introduction on p. 32.

(2) Although both texts tend towards a *plene* spelling with *yod* in words which are not commonly so spelled in Babylonian Aramaic, e.g. **lybrh, ʾyqṭwl, ʾyḥnwq, ʾyḥbwl, myštbʿnʾ**, as well as in the relative **dy-** (e.g. **dymyḥd, dynḥšh**), the New York bowl has such a spelling sometimes with the conjunction **w- (wyṣwḥt, wyrdpw, wygbʿwt** [Hebrew], **wydhwn)**, a feature which is again found also in other texts (see Commentary to Bowl 2).

(3) The Jerusalem bowl is more explicit in several cases in the use of pronouns, while the New York bowl is more elliptic: In section IV Jer. **wʾmrt lhwn,** N.Y. **wʾmrt;** Jer. **lyt ʾnʾ ptḥʾ lkwn,** N.Y. **lyt ʾnh ptḥʾ;** in section VIII Jer. (and Hilprecht) **wʾmr lhwn,** N.Y. **wʾmr.**

(4) The New York bowl, on the other hand, is more expansive in some quotations and set phrases. Cf. the quotation in section VIII, where the full biblical quotation as well as the addition of **ʾytrḥ(m)** "I shall have mercy" occur only in the New York bowl; similarly in section IX we have in N.Y. the addition of the phrase **mn ywmʾ dnn wlʿlm ʾmn ʾmn slh hllwyh.**

(5) Some differences of detail indicate that the text of N.Y. is inferior to that of Jer.: Jer. has the name **sdrws** as against **srgys** in N.Y. (cf. Appendix to Amulet 15); Jer. **lḥd ṭwrʾ dymyḥd bʿlmʾ šmyh** seems the original version as against N.Y. **lṭwrʾ ḥd mʾḥyd šmyh;** Jer. **dwktʾ dnʿbr wnyʿwl ʿlh** seems better than **(d)rkyh nʿbwr wnʿwl ʿlyh;** the same may apply to the omission in N.Y. section VII of the words **wbʿw (mynhwn)** which occur in Jer.

In addition to the following textual comments the reader is advised to consult the Commentary to the approriate lines in Amulet 15. The following comments are arranged by the sections as given in the transcription of the text.

I New York and Hilprecht have an introductory section mentioning the client while Amulet 15 and Jerusalem start with the *historiola.*

II Jer. **sdrws** supported by the traces in Amulet 15; N.Y. gives **srgys,** which is evidently a corruption. Cf. also Ethiopian Werzelya (see Appendix to Amulet 15).

III **dymyḥd bʿlmʾ šmyh:** There seems to be no room in Amulet 15 for such an epithet, although a reference to a mountain may be reconstructed there.

For the phrase Jer. **lḥršyn dynḥšh** N.Y. gives **mqdšh dynḥš**. The whole phrase seems to be a corruption from an original text where instead of **ḥršyn** the similar-looking word **trʿyn** was written, as in Amulet 15.

wʿbdyn dprzlʾ: In Hilprecht we may read **wʿbdy dprzlʾ wʾtʾ** (Gordon 1941, p. 346).

IV **sʾwny wssʾwny wsngrw wʾrtyqw:** The division of words here is ascertained from a comparison of all the places in which the names occur in the two bowls, in the amulet and in the later traditions.

ʾrtyqw, which is the verb meaning "and they knocked (on the door)", as in Amulet 15, was misunderstood by the writers of our bowls and they took it to be a part of the series of names. It is likely that they regarded **sngrw** as a word with the same shape.

Our two bowls seem to waver between taking these three characters as a singular entity or as a plural. Thus we have **wʾtʾ... wʾmrw lh.. wptḥt lhwn... wṣwḥt ʿlwhy,** etc. The Greek version of the Gyllou story (see Appendix to Amulet 15) treats Sisinios, Sinēs and Sēnodōros as a singular (ὁ ἅγιος); this point occurs in the story more than once. These three names are seemingly phonetic variations on a single form, a point which is strengthened by the observation that the names are once given in the Greek text in the vocative ὦ Σισίνιε, Σίνη καὶ συνοδία (Sisinios, Sines and company). In Amulet 15, which seems closest to the original version, the three names consistently attract plural form.

dwktʾ dnʿbr wnyʿwl ʿlh: This may be a corruption of a phrase in the original version; Amulet 15 does not provide us with the possibility of a satisfactory reconstruction. The N.Y. version presents us with another unusual phrasing.

V This paragraph implies that a new son was born to Smamit in the meantime. This is said explicitly in the Greek version (see Appendix to Amulet 15). The sequence "to kill and to strangle", which may strike one as illogical, occurs twice at least (cf. sections VII and VIII), although in N.Y. line 12 the sequence is "strangle", "kill". Amulet 15 uses the verb "to kill" exclusively.

V–VI In Hilprecht we may reconstruct (cf. Gordon 1941, p. 346): **[w]ḥnq ywtyh wqmt wṣwḥt *ʿlhy ʾsʾwny wssʾwny wsngrw wʾrtyqw.**

VI The spelling **ʾsʾwny** in the Jer. and Hilprecht bowls suggests the Greek vocative participle attached to the name in the appropriate syntactic situation, which makes it possible that there existed a Greek *Vorlage* from which the Aramaic version derived. The Greek text of Perdrizet 1922 indeed has a vocative form of address at this point (see Appendix to Amulet 15).

VII Jer. **btryh,** N.Y. **btrwhy:** Both forms are attested; cf. Rossel 1953, pp. 21 f., 58.

wʾdrykw ywtyh, "they found him", was misunderstood by the writer of the bowls as meaning "they led him"; see Commentary to Amulet 15:15–16.

lgw: Mistake for **bgw.**

plgws ymʾ rbh: See Commentary to Amulet 15:16.

wbʿw mynhwn: This phrase is not given in N.Y. **mynhwn** seems to be a mistake.

VIII The short quotation from Is. 40:12, as given in Jer., occurs also in *Sefer ha-razim,* I:226. In Hilprecht we reconstruct **[bšʿ]wlw mym dkl ʾtr...**(cf. Gordon 1941, p. 347), where we also have the short quotation. Amulet 15 gives an Aramaic version of the short quotation.

kl ʾtr d-: See Commentary to Amulet 15:19.

IX The feminine name Qarqoy occurs also in Isbell 1975, p. 110 (No. 48) and Qaqay (fem. pr. n.) in Isbell 1975, Nos. 47 and 32 (spelled **qʾqy**). The name Qaqay is Iranian from *Kaka* "uncle, brother-in-law".

The N.Y. names give more the impression of being Semitic than Iranian.

X For the phrase **mk(h) wrwph** cf. Gordon 1941, p. 352 **ברוך מכה ורופא** and Amulet 1:20.

XI The verse Cant. 3:7 occurs also in Isbell 1975, No. 66:3–4.

Bowl 13

Collection of V. Klagsbald, Jerusalem

Plates 30-31

Within the central circle:

(1) להדא (לי)ליתא

דשריא עים יויתאי בת חתאי

(2) וברוב גאונך ת[רע]ץ קומך תשלח חרונך יכלמו כקש

Outside the circle:

(3) בחיליה דרבה ובמימרא דמלאכי ובישמיה דמריא בגדנא אזיזא רבה דאילהי ומלכה ראישה דשיתי מלכותא חיליה חילא (דזיקא) חומתיה (4) חומתא דנורא סוגייה סוגיא דקטלא מרדותיה מרדותא דיקרבה דחי אכיל דלא מזיג שתי ראישיה ראישא דאריא ככיה ככי דדיבתה שיניה (5) שיני דנמרא סירפי פומיה אדוגי דנורא עיניה ברקין דיקדין (כ)פידיה גילגלי בעננא צידיה סדנא דפרזלא איבריה תרתי ארזפתא חדייה חדיא דגברא לטבא (6) כרסיה ימא דלא ביבי גביה גבא דיגילא שקיה שקי נחשה ופרזלא סנדליה סנדלי פריחי מרכבתיה מרכבא לטבי {ת}יתי בידיה חרבא דקטלא את<א> מריא אתא גיס (7) קריב עליהון על שידי ועל דיוי ועל ליליתא בישתא דשריא עים יויתאי בת חתאי ועל דנחיש ועל דיני ועל זכיא ועל פתכרא ועל ליליתא בישתא ועל מלויתא חציפתא דלויא עים (8) יויתאי בת חתאי ועים זוריגאי בר אימא דקטלא מינהון בניהון ובנתהון רמי לה פולקתא בפומה תבר שינה בפומה שפיד מוקרה קמה מחונה בחרבא דקטלא על מוקדה חביל קומה (9) כל בישה ובטילו אזה מן יויתאי בת חתאי ומן זוריגאי בר אימא אתא ב־שלם גברא (דא)ישתגר אתא עליהון דשידי ודיוי בני חילי חשוכה בני אתרא דנורא בני אתרא

Bowl 13

Translation

Within the central circle:

(1) For that Lilith who dwells with Yawitai, daughter of Ḥatai.

(2) "In the fullness of thy triumph thou didst cast the rebels down, thou didst let loose thy fury, it consumed them like chaff" (Ex. 15:7).

Outside the circle:

(3) By the power of the Great One, and by the command of the angels, and by the name of the lord Bagdana Aziza, the great one of the gods, and the king, head of sixty kingdoms, whose power is the power of a blast, whose heat (4) is the heat of fire, whose practice is the practice of slaying, whose chastisement is the chastisement of battle, that which is alive he eats, that which is unmixed he drinks. His head is the head of a lion, his molar teeth are the molar teeth of a she-wolf, his teeth are (5) the teeth of a tiger, the draughts of his mouth are furnaces of fire, his eyes are glowing lightnings, his shoulders are the spheres in a cloud, his temples are an anvil of iron, his arms are two hammers, his chest is the chest of an evil man, (6) his belly is a lake without canals, his back is alum, his legs are legs of brass and iron, his sandals are sandals of sparks, his chariot is the chariot of the evil ones; he(?) comes and in his hand there is a sword of slaying.

There came the lord, there came the troop. (7) He came against them, against the demons, against the dēws, against the evil Lilith, who dwells with Yawitai d. of Ḥatai, against Danahiš, against the judges, against he who is acquitted, against the idol, against the evil Lilith, against the impudent female companion who accompanies (8) Yawitai d. of Ḥatai and Zorigai son of Imma, who kills their sons and daughters. He cast a hatchet in her mouth, he broke her teeth in her mouth, he pierced her brain before her (i.e. before the client), they smote her on the top of her head with a sword of slaying, he destroyed all evil (9) from her presence, they annihilated **ʾzh** from Yawitai d. of Ḥatai and from Zorigai s. of Imma.

There came in peace the man who was sent, he came against them, against the demons and dēws, sons of the troops of darkness, sons of the place of fire, sons of the place of black waters, sons of those women who

דמיא איסיוי בני פגרתא (10) וילדתא בני ריגותא וזינוא בני יחטי בני בתולתא בני בתי חרבי בני כדי פסיסי בני גיבורין דהוו חלישין בני ארעא מקטלא דירה מיכליכון בשר הדדי ומישתייכון מיא איסיוי נבחיתון כיכלבי נצריתון (11) כיחזירי ומישתרקיתון כיתניני בישמיש {מי} מיתקריתון מיתחזתון לה ליויתאי בת חתאי בחילמי בישי בידמותא סניתא מיתחזתון לה בדהבא וכספא אנכא נחשא ואברא מיתחזתון לה בידמות (12) אזרא ואילנא דמות אסא שוניא וארני מיתחזתון לה ליויתאי בת חתאי בגמלי בתורי וביחמרי באריוי בדיבי ובנמרי בשורני ובקופ[י] צילמתא יהוו כצילמתא דמיתי באבא ואימא בסבא וסבתי בעולימא ועולמתא בבטנתא (13) וילדתא בקברי סרודתא בחיתא דכצומי וכלדאי בתנורי שגירי בנוולי דלא מתקני מתחזתון לה ליויתאי בת חתאי בחיות גפא דארעא ובפרחותא דישמיה אתא עליכון מריא בגדנא כנשונכו כבשונכו ואחיתונכו תחות טורא רב(ה) דפרזלא (14) <א>(ת)א פרגוד רמנכו דיוי נקש לכו בליביכו אצמומי דפרזלא אחית עליכון טינרא רבה דיגלל אטף עליכון ימא וכיפיה שלם דלא יהוי עליכון דיוי ליומא רבה דדינא דימינא ודלא ימינא יהוי עליכון רוחי בישתא ואידי שמיה חילוותא איסתרתא (15) בני בתי חרבי בני כדי פסיסי דאמריתו ניזי נורי גאוני גברא מיגיני בארעא כי איסתרא דליות אתיא ברישיכו {רכיבי} אריא רכיבא מורניתא בידה נקיטא מנסבא {גוּנא לאילהי} זרגונא לאילהי וזרגונא לאיסתרתא חף כלהו לאילהי דחרשי לא ידעיתון דיוי (16) דגברא מילבר אתא עליכון קנטיואל שמיה סכין גודדא בידיה נקיט לי<ה> וחרבא סטנא בבית אצבעתיה ואתא למיסחף בתי דאילהי וסחוף כל איסתרתא סחפונהו לפתורהו שדונהו לאגנהו זלח להו חלבא בארבעא זויתא בסיא לקרניהו תברו לשיפורהו (17) שויא לחדותהו נסיסא כד מידכריתון

are idle (?) (10) and those women who give birth, sons of lust and prostitution, sons of abortions, sons of virgins, sons of destroyed houses, sons of broken jars, sons of mighty ones who were weak, sons of a land which kills its inhabitants. Your food is the flesh of each other, your drink is black water; you bark like dogs, you grunt (11) like pigs, you hiss like snakes, you are called by Shamish(?).

You make yourselves visible to Yawitai d. of Ḥatai in bad dreams, in a hateful shape. You make yourselves visible to her in (the shape of) gold and silver, plumb, brass and lead. You make yourselves visible to her in the shape (12) of cedar (?) and tree, in the shape of myrtle, tree of chastity and pines. You make yourselves visible to Yawitai d. of Ḥatai in (the shape of) camels, oxen, donkeys, lions, wolves, tigres, cats and monkeys. (Your) forms will be like the forms of the dead. (You make yourselves visible in the shape of) father and mother, grandfather and grandmother, a lad and a lass, a pregnant woman (13) and a child-bearing woman, tombs of fright, midwives of diviners and soothsayers, burning ovens, unmended looms. You make yourselves visible to Yawitai d. of Ḥatai (in the shape of) winged animals of the earth and birds of the sky.

There came to you the lord Bagdana. They gathered you, they suppressed you, they brought you down underneath the big mountain of iron. (14) There came attendants (?), they cast you, dēws, they struck against your hearts arrows of iron, he brought down upon you a large flint rock of unhewn stone, he caused the sea and its cliffs to flow over you.

Peace without peace shall be upon you, dēws, for the great day of judgement. That which is on the right hand and that which is not on the right hand shall be upon you, evil spirits and the evil fates of the sky, troops, goddesses, (15) sons of destroyed houses, sons of broken jars.

That which you say, "Let us go and shoot(?) the pride(?) of the mighty one, the protectors on the earth, like the goddess Deliwat (who) comes at your head, mounting a lion, holding a lance in her hand, handing over a *zargona* to the gods and a *zargona* to the goddesses, they all covered the gods of the sorcerers" — you do not know, dēws, (16) that a man come against you from the outside, whose name is Kantioel. He holds in his hand a cutting knife, and (he holds) between his fingers a Satan's sword; he came to wreck the houses of the gods, and he wrecked all the goddesses, they wrecked their table, they cast away their chalice, they sprinkled fat in the four corners, they trampled upon their horns, they broke their trumpets, (17) they turned their joy into grief.

דיוא רבה כמינקדם הוהוא קרבה נפקיתון מישתעבדיתון ליה לאורוס דיוא תקיפא חומרי בישתא חומרי טמיתא חומרי זידניתא תלת אלוא אסא שוו לכו ברישיכו מיגופנא זניא דליות לא ידיעיתון דיוי דגברא מילבר אתא עליכון (18) נוריאל רבה נוריאל שמיה נורא לביש ונורא מכסי שלהביתא דנורא נפקא מיפומיה כד מידכריתון דיוא רבה כמינקדם הוהוא קרבא נפקיתון מישתעבדיתון ליה לזרני דיוא תקיפא קרני קריתון שיפורי מיבביתון פתורי מכשטיתון אגני מזגיתון כלילי גדליתון (19) וריחא רמיתון דאמריתו ניזי להו לידמות א(ד)ם ולא נישבוק להו חיה בדיריהו ניקטול סבי באסניהו ואלימני באישכריהו ני[סחו]פינהו לדר[ד]קי בשוקי נירדופינהו בפגריהו נירדופינהו בארחתהו לא ידעיתון דיוי דגברא מילבר אתא עליכון ודהבה שמיה (20) דארעא כולה נהרא בזיוה וטורי כולהון צמחי בידמותיה אישתפל גברי חשוכא איבטל אידי שמיה חילוותא איתזח קצירי אישתפי כורה[נא ביש]א דיוא (ננא) אגביה לטורא טורא קדח ויליל רוחי בי[שתא ...]אה וי וי עליכו דיוי דמיתחזתון לה ליויתאי בת חתאי ולזוריגאי (21) בר אימא דאישתגר ואתא עליכון דיוי שמיש ליקרבה עשרא מלאכיהון דאיתו קדם שמיש חמשה ראזי מיבית שידיה דשמיש מלאכי דאיתו קדם שמיש נורא לבישין ונורא מכסי של[הביתא ד]נורא נפקא מיפומיהון תרע[מה ע]ליך שידא ודיוא ודנחיש (22) ודיני וזכיא ופתכרא וליליתא דיכרא וניקבתא דשריא עים יויתאי הרפתקא דדמא קטלא ית כולא כיבסחפי דדמא ורוגזא קריב קרבא בשידי קטיל קטלא בחומרי טמיתא ובו[חומרי ב]ישתא

When you recall the great dēw, as there was a battle in old times, you go out and make yourselves slaves of **ʾwrws** the violent dēw, the evil amulet-spirits, the impure amulet-spirits, the impious amulet-spirits; place three aloes <and> myrtle on your heads from the prostitute(?) vine <of> Deliwat (?) - you do not know, dēws, that a man from the outside came against you, (18) Nuriel, the great Nuriel is his name. He is clad with fire and is covered with fire (and) a flame of fire comes out of his mouth.

When you recall the great dēw, as there was a battle in old times, you go out and make yourselves slaves of Zarne, the violent dēw, you blow horns, you sound trumpets, you set tables, you mix (drink in) chalices, you dress up wreaths, (19) and throw about perfume.

That which you say, "Let us go and (make ourselves visible) to them in the shape of a human being and we shall not spare a living creature in their dwellings; let us kill the old in their granaries, and the dumb in their wagons; let us sweep away the children in the market places, let us chase them in their bodies, let us chase them in their roads" — you do not know, dēws, that a man from the outside came against you, whose name is Dahba; (20) the whole earth is aglow with his splendour, and all the mountains are resplendent with his shape. The men of darkness were lowered, the evil fates of the sky (and) the troops were annulled, the sick rose, the [evil i]llness was healed, the dēw Nana(?) lifted (?) the mountain, the mountain moaned and wailed; the evil spirits...

Woe, woe upon you, dēws, that you make yourselves visible to Yawitai d. of Ḥatai and to Zorigai (21) s. of Imma, that there was sent and there came upon you, dēws, Shamish for battle. Ten of their angels who came to the presence of Shamish, five mysteries from the demon house of Shamish, angels who came to the presence of Shamish, are clad with fire and covered with fire, and a flame of fire comes out of their mouths.

Commotion(?) upon you, demon and dēw, and Danahiš (22) and judges and an acquitted person, and idol, and male and female Lilith, who dwells with Yawitai. A bloody destiny is killing all, as in inundations of blood and wrath. The battle against the demons is approaching, the slaughter of impure and evil amulet-spirits is killing.

This bowl, from the Victor Klagsbald Collection, was put together from fragments by Mr. Rafi Brown. Almost the whole bowl was restored, with only a small fragment missing near the rim.

This is the largest bowl of its kind seen by us, and may be the largest recorded so far. The most common size of Aramaic incantation bowls "is of about 16 cm. diameter at top, by 5 cm. full depth" (Montgomery 1913, p. 13), and the size of "one large bowl" is 28x16 cm. (ibid.; cf. also Montgomery 1913, pp. 321–326). The present bowl, in contrast, measures 30–34 cm. in outer diameter (the measurement varies because the rim of the bowl is not a perfect circle), and the height, measured from the outside, is 14–15 cm. (again there are variations in the height of the bowl around the rim). Apart from the physical size of the bowl, it is also remarkable for its inordinately long text, as well as for the fact that it contains several phrases and expressions that are found here for the first time. For this reason some points in the text remain obscure. The structure of the text is unique, with its detailed description of the magical force appealed to, which is called Marya Bagdana.

The drawing in the centre of the bowl depicts a standing human figure with arms which touch each other as if meant to be crossed. A circle seems to be drawn round the feet of the figure. Around the whole figure a serpent is drawn as a *uroboros,* and another serpent is shown inside the circle formed by the first one, surrounding the figure on three sides, but not at the bottom. The inscription inside the circle identifies the figure as Lilith, although it has no features which would identify it as feminine.

1 The reading **(ly)lytʾ** is not absolutely certain, but the comparison of the phrase with what occurs in lines 7 and 22 shows that it must be Lilith, for this is the demonic being that is consistently said to be "dwelling" **(šryʾ)** with the client.

The name Yawitai/Yoitai may be a variant of Ya'ita (see Amulet 2), with the characteristic Babylonian ending *-ay* (as in Zorigai), which seems akin to the ending *-oy,* also attested widely in Babylonian names. These endings may be of Persian origin; see Commentary to Bowl 3:2.

Ḥatai, a name which is attested under the form Ḥatoi (e.g. Isbell 11:3, 9 and other places; see index to Isbell, p. 90), is almost certainly a derivative of *ʾaḥat* "sister", with the proper-name ending *-ay/oy.*

2 The spelling of the verse shows the interesting rendering of the *qamaṣ* with *waw* in **qwmk.** The third word in the original verse is **thrs,** and it was replaced apparently by a different verb, of which the last letter is *ṣade*; the verb may thus possibly be **trʿṣ,** which occurs in verse 6, or **ttṣ. yklmw** stands for the biblical **yʾklmw.**

3 The opening formula is vaguely reminiscent of the formula in Montgomery 1913, No. 2, where, however, the expressions used are in the first person singular. The combination **ḥylyh ... mymrʾ** occurs also in a Mandaic incantation text, where we have **bhilak umimrak utušbhtak** (Yamauchi 1967, No. 22:187–188).

rbh is used as a name of the deity, as in Bowl 6:9 **byšmyh ⌜d⌝rbʾ wdḥylʾ.** A similar usage can be detected in Amulet 1:8 **rbʾ gybrʾ wdḥylʾ;** Amulet 7:15 ... **krsyh dʾlh rbh ḥsynh wdḥylh.** In the first of these cases **rbʾ** may still be a noun, qualified by **gybrʾ wdḥylʾ,** although it reflects the Jewish liturgical sequence האל הגדול הגבור והנורא, while in the last case **rbh ḥsynh wdḥylh** are evidently all epithets of **ʾlh.** However, in the Syriac Amulet 6:1–2, the sequence **br tʾwn, rbʾ ḥṣynʾ, qdyš ʾylʾ** gives us the names of three deities, the second of which is "the mighty Rabbā", with *Rabbā* serving as proper name. It is doubtful whether **rbh dʾylhy,** which we may have been tempted to translate "Lord of the gods" belongs here, as it has a clear parallel in Montgomery 1913, No. 19:5 **mryʾ rbʾ dʾylhy** (according to the reading of Epstein 1921, p. 49), which in its turn corresponds to **mlktʾ rbtʾ dʾystrʾtʾ** (No. 19:6). In Montgomery No. 19 **rbʾ, rbtʾ** are adjectives qualifying **mryʾ, mlktʾ.**

bgdnʾ: The term is quite familiar. It is used both generically for deities or demons, and as a proper name of the king of the demons (cf. Montgomery 1913, No. 11:5, and No. 19:6, with commentary on p. 198). The original meaning of the Persian word is evidently *bag-dāna* "a temple" (see Shaked, forthcoming). The name is attested apparently also as a proper name of a person in official Aramaic, see Cowley 1923, No. 17:1. The deity Bagdana, although he is described as the chief of the demons, occurs as a divine figure which is addressed in magic texts in supplication for help, as is the case here.

ʾzyzʾ: The spelling of this word with an *alef* suggests that it is not the adjective "strong, powerful", but perhaps a proper name (possibly derived from the adjective; cf. **ʾzzyʾl,** Montgomery 1913, No. 19:18), which may have been used in apposition to Bagdana. An analogical usage of the epithet **ʿzyz** can be seen in Montgomery 1913, No. 28:5 **bšmh ddlybt ʿzyztʾ.** For a deity **ʿzyzʾ** one may compare Nabataean **ʾlʿzʾ,** Arabic *al-ʿUzzá*, see Cantineau 1930–1932, vol. 2, pp. 128–129; *Encyclopaedia of Islam,* s.v. *al-ʿUzzā.*

r'yšh dšyty mlkwt' seems to be in apposition to **mlkh.** This is hardly a case of **r'yšh** being used as an adjective for **mlkh,** as in Biblical Hebrew **hkhn hr'š** (II Chron. 31:10; Ezra 7:5), a usage which is unattested in a later period either in Hebrew or in Aramaic (in Jer. 52:24 **khn hr'š** is rendered in the Targum **khn' rb').** The phrase **r'yšh dšyty mlkwt'** does not mean "his head is of sixty kingdoms"; we have a description of the head further on in line 4 **r'yšyh r'yš' d'ry'.**

šyty is the form for "sixty", besides **šytyn,** cf. Epstein 1960, p. 127. The number "sixty" is fairly widespread in magic texts, sometimes together with "eighty". Cf. Montgomery 1913, No. 19:8–9; Yamauchi 1967, Nos. 20:16f.; 27:13. Like **šyty/šytyn** there is also **tmny** (Montgomery 1913, No. 19:9)/**tmnyn** (as well as **tmnn**), although the form **tmny** is not recorded in Epstein 1960 or in Rossell 1953. (The latter, p. 34, quotes Montgomery 1913, No. 19:9 as reading **tmnn,** which is an error. Rossell himself, on p. 110, gives the same text with the correct reading **tmny**).

ḥyl' (dzyq'): Cf. Montgomery 1913, No. 12:8 **nšpyn kyzyq' brqyn kybrq'** "blowing like the blast, lightening like the lightning".

4 **swgy'** could also be translated "walking".

kkyh: For this ending of the plural noun with 3rd per. sg. m. possessive pronoun see Epstein 1960, p. 123; Rossell 1953, p. 38, and our Introduction, p. 32.

dybth might be read **dwbth** "a she-bear", but this is less likely. **dibia** "wolves" occurs as a killing agent in the Mandaic text published in Yamauchi 1967, No. 33:11. Wolves are commonly associated with demons in Iranian texts. On the confusion between "bear" and "wolf" in Jewish sources see Kook 1943/44.

5 **syrpy pwmyh:** We have assumed that **syrpy** is derived from the root **SRP** "to swallow, gulp down" (cf. **ŚRP** in Jastrow for Jewish Aramaic, **SRP** in Drower and Macuch for Mandaic, and in Brockelmann for Syriac); the alternative senses of the root **SRP** may also give suitable meanings: "burning" or "resin". A similar expression is found in Montgomery 1912, line 4: **dsrpyhwn brq'** (= Hamilton 1971, No. 1:4).

'dwgy dnwr': For **'dwg'** cf. Brockelmann, p. 5b; Drower and Macuch, p. 7. In Mandaic both forms, **adugia** and **dugia,** occur. The expression in Bavli Ḥullin 111b **by dwgy** is said to designate a receptacle for fat drippings, but one wonders whether it does not mean literally "(that which is) in the oven".

(k)pydyh is a compound of **kp-yd,** with the first element remaining unchanged in the plural. The literal translation is of course "the palm of the hand", but the combination **kpʾ dydʾ** is used in Bavli Ḥullin 54a in the sense of "shoulder" (see Rashi). The writer of this bowl may have been particularly well-versed in Talmudic expressions; cf. Commentary on **gygly bʿnnʾ** and on **gbʾ dygylʾ** below.

gygly bʿnnʾ seems to recall the expression **ʿnny bglglʾ** in Bavli Berakhot 59a, which comes as an explanation of "thunders" (based on Ps. 77:19).

ṣydyh stands for **ṣydʿyh.**

sdnʾ dprzlʾ: The same expression occurs also in a Mandaic magic text, cf. Drower 1938, p. 3:22.

6 **gbʾ dygylʾ:** This combination of words occurs in Bavli Shabbat 110a and Menahot 42b: **gbyʾ gylʾ**, meaning "alum". It may contain the Persian element *gil* "clay". The back **(gbʾ)** is compared to alum **(gbʾ dygylʾ)** possibly because of the pun element involved.

šqyh šqy nḥšh wprzlʾ is reminiscent of Dan. 2:33 **šqwhy dy przl.** Much of this passage is constructed like the description in Dan. 2.

pryḥy: The root **PRḤ** means "to bloom", "to fly", as well as "to shine, spark". On the semantic relationship of "to bloom" with "to shine" see Morag 1972, pp. 4 f., and below Commentary to line 20, **ṣmḥy.** For our translation "sandals of sparks" cf. the Mandaic expressions **sandlia ḏ-ziua** (e.g. *Ginza S.* 97:19); **sandlia ḏ-kima; sandlia iaqdana** (*Johannesbuch* 100:7), quoted in Drower and Macuch, p. 313.

mrkbtyh mrkbtʾ lṭby: Cf. the Syriac bowl in Hamilton 1971, No. 1:56 **mrkbthwn mrkbt lṭʾb̈ʾ**. Our text is irregular; it should have read either **mrkbʾ <d>lṭby** or, as in the Syriac, **mrkbt lṭby.**

tyty: The feminine form, written by mistake, may have been caused by the word **mrkbtʾ.**

gys: We should normally have a final *alef* here, for which there is space on the surface of the bowl, but it does not seeem to have been written. An analogy for such an unexpected *status absolutus* in the same position is found in line 14 **ʾtʾ prgwd.** Gaster 1896, p. XVIII:31 has **ʾm npl ʿlk gysʾ.**

7 **qryb** is perf. in the *peʿal* form.

ʿl šydy wʿl dywy etc.: This has a parallel in lines 21–22.

dnḥyš: Probably of Persian derivation, cf. Shaked (forthcoming).

mlwytʾ: Cf. the expression in Montgomery 6:3 **dlwyn ʿmhwn wdšryn bgw btyhwn.**

zwryg'y contains probably *zōrīg* from Persian *zōr* "power", though it could be read as *zīrīg*, from Persian *zīr* "wise".

8 **pwlqt'** seems to be a form related to *pelqā*, attested in Syriac, and Mandaic **pilqa** with the meaning "axe, hatchet", and in Jewish Aramaic **plq** "fissure, wound". The Jewish Aramaic verb **PLQ** is only attested once in the variants to Bavli Giṭṭin 69a, and thus may be regarded as a denominative. The ultimate origin of the word seems to be Greek πελεκύς, cf. Brockelmann 1928, p. 576a; Jeffery 1938, p. 229 (on Arabic *falaqa*); Kaufman 1974, pp. 82f. (where the alleged Semitic root is relied upon with no good reason).

mwqrh, mwqdh: Aramaic seems to possess two words which look similar, and which have caused some confusion because of the similarity of *dalet* and *resh* in the Hebrew script. The one word, **mwqr'**, has the sense of (1) "brain, marrow", (2) "yolk of an egg". This word is attested in Jewish Aramaic (where only the first sense is known, cf. Targum Job 21:24. Targ. Jonathan Deut. 28:28 has for *šiggā'ōn:* **šwwyywt' dmṭpš' mwqd'**, where **mwqd'** is evidently miswritten for **mwqr'**); Syriac (where two forms, *mūqrā* and *mūqlā*, are attested, both having the sense of "yolk"); and Mandaic (where both senses are known). The Arabic *muqla* "pupil of the eye" has been pointed out as a cognate. The other word, which exists only in Jewish Aramaic, is **mwqd'**, and is the equivalent of Hebrew *qodqod* in the Targum (Ps. 7:17, Targ. Jonathan Deut. 28:35), meaning obviously "top of the head".

In our text we seem to have for the first time in Aramaic literature the two words attested side by side. Although the difference between *dalet* and *resh* in our bowl is not always very pronounced, the two letters can be differentiated in most cases. In this particular case a distinction between *resh* in the first word and *dalet* in the second is clearly present.

't'...qryb...rmy...tbr...špyd...mḥwnh...ḥbyl...bṭylw: This sequence of verbs presents a confusing picture. Some of the verbs are in the singular, others (**mḥwnh, bṭylw**) are in the plural. A similar problem exists below, lines 13 f., where we have **'t'...knšwnkw kbšwnkw w'ḥytwnkw ... 't' ... rmnkw ... nqš lkw...'ḥyt 'lykwn...'ṭp 'lykwn.** Another series occurs in line 16: **'t' ... sḥwp ... sḥpwnhw ... šdwnhw ... zlḥ lhw ... bsy' ... tbrw ... šwy'**; in the last series the forms of the verbs include not only singular m. and plural m., but also two forms of what looks like singular feminine (**bsy', šwy'**). One may try to explain the divergence of number by assuming that the text uses without distinction a reference either to

mry' or to **gys/prgwd** (the latter nouns being considered as plural), but the last sequence (line 16) has no plural noun which one may refer to. The alternative explanation could be that the distinction between singular and plural in the perfect 3rd. person was weak, because, perhaps like in Syriac, the final vowel of the third pl. m. was not pronounced. The forms with object suffixes where the plural forms are fully pronounced indicate that all the forms of the verbs (except the initial **'t'**) may have been intended as plural 3rd. m., referring perhaps to the host of agents helping the main figure. **sḥwp** may be compared to the Jewish Babylonian Aramaic like **'mwr** "they said" etc., cf. Epstein 1960, pp. 34 ff. The forms **'yštpl, 'ybṭl** etc., line 20, belong to the same category. The two forms **bsy'** and **šwy'** remain unexplained.

qwmh: The spelling with *waw* indicates that the first vowel was pronounced *o,* i.e. *ḥolam* for *qamaṣ*. On this phenomenon see above, Commentary to Bowl 12, and Introduction, p. 32. Earlier the same word is spelled **qmh.** Another instance of the same phenomenon may exist in the proper name **ywyt'y:** perhaps Yo'itay for Ya'ita.

9 **'zh:** The meaning is uncertain. It may indicate some disease, perhaps to be associated with the root **'ZY, 'Z'** (cf. Jastrow, s.v.). Montgomery 1913, 24:2, reads **'zyt'**, but the correct reading is **'ryt'**, cf. Commentary to Amulet 9:1–2. **'zh** could hardly be connected to **'zyz'** in line 3.

***(d')yštgr:** The bowl has clearly **ṭyštgr.** It should be emended according to line 21.

'ysywy: The combination **mia siauia** "black water" occurs in Mandaic, cf. Drower and Macuch, p. 265b, where many passages are quoted. The combination **my' syw'** occurs also in Gaster 1896, p. XXVI:7 (miswritten **pyw'y** in line 4). The word is of Iranian origin, from Parthian *siyāw* (cf. Widengren 1960, p. 100).

pgrt': This is perhaps from **PGR** "to be lax, faint", possibly referring to women who do not bear children, in opposition to **yldt'.** If we read **pgdt'** (though *resh* seems the better reading) we may have the sense of "women who hold back, who restrain" (as from **PGD** in Syriac) or, as a noun, "disaster" (as **pagadta** in Mandaic).

10 **psysy** cf. Jewish Aramaic **PYS,** Mandaic **PSS,** "to destroy, break, wreck". For the sense cf. Bereshit Rabba (quoted in three versions in Sokoloff 1982, p. 201) where "broken jars" **(qnqnym mrw'r'ym)** are compared to wicked people.

ʾrʿh mqṭlʾ dyrh: Cf. Num. 13:32, where the Targum Onqelos has **ʾrʿʾ mqṭlt ytbhʾ**; Targum Jonathan has **ʾrʿʾ mqṭlʾ ytbhʾ**.

10–11 The noises made by the demons are compared to those of various animals; a similar theme occurs in an Arabic text given by Winkler 1931, p. 5.

11 **dhbʾ, kspʾ, ʾnkʾ, nḥšʾ, ʾbrʾ:** Daniel 2:32 has the sequence **dhb, ksp, nḥš, przl, ḥsp.**

12 **ʾzrʾ** is perhaps a metathesis or mistake for **ʾrzʾ**.

šwnyʾ is attested in Syriac.

bšwrny: The word had two dialect forms in Jewish Aramaic: **šwrnʾ** and **šwnrʾ**, as can be seen from Bavli Berakhot 56b, according to Ms. Munich, where the text reads: "If one sees a cat in one's dream — where it is called *šunnara,* it means that a change for the bad (*šinnuy raʿ*) will come upon him; where it is called *šurana* it means that he will have a nice song (*šira naʾa*)", cf. Jastrow, p. 1537b. Old Aramaic has **šrn,** Sefire I, A33, cf. Fitzmyer 1971, p. 50.

wsbty: For this plural form cf. Epstein 1960, p. 119, where this form is conceded for pl. fem. in adjectives only. Here it is clearly used for a noun.

13 **srwdtʾ** cf. Commentary to Bowl 1:3.

dkṣwmy wkldʾy: Cf. the same combination in Mandaic: **kaṣumia ukaldaiia,** frequently (v. Drower and Macuch, p. 200b).

bḥywt gpʾ wbprḥwtʾ: The Targum for Prov. 1:7 has for *baʿal kanaf:* **prḥtʾ dgpʾ.**

knšwnkw etc.: For the verbs cf. above, Commentary to line 8.

ṭwrʾ...dprzlʾ: The recurring Mandaic phrase is **šura ḏparzla,** cf. Drower and Macuch, p. 364a.

14 <ʾ>**(t)ʾ**(?) **prgwd:** The reading of the first word is doubtful. The supposed *taw* is uncertain, but no better reading has presented itself. **prgwd** basically means "curtain", but it may have developed to mean "attendants, guardians"; this is based on the occurrence in Hebrew of the phrase לא דומה שומע מפי פרגוד לשומע מפי המלך (cf. Jastrow, p. 1214a). In Mandaic the equivalent term **br guda** (Drower and Macuch, p. 69a), acquired the meaning of "member of a group", perhaps because of the popular etymology of the word, which was deemed to be constructed of **br+guda** the final element meaning "band". In Syriac similarly we encounter the phrase **bny gwd᾽** "adherent of a party". It is doubtful whether in Jewish Aramaic **prgwd᾽** could undergo the same development of meaning, although if our reading is correct, **prgwd** seems to be used of a group of people, as it stands in parallel to the term **gys** (above, line 6), a term which also stands in juxtaposition to **mry᾽**.

A possible alternative reading could be {᾽} **᾽prgwd rmnkw** "they cast you against the curtain". This would entail regarding the first letter as a badly executed *alef,* which was then repeated and drawn in a proper manner. The difficulty here lies in the fact that this may be the only occurrence of the use of the preposition **᾽-** for **ʿl** in Jewish Aramaic of the bowls. The usage is very common in the Talmud, but for some reason it seems so far to be completely absent from the magic bowls.

rmnkw: Probably a mistake for **rmwnkw.**

᾽ṣmwmy: Cf. Mandaic **sṭmuma** with variants, in Drower and Macuch, p. 324a, derived from Greek στόμωμα.

wkypyh: See Commentary to Bowl 5:2.

ywm᾽ rbh ddyn᾽: Cf. Montgomery 1913, No. 4:4–5; Isbell 1975, No. 62:6.

dymyn᾽ wdl᾽ ymyn᾽: The translation is based on the assumption that the right hand indicates winning a trial. Alternatively, **ymyn᾽** could mean "I swear, I adjure". The translation would then be: "that which I swear and that which I do not swear be upon you".

ḥylwwt᾽: Montgomery, No. 7:14 has **ḥylwnyn byšyn** according to Epstein 1921, p. 35, where **ḥylwt᾽** is also discussed.

15 From here onwards we have a series of stereotype phrases:

(1) lines 15–16	**d᾽mrytw ... l᾽ ydʿytwn**
(2) line 17	**kd mydkrytwn ... l᾽ ydʿytwn**
(3) line 18	**kd mydkrytwn ...** [something missing?]
(4) line 19	**d᾽mrytw ... l᾽ ydʿytwn**

After **d᾽mrytw** the verb **nyzy** occurs. After **l᾽ ydʿywtn** the constant phrase is: **dywy dgbr᾽ mylbr ᾽t᾽ ʿlykwn w-X šmyh.** The name of this **gbr᾽** is **qnṭyw᾽l, nwry᾽l** or **dhbh.** The phrases beginning with **kd mydkrytwn** go on in a uniform manner: **dyw᾽ rbh kmynqdm hwhw᾽ qrbh npqytwn myštʿbdytwn lyh l-X dyw᾽ tqyp᾽**. The name of the mighty demon is in one case **᾽wrws,** and in the other **zrny.**

The stereotype phrases are evidently built in the form of an argument, with an assumption made by one party: **d᾽mrytw...,** or **kd mydkrytwn...;** and this assumption is refuted by the phrase **l᾽ ydʿytwn,** which identifies the persons addressed by the vocative **dywy.** The text seems lacunary at one point, when in lines 18–19 there is no response to **kd mydkrytwn.**

nwry g'wny gbr': The reading is uncertain. Another possible division of words is **nyrwg 'wny gbr'** "we shall desire the dwellings of the mighty one".

mygyny b'r'': Cf. the Hebrew phrase **mgny 'rṣ** (Ps. 47:10). The initial **my-** is peculiar (as if the word had an initial preposition **mn**), though the *yod* may represent a *shva.*

dlywt: An unusual spelling for this name, which is commonly spelled **dlybt, dlbt,** cf. Montgomery 1913, p. 217. Reading **dlwwt** "who is together" seems less satisfactory.

{rkyby}, {gwn' l'ylhy} in both cases the scribe seems to have corrected himself without crossing out the wrong words.

'ry' rkyb': Cf. Gollancz 1898, p. 88: **'ry' rkybn' wbrtnyn'.**

mwrnyt' bydh nqyṭ': Cf. line 16 **skyn gwdd' bydyh nqyṭ ly<h>,** said of **qnṭyw'l.**

zrgwn' is a word of Iranian origin, meaning "yellow, gold coloured". In the Avesta *zairi gaona* (Bartholomae 1904, col. 1680) describes the *haoma* plant. It seems very close in origin to **zrny.** In Jewish Aramaic it designates a certain plant (beet or vine, cf. Kohut 1955, III, p. 319b; Löw 1924-34, I, p. 69; III, p. 449). Arabic *zarajūn* means both "vine" and "wine" (v. Ibn Qutayba 1900, p. 526, and Geiger *apud* Krauss 1955, pp. 169b f.). Talmudic Aramaic *zaryon,* a derivative of the same word, may mean "grape-wine" or "gold-coloured (wine)", cf. Geiger, loc. cit.

ḥp klhw: The verb seems to refer in the perfect to the two *zargona*-s (unless we refer **klhw** to the **'ylhy dḥršy** which follows, and translate "covering all the gods of the sorcerers"). It is noteworthy that *zargona* occurs in Yerushalmi, Sukka III, p. 53c, where we have the same verb used: עץ שענפיו חופין את רובו ועולה כמין קליעה ... אין תימר זרגונה ענפיו חופות את רובו ואינו עולה כמין קליעה ואיזה זה זה הדס

16 **wḥrb' sṭn':** We have **ḥrb' dqṭl'** in line 6.

bsy'...šwy': See above, Commentary to line 8.

17 **hwhw':** This should probably be read *hāwe (h)wā,* "there was", a typical Syriac expression (cf. Nöldeke 1898, § 277). It occurs in the group of texts Montgomery 1913, Nos. 32:3; 33:2; 9:2, which should be read with the comments and corrections offered by Epstein 1921, pp. 37 f.

'wrws is probably the god Horus. Montgomery 1913, No. 19:11 may have the same name (spelled **'wrs**?). **'wrws** is here parallel to **zrny** in line

18. A reading **ʾyrws**=Eros should also be considered, although it seems less likely. A third possibility is Ares, which occurs in Arabic magical literature (cf. Ps.-Majrīṭī 1933, p. 212).

tlt ʾlwʾ ʾsʾ: The text is difficult, and may be corrupt. A possible hypothetical reconstruction could be **tlt**<**ʾ**> <**ʾylny**> **ʾlwʾ ʾsʾ** <**w...**> **šww lkw bryšykw** "place on your heads three trees: aloe, myrtle and ..." On **ʾlwh, ʾlwws,** etc. see Löw 1924–34, III, pp. 342, 411 ff.

gwpnʾ is apparently used as a general term for a plant.

znyʾ is probably used in the botanical sense of "creeping, spreading in all directions", for a plant. A similar metaphor seems to be present in Jer. 2:20–21, where the expression סורי הגפן נכריה symbolizes a prostitute woman.

18 **nwrʾ lbyš wnwrʾ mksy**: Cf. Geniza 6, p. 3:6 for a similar expression. The same phrase occurs also in T–S AS 143.113.

zrny has an obvious Iranian etymology: *zarana-, zaranya-* "golden". The demon occurs in Montgomery 1913, No. 11:6, where we have a female genealogy: **zrny lylyth** is the grandmother of **ḥlbs** or **ḥldʾs lylytʾ**. The text is attested in two Judaeo-Aramaic versions and in one Mandaic text. This Lilith is apparently part of the retinue of Bagdana. In our text **zrny** is evidently a masculine figure. As a personal name Zarniya seems to be present in an Elamite text (cf. Mayrhofer 1973, p. 231, No. 8.1505), and Zarina, Zarinaia in Greek transmission (cf. Justi 1895, p. 382). The Pahlavi name Zarr-mihr (cf. Gignoux 179, p. 78) may be a *dvandva* compound of Zarniya and Mihr, both divine names (?).

qrny qrytwn, šypwry mybbytwn: These are unusual expressions, where the indirect object is given without an instrumental preposition **b-**.

mkšṭytwn: KŠṬ and **QŠṬ** in the sense of "to dress, set, adorn" seem to be interchangeable in Aramaic.

19 **ʾ(d)m**: The reading is uncertain, and so is the translation. The second letter could be a *kaf.*

sby...ʾlymny...drdqy: Three groups of helpless people.

dhbh: This name seems to be the Aramaic equivalent of Iranian **zrny** (line 18).

20 **ṣmḥy**: This verb like **PRḤ** has the double meaning of "blooming, growing" and "shining". Cf. above, line 6, to **pryḥy.**

ʾyštpl...ʾybṭl...ʾytzḥ: These verbs belong to subjects in the plural: **gbry, ʾydy šmyh, qṣyry.** Their singular forms confirm the supposition that the plural endings of verbs in the perfect were unpronounced (unless followed by a suffix). See above, Commentary to line 8 on **ʾtʾ** etc.

ʾytzḥ: The phrase corresponds closely to Bavli Bava Batra 16b **ʾydly ywmʾ ʾydly qṣyrʾ** "the day has risen, the sick man has risen", which is quoted there as a popular proverb.

ʾgbyh: This verb is seemingly derived from **GBY** "to seize (for taxes)", or, as in Syriac, "to choose". As none of these senses goes well with our context, we prefer to see this verb as belonging to **GBH** (which should have given **ʾgbhyh**) "to raise, lift".

qdḥ is a magic verb, as evidenced by Montgomery 1913, No. 10:11. See Epstein 1921, pp. 41 f., who overemphasizes, it seems, the sense of "to rise, pierce", while several passages make it plain that the verb has also the sense of "to wail, moan", as noted by Epstein himself, ibid., p. 42, notes 1–2. Cf. especially Yamauchi 1967, No. 22:162f. (=Lidzbarski 1909) **ašlit illit uqhdit uṣinpit uamrit** "I shrieked, wailed, howled, screamed and said". For **QDḤ** in the sense of "to flee" see Bowl 10:11.

21 **šmyš:** For a similar role of this deity cf. Montgomery 1913, No. 36:2–3.

mlʾkyhwn: The possessive suffix is somewhat unexpected. One might think of an error for **ʿšrʾ mlʾky h<yn>wn** "they are ten angels", or the like.

dʾytw: It seems that this is a *peʿal* form in the perfect tense, spelled with a *yod* for traditional Jewish Aramaic *ḥataf pataḥ*.

mybyt šydyh: This expression seems to correspond to the original meaning of Iranian **baga-dāna-,* Old Persian *daiva-dāna-* "house of deities, temple". Cf. Shaked (forthcoming).

trʿ[mtʾ] or **trʿ[mʾ]** "quarrel, complaint"; an alternative reading could be **trʿ[tʾ]** "break, breach" (which the Targum uses for Hebrew פרץ).

III. Amulets and Fragments of Magic Books from the Cairo Geniza

Geniza 1

Amulet on cloth
T–S A.S. 142.174
Plate 32

 או או ה ה ה ה
ה ה ייות אתון כל קטיריה קדישיא וכל אתיה משבחיה אלהבו
ואבערו לביה דטרשכין בן אמה אללה בתר גדב בת תפאחה
אמן

For the writing of an amulet on a piece of cloth, see below, Geniza 6, p. 1:15, **kyrqh gdydh** "a new cloth".

2 **kl qṭyryh:** The writer divided the word wrongly, assuming that these are two words meaning "all the knots", which he followed by **kl ᵓtyh** "all the letters". **klqṭyryh** corresponds to **klqṭyrym, krqṭyrym** (Greek

Geniza 2

Two pages from a magic book
T–S A.S. 143.229
Plate 33

page 1

بسم الله الرحمن الرحيم الحمد لله
איתי ביעתא בת יומא בוכרתא
מן זגתא בר בטינתא ועיבד
שכבת زرع וחקק עלה ג̇ חלקין
דעילא כתוב זפק רבו יקר

Geniza 1

Translation

1 (*magic characters*) **ʾw ʾw h h h**
2 **hh yywt.** You holy characters and all praiseworthy letters, kindle
3 and burn the heart of **ṭrškyn** son of Amat-Allāh (in longing) after **gdb** daughter of Tuffāḥa.
4 Amen.

χαρακτῆρες); see Margalioth 1966, pp. 4, 83–87. The phenomenon is already attested in Talmudic literature, cf. Kohut 1955, IV, p. 243a.

3 The magic aim of making someone's heart burn in longing after someone else occurs frequently in the love amulets from the Geniza. In our texts it occurs in Amulet 10.

Geniza 2

Translation

page 1

1 Bring a first-born egg of the (same) day
2 from a *bar-baṭinta* hen, and make
3 an effusion of semen, and engrave on it 3 parts.
4 On the upper one write **zpq rbw yqr**

יבר נבוג ואמצעי כתוב
אזיסקע מגד מסגייע ודלתחתא
מזריקי לאי מעטל וקבר
ביעתא בזבלא דקנינ(א) מ רוז
ובתר כן אפ(ת)[ח] ואת [מ]שכח
בה תרין צילמ[ין] חד דאדם
וחד דצפרה והנך דאדם
קברה על דרנא דמפלגא
לארבעי אורחתא ודצפרא
שחטה על זוזא חיורא
ועיביד הנך זוזא טבעת

page 2

הכה(א) (?) פנג (?) שמיה (........)
צום יום אלכמיס ולילת אלגומעה ואכתוב
יום אלגומעה באכר פי כזפה ניה פי
בית כאלי ואטרח פי אלחמאם (ב)[שֵׁם]
גבריאל ורפאל וצוריאל ודלקיאל
ועוזיאל מיכאל ושרפיאל ואקביאל
בשם אל אל אל אל אל אל אל נננננננננ
בשם עעעעעע בשם
ההההההה אתון שמהתא
קדיש[יא] ותק[יפיא] גיבריא
אוק[יד]ו וא[דליקו] ליבה ומזלה
וכוליתה דפֿ בֿ פֿ בתר פֿ בֿ פֿ
כמה דהדא חיספא מתיקדא
אמן אמן בפריע 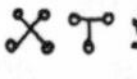
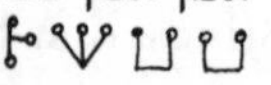 עיבידו דוצו אוחו
זריזו זלזילו ולא תעכבון

Notes to the text
p. 1:0 Addition above the line.
p. 2:0 Apparently added above the line.

5 **ybr nbwg.** On the middle one write
6 **ʾzysqʿ mgd msgyyʿ.** On the lower one
7 **mzryqy lʾy mʿṭl.** Bury
8 the egg in manure of cattle (for) forty days,
9 and after that open it and you will find
10 therein two images, one of a man
11 and one of a bird. The one of a man
12 bury in a valley which splits
13 in four ways; that of a bird
14 slaughter on a white *zuz*
15 and make of this *zuz* a ring.

page 2

1 Fast on Thursday and Friday eve night and write
2 early on Friday morning on an unbaked sherd in
3 an empty house, and throw it into (the furnace of) the bathhouse: In the name of
4 Gabriel, Raphael, Ṣuriel, Dalqiel,
5 ʿUziel, Michael, Sarafiel and Aqbiel.
6 In the name of El El El El El El El **nnnnnnnn.**
7 In the name of ʿʿʿʿʿʿʿ. In the name of
8 **hhhhhhh.** You holy and
9 mighty names, heroes,
10 kindle and inflame the heart, fortune (!)
11 and kidney of X b. Y (in longing) after A b. B,
12 just as this sherd burns!
13 Amen, Amen. Immediately. (*magic*
14 *characters*) Do, skip ...,
15 hurry, make easy and do not deter.

1:2 The term *zagta bar baṭinta* is evidently based on the Talmudic phrase **זגתא אוכמתא בי בטניתא** (Bavli Bava Meṣiʿa 86b), the meaning of which is not unequivocal. Rashi, followed by J. Levy (*Chaldäisches Wörterbuch,* s.v.), interpret it in the meaning of "a fattened black brooding hen", while Jastrow, s.v. **בטניתא**, tends to regard the phrase *Be baṭnita* as a geographic term. In Targum Jud. 15:15 **bṭyntʾ** stands for **ṭryh** "fresh" (cf. Tal 1975, p. 200, n. 25); see also Geniza 6, p. 4:10 **bydh ṭryh,** and Scholem 1965, p. 112.

1:3 **škbt zrʿ:** The second word in this Biblical Hebrew term is written in Arabic letters, with the possible aim of making the phrase difficult to decipher, perhaps because of its sexual connotation.

1:8 **rwz** is a Persian word.

1:11 **hnk** is here used for the singular, although it is otherwise consistently attested for the plural, both in the Talmudic literature and in the magic bowls (Montgomery 1913, No. 4:3), the latter under the form **ʾhnyk.** Cf. Epstein 1960, p. 26.

1:12 **drnʾ**: The reading is certain. The word is not Aramaic, unless we assume a corruption from **drkʾ** "road". **drn** is attested in Judaeo-Persian Bible translations for rendering Hebrew *ʿemeq* "valley" (cf. e.g. Paper

Geniza 3

Amulet

T–S A.S. 143.403

Plate 34

1 בשם אומר ועושה
2 מזמן הדין שמא לדלאל בת ציא
3 באהבת עשיר בן וצאיף שימני
4 כחותם על לבה ד˺ד˹לאל בת ציא וכחותם
5 על זרועך את דלאל בת ציא כי
6 עזה כמות אהבת דלאל בן(!) ציא

1972, Gen. 14:3,7,8; the editor read incorrectly **ddn**). The occurrence of two Persian words in this text, **rwz** and (presumably) **drn**, shows that the text derives from a Judaeo-Persian *milieu.*

2:2 *bākir* is evidently an Arabic word.

kzph nyh: Cf. also Geniza 5, p. 3:12 **šqph nyh;** Geniza 6, p. 1:3 and p. 4:4 **pkr ny,** all referring to an unbaked potsherd, and in all cases (with the possible exception of Geniza 6, p. 4:4) love charms are involved. For an example of an actual love amulet written on "unbaked clay" see Amulet 10, and the Commentary *ad loc.*

2:10 **lybh wmzlh wkwlyth:** The word **wmzlh** stands for **whwnh,** cf. Geniza 6, p. 1:13 **kn thpkwn lbh whwnh wkwlyth** ...The word **hwnʾ** *(=hawnā)* means "mind, intelligence", but the writer associated this word with the Biblical Hebrew *hōn* "wealth, fortune"; the latter is translated in the Targum of Psalms (e.g. 112:3) and Proverbs (8:18; 19:4; 24:4; 29:3) by **mzlʾ,** where in some manuscripts it is written **mwdlʾ.**

2:13 **bpryʿ** corrseponds to Greek ταχύ, cf. Reitzenstein 1904, p. 292, notes. For Aramaic **pryʿ** cf. Kutscher 1976, p. 82. A similar expression in Aramaic is **bʿglh wlʾ ttʿkb;** cf. Scholem 1965, p. 111.

2:15 **tʿkbwn** cf. Amulet 3:15.

Geniza 3

Translation

1 In the name of He who says and creates.
2 This spell (*lit.* name) is designated for Dallāl daughter of Ḍiyāʾ
3 for the love of ʿAšīr son of Waṣāʾif. Set me
4 as a seal upon the heart of Dallāl d. of Ḍiyāʾ and as a seal
5 on your arm, you, Dallāl d. of Ḍiyāʾ. For
6 the love of Dallāl d. of Ḍiyāʾ

7 לעשיר בן וצאיף קשה כשאול קנאה
8 רשפיה רשפי אש שלהבתיה מים
9 רבים לא יוכלו לכבות את אהבת דלאל
10 בן(!) ציא לעשיר בן וצאיף ונהרות לא
11 ישטפוה אם יתן איש א כל הון ביתו
12 בא בוז יבוזו לו ויהי יי את עשיר בן
13 [וצ]איף ויט [אליו חסד ויתן חנו בעיני]
14 [דלאל בת ציא ...]

3–12 The text is based on Cant. 8:6–7.

6 The writer uses here and in line 10 *ben* for *bat* after Dallāl. See above, Commentary to Bowl 4:7.

Geniza 4

Amulet
T–S K 1.68
Plate 34

....
1 סלה סלה הללו[יה] בשם יי אל(הי) ישר(א)[ל]
2 על חסדך ועל אמתו[ך] יה אלהים א אלהים א א[להי]
3 מערכות ישראל געור כל רוחין בישין [ויסורין]
4 וכל פגעין וכל מזיקין וכל שטן וכל צער וכל
5 מכאוב וכל מיני רוחין ושדין בשם אהיה
6 אשר אהיה שאמר והיה העולם בשם ששמע
7 הים ונבקע שמע האש ונכבה ושמעו הסלעים
8 ונשברו ושמע האבן ויתפוצץ השבעתי א[תכם]

7 to ʿAšīr s. of Waṣāʾif is strong as death. Jealousy is cruel as Sheʾol.
8 The coals thereof are coals of fire which have a most vehement flame. Many
9 waters cannot quench the love of Dallāl
10 d. of Ḍiyāʾ to ʿAšīr s. of Waṣāʾif, nor can the floods
11 drown it. If a man would give all the substance of his house
12 for love, it would be utterly scorned. And God was with ʿAšīr s. of
13 Waṣāʾif and showed [him mercy and gave him favour in the sight of Dallāl]
14 [daughter of Diya...   ]

12–13 Based on Genesis 39:21.

Geniza 4

Translation

1 Selah Selah Selah Hallelujah. In the name of **yy** the God of Israel,
2 for thy loving-kindness and for thy truth (Ps. 138:2). Yah God, ʾ, God, ʾ, the God of
3 the armies of Israel (I Sam. 17:45), drive out all evil spirits [and afflictions]
4 and all blows and all harmful spirits and every Satan and all grief and all
5 pain and all kinds of spirits and demons. In the name of
6 I-am-who-I-am, who spoke and the world came into being. In the name of He who, (when) the sea
7 heard (his voice) it split, (when) the fire heard it was extinguished, (when) the rocks heard
8 they broke, (when) the stone heard it exploded. I adjure you,

9 רוחא ושידא בשם המפורש היושב על כנ(פי) [רוח]
10 היושב על ערבות ביה שמו היושב בעבי
11 שחקים היושב בשמי שמים ועוד השבעתי
12 אתכם כל רוחין וכל שדין וכל [מ]זיקין וכל סטנין
13 וכל צער וכל מכאוב וכל מיני פורעני[ות בשם]
14 מיכאל וגבריאל ו(ר)[פאל] וצוריאל ו(נו)ריאל וברקיאל
15] ושר]פיאל ועוד [השבעתי אתכם]
16 כל רוחין ושדין ו[מז]יקין בשם] [
17 שלמה] [
18 ותתע(ר)] [

In the margin:

[אהו יהא יהו] חח אאא ה בב או מ אב אמן אמן סלה

6 ff. "In the name of He who, (when) the sea heard (his voice) it split" etc: This sequence of adjurations is strongly reminiscent of the Hadrumetum love charm in Greek, quoted in Blau 1898, pp. 97 ff., especially lines 19 ff. Cf. also Geniza 7:8 ff.

Geniza 5

Four pages from a magic book
T–S K 1.70
Plates 35-36

page 1

1  לאישתא רקיקתא ٢٧
2 ולעיריותא: משבענא בשם
3 חי האל ובשם צוריאל וכדותיאל
4 על מחושה מי שיהיה עליו הכתב
5 הזה דאיתסי בשם 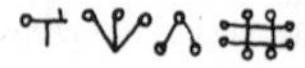

9 spirit and demon, in the name of the Tetragrammaton, who sits on the wings of the wind (II Sam. 22:11),
10 who sits on clouds, Yah is his name (Ps. 68:5), who sits in thick clouds
11 of the skies (II Sam. 22:12), who sits in the heavens of heavens (Ps. 68:34). Further I adjure
12 you all spirits and harmful spirits, and all Satans,
13 and all grief and all pain and all kinds of troubles. In the name of
14 Michael, Gabriel, Raphael, Ṣuriel, Nuriel, Barqiel,
15 [... Sara]fiel. Further [I adjure you]
16 all spirits and demons and harmful spirits. In the name of [...]
17 ...

9 On the concept of *šem hammeforaš* as used in magic texts cf. Blau 1898, pp. 123 ff.

The reconstruction of the letters in the margin is based on T-S K 1.168, lines 38–39.

Geniza 5

Translation

page 1

1 [xxvii] For fever, hectic fever,
2 and for shivering: I adjure in the name
3 of the God who lives and in the name of Ṣuriel and Kadutiel,
4 against pain. He who wears this writing
5 may he be healed. In the name of (*magic characters*)

6 ג ג ג :
7 אחר׳ קמיע טוב׳ ٢٨
8 אסותא דרחמנא למי שיהיה עליו
9 הקמיע הזה שהוא ממשפחת ישראל
10 אשביעך רוח ביהוה אלהי השמים
11 ובשביל סנדלפון ובשביל מיטטרון
12 שיתן צ(ינ)ים שיש על מי שיהיה עליו

page 2

1 הכתב הזה לגוים ואל יתן אתו לפֿ
2 בֿ פֿ שהוא מישראל ו˺י˹אמר יעקב
3 כאשר ראם מחנה אלהים ˺זה˹ ויקרא
4 שם המקום ˺ההוא˹ מחנים : ויצעק העם
5 אל משה ויתפלל משה אל יהוה
6 ותשקע האש : אחישה מפלט
7 לי מרוח סעה מסער : אֿ בֿ גֿ דֿ
8 יהוה ... יהא עוזר וסומך לפֿ בֿ פֿ
9 מיכאל מימינו וגבריאל משמאלו
10 רפאל רפא אתו׳ יהוה אל באפך
11 תוכיחני ואל בחמתך תיטרני :
12 חנני יהוה כי אמלל אני רפאני יהוה כי

page 3

1 נבהלו עצמי :
2 קמי[ע] לשנתה׳ ٢٩
3 [ ] (ד)שמאלא
4 שמה רבה בר(וך) ברוך דהוא רמה
5 שנת תרדימה על אדם ודמך כן
6 ידמוך פֿ בֿ פֿ אמן אמן סלה :
7 למן דחשש ראשיה ٣٠
8 כתֿ שמה דהדין מלאכה פולתמה
9 געור צערה דהדן שנה בין בימינה
10 בין בשמאלה אמן אמן סלה :
11 לאהבה׳ ٣١
12 כתוב עלי שקפה ניה ואלקיהא פי

6 (*a magic character*) **ggġ**
7 [xxviii] Another (matter). A proper amulet.
8 Healing of the Merciful to him who wears
9 this amulet, who is of the family of Israel.
10 I adjure you, spirit, in (the name of) **yhwh,** the God of heaven,
11 and for Sandalfon and for Metatron,
12 that he should give shields (?) of marble (?) to him who wears

page 2

1 this writing, against (?) the Gentiles, but he should not give it
2 against (?) X b. Y, who is of Israel. And when Jacob
3 saw them (the angels) he said: this is God's camp, and he called
4 the name of that place Mahanayim (Gen. 32:3). And the people cried out
5 to Moses, but Moses prayed to the Lord
6 and the fire quenched (Num. 11:2). I would hasten to find a refuge
7 for myself from the windy storm and the tempest (Ps. 55:9). **ʾ b g d**
8 **yhwh** (...) will help and support X b. Y.
9 Michael is on his right side, Gabriel is on his left side,
10 Raphael cure him. O Lord, rebuke me not in thy anger,
11 nor chasten me in thy hot displeasure.
12 Have mercy upon me, O Lord, for I am weak, O Lord, heal me for

page 3

1 my bones shudder (Ps. 6:2–3).
2 [xxix] An amulet for sleep.
3 [...] of the left side.
4 His great name be blessed. Blessed is He who caused
5 a deep sleep to fall upon Adam and he slept, so shall
6 X b. Y sleep, Amen Amen Selah.
7 [xxx] For him who has a headache.
8 Write the name of this angel Pultama (?).
9 Drive out the pain of this tooth (?) either on his right side
10 or on his left side, Amen Amen Selah.
11 [xxxi] For love.
12 Write on an unbaked sherd and throw it into

page 4

אלנאר· בשם עזריאל פוריאל
לפֿ בֿ פֿ אמן אמן סלה[:] יום דֿ
[ ] ٣٢
יכתב פי רק בס(ך) [וזע]פראן פי יום
אלג וידפן פי באב אלדאר והדה
כתאבתה· מזמן הדין לאפרוחי
ית פֿ בֿ פֿ בתר פֿ בֿ פֿ אשבעית יתך
נוריאל דיתיב על תרעי נורא· ואת
שמשיאל דיתיב על [ג]לגלי שמשא
וכן כתוב אשבעית עליכון בשום
שמקח הלוך פקח ענבים ד(או)פע
דתידלקון ותיזחון ליביה דפֿ בֿ פֿ

This is a fragment from a book of magical recipes. The individual sections are marked by Arabic numerals (27–32) on the outside margin.

1:1 For the medical terms which occur here cf. the Commentary to Amulet 2. **rqyqt'** is an error for **dqyqt';** other corruptions of these terms see in Geniza 6, p. 3:12 and p. 4:1–2.

1:3 **ḥy h'l:** Cf. Amulet 1:23.

1:12 **ṣynym:** The reading is somewhat doubtful, but this seems to be the only possible interpretation of the letters. The word is probably connected with one of the group of words attested in Biblical Hebrew: *ṣinna, ṣinnim, ṣinnot, ṣninim,* the meanings of which cover the following range: (1) shield; (2) prick, thorn; (3) fishing hook or spear; (4) chill, cold (cf. Gesenius-Robinson-Browne, *Hebrew and English Lexicon of the Old Testament,* Oxford 1975, s. vv.), or, less likely, with Talmudic *ṣinna* "basket". The association of this word with **šyš,** which apparently means "marble, alabaster", is unclear. An alternative reading might be

page 4

1 the fire. In the name of Azriel, Puriel,
2 for X b. Y, Amen Amen Selah... On Wednesday.
3 [xxxii] [...]
4 It will be written on leather with *sukk* (?) and saffron, on
5 Tuesday, and will be hidden in the door of the house. And this is
6 the writing on it: This is designated to cause X b. Y
7 to chase after A b. B. I adjure you,
8 Nuriel, who sits on the gates of fire, and
9 Shamshiel, who sits on the sun-globes.
10 And write as follows: I adjure you in the name of
11 **šmqḥ hlwk pqḥ ʿnbym dʾwpʿ**
12 that you should kindle and move the heart of X b. Y

šeyyēš, which would give an ungrammatical construction, unless some error is assumed in the writing.

2:1 In **lgwym,** as afterwards in **lp. b. p.**, the initial *lamed* seems to be used in the unusual sense of "against", or possibly "for (fighting against)".

3:4–5 Our text is based on Targum to Gen. 2:21.

3:7–10 The headache referred to in this amulet seems to be a toothache.

3:12 For **nyh** cf. Geniza 2, p. 2:2.

4:4 For **sk** cf. also Geniza 6, p. 2:8 **swk**. The word signifies a certain combination of elements, which make up a well known medical preparation; cf. e.g. Garbers 1948, pp. 329–331; Ps. Majrīṭī 1933, pp. 220:1, 275:7.

Geniza 6

Four pages from a magic book
T–S K 1.73
Plates 37–38

page 1

לבה דפ̇ ב̇ פ̇ ולא יהווי לפ̇ ב̇ פ̇ אסו עד
מן דיעבד צביוני נפשה דפ̇ ב̇ פ̇ א̇ א̇ א̇
ס̇ ה̇ חורן יוכתב עלא פכר ני ויטרח
פי אלוקיד והדה אלדי תוכתב בשם
אומר ועושה מזמן הדן כתבה לפ̇ ב̇ פ̇
דירחום ית פ̇ ב̇ פ̇ ויהווי ליבה יקד הך
מא דהדן חספא יקד כן יהווי לבה דפ̇ ב̇ פ̇
יקד בתר פ̇ ב̇ פ̇ בשם נוריאל מלאכה
רבה דמני על חסדא ו(א) וחנה אחת
נור מן נורך ואשה מן אשתך ואק(ו)ד
לבה דפ̇ ב̇ פ̇ בשם א̇ב̇ר̇ס̇כ̇ס̇
מלאכה רבה דהפוך את סדום את
עמרה כן תהפכון לבה והונה וכוליתה
דפ̇ ב̇ פ̇ בתר פ̇ ב̇ פ̇ אא̇א̇ סה̇: חורן
כוד כירקה גדידה וכתוב עליהא
הדא אלכלם ואגעלהא פי אנבובה
קצב ואדפינהא פי שפת

page 2

נהר גרי בשם רחמנא מזמ<ן> הדן רז[ה]
לרחמתא רבה דירחום ית פ̇ ב̇ פ̇
בשם א̇ א̇ הלוציאל הניא<ל> יה אהנהאל
צוריאהאל א̇ א̇ א̇ ס̇ ה̇ אתון אתייה
קדישייה אלהבו ולק(טף)א ודלקו לבה
דפ̇ ב̇ פ̇ בתר פ̇ ב̇ פ̇ ויהוי רחם לה אמן
סלה הלו ○ חורן כתוב עלא ריק גזל

Geniza 6

Translation

page 1

...(1) the heart of X b. Y, and that there should be no healing to X b. Y until (2) he does the desires of A b. B's soul. A(men) A(men) A(men) (3) S(elah) H(allelujah).

Another (charm). It should be written on an unbaked potsherd and thrown (4) into the fire. This is what should be written: "In the name of (5) He who says and does. This writing is designated for X b. Y (6) that he should love A b. B, and that his heart should burn, just (7) as this piece of pottery burns, so should X b. Y's heart (8) burn (in longing) after A b. B. In the name of Nuriel the great (9) angel who is appointed over grace and loveliness! Bring down (10) a light from your light and a fire from your fire and kindle (11) the heart of X b. Y. In the name of Abrasax (12) the great angel who overturned Sodom and (13) Gomorrah, so should you turn the heart, the mind and the kidney (14) of X b. Y (in longing) after A b. B. A(men) A(men) A(men) S(elah) H(allelujah)."

Another (charm). (15) Take a new (piece of) cloth and write on it (16) these words and put it in a pipe of (17) reed and bury it in the bank of

page 2

(1) a running river: "In the name of the Merciful! This mystery is designated (2) for a great love that (X b. Y) should love A b. B. (3) In the name of ʾ, ʾ, Haluṣiel, Haniel, Yah, Ahanahel (4) Ṣuriahel A(men) A(men) A(men) S(elah) H(allelujah)! You holy (5) letters, kindle and ... burn the heart of (6) X b. Y (in longing) after A b. B, that he should love her, Amen (7) Selah Hall(el)u(jah)."

8 בסוך וזעפרן ועלקוה עליך בשם
9 יי נעשה ונצליח מזמן הדן רזה
10 לשפראטא דפֿ בֿ פֿ דירחום ית פֿ בֿ פֿ
11 בשם כלבו בדו בלהו ריסודוס ד(ז)
12 הווה וזה בא גטית אתון אתייה
13 קדישייה משבחייה אלהבו ואד˺ל˹ק[ו]
14 לבה <ד>פֿ בֿ פֿ בתר פֿ בֿ פֿ ברחמה רבה
15 אֿ אֿ סֿ הֿ Θ חורן לילמרדֿ ולגרב גי(ד)
16 כוד בידֿה מדֿרה ואטמרהה פי
17 קבר והאדא אלדי תו˺כ˹תוב מזמן
18 הדן כתבה לפֿ בֿ פֿ דיהווי שייח

page 3

1 ומדנק באשתא אש תמיד תוקד על
2 פֿ בֿ פֿ לא תכבה בשם נֹטֹרֹוֹסֹ סֹיֹהֹ דגהנ(ם)
3 ובשם סמאל סטנא XXXXXX 
4  אש תמיד תוקד על פֿ בֿ פֿ לא
5 תכבה אש תלהט אש תורד על
6 פֿ בֿ פֿ ויהווי בנורא נפק בנורא לבש בנורא
7 נפ(ק) שחמה ועד דנצבי אֿ אֿ סֿ הֿ חורן ליל[...]
8 כוד דלף ואכתוב עליה מזמן הדן כתבה
9 לפֿ בֿ פֿ דיהווי עלל באשתא ונפק באשת(א)
10 בשם עובה דבר עבראות ילו יסר נֹיֹנֹוֹתֹ
11 כֹוֹנֹיֹתֹ כֹוֹנֹיֹתֹ אתון שמהתה קדישייה
12 שלחו אשתא ועריתא וזעקה על פֿ בֿ פֿ
13 מן הדן יומה ועד דנצבי אמן אֿ סֿ הֿ ○
14 חורן יוכתב עלא צפיחת אנך ויטמר
15 פי אלבית אלדי תריד והאדא אלדי תֹוֹכֹ<תב>
16 מזמן הדן כתבה לפֿ בֿ פֿ דיהווי שיח ודייב
17 ומדנק ומטלק בערס מרעה בשם אוֹ אוֹ
18 נֹוֹקֹאֹךֹ קֹהֹתֹךֹ קדיתך אפלוק או או
19 כיתאון ושאקצו שמו

Another (charm). Write on the hide of a deer (8) with *sukk* (?) and saffron and hang it on you(rself): "In the name of (9) God we shall do and succeed. This mystery is designated (10) for the endearment (?) of X b. Y that he should love A b. B. (11) In the name of **klbw bdw blhw ryswdws dz** (12) **hwwh wzh bʾ gṭyt.** You, praiseworthy holy (13) letters, kindle and burn (14) the heart of X b. Y (in longing) after A b. B with great love, (15) A(men) A(men) A(men) S(elah) H(allelujah)."

Another (charm). For sickness and for scab. Effective. (16) Take a fresh egg and bury it in (17) a tomb, and this is what you should write: "This writing (18) is designated for X b. Y that he may melt

page 3

(1) and groan in the fire. There should burn a perpetual fire over (2) X b. Y, unextinguished. In the name of **nṭrws syh** of gehenna (3) and in the name of Samael the Satan (*magic symbols*) (4) There should burn a perpetual fire over X b. Y, un-(5)extinguished, there should blaze a fire, there should descend (?) a fire over (6) X b. Y, and may he be going out in fire, being clothed in fire, (7) its blackness (?) coming out as long as I desire. A(men) A(men) S(elah) H(allelujah)."

Another (charm). For ... (8) Take a hoof (?) and write on it: "This writing is designated (9) for X b. Y, that he may be going into fire and going out in fire. (10) In the name of **ʿwbh dbr ʿbrʾwt ylw ysr nynwt** (11) **kwnyt kwnyt.** You holy names, (12) send fire and fever and crying over X b. Y (13) from this day and as long as I desire, Amen A(men) S(elah) H(allelujah)."

(14) Another (charm). There should be written on a sheet of lead and buried (15) in the house which you desire. This is what should be written: (16) "This writing is designated for X b. Y, that he may melt and drip (17) and groan and be cast away on a sick-bed. In the name of **ʾw ʾw** (18) **nwqʾk qhtk qdytk ʾplwq ʾw ʾw** (19) **kytʾwn wšʾqsw šmw.**

page 4

1 אתון אתייה קדישייה אפלון על פ̇ ב̇ פ̇ אש[תה]
2 זעריתה ודנוקה ויהווי מטלק בערס מארעה
3 ולא יהווי לה אסו עד זמן דנצבי א א̇ ס̇ ה̇ ○
4 חורן יוכתב עלא פכר ני ויטמר פי מוקדה
5 אש תמיד תוקד על פ̇ ב̇ פ̇ לא תכבה כי אש
6 קדחה באפ בפ̇ ב̇ פ̇ ותיקד עד שאול
7 תחתית ותאכל ארץ ויבולה ותלהט פ̇ ב̇ פ̇
8 לילה וימם לא תכבה האש מן פ̇ ב̇ פ̇ הנה
9 יד ײ בפ̇ ב̇ פ̇ א א̇ ס ה̇ חורן לסינה יוכתב
10 עלא בידה טריה ותודפן יום אלגומעה
11 פי קבר מזמן הדן כתבה לפ̇ ב̇ פ̇ דיסני
12 לפ̇ ב̇ פ̇ בשם ײ וישנאה פ̇ ב̇ פ̇ לפ̇ ב̇ פ̇
13 שינאה גדולה עד מאד כי גדולה
14 השינאה אשר שנא פ̇ ב̇ פ̇ לפ̇ ב̇ פ̇
15 מאהבה אשר אהבו בשם אכתריאל
16 הפכיאל ודפוניאל כן יתהפך לבה
17 והונה דפ̇ ב̇ פ̇ ויסני ית פ̇ ב̇ פ̇ הך מא
18 דאכלבה סני לחזירה וחזירה לכלבה
19 אמן אמן ה ○

1:1–2 **ʿd mn** for **ʿd mʾ**. The phrase **ʿd mn dyʿbd ṣbywny npšh** can be compared with the formula **ʿd dnṣby** below p. 3:7, 13 etc.

1:3 **pkr ny:** See Commentary to Geniza 2, p. 2:2 and to Amulet 10.

1:9 **dmny** for **dmmny**.

wʾ wḥnh is an error for **wʿl ḥnh.**

1:13 **whwnh:** The word **hwnʾ** may be connected to the Targumic and Syriac word *hawnā* "mind, intelligence", rather than to the Hebrew *hōn* "wealth". For **lbh whwnh wkwlyth**, Geniza 2, p. 2:10–11 has **lbh wmzlh wkwlyth**; see Commentary there and to Amulet 10.

1:16 **ʾlklm** for *al-kalām* (usually spelled in Jewish Arabic **ʾlklʾm).**

1:17 The expression **špt nhr gry** is somewhat incongruous, if the reading is correct. One might expect the Arabic *ḍaffa* rather than the Hebrew *śafa* or the Aramaic *siftā*.

page 4

(1) You holy letters, cause there to fall on X b. Y fire (2) and fever and groaning and may he be cast away on a sick-bed (3) and may he have no healing as long as I desire. A(men) A(men) S(elah) H(allelujah)."

(4) Another (charm). There should be written on an unbaked potsherd and buried in a furnace (as follows): (5) "The fire shall ever be burning upon X b. Y, it shall never go out. For fire (6) is kindled by my anger against X b. Y, it burns to the depths of (7) Sheol; it devours earth and its harvest and it glows at X b. Y. (8) Day and night shall the fire keep (burning) unextinguished at X b. Y. Behold, (9) the hand of the Lord is upon X b.Y. A(men) A(men) S(elah) H(allelujah)."

Another (charm). For hatred. There should be written (10) on a fresh egg, which will be buried on Friday (11) in a tomb (as follows): "This writing is designated for X b.Y, that he may hate (12) A b. B in the name of God. Then X b. Y hated A b. B (13) exceedingly, so that the hatred (14) with which X b. Y hated A b. B (15) was greater than the love with which he had loved him. In the name of Akatriel, (16) Hafkiel and Dfuniel, so should the heart (17) and mind of X b. Y change to hate A b. B like the way (18) a dog hates a pig and a pig hates a dog. (19) Amen Amen Selah Ha(llelujah)."

2:1 **gry** should be **gʾry** (Arabic *jārī*).
2:5 **ʾlhbw wlqṭpʾ wdlqw** seems to be an error for **ʾlhbw wʾdlqw**.
2:7 **gzl** should be **gzʾl**.
2:8 **swk**: Cf. above, Geniza 5, p. 4:4.
2:10 **lšprʾṭʾ** may be a corruption from **lšpr bʿynh** "finding grace" (?).
2:15 *lilmaraḍ*, as also *bayḍa*, *maḍira*, are spelled with *dalet*; cf. Blau 1980, pp. 35 f., § 2:15; pp. 38 f., § 2:21; Blau 1981, p. 76, note 1. "For sickness" means obviously "in order to inflict sickness on your enemy". Many of the recipes in this fragment deal with malicious effects which the magician tries to direct towards his enemy.
2:16 **mdrh** probably Arab *maḍira* "fresh". Professor Blau has suggested the reading *maḏira* "rotten (egg)", but the recipes usually call for fresh objects; cf. also p. 4:10 **bydh ṭryh**, as well as Geniza 2, p. 1:1–2.

2:18 **šyyḥ** from **ŠWḤ** "to melt, be consumed, waste away by fire".

3:1–2 The phrase here recalls Lev. 6:6.
3:5 **twrd** should be perhaps **twqd**?
3:7 **npp** or **npq**?
dnṣby may be either first person singular or plural; cf. Dalman 1905, p. 265; Kutscher 1971, col. 272. The singular seems preferable in this context; cf. T—S K 1. 95: **bḥtmʾ dḥtymyn... wlʾ ʾyštryn ʿd dʾnh ʾyṣby**.
3:8 **dlp** may represent Arabic ظلف.
3:12 **ʾštʾ wʿrytʾ wzʿqh**, cf. p. 4:1–2 **ʾš[th] zʿryth wdnwqh**, and Amulet 2:12 **ʾšth wʿryth wdqyqth**. The latter is the correct version meaning "fever, shivering and hectic fever".
3:16 **dyyb** from **DWB** (Hebrew **ZWB**) "to drip, to flow".
3:17 **ʿrs mrʿh** is not known to us from other sources. It obviously means "a sick-bed", as Hebrew **ʾrś dwy** in Ps. 41:4.

4:1–2 See above Commentary to p. 3:12 as well as Commentary to Amulet 2:2, 12.
4:5 After Lev. 6:6.
4:5–7 After Deut. 32:22.
4:8–9 After Ex. 9:3.
4:12–15 After 2 Sam. 13:15.
4:18 **dʾklbh** should be **dklbh**.

Geniza 7

Amulet
T–S K 1.127
Plate 39

1 בשמך ײ̂ צבאות אלהי ישראל יושב הכרובים שם
2 המפורש בשבעים שמות אל חנון ורחום אל מוחץ
3 ורופא שלח רפואה ותרחם לבנינה בנת ימן ותשלח לה
4 רפואה שלמה על חסדך ועל אמתך בך בטחתי אלהי
5 ישראל ענה אותי ב(ע)ת צרתי משביע אני עליכם
6 הרוחות והשדות ועין רע ופגע רע ושטן רע וכל
7 מיני פורעניות בשם אהׄיׄהׄ אשר אהׄיׄהׄ המרעיש
8 את העולם כולו בשם ששמע הים ונבקע
9 ששמע האש ונכבה ושמעו סלעים ונשתברו
10 ושמע האבן ויתפוצץ כן תצאו ותלכו ותתרחקו
11 ולא תגעו לבנינה בת ימן מן היום הזה ועד לעולם
12 אמן אמן אמן סלה  על שמך רחמנא אסותא
13 מן שמיא תהוי לה לבנינה בת ימן ותיתסי ברחמי
14 שמיא ותהוי לה אסותא מן כל עינא בישא
15 ורוחא בישא ופגעא בישא ומרעין בישין
16 ומכתשין ויסורין ואשתא וערויתא וכל זיקין
17 ומזיקין בישין אנא מומינא לכון ומשבענא
18 עליכון בשם גׄבריאל מיכאל ורפאל דתזועון
19 ותפקון מן בנינה בת ימן מן גופה ומן
20 רישה ומן צידעה ומן מאתן וארבעין
21 ותמנה איברין דאית בה אׄ אׄ סׄ הללויה
22 בן פורת יוסף בן פורת (ע)[לי עין] בנות צעד[ה]
23 עלי שור אחישה מפל[ט לי מ]רוח סועה
24 מסער מסער סועה מרוח לי מפלט
25 אחישה 
26 כי עם בציון ישב בירושלם בכה לא
27 תבכה חנון יחנך לקול זעקך כשמעתו
28 ענך ויענך ורע שר לא יאונך אׄ אׄ סׄ

29 פיומיאל אדרמלאל אברסכס סמראל
30 אנטיכוס מנטיפוס שבר שניר
31 שינר ויסיסים וסם ובתכיסן ויכר
32 מצוץ יקטקוטה מעשה ברוחא
33 והן אן בהם א א א ס׳ יברכך יי וישמרך
34 אנקתם יאר יי פניו אליך פסתם
35 ישא יי פניו אליך וישם לך שלום
36 פספסים ושמו את שמי על בני
37 ישראל ואני אברכם ודיוניסים
38 והפשיט את העלה ונרצה לו לכפר עליו

It has seemed unnecessary to give a translation of this text, which is largely based on biblical verses and contains parallels to other Geniza charms.

2–3 For **mwḥṣ wrwp**ʾ cf. Dt. 32:39; Is. 30:26; Job 5:18.
3 The name of the client seems to be Bunayna daughter of Yaman (or Yumn).
5 Cf. Ps. 20:2.
8 For these formulae see Geniza 4:6 ff.
22 Gen. 49:22.
23–24 Ps. 55:9. The verse is repeated backwards.
26 ff. Is. 30:19.
28 **šr** seems to be the Arabic equivalent of Heb. *raʿ*, introduced as a gloss. The Hebrew phrase is a paraphrase of Ps. 91:10.
33 ff. Num. 6:24.
38 Lev. 1:6; 1:4.

Geniza 8

Amulet
T–S K 1.137
Plate 40

1 על שמך ועל חילך מרי
2 דעלמא יהׄ יהׄ צור
3 ויזא̂ (?) נושא הכתב הזה
4 מכל חולי ומכל נגע ומכל
5 דבר רע ומכל קנאה בישא
6 יהׄ
7 אהׄהׄ חסין יה יחישה 8 יהׄ אהׄהׄ
9 חסין יחישה ושמתיה אתון
10 מלאכיא קדישיא יהׄ אהׄהׄ
11 חסין יחיש טולו ושיזבו מן
12 נושא הכתב הזה חרשין
13 בישין ומכל לווטין בישין יהׄ
14 אהׄהׄ יחיש ופרחיה שדין בישין
15 ומכל פגעים בישין ומכל
16 רוחין בישין לילא ויממא
17 וצהריא ויתגערון ויתרח<ק>ון
18 ויפ(ק)ון מן נושא כתבי זה
19 ומן מאתים ושמונה וארבעים
20 אברים בשם אל חי וקיים
21 מוחץ ורופא והסיר יי̂ ממך
22 כל חולי ויאמר אם שמוע תשמע
23 בקול יי̂ אלהיך והישר בעׄיניו
24 תעשה והאזנת למצותיו ושמרת
25 כל חוקיו וכל המחלה אשר שמתי
26 במצרים לא אשים עליך כי אני
27 יי̂ רופאיך מרׄמרׄאׄותׄ
28 וערׄבׄת שמירות קרובי

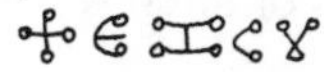

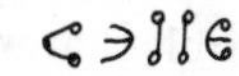

In the margin:

לב̊רו יתי̇ה̇ תסגוגא רפא ותי̇א̊ו ותי(נ)או וי(ר̇ג̇י̇ה̇)

At the top, inverted:

והוא ג̇ע̇ר̇ה̇ א̇ה̇ אה̈ סלה
לעולם ועד אמן (אמן)

This fragment too does not seem to require translation. In the following some comments on points of interest will be made.

3 **wyzʾ:** We should have expected a verb meaning "to save", like **ṭwlw wšyzbw** in line 11. It is possible that **wyzʾ** is a corruption of **šyzb**. On the other hand it could belong to the verb attested in similar contexts under the forms: **wtyzh mnh mbkltʾ** (Bowl 1:11 and Montgomery 1913, No. 32:2); **dyzh wytrḥq mynyh dywʾ byšʾ wsṭnʾ byšʾ** (Montgomery 1913, No. 3:2). Montgomery 1913, p. 130, explains this verb as derived from **ZḤḤ** or **ZWʿ**, but it is also possible to regard it as deriving from **ʾZL**, with the *lamed* dropped, as frequently in Eastern Aramaic (see Epstein 1960, pp. 58 f.). In that case the phrase would mean: "May the bearer of this writing go away from all illness...". The difficulty about this interpretation is that it does not form a good parallel with lines 11–12 and that it is not built around any otherwise attested formula, for the bowl-texts use this verb in relation to the evil things which should depart from the person. In addition it would be strange to find here an East Aramaic form. Our suggestion that **wyzʾ** is a corruption of something like **wyštzyb** seems therefore preferable.

7 **yḥyšh:** Cf. Commentary to Amulet 3:2.

11–13 The syntax here is confused. Read טולו ושיזבו נושא הכתב הזה מן חרשין בישין ומכל לווטין.

17 **wṣhryʾ:** This is a Hebraism in Aramaic.

21 **mwḥṣ wrwpʾ:** See Commentary to Amulet 1:20 and Geniza 7:2–3.

Bibliography, Glossary and Indices

ABBREVIATIONS

AASOR	*Annual of the American Schools of Oriental Research*
ADAJ	*Annual of the Department of Antiquities, Jordan*
AIPHOS	*Annales de l'Institut de Philologie et d'Histoire Orientales et Slaves*
AJSLL	*American Journal of Semitic Languages and Literatures*
BASOR	*Bulletin of the American Schools of Oriental Research*
BEO	*Bulletin d'Etudes Orientales de l'Institut Français de Damas*
BSOAS	*Bulletin of the School of Oriental and African Studies*
CRAIBL	*Comptes-Rendus de l'Académie des Inscriptions et Belles-Lettres*
IEJ	*Israel Exploration Journal*
IOS	*Israel Oriental Studies*
JA	*Journal Asiatique*
JNES	*Journal of Near Eastern Studies*
JQR	*Jewish Quarterly Review*
JRAS	*Journal of the Royal Asiatic Society*
MSL	*Mémoires de la Société de Linguistique*
NTS	*New Testament Studies*
PSBA	*Proceedings of the Society for Biblical Archaeology*
QDAP	*Quarterly of the Department of Antiquities, Palestine*
RA	*Revue d'Assyriologie*
REJ	*Revue des Etudes Juives*
RHR	*Revue de l'Histoire des Religions*
SPAW	*Sitzungsberichte der Preussischen Akademie der Wissenschaften zu Berlin,* Philosophisch-historische Klasse
TSBA	*Transactions of the Society for Biblical Archaeology*
WZKM	*Wiener Zeitschrift für die Kunde des Morgenlandes*
ZA	*Zeitschrift für Assyriologie*
ZDMG	*Zeitschrift der Deutschen Morgenländischen Gesellschaft*
ZK	*Zeitschrift für Keilschriftforschung*
ZPE	*Zeitschrift für Papyrologie und Epigraphik*

BIBLIOGRAPHY

The main dictionaries (Brockelmann, Jastrow, Payne-Smith, Drower and Macuch) have often been quoted without the date of publication. "Montgomery" indicates Montgomery 1913.

Abt, Adam
1908 *Die Apologie des Apuleius von Madaura und die antike Zauberei. Beiträge zur Erläuterung der Schrift de magia* (Religionsgeschichtliche Versuche und Vorarbeiten, IV,2) Giessen

Adler, E.N.
1911 "Un fragment araméen du Toldot Yéschou", *REJ* 61, pp. 126–130

Aešcoly, A.Z.
1932 "Les noms magiques dans les apocryphes chrétiens des Ethiopiens", *JA* 220, pp. 87–137

Alfaric, Prosper
1918/9 *Les écritures manichéennes,* I–II, Paris

Andreas, F.C., and Walter Henning
1932/3 *Mitteliranische Manichaica aus Chinesisch-Turkestan,* I (*SPAW,* pp. 175–222), II (*SPAW*, p. 293—363) Berlin

Anstock-Darga, Muhibbe
1950/1 "Semitische Inschriften auf Silbertäfelchen aus dem Bertiz-Tal (Umgebung von Maraş)", *Jahrbuch für Kleinasiatische Forschung* I, pp. 199–200

Avi-Yonah, Michael
1940 *Abbreviations in Greek inscriptions (The Near East, 200 B.C.-A.D. 1100)* (Supplement to *QDAP,* vol. 9) Jerusalem

Babelon, E., and M. Schwab
1882 "Un vase judéo-chaldéen de la Bibliothèque Nationale", *REJ* 4, pp. 165–172

Bailey, H.W.
1943 *Zoroastrian problems in the ninth-century books,* Oxford [Reprint: 1971]

Bammel, E.
1966/7 Christian origins in Jewish traditions", *NTS* 13, pp. 317–335

Bar-Asher, Moshe משה בר־אשר
1983 "נשכחות בלשון התנאים", מחקרי לשון מוגשים לזאב בן־חיים. ירושלים, עמ' 83–110
Barb, A.A.
1963 "The survival of magic arts", in: Arnaldo Momigliano (ed.), *The conflict between paganism and Christianity,* Oxford, pp. 100–125
Bar-Hebraeus
1892 *Die Scholien des Gregorius Abulfaragius Bar-Habraeus zum Weisheitsbuch des Josua ben Sira,* ed. S. Kaatz, Halle
Basset, René
1894 *Les apocryphes éthiopiens, traduits en français.* IV. *Les légendes de S. Tétrag et de S. Sousnyos.* Paris
1922 *Le synaxaire arabe jacobite (Rédaction copte).* Patrologia Orientalis, ed. R. Graffin and R. Nau, vol. XVI, fasc. 2, IV. Paris
Ben-David, A. א. בן־דוד
1971 לשון מקרא ולשון חכמים. תל אביב
Ben-Ḥayyim, Z. זאב בן־חיים
1943 "ספר אסטיר", תרביץ יד, עמ' 104–125, 174–190
1957 עברית וארמית נוסח שומרון. כרך ב'. ירושלים
1967 עברית וארמית נוסח שומרון. כרך ג', ספר ב'. ירושלים
Benveniste, Emile
1929 *Essai de grammaire sogdienne,* II (Mission Pelliot en Asie Centrale, Série petit, III) Paris
1966 *Titres et noms propres en iranien ancien* (Travaux de l'Institut d'Etudes Iraniennes de l'Université de Paris, 1) Paris
Ben-Zvi, Izhak יצחק בן-צבי
1976 ספר השומרונים. ירושלים
Betz, Hans Dieter
1980 "Fragments from a catabasis ritual in a Greek magical papyrus", *History of Religions* 19, pp. 287–295
Bezold, Carl
1888 *Die Schatzhöhle,* Syrisch und deutsch herausgegeben. Leipzig
Bibliotheca Sanctorum
Istituto Giovanni XXIII della Pontifica Università Lateranense, vol. XI, col. 1246 f., s.v. "Sisinnio (Susinus), santo, martiro di Antiochia"

Bivar, A.D.H.
1967 "A Parthian amulet", *BSOAS* 30, pp. 512–525
1969 *Catalogue of the Western Asiatic seals in the British Museum. Stamp seals.* II: The Sasanian dynasty. London
Black, M.
1954 *A Christian Palestinian Syriac horologion* (Berlin Ms. Or. Oct. 1019), ed. by M. Black (Texts and Studies. Contributions to Biblical and Patristic Literature, N.S. 1) Cambridge
Blau, Joshua יהושע בלאו
1980 דקדוק הערבית היהודית. ירושלים
1981 *The emergence and linguistic background of Judaeo-Arabic. Jerusalem* [Reprint of the first edition, Oxford 1965]
Blau, Ludwig
1898 *Das altjüdische Zauberwesen* (Jahresbericht der Landes-Rabbinerschule in Budapest für das Schuljahr 1897-98) Budapest
Bonner, Campbell
1950 *Studies in magical amulets, chiefly Graeco-Egyptian.* Ann Arbor-London
1951 "Amulets chiefly in the British Museum. A supplementary article", *Hesperia, Journal of the American School of Classical Studies at Athens* 20, pp. 301–345
Borisov, A. Ja.
1969 "Epigrafičeskie zametki", *Epigrafika Vostoka,* 19, pp. 3–13
Bowman, Raymond A.
1970 *Aramaic ritual texts from Persepolis* (The University of Chicago Oriental Institute Publications, vol. XCI) Chicago
Boyarin, Daniel דניאל בויארין
1978a "קריאה מתוקנת של הקטע החדש של 'תולדות ישו' ", תרביץ מז, עמ' 249–252
1978b "On the history of the Babylonian Jewish Aramaic reading traditions: The reflexes of *a and *ā", *JNES* 37, pp. 141–160
Boyce, Mary
1954 *The Manichaean hymn-cycles in Parthian* (London Oriental Series, 3) London
Brauer, Erich א. בראואר
1944 "יהודי אפגאניסטאן", סיני יד, עמ' שכד-שמב

Brockelmann, Carl
1928 *Lexicon syriacum.* 2. Ausgabe. Halle
Budge, E.A. Wallis
1930 *Amulets and superstitions.* London
Cantineau, J.
1930–2 *Le Nabatéen,* I–II, Paris
Caquot, A.
1972 "Un phylactère mandéen en plomb", *Semitica* 22, pp. 67–87
Casanowicz, I.M.
1917 "Two Jewish amulets in the United States National Museum", *JAOS* 37, pp. 43–56
Chabot, J.-B.
1898 "La lettre du chatholicos Mar Aba II aux membres de l'école partiarcale de Séleucie", *Actes du onzième congrès international des orientalistes, Paris 1897, Quatrième section,* Paris, pp. 295–335
Chwolson, D.
1882 *Corpus inscriptionum hebraicarum,* St. Petersburg ("Die Inschriften auf den babylonischen Thongefässen," cols. 103–120)
Clédat, Jean
1904 *Le monastère et la nécropole de Baouit* (Mémoires de l'Institut Français d'Archéologie Orientale du Caire, XII) Cairo
Cohen, Shaye J.D.
1981 "Epigraphical rabbis", *JQR* 72, pp. 1–17
Cowley, A.
1923 *Aramaic papyri of the fifth century B.C.* Oxford
Cross, F.M.
1973 "Heshbon Ostracon II", *Andrews University Seminary Studies* 11, pp. 126–131
Daiches, Samuel
1913 *Babylonian oil magic in the Talmud and in the later Jewish literature* (Jews' College Publication No. 5) London
Dalman, Gustaf
1905 *Grammatik des jüdisch-palästinischen Aramäisch.* Leipzig
Del Medico, H.E.
1949 "La lamelle Virolleaud", *AIPHOS* 9, pp. 179–192

Dieterich, Albrecht
1891 *Abraxas. Studien zur Religionsgeschichte des spätern Altertums.* Leipzig
Doutté, Edmond
1908 *Magie et religion dans l'Afrique du Nord* (La Société Musulmane du Maghrib) Alger
Drijvers, H.J.W.
1980 *Cults and beliefs at Edessa* (Etudes Préliminaires aux Religions Orientales dans l'Empire Romain, 82) Leiden
Driver, G.R.
1930 "A magic bowl", *RA* 27, pp. 61–64.
Drower, E.S.
1937 "Shafta ḏ Pishra ḏ Ainia (A Mandaean magical text)", *JRAS,* pp. 589–611
1938 Idem, pp. 1–20
1939 "Three Mandaean phylacteries", *JRAS,* pp. 397–406
1943 "A Mandaean book of Black Magic", *JRAS,* pp. 149–181
1946 "A phylactery for rue", *Orientalia* 15, pp. 324–346
Drower, E.S. and Rudolf Macuch
1963 *A Mandaic dictionary.* Oxford
Du Mesnil du Buisson, Comte
1962 *Les tessères et les monnaies de Palmyre.* Paris
Dupont-Sommer, André
1942-4 "La tablette cunéiforme araméenne de Warka", *RA* 39, pp. 35–62
1946 *"La doctrine gnostique de la lettre "Waw" d'après une lamelle araméenne inédite* (Bibliothèque archéologique et historique, tome XLI) Paris
1950/1 "Deux lamelles d'argent à inscription hébréo-araméenne trouvées à Ağabeyli (Turquie)", *Jahrbuch für Kleinasiatische Forschung* I, pp. 201-217
1951 "Remarques sur la 'lamelle Virolleaud' ", *AIPHOS* 11, pp. 113–128
Ellis, Thomas see Layard 1853
Encyclopaedia Biblica אנציקלופדיה מקראית. ירושלים
Epstein, J.N. יעקב נחום הלוי אפשטיין
1913 "Zum magischen Texte (*JAOS* 1912, p. 434 seq.)", *JAOS* 33, pp. 279–280

1921 "Gloses babylo-araméennes", *REJ* 73, pp. 27–58
1922 Idem, *REJ* 74, pp. 40–72
1960 דקדוק ארמית בבלית. ירושלים

Falk, Zeev זאב פלק
1978 "קטע חדש מ׳תולדות ישו׳", תרביץ מו, עמ׳ 319–322

Février, J.G.
1931 *La religion des palmyréniens.* Paris

Fitzmyer, Joseph A.
1971 *The Genesis Apocryphon of Qumran Cave I: A commentary.* 2nd ed. (Biblica et Orientalia, 18a) Rome

Fitzmyer, Joseph A., and Daniel J. Harrington
1978 *A manual of Palestinian Aramaic texts* (Biblica et Orientalia, 34) Rome

Fraenkel, Siegmund
1886 *Die aramäischen Fremdwörter im Arabischen.* Leiden [Reprint: Hildesheim 1962]
1890 "Miscellen", *WZKM* 4, pp. 332–341

Frank, C.
1910 "Zu babylonischen Beschwörungstexten", *ZA* 24, pp. 157–165

Frey, Jean-Baptiste
1936 *Corpus inscriptionum iudaicarum,* I, Europe. Rome [Reprint, with Prolegomenon by B. Lifshitz: New York 1975]
1952 *Corpus inscriptionum iudaicarum,* II, Asie-Afrique. Rome
1975 See Frey 1936

Fries, Karl
1893 "The Ethiopian legend of Socinius and Ursula", *Actes du 8e congrès international des orientalistes,* Section I: Sémitique (B), Leiden, pp. 53–70

de la Fuÿe, Allotte
1925 "Une coupe magique en écriture manichéenne", *CRAIBL,* pp. 388–399

Garbers, Karl
1948 *Kitāb kīmiyā al-ʻiṭr wat-taṣʻīdāt...* von Yaʻqūb b. Isḥāq al-Kindī (Abhandlungen für die Kunde des Morgenlandes, XXX) Leipzig

Gaster, Moses
1896 "The Sword of Moses. An ancient book of magic published

for the first time from an unique manuscript (Cod. Heb. Gaster 178), with introduction and translation", *JRAS*, pp. 149–198, I–XXXV [Reprinted in Gaster 1928, I, pp. 288–337; III, pp. 69–103]

1900 "Two thousand years of a charm against the child-stealing witch", *Folk-Lore* 11 (46), pp. 129–162 [Reprinted in Gaster 1928, II, pp. 1005–1038]

1928 *Studies and texts in folklore, magic, mediaeval romance, Hebrew Apocrypha and Samaritan archaeology,* I–III. London [Reprint: New York 1971, with Prolegomenon by T. Gaster]

Gaster, Theodor H.

1942 "A Canaanite magical text", *Orientalia* 11, pp. 41–79

1955 *The holy and the profane,* New York. Chapter 4: "The wiles of Lilith", pp. 18–28

1971 "Prolegomenon" to a reprint of M. Gaster 1928

Geller, Markham J.

1976 "Two incantation bowls inscribed in Syriac and Aramaic", *BSOAS* 39, pp. 422–427

1980 "Four Aramaic incantation bowls", *The Bible world. Essays in honor of Cyrus H. Gordon* (ed. by J. Rendsburg et al.), New York, pp. 47–60

Gershevitch, Ilya

1954 *A grammar of Manichaean Sogdian* (Publications of the Philological Society, XVI) Oxford

1969 "Amber at Persepolis", *Studia classica et orientalia Antonino Pagliaro oblata,* Rome, vol. II, pp. 167–251

Gignoux, Philippe

1978 *Catalogue des sceaux, camées et bulles sasanides de la Bibliothèque Nationale et du Musée du Louvre.* II, Les sceaux et bulles inscrits. Paris

1979 *Pad nām i Yazdān. Etudes d'épigraphie, de numismatique et d'histoire de l'Iran ancien,* par Ph. Gignoux et R. Curiel, R. Gyselen, Cl. Herrenschmidt (Université de la Sorbonne Nouvelle. Travaux de l'Institut d'Etudes Iraniennes, 9) Paris

Ginza: Y, S *Thesaurus sive Liber magnus,* ed. H. Petermann. T. 1, Pars 1: s. dextra; T. 1, Pars 2: s. sinistra. Lipsiae 1867

Göbl, Robert

1971 *Sasanian numismatics* (Manuals of Middle Asian

Numismatics, I) Braunschweig

Goldziher, Ignaz

1872 "Linguistisches aus der Literatur der muhammedanischen Mystik", *ZDMG* 26, pp. 764–785

1894 "Hebräische Elemente in muhammedanischen Zaubersprüchen", *ZDMG* 48, pp. 358–360

1907 "Eisen als Schutz gegen Dämonen", *Archiv für Religionswissenschaft* 10, pp. 41–46

Gollancz, Hermann

1898 "A selection of charms from Syriac manuscripts", *Actes du onzième congrès international des orientalistes, Paris 1897, 4e Section,* Paris, pp. 77–97

1912 *The Book of Protection. Being a collection of charms...* London

Goodblatt, David

1976 "**ʾyprʾ hwrmyz** Mother of King Shapur and **ʾprʾ hwrmyz** Mother of Khusro: A note on the name **ʾyprʾ/ʾprʾ hwrmyz**", *JAOS* 96, pp. 135–136

Gordon, Cyrus H.

1934a "An Aramaic incantation", *AASOR* 14, pp. 141–143

1934b "Aramaic magical bowls in the Istanbul and Baghdad Museums", *Archiv Orientální* 6, pp. 319–334

1934c "An Aramaic exorcism", *Archiv Orientální* 6, pp. 466–474

1937 "Aramaic and Mandaic magical bowls", *Archiv Orientální* 9, pp. 84–106

1937–9 "The Aramaic incantation in cuneiform", *Archiv für Orientforschung* 12, pp. 105–117

1940 "The cuneiform Aramaic incantation", *Orientalia* 9, pp. 29–38

1941 "Aramaic incantation bowls", *Orientalia* 10, pp. 116–141, 272–284, 339–360

1949 "An incantation in Estrangelo script", *Orientalia* 18, pp. 336–341

1951 "Two magic bowls in Teheran", *Orientalia* 20, pp. 306–315

1953 "Holy Waw? A case of contrasting methodologies", *Orientalia* 22, p. 415

1957 *Adventures in the nearest east,* London (Chapter 12: "A world of demons and Liliths", pp. 160–174)

1978 "Two Aramaic incantations", in: Gary A. Tuttle (ed.), *Biblical and Near Eastern Studies. Essays in honor of W.S. LaSor,* Grand Rapids, Mich., pp. 231–244

Gottheil, J.H.
1969 *A selection from the Syriac Julian Romance,* ed. by J.H. Gottheil. Reprinted, Leiden

Grantovskij, E.A.
1970 *Rannjaja istorija iranskix plemen perednej Azii.* (Akademija Nauk SSSR, Institut Vostokovedenija) Moscow

Greenfield, Jonas C.
1973a "Notes on some Aramaic and Mandaic magic bowls", *The Journal of the Ancient Near Eastern Society of Colombia University* 5 (The Gaster Festschrift), pp. 149–156
1973b "Prolegomenon" [to the 1973 reprint of Odeberg 1928]
1980 "The Genesis Apocryphon—Observations on some words and phrases", in: G.B. Sarfati (ed.), *Studies in Hebrew and Semitic languages,* Ramat Gan, pp. XXXII–XXXIX

Gruenwald, Ithamar
1980 *Apocalyptic and Merkavah mysticism* (Institutum Iudaicum, Tübingen: Arbeiten zur Geschichte des antiken Judentum und des Urchristentums, Bd. XIV) Leiden-Köln

Grünbaum, M.
1885 "Einige Bemerkungen mit Bezug auf den Aufsatz 'Sur un vase judéo-babylonien' etc.", *ZK* 2, pp. 217–230 [On Hyvernat 1885]

Halévy, J.
1877 "Observations sur un vase judéo-babylonien du British Museum", *CRAIBL,* 4e série, t. 5, pp. 288–293

Hambroer, Johannes
1962 *Armenischer Dämonenglaube in religionswissenschaftlicher Sicht.* Wien

Hamilton, Victor Paul
1971 *Syriac incantation bowls.* Brandeis University Ph.D., University Microfilms. Ann Arbor, Michigan

Hanauer, J.E.
1907 *Folk-Lore of the Holy Land.* London

Harkavy, A. (A. Garkavi)
1889 "Neskol'ko zamečanij ob aramejskoj nadpisi na vaze,

naxodjaščejsja v Moskve", *Zapiski vostočnago otdelenija imperatorskago russkago arxeologičeskago obščestva* 4 (St. Petersburg 1890), pp. 83–95

Harviainen, Tapani

1978 *A Syriac incantation bowl in the Finnish National Museum, Helsinki. A specimen of Easterm Aramaic "koiné"* (Studia Orientalia, edited by the Finnish Oriental Society, 51:1) Helsinki

1981 *An Aramaic incantation bowl from Borsippa. Another specimen of Easterm Aramaic "koiné".* Appendix: A cryptographic bowl text or an original fake? (Studia Orientalia, edited by the Finnish Oriental Society, 51:14) Helsinki

Henning, W.B.

1947 "Two Manichaean magical texts with an excursus on the Parthian ending *-ēndēh*". *BSOAS* 12, pp. 39–66

Heim, Ricardus

1892 *Incantamenta magica graeca et latina.* Lipsiae

Hilprecht, H.V.

1903 *Explorations in Bible lands during the 19th century.* Philadelphia

Hinz, Walther

1975 *Altiranisches Sprachgut der Nebenüberlieferungen* (Göttinger Orientforschungen, III. Reihe: Iranica, Bd. 3) Wiesbaden

Hoffmann, Georg

1880 *Auszüge aus syrischen Akten persischer Märtyrer* (Abhandlungen für die Kunde des Morgenlandes, VII. Band, No. 3). Leipzig [Reprint: Nendeln, Liechtenstein, 1966]

Horn, Paul

1893 *Grundriss der neupersischen Etymologie* (Sammlung indogermanischer Wörterbücher, IV) Strassburg

1898–1901 "Neupersische Schriftsprache", in *Grundriss der iranischen Philologie,* Strassburg, 1. Band, 2. Abteilung, pp. 1–200

Hübschmann, Heinrich

1895 *Persische Studien,* Strassburg

1897 *Armenische Grammatik,* I. Leipzig [Reprint: Hildesheim 1972]

Hull, John M.

1974 *Hellenistic magic and the Synoptic tradition* (Studies in

Biblical Theology, 2nd series, 28) London
Hurwitz, Siegmund
1980 *Lilith, die erste Eva.* Zürich
Hyvernat, Henri
1885 "Sur un vase judéo-babylonien du musée Lycklama de Cannes (Provence)", *ZK* 2, pp. 113–148
Isbell, Charles D.
1975 *Corpus of the Aramaic incantation bowls* (Dissertation Series 17, Scholars Press) Missoula, Montana
1976 "Two new Aramaic incantation bowls", *BASOR* 223, pp. 15–23
1978 "The story of the Aramaic magical incantation bowls", *Biblical Archaeologist* 41, No. 1, pp. 5–16
Jacobson, Howard
1980 "Greco-Roman light on rabbinic texts", *Illinois Classical Studies* 5, pp. 57–62
Jastrow, Marcus
1950 *A dictionary of the Targumim, the Talmud Babli and Yerushalmi and the Midrashic literature.* I–II. New York [Reprint of an earlier edition]
Jeffery, Arthur
1938 *The foreign vocabulary of the Qur'ān.* Baroda
Jeruzalmi, Isak
1963 *Les coupes magiques araméennes de Mésopotamie.* Thèse pour le doctorat du troisiéme cycle présentée à la Faculté des Lettres et Sciences Humaines de l'Université de Paris. Paris [mimeographed]
Justi, Ferdinand
1895 *Iranisches Namenbuch.* Marburg
Kaplan, J.
1967 "Two Samaritan amulets", *IEJ* 17, pp. 158–162
Kaufman, Stephen A.
1973 "A unique magic bowl from Nippur", *JNES* 32, pp. 170–174
1974 *The Akkadian influences on Aramaic* (The Oriental Institute of the University of Chicago, Assyriological Studies, 19) Chicago and London
1975 "Appendix C: Alphabetic texts", in McGuire Gibson (ed.), *Excavations at Nippur, Eleventh Season* (The Oriental

Institute of the University of Chicago, Oriental Institute Communications 22) Chicago and London, pp. 151–152

Kent, Roland G.

1911 "The etymology of Syriac *dastabira*", *JAOS* 31, pp. 359–364

Kimron, Elisha אלישע קמרון

1980 "שמות רוחות השמיים במקורותינו הקדומים", בית מקרא א (פ), עמ' 41–47

King, C.W.

1864 *The gnostics and their remains, ancient and mediaeval.* London

Klein, Michael L.

1980 *The Fragment-Targums of the Pentateuch according to their extant sources,* I–II. Rome

Kleine-Franke, Felix

1971 "Eine aramäische Tabella devotionis", *ZPE* 7, pp. 47–52, and Tafel III

Kloner, Amos

1980 "Ḥurvat Rimmon, 1979", *IEJ* 30, pp. 226–228

1981 "Ḥurvat Rimmon, 1980", *IEJ* 31, pp. 241–242

Kohut, Alexander אלכסנדר קאהוט

1955 *Aruch Completum*, I–VIII (הערוך השלם) New York [Reprint of an earlier edition; see also Krauss 1955]

Kook, S.H. ש.ח. קוק

1943/4 "הערות לשמות בעלי חיים", סיני י"ד (תש"ד) עמ' שמג־שמו

1959 עיונים ומחקרים, א. ירושלים

Krauss, Samuel

1898 *Griechische und lateinische Lehnwörter im Talmud, Midrasch und Targum,* I. Berlin

1911a "Fragments araméens du Toldot Yéschou", *REJ* 62, pp. 28–37

1911b "Un texte cabbalistique sur Jésus", *REJ* 62, pp. 240–247

1955 *Additamenta ad Aruch Completum* (=Kohut 1955, IX). תוספות הערוך השלם להרב קאהוט New York [Reprint of an earlier edition]

Kriss, Rudolf and Hubert Kriss-Heinrich

1962 *Volksglaube im Bereich des Islam,* II. Wiesbaden

Kutscher, E.Y. יחזקאל קוטשר

The articles 1957–1971 are reprinted in Kutscher 1977

1957 "The language of the Ġenesis Ȧpocryphon. A preliminary study", *Scripta Hierosolymitana* 4, Jerusalem, pp. 1–35
1961 "לשונן של האיגרות העבריות והארמיות של בר כוסבה ובני דורו", לשוננו כה, עמ' 117–133
1963 "לשון חז"ל", ספר חנוך ילון, ירושלים, עמ' 246–280
1968 "הארמית של השומרונים", תרביץ לז, עמ' 397–419
1969 "Two 'passive' constructions in Aramaic in the light of Persian", *Proceedings of the International Conference on Semitic Studies held in Jerusalem, 19–23 July 1965,* Jerusalem 1969, pp. 132–151
1971 "Aramaic", *Encyclopedia Judaica,* III, cols. 259–287
1976 *Studies in Galilean Aramaic* (Tr. by Michael Sokoloff) Ramat-Gan
1977 *Hebrew and Aramaic studies* (ed. by Z. Ben-Ḥayyim et al.) Jerusalem

Lacau, P.
1896 "Une coupe d'incantation", *RA* 3, pp. 47–51

Layard, Austen H.
1853 *Discoveries among the ruins of Nineveh and Babylon,* New York [A description and decipherment with translation of magical bowls, under numbers 1–7, by Thomas Ellis, pp. 434–445]

Levine, Baruch A.
1970 "The language of the magical bowls". Appendix in: Jacob Neusner, *A history of the Jews in Babylonia,* V, Leiden, pp. 343–375

Levy, M.A.
1855 "Über die von Layard aufgefundenen chaldäischen Inschriften auf Topfgefässen. Ein Beitrag zur hebräischen Paläographie und zur Religionsgeschichte", *ZDMG* 9, pp. 465–491

Levy S. et alii
1960 "The ancient synagogue of Ma'on (Nirim)", *Bulletin, L.M. Rabinowitz Fund for the Exploration of Ancient Synagogues,* 3, pp. 6–40

Lewy, Hans
1978 *Chaldaean oracles and theurgy.* Nouvelle édition par M. Tardieu. Paris

Lidzbarski, Mark
1902 *Ephemeris für semitische Epigraphik*, I, 1900–1902. Giessen

1909 "Ein mandäisches Amulett", *Florilegium ou recueil de travaux d'érudition dédiés à M. Melchior de Vogüé.* Paris, pp. 349–373

1916 "Die Herkunft der manichäischen Schrift", *SPAW,* pp. 1213–1222

1920 *Mandäische Liturgien* (Abhandlungen der Königlichen Gesellschaft der Wissenschaften zu Göttingen, philol.-hist. Klasse, N.F. XVII, 1) Berlin

Lieberman, Saul שאול ליברמן

1946 "Palestine in the third and fourth centuries", *JQR* 36, pp. 329–370

1947 Idem, *JQR* 37, pp. 31–54

1957/8 "משהו על השבעות בישראל", תרביץ כז, עמ' 183–189

1961/2 תוספתא כפשוטה, חלק ג': סדר מועד. נויארק

1962 יוונית ויוונות בארץ-ישראל. ירושלים

1974 מדרש דברים רבה, מהדורה שלישית. ירושלים

Löw, Immanuel

1912 "Aramäische Lurchnamen", *ZA* 26, pp. 126–147

1924-34 *Die Flora der Juden,* I–IV, Wien

Maas, Paul

1942 "The Philinna papyrus", *The Journal of Hellenistic Studies* 92, pp. 33–38

Macler, F.

1908 "Formules magiques de l'Orient chrétien", *RHR* 58, pp. 9–33

Macuch, Rudolf

1967 "Altmandäische Bleirolle", in: F. Altheim and R. Stiehl, *Die Araber in der alten Welt,* IV, Berlin, pp. 91–203

1968 Idem, vol. V, 1, pp. 34–72

Ps. Majrīṭī

1933 *Ġāyat al-ḥakīm "Picatrix",* ed. H. Ritter *(Studien der Bibliothek Warburg, XII).* Leipzig [German translation by H. Ritter and M. Plessner, London 1962]

Mancini, Ignazio

1977 *L'archéologie judéo-chrétienne. Notices historiques* (Publications du Studium Biblicum Franciscanum, Collectio minor 10) Jerusalem

Margain, Jean

1979 "La racine ŠWY en araméen samaritain", *Semitica* 29, pp. 119–130

Margaliot, Reuven ראובן מגליות
1964 מלאכי עליון, המוזכרים בתלמוד בבלי וירושלמי, בכל המדרשים, זהר ותקונים, תרגומים וילקוטים עם ציונים לספרי קודש של הקבלה (ירושלים תש"ה) מהדורה שנייה תשכ"ד
Margalioth, Mordecai
1966 See: *Sefer har-razim*
Mayrhofer, Manfred
1973 *Onomastica persepolitana* (Österreichische Akademie der Wissenschaften, phil.-hist. Klasse, Sitzungsberichte, 286. Band) Wien
1979 *Iranisches Personennamenbuch.* Band I, Faszikel 2 und 3, Die altpersischen Namen und Indices (Österreichische Akademie der Wissenschaften, phil.-hist. Klasse, Sonderpublikation der iranischen Kommission) Wien
McCullough, W.S.
1967 *Jewish and Mandaean incantation bowls in the Royal Ontario Museum.* University of Toronto Press [Cf. Segal 1970; Yamauchi 1970]
Milik, J.T.
1967 "Une amulette judéo-araméenne", *Biblica* 48, pp. 450–451
1976 *The books of Enoch. Aramaic fragments of Qumran Cave 4.* Ed. by J.T. Milik with the collaboration of M. Black. Oxford
Milik, J.T. and J. Starcky
1975 "Inscriptions récemment découvertes à Pétra", *ADAJ* 20, pp. 111–130
Montgomery, James A.
1907 *The Samaritans. The earliest Jewish sect. Their history, theology and literature.* Philadelphia
1911 "Some early amulets from Palestine", *JAOS* 31, pp. 272–281
1912a "The original script of the Manichaeans on texts in the Museum", *The Museum Journal, University of Pennsylvania Museum,* 3, pp. 25–29
1912b "A magical bowl-text and the original script of the Manichaeans", *JAOS* 32, pp. 434–438
1913 *Aramaic incantation texts from Nippur* (University of Pennsylvania, The Museum, Publications of the Babylonian Section, Vol. III) Philadelphia
1917/8 "A Syriac incantation bowl with Christian formula", *AJSLL* 34, pp. 137–139

Morag, S. שלמה מורג
1972 "ומתערה כאזרח רענן", תרביץ מא, עמ' 1–23
1973 "מחקר הארמית הבבלית וכתבי היד של הגניזה", תרביץ מב, עמ' 60-78
1979 "משניות מן הפרק 'במה מדליקין' בשני כתבי יד של גניזת קאהיר", חקרי מזרח לזכר ד"צ בנעט, ירושלים, עמ' 111–123

Mouterde, René
1930 "Le glaive de Dardanos. Objets et inscriptions magiques de Syrie", *Mélanges de l'Université St. Joseph,* Beyrouth, Tome XV, fasc. 3, pp. 53–136

Müller, Friedrich
1891 "Kleine Mittheilungen", *WZKM* 5, pp. 250–270, 348–356

Myhrman, David W.
1909 "An Aramaic incantation text", *Hilprecht Anniversary Volume.* Leipzig-London-Paris-Chicago, pp. 342–351

Narqis, M. מרדכי נרקיס
1935 "השבעה ארמית (בבית הנכאת הלאומי בצלאל)", תרביץ ו, ספר א, עמ' 106–107

Nash, W.L.
1906 "A Hebrew amulet against disease", *PSBA* 28, pp. 182–184

Naveh, Joseph יוסף נוה
1975 "Another Mandaic lead roll", *IOS* 5, pp. 47–53
1978 על פסיפס ואבן. הכתובות הארמיות והעבריות מבתי הכנסת העתיקים. ירושלים
1979a "A Nabatean incantation text", *IEJ* 29, pp. 111–119
1979b "Varia epigraphica judaica", *IOS* 9, pp. 17–31
1980 "An Aramaic consolatory burial inscription", *'Atiqot,* English Series, 14, pp. 55–59
1983 "A recently discovered Palestinian Jewish Aramaic amulet", in: M. Sokoloff (ed.) *Arameans and Aramaic literary tradition.* Ramat Gan. pp. 81–88

Neusner, Jacob
1968 "Jews and Judaism under Iranian rule: bibliographical reflections", *History of Religions* 8, pp. 159–177
1975 "How much Iranian in Jewish Babylonia?", *JAOS* 95, pp. 184–190

Niditch, Susan
1979 "Incantation texts and formulaic language: A new etymology for **ḥwmry**", *Orientalia* 48, pp. 461–471

Niggemeyer, J.H.
1975 *Beschwörungsformeln aus dem 'Buch der Geheimnisse'.* Hildesheim and New York

Nöldeke, Theodor
1875 *Mandäische Grammatik.* Halle
1879 *Geschichte der Perser und Araber zur Zeit der Sasaniden,* aus der arabischen Chronik des Tabari übersetzt... Leyden
1885 [Notes on Hyvernat 1885], *ZK* 2, pp. 195–197
1888 "Persische Studien", *Sitzungsberichte der philosophisch-historischen Klasse, K. Akademie der Wissenschaften,* Wien Bd. 116, pp. 387–423
1892a "Kleinigkeiten zur semitischen Onomatologie", *WZKM* 6, pp. 307–316
1892b *Persische Studien* II (Sitzungsberichte der Kais. Akademie der Wissenschaften in Wien, philos-hist. Klasse, Band 126, XII) Wien
1898a *Kurzgefasste syrische Grammatik.* Leipzig
1898b [Review of: Pognon 1898], *WZKM* 12, pp. 141–147, 353–361

Obermann, Julian
1940 "Two magic bowls: New incantation texts from Mesopotamia". *AJSLL* 57, pp. 1–31

Odeberg, Hugo
1928 *3 Enoch or the Hebrew Book of Enoch,* Ed. and translated ... Cambridge [Reprinted, with Prolegeomenon by Jonas C. Greenfield. New York 1973]

Paper, Herbert H.
1972 *A Judeo-Persian Pentateuch.* British Museum Ms. Or. 5446. Jerusalem

Patai, Raphael
1967 *The Hebrew goddess.* New York: Ktav Publishing House. Chapter VIII: "Lilith", pp. 207–245

Payne-Smith, R.
1890 *Thesaurus syriacus.* Oxford

Perdrizet, Paul
1922 *Negotium perambulans in tenebris. Etudes de démonologie gréco-orientale* (Publications de la Faculté des Lettres de l'Université de Strasbourg, fasc. 6) Strasbourg

Petermann See *Ginza*

Peterson, Erik
1926a Εἷς Θεός. *Epigraphische, formegschichtliche und religionsgeschichtliche Untersuchungen* (Forschungen zur Religion und Literatur des Alten und Neuen Testaments, N.F. 24[=41]) Göttingen
1926b "Engel- und Dämonennamen. Nomina Barbara", *Rheinisches Museum für Philologie,* N.F. 75, pp. 393–421
Pognon, Henri
1894 "Une incantation contre les génies malfaisants en mandaïte", *MSL* 8, pp. 193–234
1898 *Inscriptions mandaïtes des coupes de Khouabir,* Paris [Reprint: Amsterdam 1979]
Pope, Arthur Upham, and Phyllis Ackerman
1938 *Survey of Persian art,* I. London and New York
Preisendanz, Karl
1928 *Papyri graecae magicae. Die griechischen Zauberpapyri,* I, Leipzig-Berlin
1931 Idem, II
1941 Idem, III. Unpublished index to above, photocopied from author's page proofs at the Warburg Institute, London [A xerox copy in the possession of Prof. G. Scholem was used by kind permission]
Rahmani, L.Y.
1960 "The ancient synagogue of Ma'on (Nirim). B. The small finds and coins", *Bulletin, L.M. Rabinowitz Fund for the Exploration of Ancient Synagogues,* 3, pp. 14–18
Reich, S.
1937/8 "Quatre coupes magiques", *BEO* 7–8, pp. 159–175
Reitzenstein, Richard
1904 *Poimandres. Studien zur griechisch-ägyptischen und frühchristlichen Literatur.* Leipzig [Reprint: 1922]
Rettig, David
1934 *Memar Marqa—Ein samaritanischer Midrash zum Pentateuch.* (Bonner Orientalische Studien, Heft 8) Stuttgart
Rodwell, J.M.
1873 "Remarks upon a terra-cotta vase", *TSBA* 2, pp. 114–118
Rosenthal, Franz
1939 *Die aramaistische Forschung seit Th. Nöldeke's Veröffentlichungen.* Leiden [Reprint: 1964]

Rossell, William H.

1953 *A handbook of Aramaic magical texts* (Shelton Semitic Series, Number two) Skylands, Ringwood Borough, New Jersey

Salemann, C.

1930 *A Middle Persian grammar.* Trans. L. Bogdanov. Bombay

Scheftelowitz, I.

1920 *Die altpersische Religion und das Judentum—Unterschiede, Übereinstimmungen und gegenseitige Beeinflussungen.* Giessen

Schiffman, L.H.

1963 "A forty-two letter divine name in the Aramaic magic bowls", *Bulletin of the Institute of Jewish Studies* 1, pp. 97–102

Scholem, Gershom G. — גרשם שלום

1948 "פרקים חדשים מענייני אשמדאי ולילית", תרביץ יט, עמ' 175–160

1965 *Jewish gnosticism, Merkabah mysticism, and Talmudic tradition.* (Second edition), New York [The first edition appeared in 1960]

1974 "Jaldabaoth reconsidered", *Mélanges d'Histoire des Religions offerts à H.-C. Puech,* Paris, pp. 405–421

1980/1 "הבדלה דר' עקיבא—מקור למסורת המאגיה היהודית בתקופת הגאונים", תרביץ נ, עמ' 281–243

Schrire, T.

1966 *Hebrew amulets—Their decipherment and interpretation,* London

Schulthess, Friedrich

1924 *Grammatik des christlich-palästinischen Aramäisch.* Tübingen

Schwab, Moïse

see also Babelon and Schwab

1886 "Une coupe d'incantation", *RA* 1, pp. 117–119

1890 "Les coupes magiques et l'hydromancie dans l'antiquité orientale", *PSBA,* April 1890, pp. 292–342

1891 "Coupes à inscriptions magiques", *PSBA,* June 1891, pp. 583–595

1892 "Deux vases judéo-babyloniens", *RA* 2, pp. 136–142

1897 *Vocabulaire de l'angélologie d'après les manuscripts hébreux de la Bibliothèque Nationale.* Paris

1906 "Une amulette judéo-araméenne", *JA,* 2e série, vol. 7, pp. 5–17

1916/7 "Amulets and bowls with magic inscriptions", *JQR* 7, pp. 619–628

Sefer ha-razim ספר הרזים. ההדיר מרדכי מרגליות. ירושלים 1966

Segal, J.B.

1970 [Review of McCullough 1967], *BSOAS* 33, pp. 609–611

Shachar, Isaiah ישעיהו שחר

1971 אוסף פויכטונגר – מסורת ואמנות יהודית. מוזיאון ישראל. ירושלים

Shaked, Shaul שאול שקד

1979 *The wisdom of the Sasanian sages* (Denkard VI), by Āturpāt-i Emetētān. Translated by S. Shaked (Persian Heritage Series, 34) Boulder, Colorado

1983 "על ספרות הכישוף היהודית בארצות האסלאם, הערות ודוגמאות", פעמים 15, עמ' 15–28

[Forthcoming] "Bagdana, King of the Demons, and other Iranian terms in Babylonian Aramaic magic", *Acta Iranica, Monumentum M. Boyce*

Sharvit, Shimon שמעון שרביט

1974 "העדר ניגוד בין קמץ לחולם ובין סגול לפתח (בכתב יד שהגייתו בבלית)", ספר זיכרון לחנוך ילון. ירושלים, עמ' 547–555

Siddiqi, A.

1919 *Studien über die persischen Fremdwörter im Klassischen Arabisch.* Göttingen

Smith, Morton

1982 "Helios in Palestine", *Eretz Israel* 16, pp. 199*-214*

Sokoloff, Michael מיכאל סוקולוף

1982 קטעי בראשית רבה מן הגניזה. ירושלים

Stark, Jürgen Kurt

1971 *Personal names in Palmyrene inscriptions.* Oxford

Sperber, D.

1966 "On a meaning of the word מלה", *REJ* 125, pp. 385–389

Sukenik, E.L. א. ל. סוקניק

1930 "השם 'שלון' בגלוסקמאות", תרביץ א/ג, עמ' 154

Sword of Moses See Gaster 1896

Tabarī, Abū Jaʿfar Muḥammad B. Jarīr

Taʾrīkh al-rusul wa-l-mulūk, ed. Muḥ. Abū-l-Faḍl Ibrāhīm. 10 vols. Cairo, 1960 ff.

Tal (Rosenthal), Abraham אברהם טל

1975 לשון התרגום לנביאים ראשונים ומעמדה בכלל ניבי הארמית. תל אביב

1980/1 התרגום השומרוני לתורה. מהדורה ביקורתית. תל אביב

Tavadia, Jehangir C.
1930 *Šāyast-nē-šāyast,* edited by J.C. Tavadia. Hamburg

Teixidor, Javier
1962 "The Syriac incantation bowls in the Iraq Museum", *Sumer* 18, pp. 51–62

Testa, Emmanuel
1962 *Il simbolismo dei Giudeo-cristiani* (Publications du Studium Biblicum Franciscanum, No. 14) Jerusalem
1967 *L'huile de la foi. L'Onction des malades sur une lamelle du 1er siècle.* Traduit et adapté de l'italien par O. Engelbert (Publications du Studium Biblicum Franciscanum, Collectio minor, 3). Jerusalem [Cf. Milik 1967; Testa 1968]
1968 "Una falsificazione della laminella dell'unzione", *La Terra Santa* 44, pp. 55–58

Thompson, R. Campbell
1906 "The folklore of Mossul", *PSBA* 28, pp. 76–86, 97–109

Trachtenberg, Joshua
1939 *Jewish magic and superstition* [Reprint: New York 1970]

Urbach, Ephraim E.
1975 *The Sages—their concepts and beliefs.* Jerusalem

Utas, Bo
1968 The Jewish-Persian fragment from Dandān-Uiliq", *Orientalia Suecana* 17, pp. 123–136

Vanden Berghe, Louis
1970 "Luristan. Prospections archéologiques dans la région de Badr", *Archeologia,* Paris, No. 36, pp. 10–21

Viaud, Gérard
1978 *Magie et coutumes populaires chez les Coptes d'Egypte* (Éditions Présence. Collection "Le Soleil dans le Coeur') St. Vincent-sur-Jabron, Sisteron

Vincent, H.
1908 "Amulette judéo-araméenne", *Revue Biblique,* Nouvelle série 5, pp. 382–394

Wertheimer, S.A. שלמה אהרן ורטהימר
1980 בתי מדרשות. עשרים וחמשה מדרשי חז"ל. מהדורה חדשה ... מאת אברהם יוסף ורטהימר. כרכים א־ב. ירושלים

West, E.W.
1892 *Pahlavi texts,* IV. The Sacred Books of the East, ed. by F. Max Müller, XXXVII. Oxford

Westermark, E.
1926 *Ritual and belief in Morocco.* 2 vols. London

Widengren, Geo
1960 *Iranisch-semitische Kulturbegegnung in parthischer Zeit* (Arbeitsgemeinschaft für Forschung des Landes Nordrhein-Westfalen, Geisteswissenschaften, Heft 70) Köln und Opladen

Winkler, H.A.
1930 *Siegel und Charaktere in der muhammedanischen Zauberei* (Studien zur Geschichte und Kultur des islamischen Orients. Beihefte zu "Der Islam", 7) Berlin und Leipzig
1931 *Salomo und die Karina. Eine orientalische Legende von der Bezwingung einer Kindbettdämonin durch einen heiligen Helden* (Veröffentlichungen des Orientalischen Seminars der Universität Tübingen. Abhandlungen zur allgemeiner Religionsgeschichte, 4. Heft) Stuttgart

Wohlstein, Jos.
1893 "Über einige aramäische Inschriften auf Thongefässen des Königlichen Museums zu Berlin", *ZA* 8, pp. 313–340
1894 Idem, *ZA* 9, pp. 11–41

Worrell, William Hoyt
1914/5 "Studien zum abessinischen Zauberwesen (Fortsetzung und Schluss)", *ZA* 29, pp. 85–141

Yamauchi, Edwin M.
1965 "Aramaic magic bowls', *JAOS* 85, pp. 511–523
1967 *Mandaic incantation texts* (American Oriental Series, 49) New Haven, Connecticut
1970 [Review of McCullough 1967], *JNES* 29, pp. 141–144

Zand-i-khūrtak Avistāk, ed. by Ervad B.N. Dhabhar (Pahlavi Text Series, 3) Bombay 1927

GLOSSARY*

In the following, all the words and names occurring in the Amulets and Bowls published in this book are indexed. The Geniza texts have not been included in this Glossary. The main Glossary is followed by an index of divine names, names of angels and *nomina barbara,* and by an index of personal names. Biblical quotations are listed in a separate index. The individual words in such quotations are not included in the glossary.

Numbers in italics indicate that the reference is to a text in Syriac (this applies to A*6,* B*1,* and B*10*).

Verbs are placed under their root forms. Nouns are arranged in principle according to their spelling, usually in the definite form. *Matres lectionis* are ignored in the alphabetical arrangement, unless they form part of the root or of the basic nominal form. This rule has not been strictly observed in foreign words.

Restored words have not been listed. Words partly restored are indicated by parenthesis around the line number.

אבא father B 13:12. אבוכון B *1:9*
אבד to be lost. יבד B 9:4
אבל to mourn. אבילין B 6:7
אבנא stone. אבן B 6: 5,8
אברא limb. אברין A 9:3. אבריה (H) A 4:17. איבריה B 13:5
אברא lead B 13:11
אגנא chalice. אגני B 13:18. אגנהו B 13:16
אדוגא furnace. אדוגי B 13:5
אדמסא steel B *1:12*
אדם a human being B 13:(19)
אודנא ear. אודנין B 6:4. אודניהון B 6:7
או O (interj.) A *6:1, 11*
אוקינוס sea, ocean A *6:4–5*
אוריתה see עריתה
אזגנדא messenger; pl. B *1:5*
אזה perspiration (?) B 13:19
אזל to go, move out. אזלת B 12:2 אזילו B *10:9, 12.* תיזה B *1:11.* ניזי B 13:15, 19
אזרא cedar (?) B 13:12
אחא brother B *1:8*
אחד to hold, seize. יחוד B 9:5
אחד (H) one A 1:9
אחרי (H) behind. מאחריך A 1:2
אידא fate. אידי B 13:14, 20
איך like B *10:11*
אילנא tree B 13:12

*Prepared by Ḥ. Avitan

איח there is / are B *1:4;* 2:6; 5:(2),3; 7:3; 11:8; 12:IX,XI. עית B *10:6,10*

אכל to eat. תכול B 9:9. איכולי B 7:8. אכיל B *1:8;* 13:4. אכלה A 7:17,20. מוכיל *af.* B *1:8.* See also מיכלא

אכליא perdition (?) B 7:3.

אכפיא paralysis B 9:10

אל (H) God A 1:3; 2:4; 4:5,7,8. האל A 1:23. אלהי A 1:23; 4:24,34

אלהא God A 3:12; 5:3; pl. B *1:9.* אלה A 3:6; 7:5, 11, 14, 15. אילה A *6:2,22,18.* אילהי B 13:3,15. See also בית אילהי

אלוא aloe B 13:17

אילמא mute, dumb. אילמין B 6:17. אלימני B 13:19

אלתר see עלתר

אימא mother B 13:12; see also list of personal names. אמה A 12:17. דימא B 2:4

אמיתא (=אמיטתא) darkness B 7:4

אמן A 1:(6),12, 18, 19; 2:12; 4:23; B *passim.* אמין B *1:13*

אמר to say, speak A 15:17; B 6:10; 12:VIII. אמרת (1st p.) A 7:19; (3rd p. f.) B 12:IV. אמרו B 12:IV. אאמר B *1:5.* יאימר B 4:5. אמריתו B 13:15, 19. אמרן A 7:22. See also מאמר, מימרא

אן if A 3:16; 7:7; 7b:3

אנה I A 1:12; 8:3; 9:4; 10:6; 12:1; B 12b:IV. אנא B 12a:IV; 12:VIII. אני (H) A 4:28,32; B 5:1.

אנכא plumb B 13:11

אנשא man; see also בני אינשא (s.v. בר). אינשי B 6:6

אנתי you (f.) B 12b:I

אנתון see אתון

אסא myrtle B 13:12, 17

אסותא remedy, healing B 3:1. אסותה B 11:7. אסו A 3:20(?); B 5:1. אסיותא B *10:6,13.* אסיותיה A 1:15, 18

אסי *pa.* to heal. יאסי A 1:(13). אסי A 3:20 (?). אסון A 3:22. מאסיה A 2:1. *itp.:* יתסי B 11:8. אתאסי A 1:(10)

איסיוי black B 13:9,10

אסכרא choking B 9:9

אסנא granary. אסניהו B 13:19

אסקופתא threshold. אסקופת B 5:1. איסקופתיה B 11:1, (7), 8

אסר to bind. אסרתינון B 5:2, 3. אסיר B 12:IX. אסירא B 2:5; 12:XI. אסרא B 8:I. אסריא B 8:II. אסירת B 12b:I. אסירין B 2:8; 12:XI. אסרין B 8:I. אסיריתון B 5:7

איסרא imprisonment, spell B 4:2

איסתרא goddess B 13:15. איסתרתא pl. B *1:5,9;* 13:14,15,16

אף also B 4:6; 5:7

אצמומא arrow. אצמומי B 13:14

אקרא fort (?). אקרי B 6:9

ארבעא four B 13:16. ארבעין forty A 9:3. ארבעים (H) 4:17. ארבע מאות four hundred (H) 4:17–18

ארזפתא hammer B 13:5

אורחתא way B 6:10. ארחתהו B 13:19

אריא lion B 13:4,15. אריוי B 13:12

אריסותא submission B 11:4

ארנא pine. ארני B 13:12

ארעא, ארעה earth A 9:6; B *1:(3,4);* 2:2, 8; 3:4; 5:2; 6:4; 7:8; 13:10, 13, 15, 20.

ארץ (H) A 3:19

אישכרא B 13:19 wagon. אישכריהו

אשתה, אישתא fire, fever A 2:2, 8, 12; 3:22; 9:1; B 7:4, 9; 9:3. אשא A 14:2.

אש (H) A 4:29

אשלמתא spell; pl. B *10:8*; 11:4

את (H) acc. particle A 1:(3); B 12b:X

אתא omen. את(ה) B 9:13

אתון you (pl.) A 7:4; 10:3; B5:7.

אנתון B *10:8*
אתון furnace A 3:17
אתי to come. אתא B 5:5, 7; 12:IV; 13:6, 9, 13, 16, 17, 19, 21. יתי B 13:(6). יתא B 9:(13). תיתי B 9:4. תיתון B *10:5.* אתיה B *1:7.* אתיא B 13:15. אתין B *1:7. af.*: איתו B 13:20. איתכי B 7:5
אתרא place B 13:9. אתר A 3:14; B *10:10*; 12:VIII
אתתא woman. דיתתא B 2:9. יתיתתא B 2:9. אינתתיה B 12b:IX. pl. נשי B 2:4; נשא B *10:(7)*
באש to corrupt; see also ביש. מבאשה A 3:4. מבאשין B 6:7
בור pit B 6:8
בטל *pa.* to annul. בטילו B 13:9. בטלון A 5:4. *itp.*: עתבטילו B *10:12.* איבטל B 13:20
בטנתא pregnant B 13:12
ביבא canal. ביבי B 13:6
בין between, among. בין...בין whether ... or A 4:29–31. בן...בן B 5:3. בבית B 13:16
ביר well, spring B 6:8
בירא see בעירא
ביש bad, evil B *1:6*; 3:3; 6:10; 11:5. בישא B 7:3; 11:(3). בישין A 13:(5), 9; B 12:XI. בישי B 6:2; 11:(3); 13:11. בישא pl. B *1:11.* בישה f. A 3:4; 13:6; B 13:9. בישא A 14:2. בישתה A 2:3; 7:6,12. בישתא B 8:I,II, III; 12b:I; pl. B 13:7,14,17
בית to dwell, lodge. באתא(?) A 12:12
ביתא house B *1:3,8;* 5:(1). ביתה A 1:17. בית A 15:4; B:13:22. ביתה (with suffix) B *1(1:1–2),10*; 8:II, III. ביתיה B *10:5,7,;* 12:IX, XI. בתי B 13:10,15
בית אילהי temple B 2:5. בתי דאילהי B 13:16
בית כנישתא synagogue B 2:5
בית קברי cemetery B 9:14
בית see בין
בלועא throat. בלועיה B 9:9
בלע to swallow. יבלע B 9:9
בני to build. בנת A 15:4
בסי to trample. בסיא B 13:16
בעותא will, prayer. בותך A *6:10*
בעי to ask. בעו B 12:VII
בעירא cattle. בירא B *1:9.* בעריה B *10:(5),7*
בר son *passim*
בני אינשא B 2:3. בני אינשה B 5:6; 6:2, 9
ברתא/בת daughter *passim.* פת B 4:5
ברא to create. ברינא B 6:3
ברא open space (?) A 1:17
מילבר from the outside B 13: 16, 17, 19
בראשית (H) creation B 5:5
ביריאתה pl. streets B 6:9
ברך to bless. ברוך (H) A 1:(20); 3:18. ...ברוך אתה A 15:23; B 12b:X
ברכתא blessing A 12:5
ברקא lightning. ברקין B 13:5
ברוקה cataract (?), lightning (?) A 1:16
בשרא flesh. בשר B 13:10. בישריה B 7:8
בתולתא virgin B 13:10
בתר after. בתרי A 10:(6). בתרה A 15:15. בתריה B 12:VII
גאון pride (?). גאוני B 13:15
גבא back. גביה B 13:6
גבא דיגילא alum B 13:6
גבה *af.* to lift, raise (?) אגביה B 13:20
גברא man B 13:5, 9, 16, 17, 19. גברי B 2:4; 6:6; 13:20
גיברא hero, mighty A 1:8. גברא B 13:15. גבר B 5:8. גיבור A 12:(31).

גיבורין B 13:10. גיברי B 5:8. גיבריה B 6:4
גדא fortune B *1:9*
גדד to cut. גודדא B 13:16
גדוד troop. גדודהו B 3:5
גדל *pa.* magnify. מגדלה A 7:16
גדל to dress (the hair). גדליתון B 13:18
גו midst. לגו B 12:VII
גוכתא hill B 7:7
גודא troop; pl. B *1:5*
גוז to vanish. גיזו A 7:22 (?)
גופא body. גופיה B 9:3. גופה A 9:2
גיטא divorce B 5:5, 7
גידא vein, tendon. גידוהי A 1:22. גידוי A 5:(5)
גיל to rejoice. נגיל B 2:9 (?)
גילא see גבא דיגילא
גיסא troop. גיס B 13:6
גילגלא wheel, sphere. גילגלי B 13:5
גללא stone. גלל B 13:14
גלמתה hill; pl. A 9:8
גמלא camel. גמלי B 13:12
גער to drive out, exorcise. געור A 14:(9). געורו A 2:8. מגעור A 2:11. אגער *itp.* A 9:2,4
גפא wing. חיות גפא B 13:13
גופנא vine B 13:17
גופריתא sulphur B 9:3
גרבא itch B 9:(13)
גרגרתא throat. גרגרתיה B 9: 3,(9)
גרמא bone. גרמיה pl. A 1:20,21. גרמוהי A 1:22
-ד, -די of, which *passim.* דיליה B *10:8*
דאן A 7:22 (?)
דיבא wolf. דיבי B 13:12. דיבתא B 13:4
דבק to stick. ידבוק B 6:10. ידבקיה B 9:5
דבר to lead, direct. מדברין *pa.* A*6:5*
דברא open field B 2:5
דהבא gold B 13:11
דור to dwell. דירא pt. pl. B *1:8.* דירה (with f. suff.) B 13:10
דורא dwelling. דורה B *1:(1–2),10*; see also דירא
דחל to fear, frighten. תידחלי B 7:6. דחלי B 7:8. דחילא A 1:(8); B 6:9. דחילה A 7:15. דחילי B 11:4. מידחלא *pa.* pt. (?) B 7:8
די enough. דאן A 7:22 (?)
דיוא *dev,* devil, demon A *6:10,14;* B 13:17,18,21. דיוה B *1:12.* דיוין B 8:I. דיוי B 13:7,9,14,15,17,19,21. דיוא pl. B *1:3,4,11; 10:3,8*
דינא judgment B *1:10.* דינה B 9:13
דינא judge. דיני B 13:17, 22
דירא shed, tent, dwelling. דיריהו B 13:19; see also דורא
דכי pure. דכיא B *1:12*
דכר male A 7:7; 7b:3; B 5:3; 8:I. דיכרא pl. B *1:9*; 13:22. זכר (H) A 4:15
דכר to remember, mention. דכרין B 12a:VIII. מדכרין *af.* A 15:20. *itp.:* ידכר B 12b:VIII. מידכריתון B 13:17, 18
דוכרנא memory. דוכרניה B 9:(12)
דוכתא place B 12a:IV. דוכה B 3:2
דלק to burn. תידלק B 9:3. תידלוק B 9:5
דמא blood B 13:22. דמיה B 7:8
דמותא shape, form B 13:11. דמות B 13:11,12,19. דמותיה B 13:20. בת דמו B *10:9*
דמך to lie, fall asleep. ידמכון B 3:2. דמכה A 7:19, 22
דן, דנן see הדין
דנח to shine. מדנח B 7:7

דקיקתה hectic fever A 2:12
דרדקא child. דרדקא pl. B *1:8*. דרדקי B 6:6; 13:(19). דערדקיהון B 5:4. דרדוקתא B 6:6
דרום (H) south A 4:12.
דרך *af.* to find. אדריכו B 12:VII
דרך way. דרכיה B 12b:IV
הדדי each other B 13:10
הדין this B *1:4,6;* 2:9; 4:1; 5:1,7. חדין B *10:13.* הדן A 4:(1). דן A 1:(11); 3:14. דנן B 6:1; 8:(II,IV); 12b:IX. הלין A *6:3;* B 2:7. אילין B 2:8. המון A 7:16. הדא B 7:1; 13:1. חדא (=הדא) B *10: 7,11,13*
הדמא part, member. הדמאיהוא (?) B 9:(13)
הדר (H) splendour A 4:27
הוא he A 1:14; 4:(5). היא she A 1:21. ההיא B 5:6. הי B 4:5
הוי to be. הוא B *1:8,9;* 5:6; 6:10. הוהוא B 13:17,18. הוו B 13:10. הות B 5:6. יהוי B 13:14. יהי B 5:1. נהוא B *1:8.* יהוון B 6:6. ניון B *10:10.* הון B 6:6; 12:IX
הונא mind. הונה A 10:(7)
היך like B 4:4
הכין thus A 15:(13)
הכנא thus B *10:10*
הלך *pa.* to walk. מהלכה A 1:(21)
הללויה A 4:23; B 12b:IX
הן where. כל הן ד־ A 15:19
הפך to turn away, overturn. תהפכי B 4:6. הפיכא B 2:1–4. הפיכי B 2:1,3
הר (H) mountain A 4:10,11
הרבה (H) many A 1:1
הרי (H) behold, here is A 1:19
הרפתקא destiny B 13:22
־ו and *passim.* ־וי B 2:3, etc.
וי woe (interj.) B 13:20
ולדה child A 12:(4), 34
זידניתא wicked (f. pl.) B 13:17
זוח to move, rise, be elated. איתזח B 13:20
זויתא corner; pl. B 13:16
זולת (H) except for. זולתו A 4:19
זוע to shake, tremble. מזדעזעין *itp.* A 9:(8)
זיוא splendour. זיוה B 13:20
זיעא shiver B 9:5
זיקא blast, blast demon B 13:(3). זיקין A 11:8
זכי to win a trial. זכא B *1:10.* זכיא B 13:7,21
זכר see דכר
זלח to sprinkle B 13:16
זמורה (?) A 1:(16)
זמן *pa.* to appoint. מזמן B *1:(1–2)*. מזמנא B 7:1
זמר to sing, praise. זמרו A 4:11
זינותא prostitution B 13:10
זני to fornicate. זניא B 13:17
זרגונא vine (?)B 13:15
חבל to injure, destroy. איחבול B 12a:VIII. *pa.:* חביל B 13:8. חבילו B 2:9. See also מחבלה
חבילא injury, destruction B*1:10.* חבילי B 3:2
חברא companion B*1:8*
חברא sorcerer. חברי B 11:(4)
חד one B 12:III. חדה A 7:17,18. חד עסר eleven B 2:6
חדותא joy. חדותהו B 13:17
חדי to rejoice. חדא B *1:8.* מחדא *af.* B *1:8*
חדיא breast, chest B 13:5. חדייה B 13:5
חדר to surround. נחדרה B *1:11.* חדרא B *1:7*

חדש (H) month A 4:31
חדת new. חדתתא B*10:9*
חוי *pa.* to tell. מחוא B *1:6*
חוף to cover. חף B 13:15
חיזונא vision; pl. B *10:4*
חזי to see. חזין A 15:15. חזוהי B 9:4. *itp.:* יתחזי A 3:14. מיתחזתון B 13:11,13, 20
חזירא swine. חזירי B 13:11
חיא life B 4:8
חיה a living creature B 13:19
חיותא animal
 חיות גפא see גפא
חיי to live. חי B 4:8; 13:4. חיה A 9:5
חיים (H) life. בחי האל A 1:23; 12:(19)
חילא power B 13:3. חיליה B 13:3. חילי B 13:9. חילוותא B 13:14,20
חיתא midwife B13:13
חלא sand B 7:7
חלבא fat B 13:16
חלמא dream; pl. B*10:4.* חילמא pl. B *1:1–2, 11.* חילמי B 13:11
חליש weak. חלישין B 13:10
חמה (H) sun A 4:20
חמי to see. חמתון B 6:4. תתחמין *itp.* A 12:(13), 33
חמרא donkey B 13:12
חומרא charm; pl. B *1:5.* חומרי B 13:17,22
חמשה five B 13:21. חמשין fifty B 6:7
חמתה mother-in-law B 2:4
חומתא heat B 13:4. חומתיה B 13:4
חינכיא jaws, palate. חינכוהי B 9:10
חנק to strangle B 12:V. איחנוק B 12:VIII. חנקא B 5:6. למיחנק B 12:VII
חיסא rock. חיסיא B 7:7
חסמתא jealousy B 11:3
חסינא mighty A *6:2.* חסינה A*7:15*
חציף impudent. חציפתא B 13:7
חרב destroyed, wrecked, ruined. חרבי B 13:10,15
חרבא sword B 13:6,8; pl. B *1:7*
חרשא deaf. חרישין B 6:7
חרשא spell, sorcery; sorcerer; pl. B*1:1–2, 4, 11; 10:8.* חרשין B 12a:III. חרשיא B 4:6. חרשי B 3:4; 13:15
חשוכא, חשוכה darkness B 13:9,20
חשש *pa.* cause pain. תיחשין A 3:5
חתם to seal. חתמין B 2:8. חתמין B 8:(I). חתמן B 8:(I). חתימא B 2:5. חתימת B 12b:I. חתימתא B *10:9.* ניתחתים *itp.* B *1:(10)*
טב good A 1:(20); 2:1,11; 4:1; 13:2. טבא B *1:9.* טבתא goodness B *1:6*
טוף *af.* to make flow אטף B 13:14
טורא mountain B 2:5; 7:7; 12:III; 13:13,20. טור A 12:4; B 7:7. טוריה A 9:8. טורי B 13:20
טלא shaded place (?) B 3:3
טליא child A 12:3
טלם to oppress. טלמי A 4:6
טלניתה shadow spirit A 7:6,13; 7b:3. הטלנית (H) A 4:15. טלני A 13:8. טלנין A 11:8
טמא impure. טמאה (H?) A 13:(11). טמיתא B 13:17,22
טמר to hide. יטמרון *itp.* B 3:4
טינרא flint B 13:14
טרד to lock. טרדת A 15:6
יבב *pa.* to sound (a trumpet). מיבביתון B 13:18
יבל to lead. אובלתיכי *af.* B 7:5
יבש to dry out, ניבש B 9:(2). יבשון B 9:3

ידא hand. ידיה B 13:6. עדיה B *10:12.* ידה B 13:15
 לידא (?) A 15:7
ידע to know B 5:6. יאידע B 4:5. ידענא B 5:4. ידעיתון B 13:15,17,19
יובלה jubilee B 6:7
יומא day B 8:II,IV; 12b:IX; 13:14. יומה A 1:11. יום (H) A 4:29. יומי B 5:4,5; 6:8. יממא A 12:14; B *1:13.* עממא B *10:4*
יחד *pa.* to single out. מיחד unique B 12a:III. מאחיד B 12b:III
יחטא abortion. יחטי B 13:10
ילד to give birth. ילידת A 15:1; B 12:II. יליד B 7:8. ילדתא B 13:10,13
ילל *pa.* to wail, moan. יליל B 13:20
ימא sea B 5:5,7; 12:VII; 13:6,14. ימה A 9:7; 15:16
ימא to swear. מוממנא *af.* A *6:7*
ימינא right B 13:14. ימינך (H) A 1:1. ימינו (H) A 4:32
יממא see יומא
יקד to burn. יקוד A 10:5. יקדתה A 3:18. יקדין B 13:5
ירחא moon, month B 6:8
 ריש ירחא New Moon Day B 6:8
ירי to shoot. נורי *af.* (?) B 13:15. See מורניתא
ית acc. particle A 3:14; B 13:22. יתיתתא B 2:9. יתה (w. m. suff.) A 15:17. יתיה B 9:5; 12b:V,VII. יותיה B 12a:V,VII. יאתוה B *1:6.* יתה (w. f. suff.) A 13:4; B 2:9. יתכון A 10:4; B 6:3,8,9. יתהון B 12:II
יתב to sit. יתיב B *1:8.* יתבי B 6:9
כא here B 5:5,7
כבר already B 5:4,5
כבש to press down. כבשתינון B 5:3. כבשונכו B 13:13. לכבישוה B *10:13.* כביש A 11:6. כבישתון B 5:7. *itp.:* ניתכביש B *1:11,12.* יתכבשון B 3:4. יתכבשו B 9:13
כד just as, while, when B 5:6; 7:9; *10:9;* 13:17,18
כדא jar. כדי B 13:10,15
כויא scalding (?) B 9:(3)
כוכבא star. כוכבי B 2:3; 9:1
כול to measure. אכיל *af.* A 15:18
כח (H) strength A 4:32
כיפא stone, rock. כיפי B 5:2. כיפיה B 13:14. See also כפא
ככא molar tooth. ככי , ככיה B 13:4
כל, כול all *passim*
כלבא dog. כלבי B 13:10
כלדאה soothsayer. כלדאי B 13:13
כלי to terminate, extinguish. *itp.:* יתכל A 7b:2. יתכלון A 7:5,12. עתכלו B *10:12*
כלי vessel. כלין A 1:14 (?)
כלילא wreath. כלילי B 13:18
כוליתה kidney (w. suff.) A 10:7
כלתא daughter-in-law B 2:4
כלמתא vermin B 9:13.
כמא as ... כ(י)ן ... כמא/ה as ... so ... A 4:(6–)14; 10:(4–5); B 6:4; 9:12
כנישתא see בית כנישתא
כנש to gather. כנשונכו B 13:13
כסא full moon B 6:8
כסי to cover, hide. כסיי B 11:3. מכסי *pa.* B 13:18,21
כספא silver B 13:11
כפא palm (of the hand); foot כף A 12:8 (?). כיפי B 5:7. See also כיפא
 כפא דידא shoulder. כפידיה B 13:5
כפי to force. תכפין A 12:(10)

כפן to be hungry. כפנה A 7:17,20. כפנתה A 7:19

כפת to bind, tie. כפתינון B 5:2,(3). כיפיתון B 5:7

כצומא diviner. כצומי B 13:13

כורהנא illness B 13:(20). כורחנה B *1:11, 12.* כורהניא B 11:(3)

כרז to announce. כריזי *pa.* (?) B 5:7

כיריתא ditch (?) B 7:4

כורכוריא bones (?) A 11:5,10

כרסא belly. כרסיה B 13:6

כורסיא throne. כרסיה A 7:5,15; 7b:1

כשט *pa.* or *af.* to dress, set, adorn. מכשטיתון B 13:18

כתב to write. כתבת A 1:12. כתבו B 5:5,6; 11:3. כתבי B 6:9. כתיב B 9:5,7,10

לא no, not *passim.* דלא without A 11:6,(7); B 13:6,14. דלה A 9:6

לבא heart. לב (H) A 4:18. לבה (w. suff.) A 10:5. ליביה B 4:5. ליביכו B 13:14. ליביהון B 6:7

לבנה (H) moon A 4:20

לבש to be dressed. לביש B 13:18. לבישין B 13:21

לוט to curse. לטת B 2:6,9. תילוט B 2:9. ליט B 2:(1). ליטא B 4:6. ליטי B 11:4

לוטתא curse B 2:4,5–6; pl. B *1:11;* 4:6; *10:8*; 11:4

לוי to accompany. לוית B 12b:I. לויא B 13:7. See also מלויתא

לוחשה whisper, spell A 1:16

לטבא (= לא טבא) evil B 13:5. לטבי B 13:6

ליליא night A 12:14; B *10:4.* לליא B *1:13*

ליליתא Lilit B 5:6; 12a:XI; 13:(1),22; pl. B 13:7. לילתה B 8:I. לליתא B *1:3, 6, 11*

לית not B 12:IV

למא why. למת (=למה את) A 7:19,20,21

למעלה (H) above A 1:3. למעל A 14:8

ליסטא pirate B 9:14

לפני (H) in front of. מלפניך A 1:(2); 15:25

לקבל against. לקובלי B 6:5,6. לקובליה B 6:2

לקי *af.* to strike. ילקו B 9:3

לשנא tongue. לישניה B 9:2,(10). לישניהון B 6:10

מא anything; what? B 12:VI. מה A 15:13. See also כמא, למא

מאד (H) very A 1:1

מאה hundred. מתין A 9:3. מאתים (H) two hunderd A 4:16. ארבע מאות (H) four hundred A 4:17–18

מאמר speech, commandment A 3:23. See also מימרא

מבכלתא tormentor B *1:1–2, 11;* 12a:XI; 12b:I

מבעדא see מעבדא

מגלא sickle (?) B 4:(4)

מגר *pa.* to vanquish. ימגר B 9:4

מדברה wilderness A 9:7

מדינתא country, city B 6:3

מידיעם thing B 3:3; 11:5

מה see מא

מהרא (sacred) word, spell. מהרין B 11:3

מורניתא lance B 13:15

מות to die. ימות B 9:4. מיתי B 13:12

מזג to mix, fill the cups. מזיג B 13:4. מזגיתון B 13:18

מזופיתא rebuke B 9:5

מזיקא harmful spirit, destroyer.

מזקה A 7:13; 7b:2. מזיקין B 12:XI. מזקין A 11:8; 13:(5),9. מזיקי B 5:3

מזלא planet. מזלי B 2:3; 9:1. מזלותיה (H) A 4:20

מחבלה destroyer A 7:13; 7b:2

מחי to blot out; to smite. מחונה B 13:8. *itp.:* איתמחי B 9:12. יתמיח B 9:12

מחלה (H) illness. מחלתם B 9:(6)

מחמת (H) because of B 6:6

מיא water A *6:5;* B 13:9,10. מיה A 15:(19)

מיכלא food. מיכליהון B 13:10

מימרא speech B 13:3. See also מאמר

מכאובא pain A 1:11

מלא to fill. מלא משמלא (?) B 4:4

מלאכא angel; pl. B *1:7.* מלאכה A 11:6,(7); B 2:6; 9:14. מלאכין B 2:9. מלאכיה A 3:21; 7:4; 10:3. מלאכי B 13:3,21. מלאכיהון B 13:21

מלויתא companion (f.); an epithet for female demon B 13:7

מלך to advise (?); to rule (?) מלכנא B 4:4

מלכא king. מלכה B 13:3. מלך A 1:(7); 3:1,3; 4:8

מלך מלכי מלכיא A 1:(24); 12:(20)

מלכותא kingdom B 13:3. מלכות A 4:25

מלכנא see מלך

מלל *pa.* to speak. ימללון B 6:10. ממלל A 3:3; B *10:12*

מללא speech B 6:10

ממלא speech B 11:3

מילתא word, spell B 7:1. מליה pl. A 7:14. מלא pl. B *1:7*

מן who A 9:5; 15:18; B 2:7

מן from *passim.* מין B 2:9; 4:6,7,8

מנוחה repose A 1:2

מני *pa.* to appoint. ממני A 12:2

מסס to dissolve. יתמסי *itp.* B 9:2

מעבדא witchcraft, magic practice, sorcery B *10:8;* pl. B *1:5.* מבעדא B *1:11*

מעברתא ford A *6:3–4,6*

מועט diminution. מועט לבנה (H) A 4:20

מערב (H) west A 4:13

מערכות (H) battle line A 4:24

מוקדא top of the head. מוקדה B 13:8

מקדשה temple B 12b:III

מוקרא brain. מוקרה B 13:8

מראה (H) sight. מראות הדר A 4:27

מרוביא educator B *1:9*

מרדותא chastisement B 13:4. מרדותיה B 13:4

מריא lord B 10:8; 13:3,6,13. מרי A 1:18

מרתי my lady A 8:6

מריע sick. מריעין B 6:7

מרירתא bitterness. מרירת B 7:4

מרכבא chariot B 13:6. מרכבתיה B 13:6

מרעא sickness. מרעי B 11:3

מרר to embitter, afflict. מררי B 7:8

משדרנא sender. משדרניה B *10:12*

משקיפותא affliction B 4:6

מישתיא drinking, drink. מישתייכון B 13:10

מתא place, village, town B 2:5; 9:13

נבח to bark. נבחיתון B 13:10

נגע (H) plague A 1:4

נידרא vow; pl. B *1:1–2,11;* 3:2. נדרך (?) A 4:6

נהר to illuminate. נהרא B 13:20. אנהר *af.* A *6:10*

נוולא loom. נוולי B 13:13

נום to sleep. נימה A 7:18,21. נאמתה A 7:(21)

נורא fire A 3:18; B *1:7, 10;* 13:4,5,9,18,21

נוחרא nostril. נוחרה A 5:(3)

נחשא copper B 13:11. נחשה B 12a:III; 13:6. נחש A 11:(6); B 12b:(III)

נחת to descend; *af.* to bring down, introduce. אחית B 13:14. אחיתונכו B 13:13. מחית B 4:5

נטר to guard. *part.* A 12:3. טור A 12:4. *itp.:* נתנטר B *1:13.* ניתנטר B *10:6, 7, 10, 13.* ניתנטרון B *10:11*

ניא chest A 11:(5),10

נכבד (H) honourable A 4:(2)

נכי to afflict. מכה (H) A 1:20; B 12b:X

נכל (?) A 4:18

נכר *itp.* to be estranged. יתנכיר B 9:3

נמרא tiger B 13:5. נמרי B 13:12

נסב *pa.* to hand over. מנסבא B 13:15

נסיסא grief B 13:17

נער to shake off. תנער (H) *nif.* A 4:15

נפל to fall. יפול B 9:10. פולי B 7:6,8. מיפל B 7:7

נפק to go out. נפקת B 7:4. תיפקון B *10:10.* פוקו B *10:8.* נפקי B 6:10. נפקיתון B *10:9;* 13:17,18 נפקא B 13:18,21. נפקן B 10:9

נצח to be victorious. נצחין B 5:8

נצר to grunt. נצריתון B 13:10

נקבה female A 4:15 (H); A 7:7; 7b:(3). נקבא B 5:3. נוקבה B 8:I. נקבתא pl. B *1:10.* ניקבתא B 13:22

נקט to hold. נקיטא B 13:15

נקם to take revenge. תיקום B 2:9. נקום B 2:9

נקמה (H) revenge, judgment. ניקמת B 2:9
אל נקמות A 12:18

נקש to strike B 13:14

נתן to give. תיתנו B 6:4

נישמתא soul; pl. B 2:9

סבא old man; grandfather B 13:12. סבי B 13:19. סביהון B 5:4
סבתי grandmother B 13:12

סגי numerous B 6:3

סוגיא walk, practice B 13:4. סוגייה B 13:4

סדנא anvil B 13:5

סומא blind. סמן B 6:7

סחף to wreck. סחוף B 13:16. סחפונהו B 13:16. ניסחופינהו B 13:(19). למיסחף B 13:16. סחפי B 13:22

סטנא Satan B 13:16; pl. B *1:6.* סטנה B 9:(14). סטן A 14:2,9

סטרא side. בסטר A 7:15

סיפא sword, sabre B *1:7*

סכינא knife. סכין B 13:16

סכר to lock, shut. לסכורי *pa.* B 6:1. יסתכר *itp.* B 9:(3)

סכתא nail. סכת פדנא coulter B 4:4

סלה A 1:12, (18,19); 2:11; 4:23; B 3:5; 5:6; 6:10; 8:IV; 11:5,9. סלא B 4:3

סלק to rise. סלקה A 7:14. מבסק (error for מנסק or מיסק ?) B 7:7

סמך to lean, rely. יסמכו B 9:14

סממיתא spider, lizard (?) B 12b:II. סממית A 15:1. סמומית B 12a:II

סנדלא sandal, shoe. סנדלי B 13:6. סנדליה B 13:6

סני to hate. סניי B 11:3,4. סניתא B 13:11

ספרא book. סיפרי B 6:9

סרודתא terror, fright B 13:13; pl.

B *1:3,(11)*

סירפא draught. סירפי B 13:5

סרורותא dominion. סררו A 7:(3)

סתם to shut B 5:8

עבד to do, make, perform A 15:13; B 7:9. עבדת B 12:III. עבדו B 12:VI. למעבד B 9:(13). עביד B *10:6.* תיבדון B 4:8. מתעבדין *itp.* B 3:4 משתעבדיתון *išt.* B 13:17,18

עבדא servant. עבדה A 3:6

עובדא, עבדא work, magic act; pl. B *10:12.* עבדין B 3:4; 12:III

עבר to pass, transgress B 2:7. נעבר B 12:IV

עיבר bank, side. מן עיבר from across, beyond B 5:5,7

עגלא swiftness. בעגלה swiftly B 9:13

עד up to, until A 1:(12); 4:12; B 5:3,4; 7:7; 8:IV

עוק *af.* to oppress. מעיק B 3:3

עוז (H) power B 3:5

עזר (H) help. עזרי A 4:3

עינא eye. מעין A 1:16–17. עינין B 6:4. ענין B 2:9. עיני B 9:4. עינוי A 5:(5). עיניה B 13:5. עיניהון B 6:7 עינא בישתא evil eye B 8:II,III. עין בישה/א A 2:2–3. עינה בישתה A 13:6; 14:2 עין רעה (H) A 13:10

עית see אית

עכב *pa.* to detain, prevent, delay. תעכבין A 3:15,16

עכר to disturb. יתעכר *itp.* B 9:4

על upon, above; against *passim*

עלל to enter. על, עול A 15:10; B 12:V. נ(י)עול B 12:IV. עלא A 11:5

עולימא young man, lad B 13:12. עולימיהון B 5:4

עולמתא lass B 13:12

עלמא world, eternity A *6:5–7*; B 2:9; 5:3; 12a:III. עלמה B 9:12. לעלם A 1:12; B 8:II,IV; 12b:IX. עלמיה A 3:(1). עולמים (H) A 3:2

עלתר on the spot, now B 7:9

עם with A 4:9. עים B 12b:I; 13:1,7,8. ע(י)מהון A 15:(10); B 12:V

עמא population. עמיה B 6:3

עמודא colum, pillar. עמודין A 9:7

עננא cloud B 13:5

עפרא dust B 3:2

עקר to uproot. תעקרו A 11:10. *itp.:* יתעקר B 9:(12). תתעקרון A 11:4

עריתה shiver, shivering A 2:2,8,12; 3:22. בירויתא (=בערויתא) B 9:13. אוריתה A 9:1. העריה (H) A 4:29

ערק to flee, run away A 15:(14). ערקת A 15:2; B 12:II. יערקון A 11:8 ערוסו ארוקו B *10:11*

עשה (H) to do. עושה B 5:1

עשרא ten B 13:21. תרי(ן) עשר twelve B 12:II

פאר *pa.* to glorify. מפאר A 4:3. מפארה A 7:(16)

פגרתא see פגדתא

פגע affliction A 1:4

פגרא body. פגרה (w. m. suff.) B *1:10.* פגריה B *10:6,8,10,12.* פגרה (w.f. suff.) A 2:9. פגריהו B 13:19

פגרתא idle (?); pl. (?) B 13:9

פדנא plough B 4:4

פה (H). mouth פי (?) A 4:1. פיה A 4:19

פומא mouth. פום B 5:8; 6:5. פומיה B 4:5; 9:2; *10:12;* 13:5,18. פומה B 6: 1, 5, 9; (w. f. suff.) B 13: 8. פומיהון B 6:7,19; 13:21

פלגוס sea A 15:16; B 12:VII

פלט *pa.* to save. לפלטא A 13:(4)
פולקתא hatchet B 13:8
פנים (H) face, north. See also לפני
פסס to cut off, break. פסיסי B 13:10,15
פרגוד attendants (?) B 13:14
פרזלא iron B 12a:III; 13:5,6,13,14. פרזלה A 15:(5). פרזל B 12b:III. פורזיל A 11:7
פרח to flee. פרחו B *10:8*. פרחן B *10:9*
פריחא spark. פריחי B 13:6
פרחתא bird. פרחותא B 13:13
פורענותא misfortune B 9:13
פרק to loosen; *pa.* to remove, take off A *6:13*. פרקי A *6:9*
פרש to disclose, explain. פירישו B 5:4,5. פרוש (H?) wonderful, distinguished A 3:3
פשר to melt. פשרא B *10:11*
פתגמא word A 4:1; B *1:6, 8*. פידגמי B 11:(3)
פתח to open A 15:14; B 12:IV. פתחת A 15:10; B 12:V. פתחא B 12:IV
פתכרא idol (spirit) B 12a:XI; 13:7,22. פתכריה B 8:I
פתכרותא idolatry B *1:5*
פתורא table. פתורי B 13:18
צביונא will, desire. ציביוני A 10:8
צדעא temple. צידיה B 13:5
צוח to shout. צוחת A 15:(11); B 12:IV. מצוח B 7:6
צותא associate B *1:9*
צחי to be dry, thirsty. צחיה A 7:18,20. צחיתה A 7:20
צידא see צדעא
צית *pa.* to obey. מציתא B 2:8
צל (H) shadow A 4:19
צילמתא form; pl. B 13:12
צמד *pa.* to attach. מצמדנא B 4:4
צמח to grow, shine. צמחי B 13:20

צערא pain B 11:3. צערי B 11:3
ציפרא bird; pl. B *10:9*
קבל *pa.* to accept, receive. קבילת B 5:6. קבילו B *1:9*. מקביל B 1:6. מקבלא B 2:9
קבר to bury. קביר B *1:3*
קברא tomb. קברין B 7:4. קברי B 9:14; 13:13
קדח to run away. קדחו B *10:11*
קדח to wail, moan B 13:20
קדם (מן), קמ־ before, in the presence of. קדם A 1:18; 7:5; 7b:1; B 13:17,18,21. קדמין beginning A 1:23. קדמוי A 9:(8). קדמוהי B *1:7*. קדומוהי B 2:2. קדומיה B 3:4. קומה, קמה B 13:8
קדיש holy A 3:23; *6:2*. קדישא A 4:2; B *10:(8)*. קדישיא A 4:2. קדישלה A 5:2; 10:(3). קדשיה A 7:4. קדוש (H) A 12:16–17, 44
קדש *pa.* to sanctify. מקדשה A 7:11,16
קום to stand, exist. קומו, קמו B 12: VII. קמת A 15:3; B 12 :VI. קים B 12b:X. קימא B *10:5*. קימה A 9:5. קימין A 6:3; 7:4; B 1:7; 6:2,5. קימן B 6:6. אקים *af.* A 9:6. יתקים *itp.* B 9:5,6,7,(10)
קופא monkey. קופי B 13:12
קטל to kill A 15:11; B 5:8; 12:II. קטליה B 12:V. איקטול B 12:VIII. ניקטול B 13:19. קטיל B 13:22. קטלין B *1:7*. קטלא B 13:4,6,8,22. מיקטל B 12:VII. מקטול A 15:17. מקטלא *pa.* B 13:10. עתקטל itp. B *10:12*
קיא vomit. קיה B 9:(2)
קלא voice. קלא קל(?) B 4:4. קלה B 2:9. קל B 2:8
קלי to burn. קליה(?) B 4:4. מתקלא

itp. B *1:10*
קלמתא vermin B 9:13
קמ־ see קדם
קמיעא amulet B 5:1. קמיעה A 3:14. קמיע A 1:20; 2:1,11; 4:1; 13:(2)
קנינא possession, livestock. קנין B 5:2. קינין B 4:8. קיניניה B *10:7*
קפלרגיא headache A 11:5
קצירא sick. קצירי B 13:20
קרא to call. קריא B 2:8. קרינא B 6:4. קריתון B 13:18. *itp.:* מתקרא B *1:9.* מתקריה A 9:1. מתקרייא A 11:5. מיתקריתון B 13:11
קראה a biblical verse B 9:5,7,10
קרב to come near, approach. קריב B 13:7,22
קרבא war, battle B 5:8; 13:4,17, 18, 21, 22. קרוביא attack, encroachment B *1:3, 11*
קרבין (H?) intestines A 4:18
קרי to happen B 7:3. קירית B 7:3
קריא accident, mishap B 7:3
קרנא horn. קרני B 13:18. קרניהו B 13:16
קרנתא street corners B 6:9 (cf. שוקא)
ראש see רישא
ראשית see בראשית
רב great. רבא A 1:8; 3:12; *6:1;* 12:15; B 2:6; 6:9; *10:8.* רבה A 7:4,5,15; B 12:VII; 13:3,13,14,17,18. רבתא A *6:4.* רברבן A 4:(2). רברביהון B 5:(3)
רבו greatness A *6:8*
רבון lord B *6:12*
רבי Rabbi A 3:5
ריגותא lust B 13:10
רוגזא anger, wrath B *1:7;* 13:22
רגע (H) (bad) fate (?) A 1:4
רדף to chase. רדפו A 15:15; B 12: VII. נירדפינהו B 13:19
רוחא spirit A 12:9; B 9:(14). רוחה A 7:6, (12); 9:1. רוח A 1:20,21; 3:4; 4:15; 12:1,12,32; 13:7,11; 14.(3). רוחי B 13:14,20. רוחתה A 2:9. רוחות (H) A 15:25
רויתא see עריתה
רום *pa.* to lift, exalt. מרומה A 7:16
רוקא spittle. רוקיה B 9:2
רזא secret, mystery B *1:7;* 6:1. רזה B *1:3.* רז B *1:3.* רוז A 3:3. רזי B 5:2
רזם *af.* to swear (?). ארזם A *6:12*
רחם to love. רחימנא B 6:3. איתרחם *itp.* B 12b:VIII
רחמא friend B *1:8*
רחמין mercy A 7:1; 7b:1. רחמי B 11:8
ריחא odour, perfume B 13:19
ריסיא eye-lids A 5:(4)
רירא spittle. ריריה B 9:2
רישא head. ראישא B 13:4. ראישה B 13:3. רעשי (H?) A 14:8. ראישיה B 13:4. רישה (w. m. suff.) A 5:3; (w. f. suff.) A 11:4,10. רישיכו B 13:15,17
רכב to ride. רכיבא B 13:15
רמי to throw B 13:8. רמיתון B 13: 19. רמנכו B 13:14. תתרמין *itp.* A 3:17
רפא (H) to heal. רופא A 3:19. רופה B 12b:X. מרפא *pi.* A 1:20
רפוי (H) healing, curing A 3:19
רקיעא sky, heaven B 5:(2),7. רקיעה A 1:14; 7:14
רשיעה wicked B 12a:II
רתק *af.* to knock. ארתקו A 15:8. ארתיקו B 12:IV, VI, VIII
רתת *pa.* to shake. מרתתא A 14:3
שובטא an evil spirit. שופטין B 2:8

שבע to swear. *af.* אשבעת A 12:(9). משבע A 8:3; 9:4. משבענה A 1:21. משבענא B 6:8. משביע (H) A 4:28,(31). *itp.* משתבע A 15:(18). מישתבענא B 12: VIII

שבעה seven B 5:4; 6:8. שבא B *1:9.* שבעת B 5:5. שבע B 6:7

שבק to leave, let free. נישבוק B 13:19. שבוקו B 12: VIII

שבתא Sabbath, week B 6:8. שבת (H) A 4:30

שגר *pa.* to send, convey. שגרתיכי B 7:6. אישתגר *itp.* B 13:(9),21

שגר to heat, burn. שגירי B 13:13

שידא devil, demon; pl. B *1:(3), 4, 5, 11; 10:3.* שידה A 7:6,12; 7b:3; B *1:12.* שיד A 13:7. שידין B 2:8; 8:(I). שידי B 5:3; 13:7,9,22. שידיה B 13:21. שידתה f. pl. A 2:8

שדי to throw, cast. שדונהו B 13:16

שדר *pa.* to send B 5:6. שדרית B 2:9. שדרתיכי B 7:5. שדרו B 2:9; 5:5. משדר B *10:9.* See also משדרנא

שוי *pa.* to make, place. שוו B 13:17. שויו A 7:1. שויא B 13:17. משוא B *1:10*

שופטין see שובטא

שוקא market. שוקי B 13:19 שוקי קרנתא B 6:9

שורא wall B *1:11*

שיחלה a kind of disease (?) B 9:13

שחמתא blackening; heat B 11:1

שיחנה inflammation B 9:13

שחרתא blackening B 9:13

שיחה talk A 1:17

שים to put. סמו B *10:9*

שיצי to finish, complete. ישתצי *itp.* B 9:4

שיר (H) song A 3:1

שית (H) to put. תשית A 4:18

שכח *af.* to find. אשכחוי A 15:(15–16). משכח B *1:6*

שלהביתא flame B *1:7;* 13:18. שלהוביתא B 9:4. שלהפתא B 11:1

שלח to send A 3:19. שלחתיכי B 7:5. ישלח A 1:15

שלמא peace B *1:9, 10.* שלם B 6:3; 13:9,14. שלום (H) A 8:12

שלשלתא chain. שלשלן A 9:6. שושלן A 11:6

שמא name. שמהתא B 2:7. שמין B 2:6

בשם, בשום *passim.* לשם A 8:1 על שמיה ד־ B 7:1

שמאול left A 4:13. שמאולך A 1:1

שמיא heaven B *1:3, 9;* 2:(3),8; 3:1; 9:4, 11:7,8. שמיה A 1:18; 7:1; B 2:8; 13:13,14,20. שומיה A 3:6; 9:5

שמיטתא *shemiṭa,* release, the soil being let to lie fallow B 6:7

שמונה see תמניה

שמע to hear, listen. שמעית B 2:8,9. שמא B *1:8.* שמעיתון B 6:4

שימשא sun B 7:7

שמת to ban. ישתמת *itp.* B 9:4

שמתא ban B 5:6

שנה year A 4:30–31 (H). שני B 6:7

שינה tooth B 13:8. שיני B 13:5. שיניה B 13:4

שני *pa.* to move. תישנון B *10:10.* משנין B *10:9*

שוניא tree of chastity B 13:12

שנים (H) two A 1:19

שעבד see עבד

שעיתא wax B *10:11*

שעולא hollow of the hand. שעולה (w. suff.) A 15:19

שעתא talk B 2:3

שעתה moment, hour A 3:17

שפד *pa.* to pierce. שפיד B 13:8

שפי *itp.* to be relieved. אישתפי B 13:20

שפל *itp.* to be low. אישתפל B 13:20

שיפורא trumpet. שיפורי B 13:18. שיפורהו B 13:16

שקא leg. שקי B 13:6. שקיה B 9:3; 13:6

שקי *af.* to pour drink. משקא B *1:8*

שרי to dwell. שריא B 9:14; 13:1,7,22

שורנא cat. שורני B 13:12

שרק to hiss. מישתרקיתון *itp.* B 13:11

שריר (H) true B 12b:X

שושלתא see שלשלתא

שיתא six. שיתי sixty B 13:3

שתי to drink B 13:4. שתא B *1:8.* שתיה A 7:18,21. אישתאי B 7:8

שתק *pa.* to silence. תישתקין B 6:9. לשתוקי B 6:1. לשתקא B 6:5

תבר to break B 13:8. תברו B 13:16. יתבר B 9:4

תברא fracture B 9:5

תוב again B 4:1; 11:7

תורא ox B 13:12

תחת under A 7:11. תחות B 5:7; 13:13

תלי to hang. תלה A 9:5

תלתא three A *6:3.* תלת B 13:17. תלתהין A 7:17. תלתיהן A 7:22. תלתין thirty B 6:8

תמה to fear, be terrified. תמהין A 9:(7)

תמידה wine (?) A 1:14

תמניה eight A 9:3. שמונה (H) A 4:17

תנורא oven. תנורי B 13:13

תנינא snake. תניני B 13:11

תקן *pa.* to repair, mend. מיתקני B 13:13

תוקף (H) strength. תוקפו A 4:33

תקיף mighty B 5:8. תקיפא B *1:5,6;* 13:17,18. תקיפין B 11:3. תקיפי B 6:2; 11:4. תקיפתא B *1:6*

תרין two. תרתי B 13:5. תרי עשר twelve B 12a:II. תרין עשר B 12b:II

תרעה gate A 15:7. תרעין A 15:5

תרעמתא commotion B 13:(21)

תשבחות (H) praise. שיר תשבחות ode A 3:1

Names of Gods, Angels, Demons and *Nomina Barbara*

יה A 1:10; 2:6; 3:2; 4:3,4,11,22,33; 12:29; B 5:8; 10:5
יה ביה A 4:33
יהו A 1:10; 2:3; 3:11 B 10:5
יהואל B 5:(8)
יהוה A 4:7; 7:11; B 3:5; 11:5,6; 12b:X
יהפש A 4:21–22
יואל A 11:8
יונון A 1:7
יחיש A 3:2; 12:25
יייי A 1:5,6,(12); 13:(13); B 9:7,8, etc. ייי B 2:6. יי B 2:9
יפא A 4:25
יקותיאל B 2:6
יקיפס A 3:8
יקרנדריס A 3:11
ירוד B 9:14
ישמעאל A 1:8
כבשיאל B 10:(13)
כבבא B 2:7
כביבי B 2:7
כנברא B 2:7
כסיאל A 2:14
כריאל A 2:13
כרמסיס A 3:11
לבאת see אבלנה
לוזפת A 1:9
לידפת A 1:9
ליליתא see Glossary
מבכלתא see Glossary
מות B 9:14
מיכאל A 2:15; 7:2
מלויתא see Glossary
מלחמיאל A 11:3
מלך העולם A 15:24
מלך מלכי מלכיא/המלכים A 1:(24); 12:(20)
מסוסין A 1:7
מספס A 3:10–11
מפקיאיל B 10:13
מרהפתיס A 1:9
מרירי א B 2:7
מרמר A 3:13
מרמרמאות A 4:24–25
מרתין A 8:1,4
משגאל A 5:1
משנידה A 11:(2)
נאתה see אבלנה
נגדיאל A 3:10; 11: (6)
נהריאל A 3:9
נוריאל B 13:18
נחשור A 11:7
נכיר B 2:9
נימוס A 1:7
נרג B 7:9
נרקי A 4:26
סדיא B 2:7
סודריא B 2:7
סדרוס A 15:(2,11,14); B 12a:II,V
סוני A 15:7,12,(20); B 12b:IV,VI,VIII
סאוני B 12a:IV,VI,VIII
סוסוני A 15:(7–8),13,21
סאסוני B 12b:IV,VI,VIII
ססאוני B 12a:IV,VI,VIII
סוסיאל A 1:2
סוסגון בר פרונגס :סוסגון A 7:10
[...]סוסגר A 10:2
סטנא see Glossary
סכסך A 11:2
סוריאל A 11:(7)
סלסלירה A 3:8
סמרוטוש A 7:9
סניגלי A 15:8,(13),21
סנגרו B 12a:IV,VI,VIII
סינגרו B 12b:IV,VI,VIII
ססכבא B 2:6
ספתון A 10:2

Personal Names

Biblical Quotations in the Amulets and Bowls

Genesis 33:20 A 12:19 (?)
Exodus 15:7 B 13:2
15:26 A 13:22 ff.
22:23 B 9:7
Leviticus 26:29 B 9:9
26:27 B 9:5
Numbers 10:35 B 3:5
Deuteronomy 6:4 B 11:6–7
28:22 B 9:7–8
28:28 B 9:9
28:35 B 9:8–9
29:19 B 9:11–12
Isaiah 40:12 B 12:VIIII
Jeremiah 8:4 B 9:5
10:10 A 4:9–10
Micah 7:16–17 B 9:10–11
Zechariah 3:2 A 1:5–6; B 11:5–6
Psalms 69:24,26 B 9:6
91:1 B 11:6–7
94:1 A 12:17–18
Job 38:13 A 4:13–14
Song of Solomon 3:7–8 B 12a:XI

INDICES

As the Glossary gives all the words occurring in the Amulets and Bowls published in this volume, the Indices are in principle restricted to the Introduction and Commentary. Two exceptions have been made: the General Index includes divine names occurring in our Geniza texts, and the Index of Quotations incorporates references to the Amulets and Bowls as well.

The alphabetical order follows that of the roman alphabet, the two signs for *alef* (ʾ) and *ʿayin* (ʿ) coming first when used in consonantal transliterations. Greek is here given in transcription.

General Index

ʾwgryt 22
Abaho 166
Ablanathanalba 22,35
Abrasax 35,37,95,228
Adarmalel 238
Agirat 23
Ahanahel 231
Akatriel 235
aloe 213
Amen 36
ʿAmida prayer 43,72
Amorpho 119
amulet for fever 47,51,57,83, 225,233,235,237; for hatred 235; for love 24,221,224,227; for sickness 232; for sleep 227
amulet on cloth 216,231
Anahid 37
Anqatam 141,238
Aqbiel 219
Ares 213
Armenian proper names 150
ʿayin 162
Azriel 229
Babylonian Jewish Aramaic 31,194, 195
Bagdana 29,37,205,213
Bahaot 166
Bar-Maren 79
Bar-Theon 23
Bardellous 116
Barqiel 225
Belti 37,171
Beradonai 67
cemetery 16,153f.
Christian monogram 22,58
copper 36
curses 28
Dalqiel 219
Danahish 37,207

Index of Words

Index of Personal Names

'ypr'-hwrmyz 146
Anōšagzād, **'nwšz't'k** 149
Antonina, Antoninos 110
b'bnwš, bb'nwš, bbnwš 149
Baba, Babak 148
Bara- 157
Barāz-dukh 157
Berīk-Ṣebyāneh 165
brd'kt 157
Cosmas 42
Demetrios 74
dwkt'nwš 149
Frāta 156
Imma 167
Immi 156
Izdāndukh 182
kw'r'nwš 149
Mādar-āfriya 148
Māh-ized-dukh 157
Māhdād 156
Māhičya 157
*Māhidāta 157
Mam, Mama, Mamay, Mamma 148, 157,166
Merd-dukh 159
mh'nš 149
mhgwšnyd'(k)t 157
mṭy'r 183
myrdwk 158
Pahray 175
Pālī, Pālīz 175
Panāhak 183
Pap, Papa, Papak 148
Salome 42
Salon, Selonos 72
Shallum 72
Shlamṣiyyon 95
Tation 99
Tettius 101
šhd'kt 157
Xwarxšēd 161
z'd'nwš 149
Zarina, Zarinaia, Zarniya 213
Zuṭra 159

Index of Quotations

BIBLE, PSEUDEPIGRAPHA AND QUMRAN

NOTE: The order of books is alphabetical. References to Amulets and Bowls published in this volume are with the prefix A and B respectively, with reference to the text number and line. References to the Geniza and to discussions in the Commentary or Introduction are by page number. These numbers are usually introduced without a prefix.

Ben-Sira 26:26 49
Cant. 3:7–8 B12a:XI
6:10 60
8:6–7 222
II Chron 31:10 206
Dan. 2:32 210
2:33 207
3:6 51,54

TALMUD, TARGUM

MAGICAL TEXTS

No. 36 183,214
No. 37 126,128,129,183
No. 39 182
p. 183 186
p. 258 118
1917/18 160
Mouterde 1930, p. 124 79
Nash 1906 179
Pognon 1898 140,154
Preisendanz 1928, III:56 62
IV:86 79
VI:652 68
1930 IX:2 62
Schwab 1890 156
1891, p. 592 187
Sefer ha-razim 1:152 168
1:178 179
1:226 197
2:12 168
2:118 151
2:182 44
4:9,11,18 66
4:13–16 42,79
5:13–14 55
Shachar 1971, No. 2 62,118
No. 4 118
No. 966 179
No. 974 163
p. 227 141
Stübe 1895 74,166,168
Teixidor 1962 126
University of Pennsylvania University Musuem, 18059 132
Winkler 1930, p. 60 84
1931, p. 9 84
Yamauchi 1965 136ff
1967, p. 230 184
No. 18c 88
No. 20 206
No. 22 205
No. 27 206
No. 33 206
Zion Research Library, Boston, No. 48 75

PLATES

Amulet 1

PLATE 2

Amulet 2

Amulet 3

PLATE 4

Amulet 4

Note: For Amulet 5 no photo is available

Amulet 6

Amulet 7a

Amulet 7b

Amulet 8

PLATE 8

Amulet 9

Amulet 10

PLATE 10

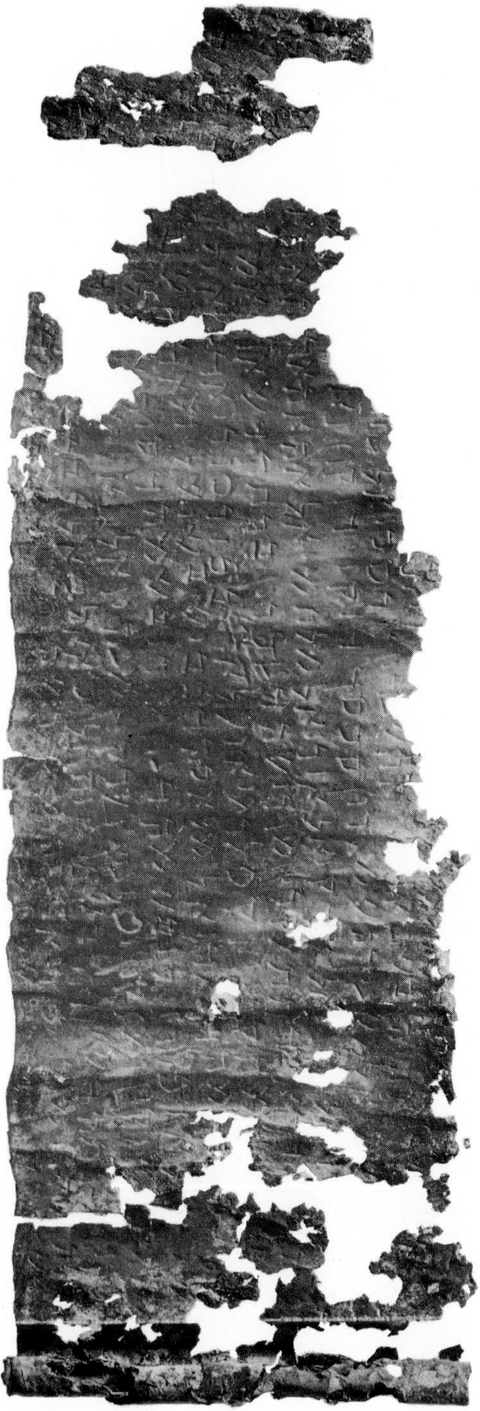

Amulet 11

Amulet 13

Amulet 12

PLATE 12

Amulet 14

Amulet 15

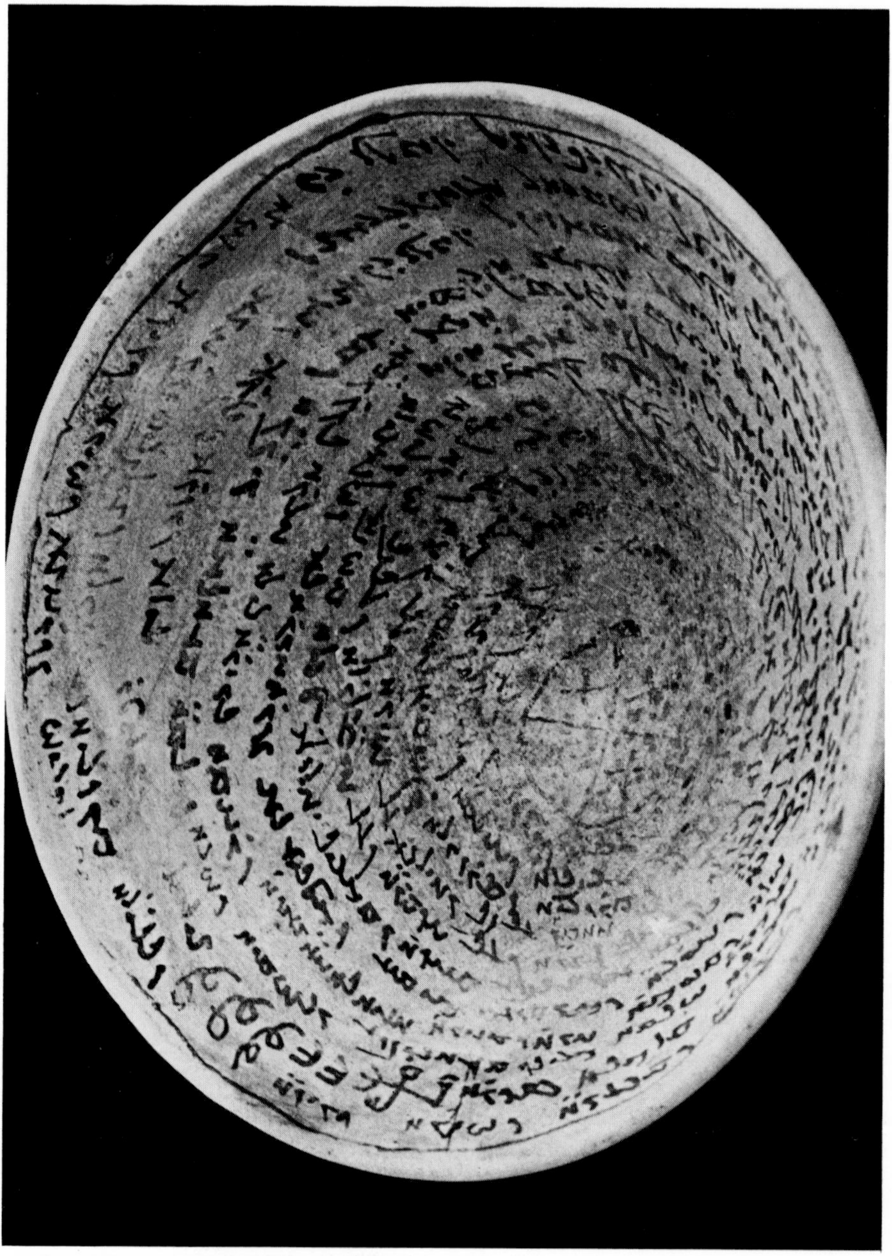

Bowl 1, left side

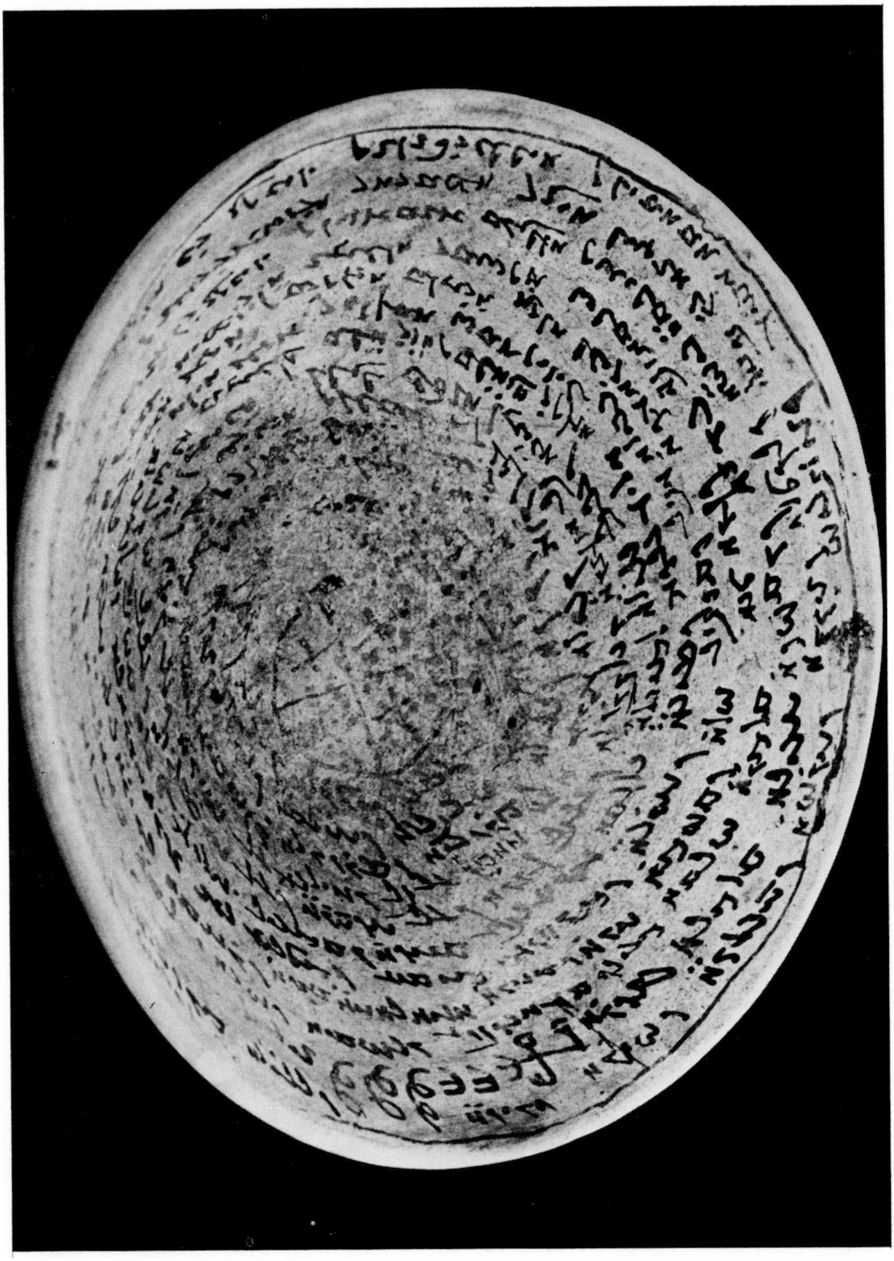

Bowl 1, right side

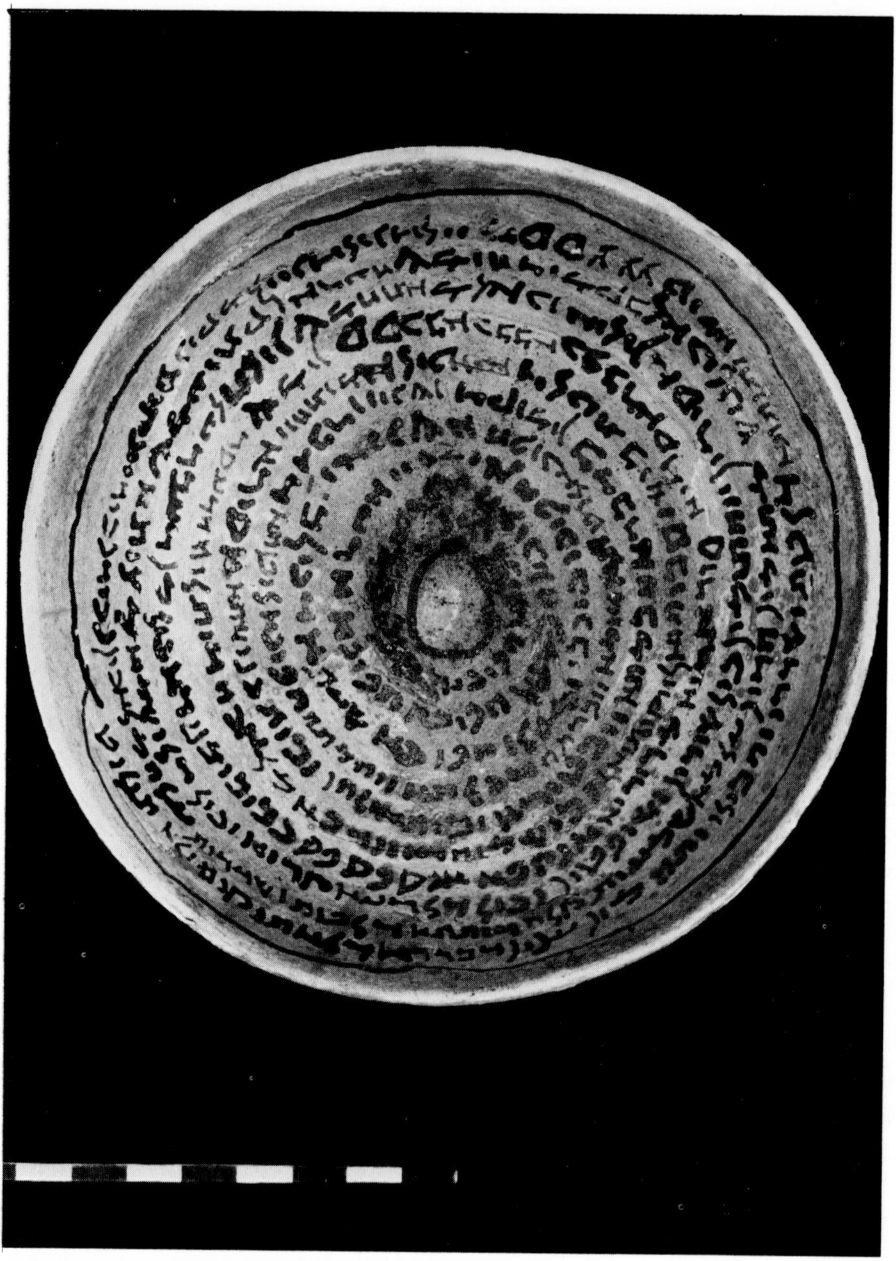

Bowl 2, inside

Bowl 2, outside

Note: For Bowl 3
see Plate 20

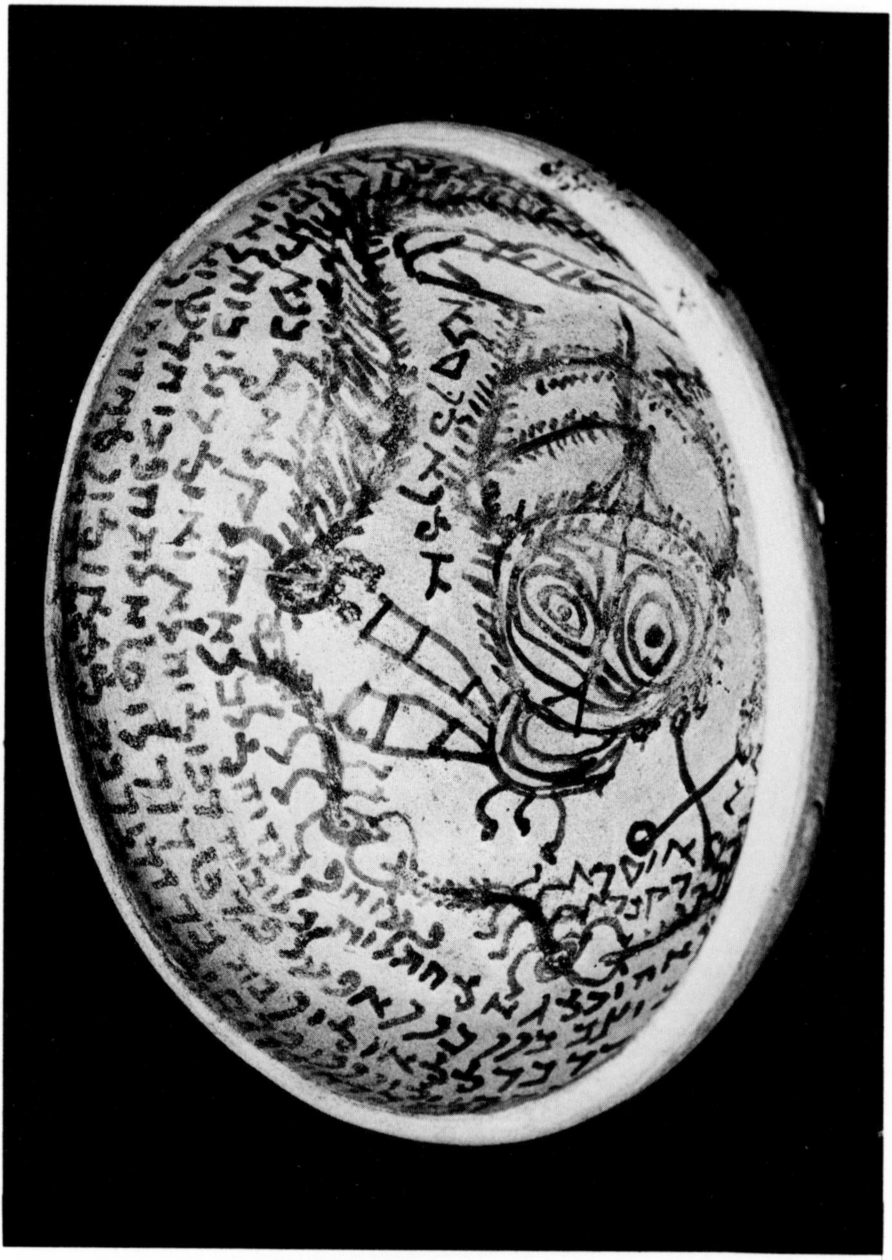

Bowl 4, left side

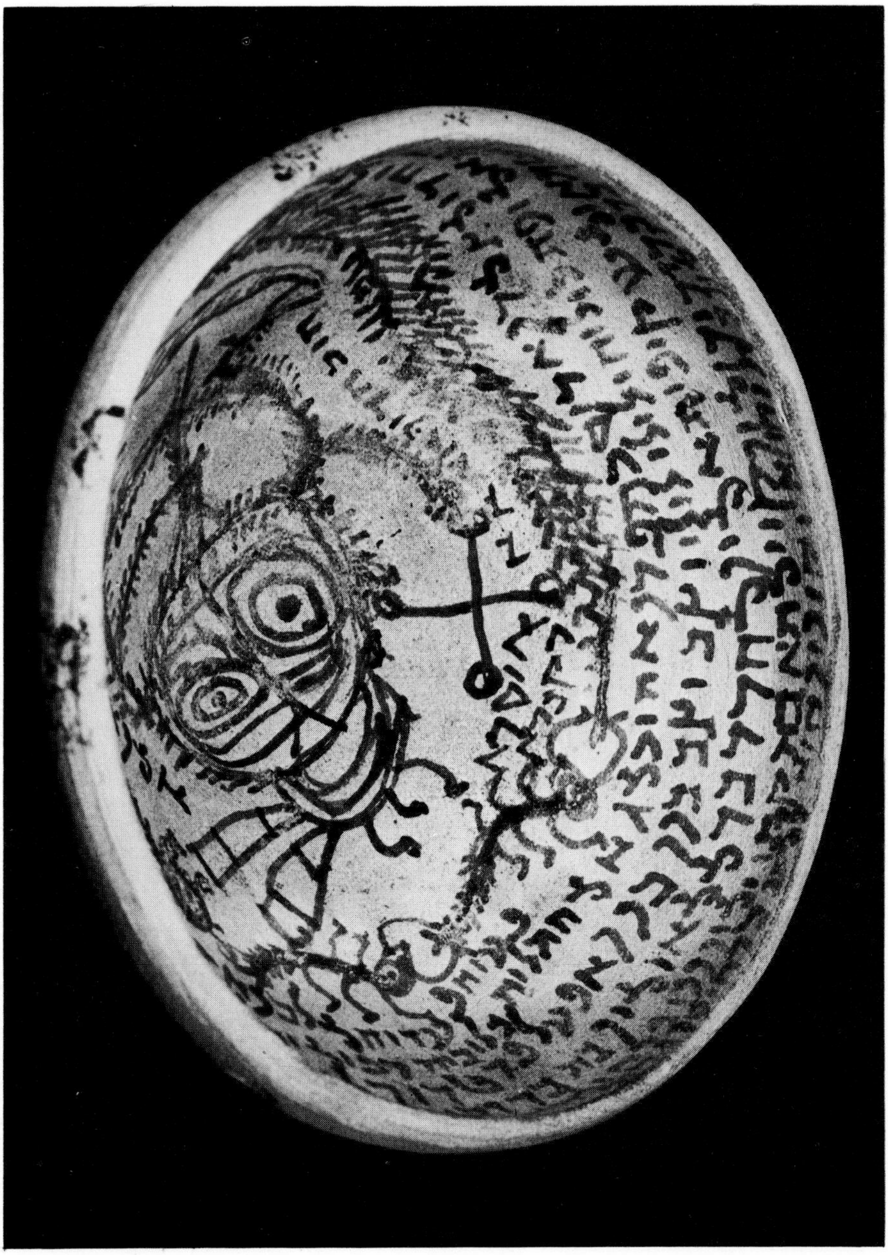

Bowl 4, right side

Bowl 3

Bowl 5

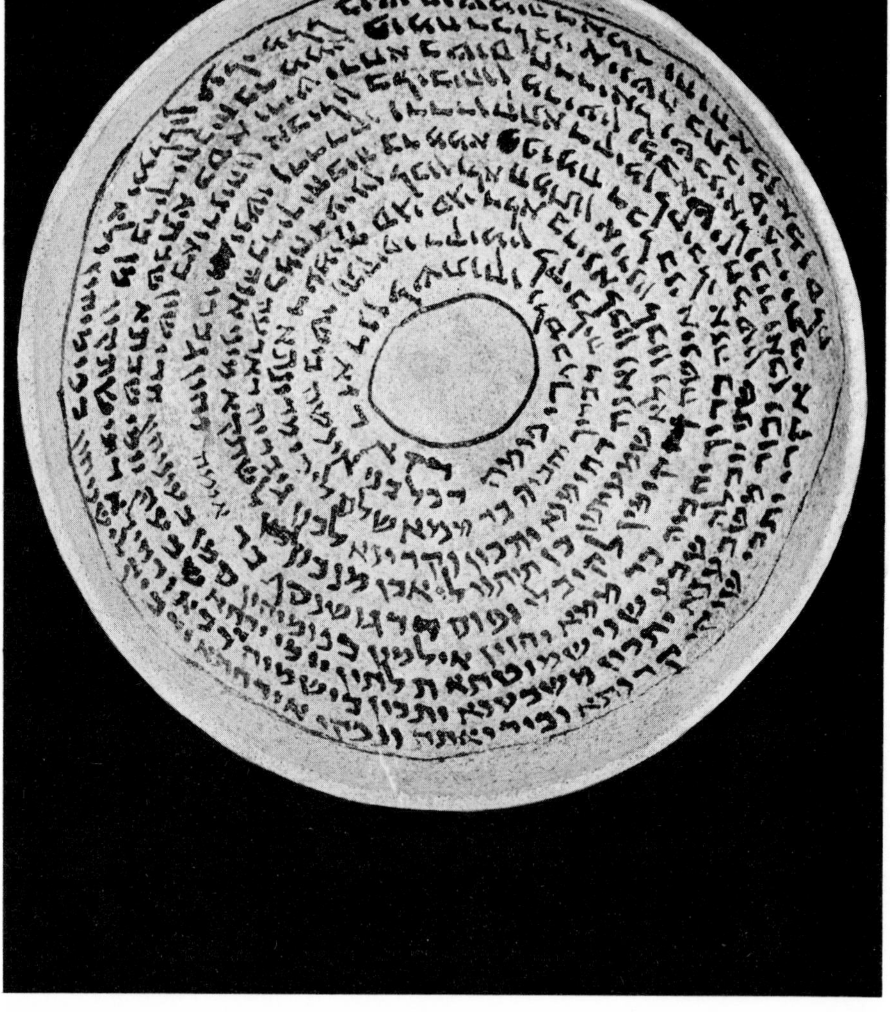

Bowl 6

Bowl 7

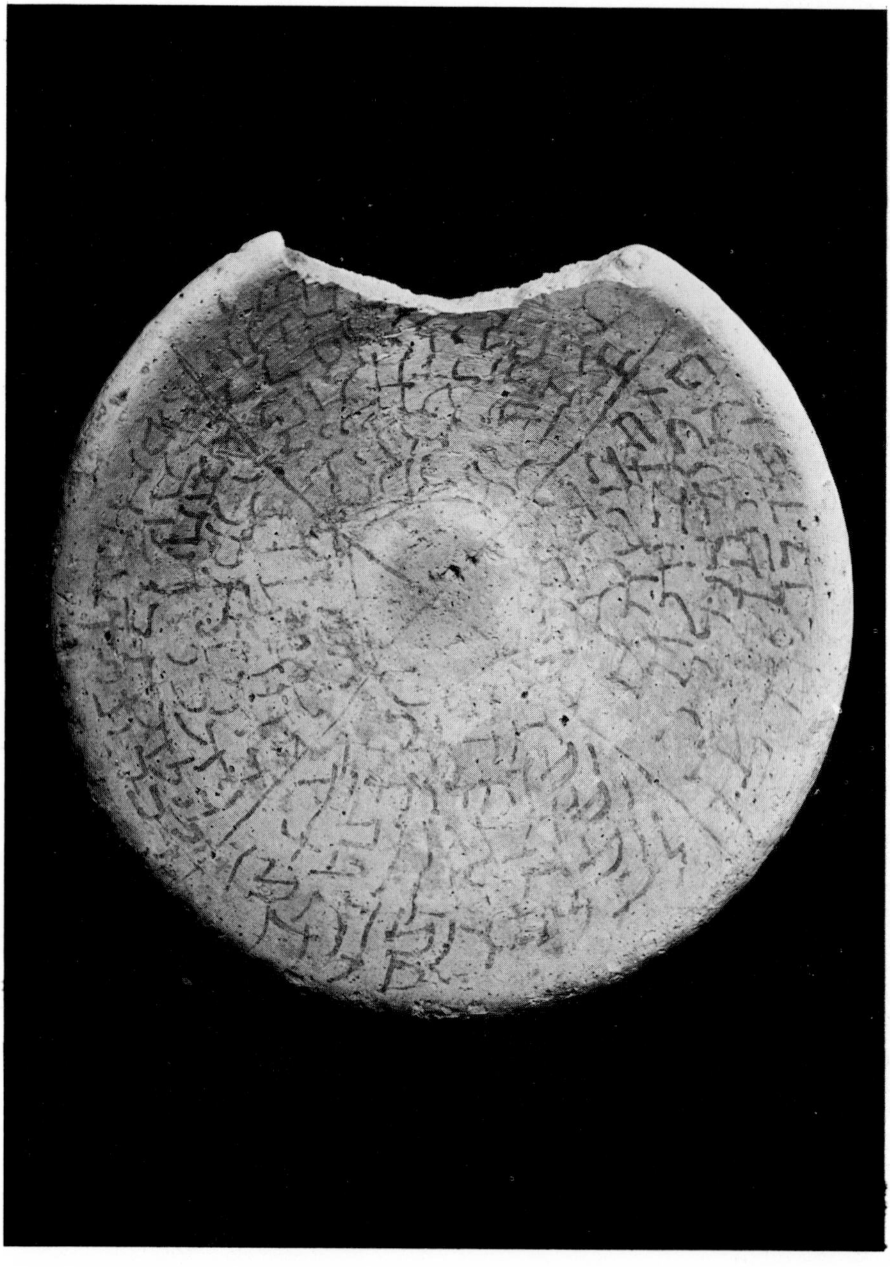

Bowl 8

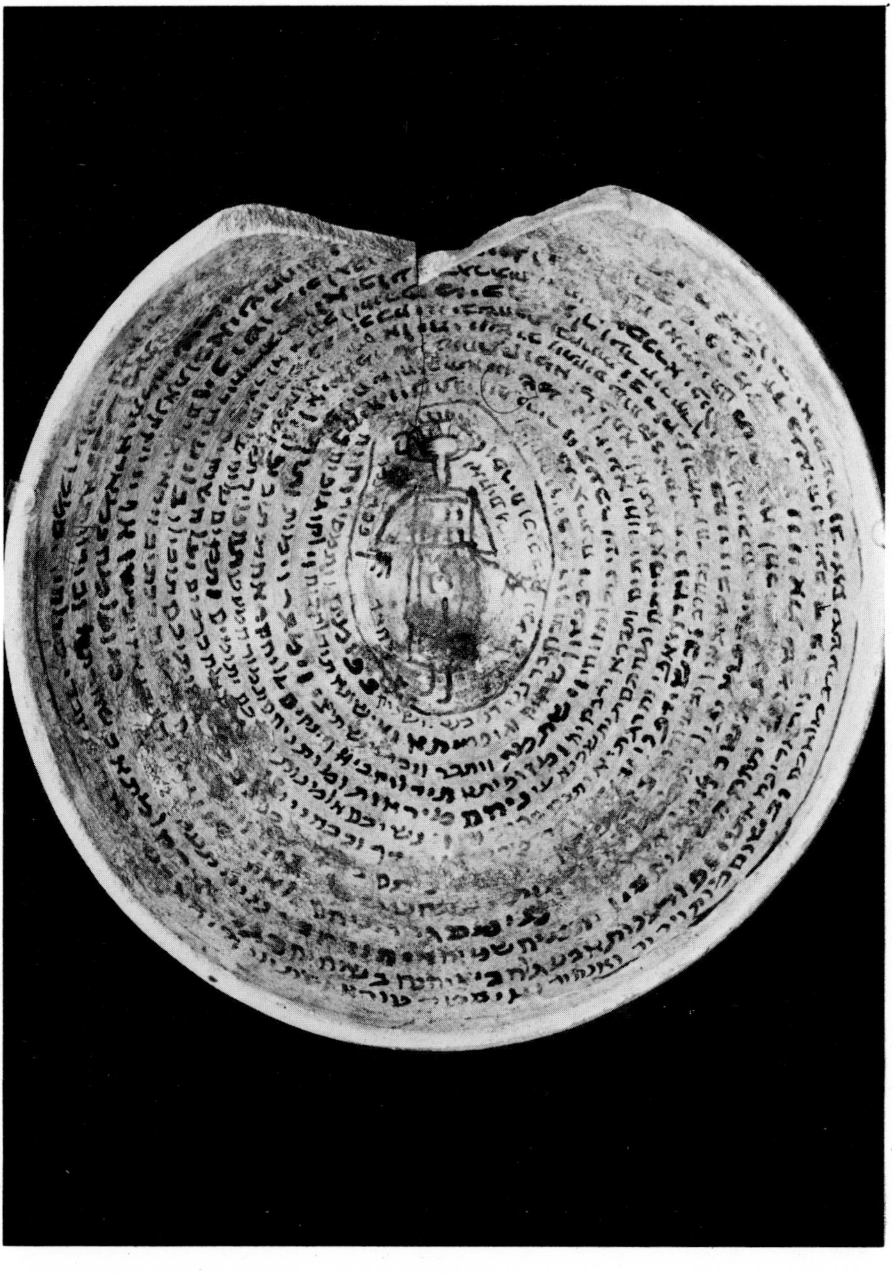

Bowl 9

PLATE 26

Bowl 10

Bowl 11

PLATE 28

Bowl 12a

Bowl 12b

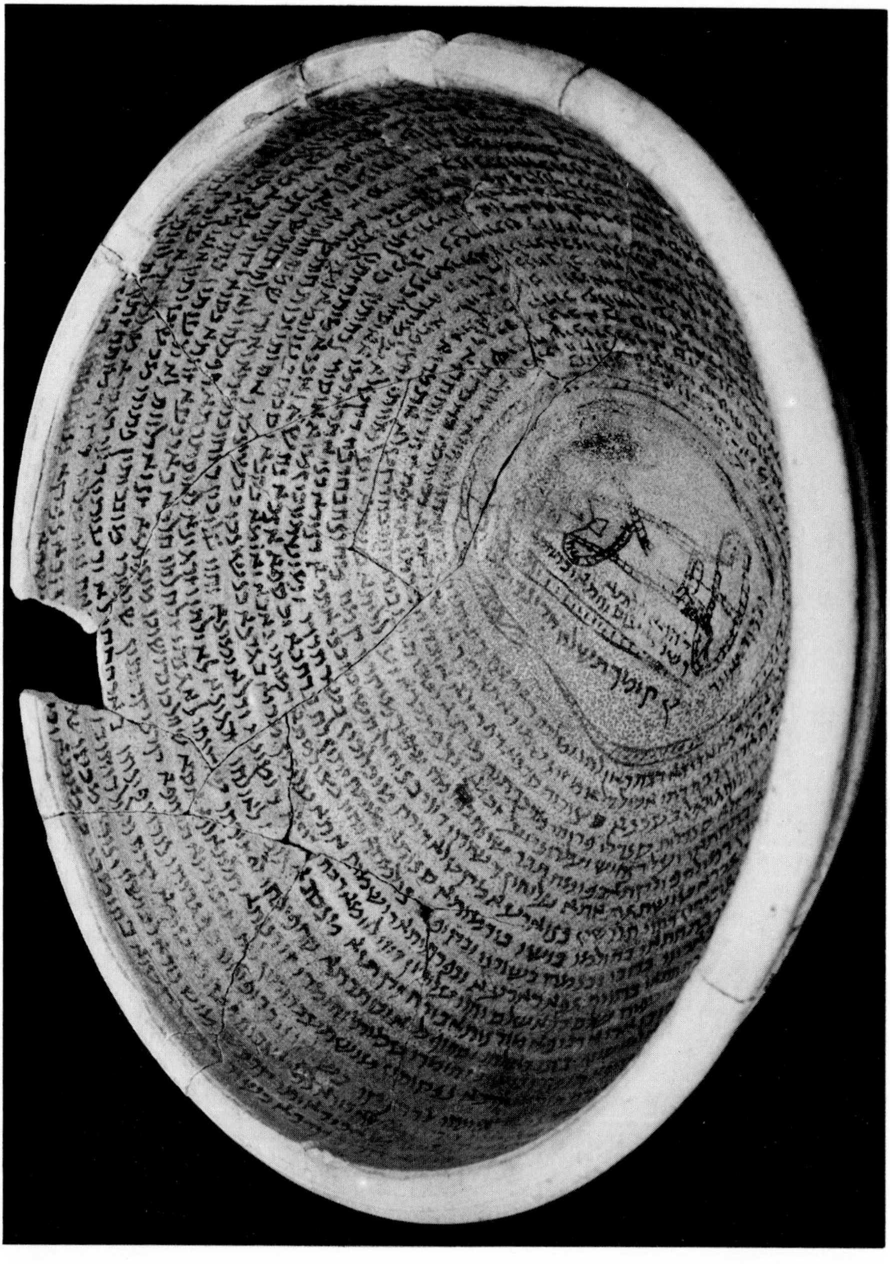

Bowl 13, left side

Bowl 13, right side

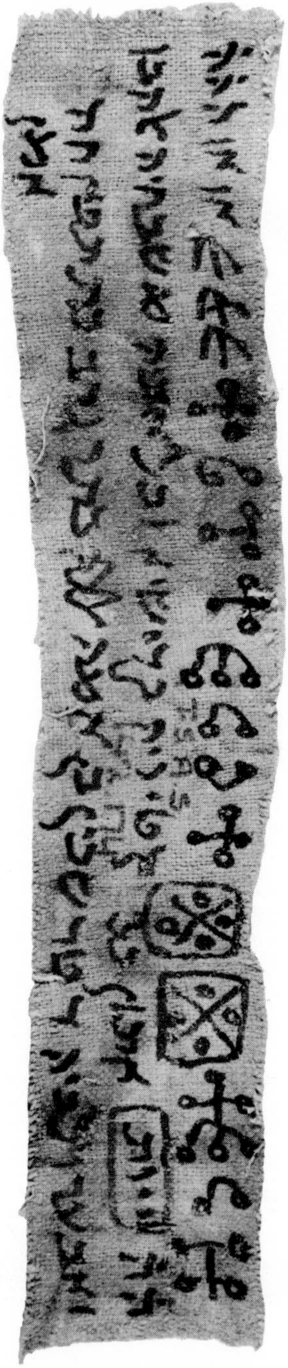

Geniza 1

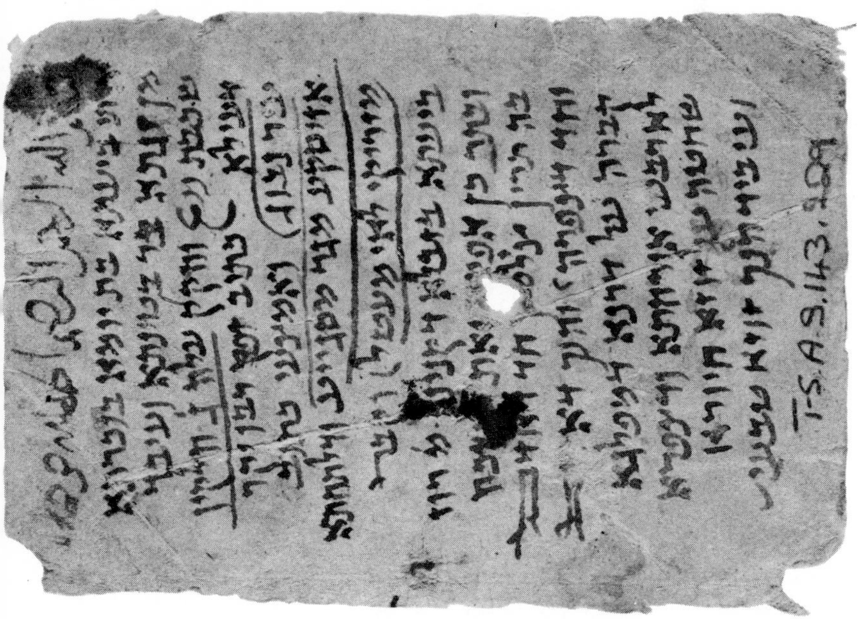

1

2

Geniza 2

PLATE 34

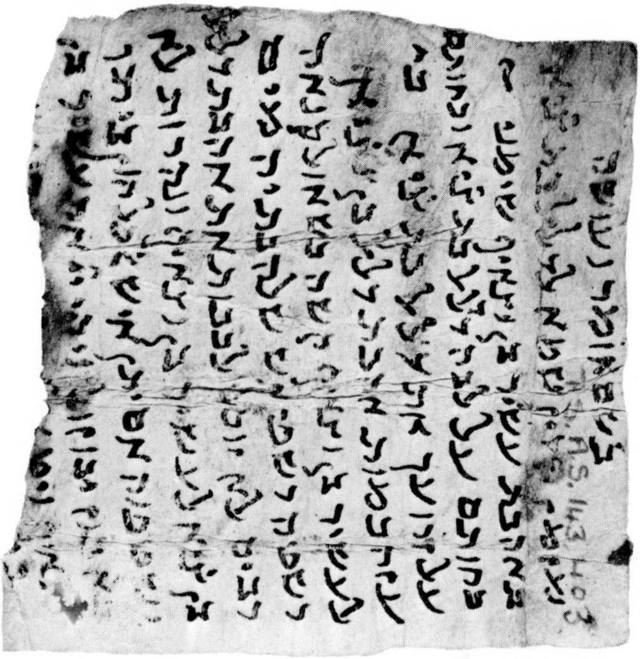

Geniza 3

Geniza 4

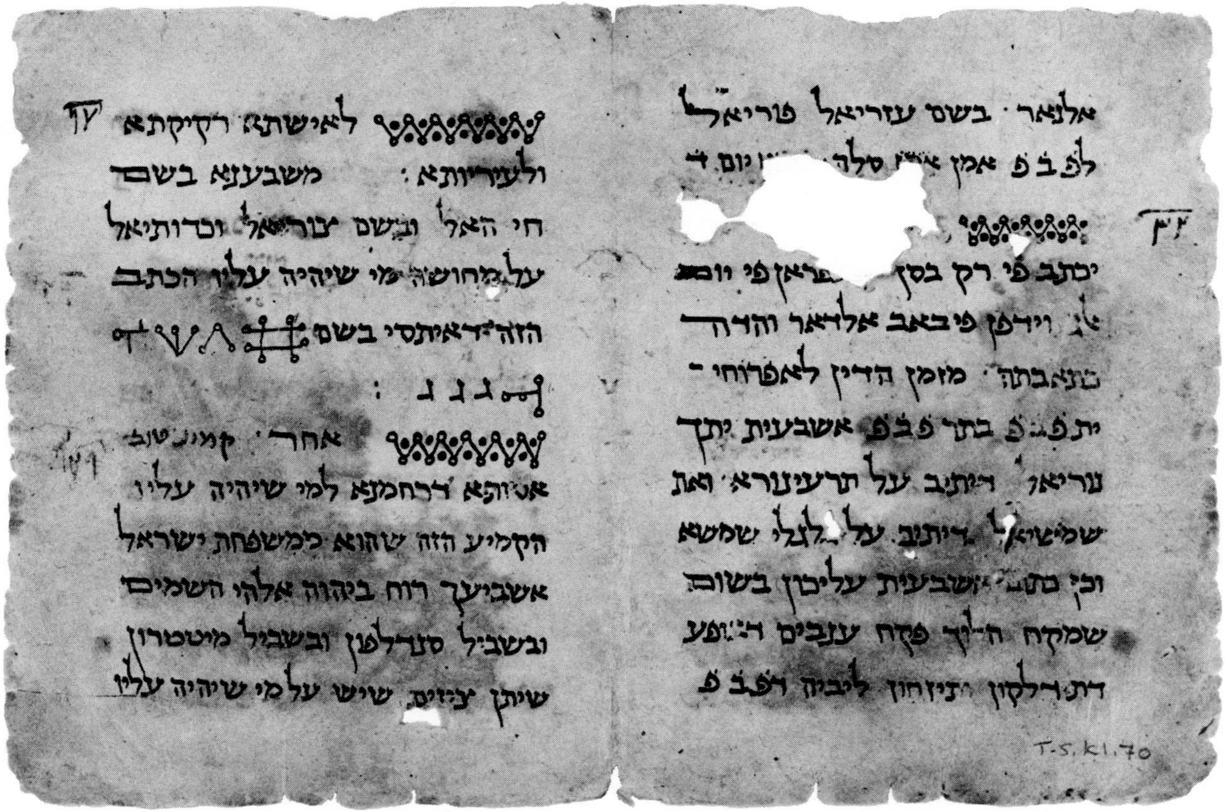

1 Geniza 5, recto 4

3

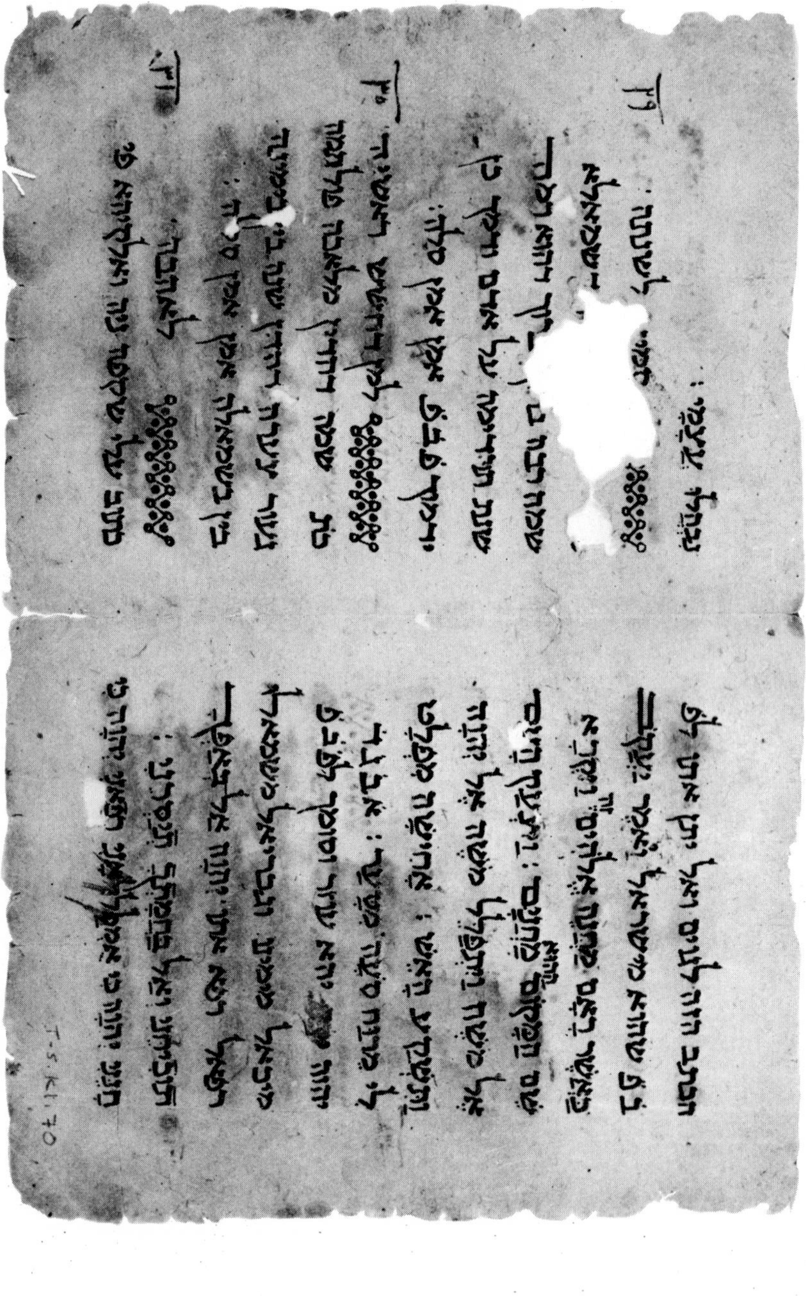

2

Geniza 5. verso

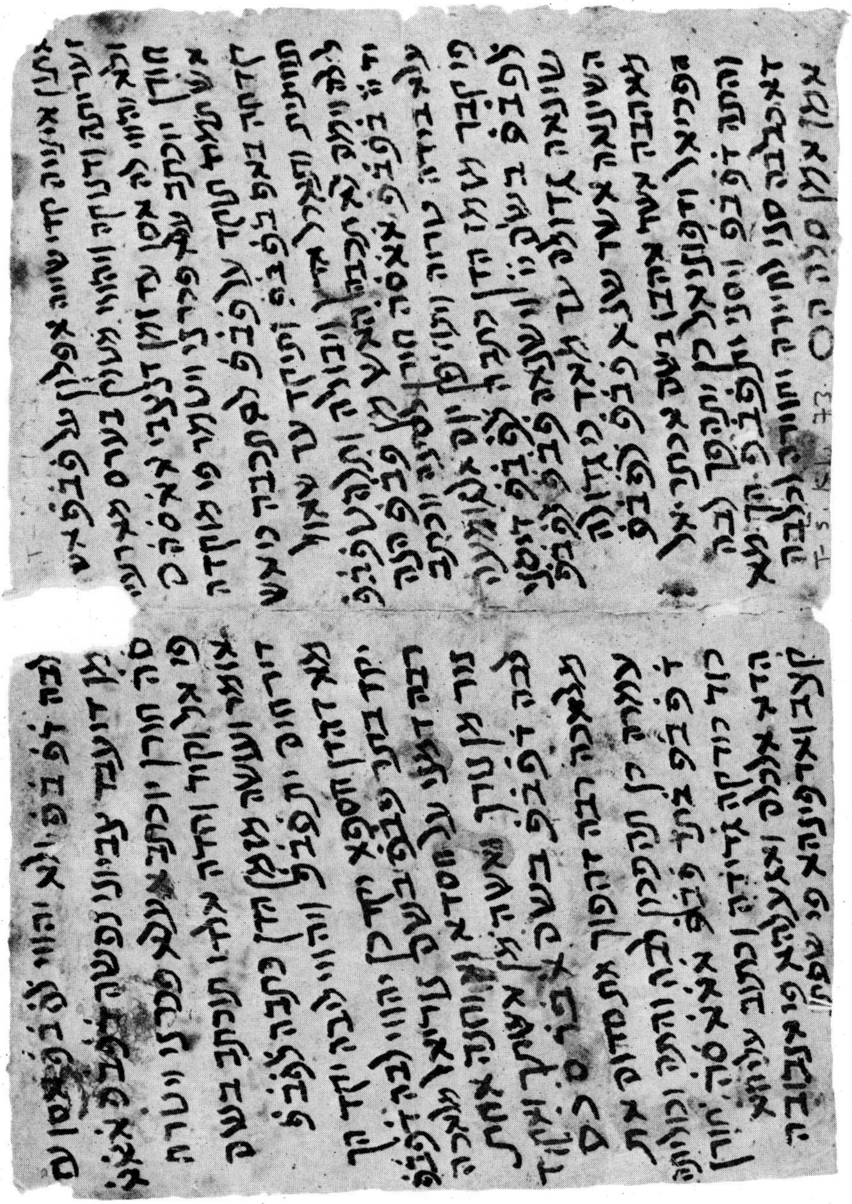

Geniza 6, recto

3

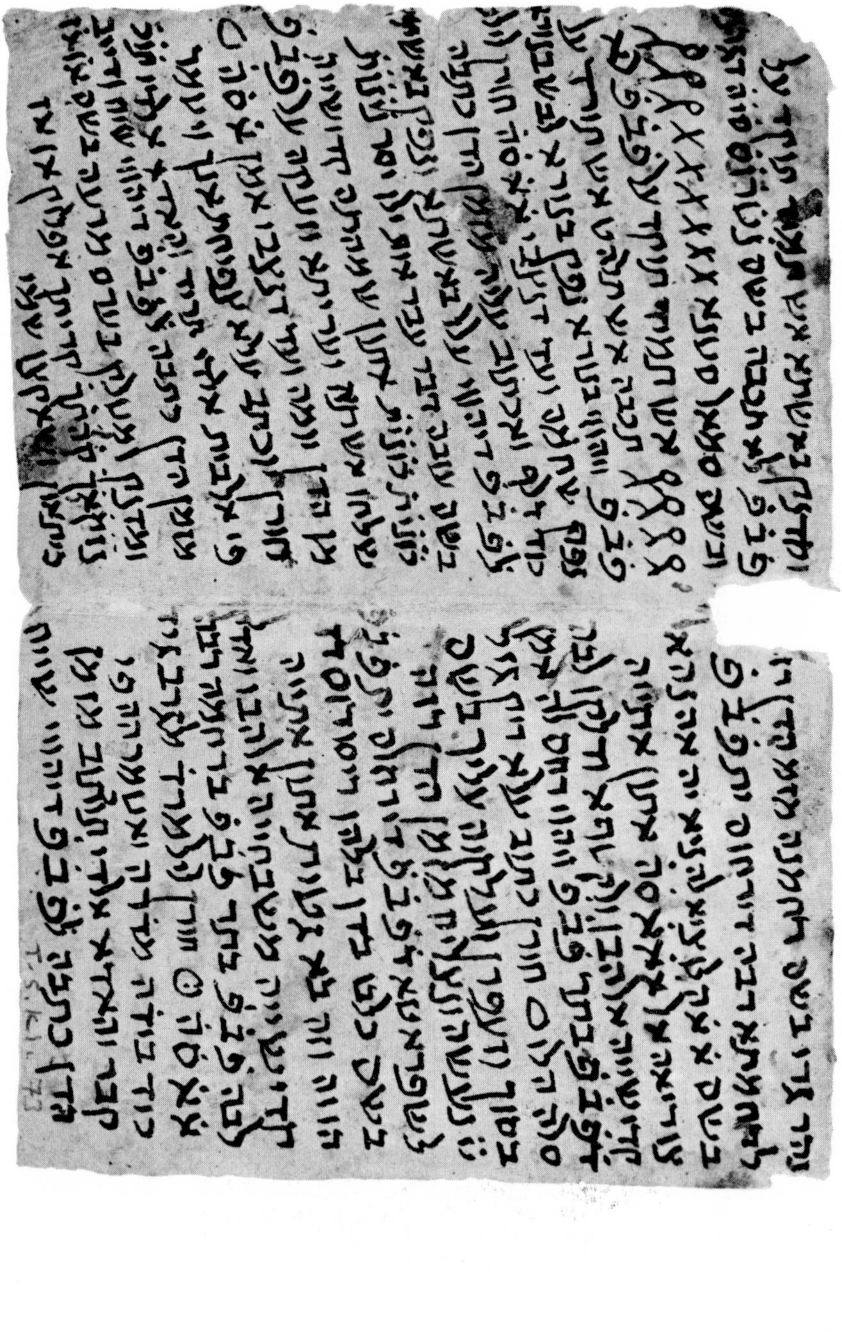

2

Geniza 6, verso

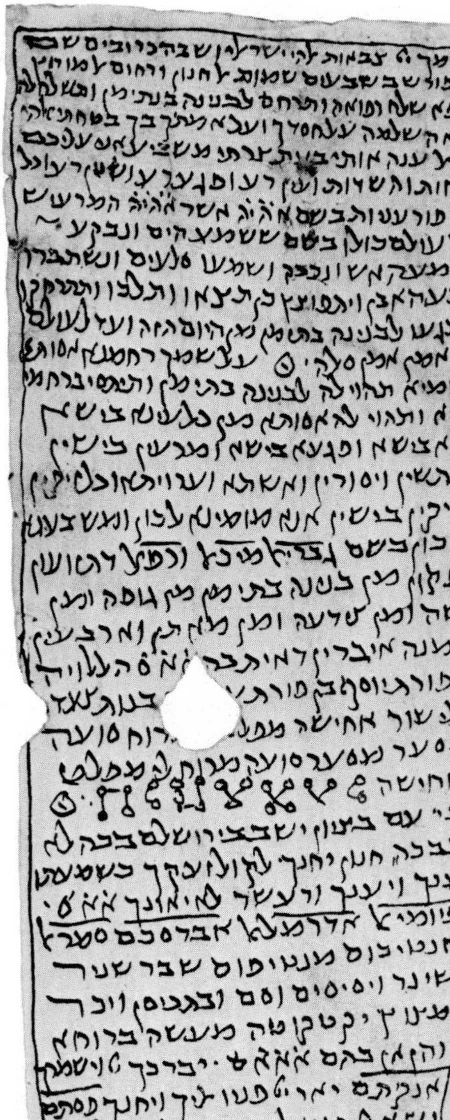

Geniza 7

PLATE 40

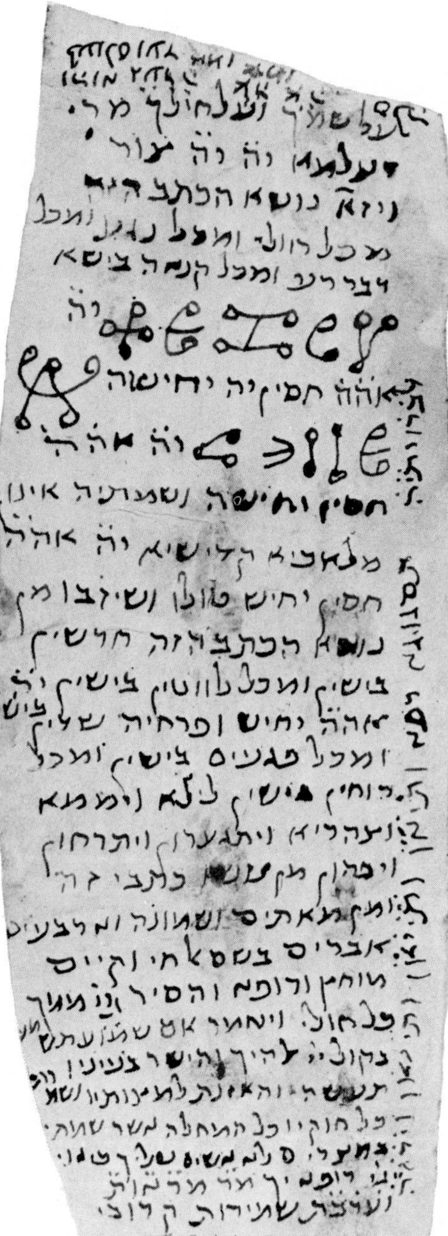

Geniza 8